CARTELS, MARKETS AND CRIME

This study of the normative justification for the use of criminal sanctions as a means of cartel control goes beyond the historical and economic viewpoints by adding a normative evaluation of anti-cartel regimes and analysing cartel control in the USA, Europe and the UK. The analysis is unique in seeking to establish why, in a liberal society, criminal sanctions should apply to individuals who participate in this sort of activity. Although cartels have been rhetorically likened to theft and fraud, there are significant differences. Notwithstanding these differences, *Cartels, Markets and Crime* presents an argument for the criminalisation of economic collusion, and, with this argument in mind, analyses the regimes of the US, EU and UK and considers the possibility of global convergence.

BRUCE WARDHAUGH is a lecturer at the School of Law, Queen's University Belfast, where his research interests include competition law and WTO law.

THE CAMBRIDGE ANTITRUST AND COMPETITION LAW SERIES

Publications within the Series consider various legal, economic and political developments related to competition law and policy. They also consider the application of competition law and policy in sector-specific as well as cross-sector contexts and deal with policy questions ranging from the formation and adoption of competition law and policy (whether at national, regional or international level) to those dealing with enforcement, and the connection between law and competition in the market place. The Series also accommodates different analytical and interdisciplinary viewpoints, such as law and economics; law and political science; law and economic geography-driven perspectives.

The Series includes publications designed to cater for academic demands as well as practitioner publications catering for the continuously evolving needs of regulators, policy-makers, and practitioners, in particular lawyers and economists (who increasingly provide advice on regulatory questions).

The editorial board of the Series welcome proposals by authors and editors who are interested in contributing to the Series through: academic monographs; revised PhD theses of high quality; practitioner texts and collections; and edited volumes.

List of books in the series:

Cartels, Markets and Crime: A Normative Justification for the Criminalisation of Economic Collusion *Bruce Wardhaugh* 9781107036307

Merger Control Worldwide (two-volume set) *General editors: Maher M. Dabbah and Paul Lasok QC* 9780521195096

Greening EU Competition Law and Policy *Suzanne Kingston* 9781107003026

A Principled Approach to Abuse of Dominance in European Competition Law *Liza Lovdahl Gormsen* 9780521767149

International and Comparative Competition Law *Maher M. Dabbah* 9780521516419

The International Dimension of EU Competition Law and Policy *Anestis S. Papadopoulos* 9780521196468

Anti-Cartel Enforcement Worldwide (three-volume set) *General editors: Maher M. Dabbah and Barry E. Hawk* 9780521897211

CARTELS, MARKETS AND CRIME

A Normative Justification for the Criminalisation of Economic Collusion

BRUCE WARDHAUGH

CAMBRIDGE
UNIVERSITY PRESS

CAMBRIDGE
UNIVERSITY PRESS

University Printing House, Cambridge CB2 8BS, United Kingdom

Published in the United States of America by Cambridge University Press, New York

Cambridge University Press is part of the University of Cambridge.

It furthers the University's mission by disseminating knowledge in the pursuit of education, learning, and research at the highest international levels of excellence.

www.cambridge.org
Information on this title: www.cambridge.org/9781107036307

First published 2014

Printed in the United Kingdom by CPI Group Ltd, Croydon, CR0 4YY

A catalogue record for this publication is available from the British Library

Library of Congress Cataloging-in-Publication Data
Wardhaugh, Bruce, 1960–
Cartels, markets and crime : a normative justification for the criminalisation of economic collusion / Bruce Wardhaugh.
pages cm. – (The Cambridge antitrust and competition)
ISBN 978-1-107-03630-7
1. Cartels – Europe – History. I. Title.
HD2757.5.W37 2014
338.8′7–dc23
2013016197

ISBN 978-1-107-03630-7 Hardback

To Jen and Jay

CONTENTS

FIGURES

PREFACE

At the time that this work went to the publisher (January 2013), the Enterprise and Regulatory Reform Bill (part of which was intended to reform the UK's competition regime) was still subject to Parliamentary consideration. The Bill was expected to receive Royal Assent in the spring of 2013. Accordingly, the discussion of reforms to the UK regime reflects the provisional nature of this legislation.

This work refers to the Articles of the various European Treaties in the way they are numbered in the Treaties. This should present no confusion to those familiar with the topic. It has also relied upon Commission Decisions (and other European materials) in authentic languages, when there is no authentic English version. I have consulted French, German and Dutch versions, though citing the French text. Unless otherwise attributed, all translations are mine.

When a work which has been reprinted over time (e.g. Locke's *Second Treatise*) is cited, citations to chapters and sections are provided, avoiding page numbers. This facilitates users of other editions to find the relevant passage. The exception to this is Mill's *On Liberty* where an authoritative text exists, and to which I refer.

The terms 'antitrust law' and 'competition law' are used interchangeably, though strictly speaking the former is American terminology. This allows for a bit of variation in my vocabulary.

All web references were verified on 30 January 2013.

ACKNOWLEDGEMENTS

Many people have assisted me in the production of this work. Parts of this work have appeared in print previously. In particular, some of the Introduction and Chapter 1 appear as part of my article 'A Normative Approach to the Criminalisation of Cartel Activity' in *Legal Studies* (2012), and part of Chapter 3 appeared as 'Closing the Deterrence Gap: Individual Liability, the Cartel Offence and the BIS Consultation' in *The Competition Law Journal* (2011).

Prior to publication, I presented versions of the *Legal Studies* article at the Socio-Legal Studies Annual Meeting in Brighton in 2011 and the Society of Legal Scholars Meeting in Cambridge, also in 2011. Part of Chapter 2 was presented at the Socio-Legal Studies Association Annual Meeting in Leicester in 2012 and at the 2012 Society of Legal Scholars meeting in Bristol. Parts of Chapter 4 were presented at the University of East Anglia/Centre for Competition Policy Conference in June of 2012. I wish to thank all who commented on these papers (including anonymous reviewers), and in particular Jonathan Galloway, Andreas Stephen, Angus MacCulloch, Bill Kovacic, Christopher Brown and Morten Hviid. The usual disclaimers apply.

I would also like to thank my wife, Jennifer, who assisted in checking references and proof reading. Of course, all errors are mine alone.

My greatest debt is to my family, Jennifer and Jason, who tolerated my work and endured my absence from them (physically, mentally and at times spiritually) during the writing of this book. I doubt I would have accomplished this task without their support, for which I thank them.

TABLE OF CASES

Canada

Canadian Dredge and Dry Dock v. *The Queen* [1985] 1 SCR 662, 19 DLR (4th) 314, 19 CCC (3d) 1 57

Irving Paper Limited v. *Atofina Chemicals Inc.* (2009) 99 OR (3d) 358 (Ont SC) 161

Pro-Sys Consultants Ltd et al. v. *Microsoft Corporation et al., Sun-Rype Products Ltd et al.* v. *Archer Daniels Midland Company et al., and Samsung Electronics Co Ltd et autres* v. *Option Consommateurs et autres* SCC Docket Numbers 34282, 342823 and 34617 (heard 17 October 2012) 255

R v. *Sault Ste Marie* [1978] 2 SCR 1299, 85 DLR (3d) 161, 40 CCC (2d) 353

European Union

Commission Decisions

Electrical and Mechanical Carbon and Graphite Products (C.36.490) [2002] OJ L100/1 96

Case COMP/39406 – Commission Decision of 28.1.2009 relating to a proceeding under Article 81 of the Treaty and Article 53 of the EEA Agreement (Case COMP/39406 – *Marine Hoses*) [2008] OJ C122/01 101

Case COMP/B/37.766 – Summary of Commission Decision of 18 April 2007 relating to a proceeding under Article 81 of the Treaty establishing the European Community (Case COMP/B/37.766 – *Dutch Beer Market*) [2008] OJ C122/01 101

Bathroom Fittings 23 June 2010, IP/10/790 (non-confidential version not yet available) 96

Case COMP/39839 *Telefónica and Portugal Telecom*; IP/11/1241, 25.10.2011 (non-confidential version not yet available) 199

Commission Decisions

EU - Courts

Court of Justice

Germany

United Kingdom

England

Office of Fair Trading and Competition Appeal Tribunal Decisions

United States

TABLE OF TREATIES, STATUTES AND LEGISLATIVE INSTRUMENTS

Treaties

European

Other

Statutes

Canada

England and Wales

United States

Other Jurisdictions

EU – Regulations

EU – Guidelines and Notices

Introduction

0.1 Cartels and calls for their criminalisation

As a means of industrial organisation, cartels have had mixed acceptance in Europe after the end of the Industrial Revolution. In the late nineteenth century there were approximately four industry-wide cartels operating in Germany. By 1923, the figure had grown to over 1,500.[1] Such organisations were a common, legal and (often) encouraged means of facilitating industrial and national development. However, by the end of the twentieth century, this complacent attitude had changed, and the European authorities were sanctioning cartel activity with apparently significant fines, some in the hundreds of millions of Euros.[2]

In contrast, on the other side of the Atlantic, the American position has apparently never wavered: since before the passage of the Sherman Act in 1890, politicians (at both the state and Federal level), economists and public opinion viewed cartel activity as a form of anti-competitive exploitation, which harmed consumers. As such, this activity was condemned by public sentiment, and later by law. In addition to criminal penalties, that Act was to provide treble damages for those harmed by such activity, and the ability to obtain legal costs (a rare procedural concession in American law). The latter half of the twentieth century in America witnessed a gradual increase in the penalties available to be (and actually) imposed on those participating in these sorts of activities. In contrast to the European system, the American system – from the beginning – imposed personal, criminal sanctions against those involved in cartel activity. While criminal sanctions were little used until the very late years of the twentieth century, the increase in penalties for breaches of the Sherman Act generally translated into an

1 This will be brought out in our discussion in Chapter 4, below.

2 For a historical account of cartels in Europe describing, *inter alia*, their pervasive nature, see Gerber, *Law and Competition in Twentieth Century Europe*, and Harding and Joshua, *Regulating Cartels in Europe*; on history of cartels and cartel control in the UK, see Mercer, *Constructing a Competitive Order*. For an American perspective, see Peritz, *Competition Policy in America*.

increase in individual penalties. The result is that people do go to Federal prisons for this activity on a frequent basis.

The justification for imprisonment is that hard-core cartel activity has a 'harmful' effect on consumers. If it were not controlled in this manner, it would become more pervasive, inflicting even greater harm on the public. Although any estimate of the extent of cartel conduct is necessarily imprecise,[3] it is clear that cartels are pervasive. In Europe, Neelie Kroes, when European Union (EU) Competition Commissioner, likened cartel activity to theft, claiming that cartels 'rip-off consumers'.[4] In this regard, one influential British scholar has remarked:

> However, if competition policy is about one thing, it is surely about the condemnation of horizontal price-fixing, market-sharing and analogous practices: on both a moral and practical level, there is not a great deal of difference between price-fixing and theft.[5]

Similar views are expressed by the Antitrust Division of the US Department of Justice:

> Price fixing, bid rigging, and market allocation are economic crimes with potentially devastating effects on the U.S. economy. Such crimes rob purchasers, contribute to inflation, destroy public confidence in the economy, and undermine our system of free enterprise.[6]

This is not merely a transatlantic phenomenon. Such opinions have also been expressed by influential international organisations such as the Organisation for Economic Co-operation and Development (OECD)[7] and the World Trade Organization (WTO).[8]

[3] This imprecision is a direct consequence of attempting to measure illegal (and hence clandestine) activity.

[4] Kroes, 'Tackling Cartels – A Never-ending Task'.

[5] Whish, 'Recent Developments' 220. [6] DOJ, *Antitrust Primer* 1.

[7] OECD, *Hard Core Cartels* 8:

> Cartels harm consumers and have pernicious effects on economic efficiency. A successful cartel raises price above the competitive level and reduces output. Consumers (which include businesses and governments) choose either not to pay the higher price for some or all of the cartelised product that they desire, thus forgoing the product, or they pay the cartel price and thereby unknowingly transfer wealth to the cartel operators. Further, a cartel shelters its members from full exposure to market forces, reducing pressures on them to control costs and to innovate. All of these effects harm efficiency in a market economy.

[8] WTO, *Provisions On Hardcore Cartels*, para. 7:

> [H]ardcore cartels are the most pernicious type of anti-competitive practice from the point of view of trade and development as well as of

To combat the pervasive nature of cartels, commentators and legislators have proposed the use of criminal sanctions. In the United States, cartel activity has been a criminal offence since 1890.[9] In Europe, Ireland,[10] the United Kingdom,[11] Estonia[12] and (to some extent) Germany[13] criminalise this sort of behaviour. Although the EU's Competition Commission metes out (apparently) substantial fines to those undertakings caught engaging in cartel behaviour,[14] some academic commentators have suggested that these monetary penalties are insufficient and need to be supplemented by criminal sanctions which include incarceration to effectively deter such activities.[15] Jurisdictions outside of the EU and North America are beginning to incorporate criminal sanctions for anti-competitive activities into their legal regimes.[16] Indeed such incorporation has the support of the WTO, whose Working Group on the Interaction between Trade and Competition Policy remarks:

> Important elements of an effective national competition law include a clear prohibition of cartel activity, backed up by substantial penalties including fines and/or imprisonment, and relevant investigatory powers. Furthermore, the suggestion has been made that particular attention should be devoted by relevant enforcement authorities to the investigation and prosecution of domestic and international cartels, given the clear anti-competitive effects of these practices and their harmful impact on the development prospects of poor countries.[17]

> competition law enforcement; that they can have the effect of undermining the benefits that should flow from international trade liberalization, and hence are an important concern for the multilateral trading system; that they impose heavy costs on consumers and user industries, and thereby also on the development prospects of poor countries; . . .

9 Sherman Act §§ 1–7; Clayton Act §§ 12–22, 52–53.

10 Competition Act 2002, ss. 4–8. 11 Enterprise Act 2002, ss. 188–190.

12 See Proos, 'Competition Policy in Estonia', in Cseres, Schinkel and Vogelaar (eds.) *Criminalization of Competition Law Enforcement* 307.

13 German criminal law prohibits bid rigging: see Vollmer, 'Experience with Criminal Law Sanctions for Competition Law Infringements in Germany', in Cseres, Schinkel and Vogelaar (eds.), ibid. 257.

14 In 2010 alone, the Commission imposed fines in excess of €3 billion for TFEU Article 101 (cartel) violations. See the Commission's website, 'Cartel Fines'.

15 See the articles contained in Ehlermann and Atanasiu (eds.), *European Competition Annual 2006*, Cseres, Schinkel and Vogelaar (eds.) (n. 12); and Wils, *Efficiency and Justice* 155–201.

16 See OECD, *Hard Core Cartels: 2000*, Annex A for an enumeration of sanctions against hardcore cartels on a member-by-member basis.

17 WTO (n. 8) para. 126.

However, these calls for criminalisation are themselves not unproblematic. Criminal laws are of a *sui generis* nature.

By threatening loss of property or liberty, criminal sanctions are a legal order's most coercive mechanism for regulating the conduct of those within its jurisdiction. Additionally, the criminal law and its sanctions carry a non-trivial element of moral (or normative) force, with its higher standards of proof and its inquiry into the defendant's mental state which bears upon the defendant's culpability. The coercive nature of the use of criminal sanctions and their purported moral content requires some normative justification for its use. The reason is fairly clear: to deprive someone of their property or liberty requires a reason; otherwise there is apparently little difference between the state and the kidnapper or burglar.[18] Likewise, it is a fair retort to anyone who expresses moral indignation regarding certain behaviour to ask them to justify their condemnation.

However, at this point it is necessary to clarify what is meant by a 'cartel' and by the sorts of harm that these arrangements cause. Clarifying these two points ensures precision in our subsequent discussion.

0.2 Cartels and their effects

0.2.1 Defining cartels

When one attempts to define certain activities for analytic purposes, one is often faced with problems of vagueness or indeterminacy. Every definition should identify (or select) paradigmatic cases which ought to be included from those which ought to be excluded; however, there may be a so-called 'grey' area, of doubtful or marginal cases. The phrases used in competition law such as 'anti-competitive practices' or 'improving the production or distribution of goods' are not exceptions to this general rule. To illustrate this, an agreement among manufacturers of, for example, elevators to allocate customers and coordinate bids on construction projects[19] would certainly be picked out by any adequate definition of the two terms. However, it is not clear that an agreement of a manufacturer

[18] Indeed, a similar criticism of e.g. John Austin's positivism is often voiced: Austin, *The Province of Jurisprudence Determined* (192–3). The best-known critic of Austin on this basis is Hart, 'Positivism and the Separation of Law and Morals', 48, 50.

[19] *Elevators and Escalators* (Case COMP/E-1/38.823).

of, for example, bicycles[20] or leather products[21] with its retailers to maintain a required minimum retail price, does (or should) fall within the same definition.

Indeed the indeterminate nature of the subject can be seen from legal instruments which define the subject matter of a jurisdiction's competition regime. In the EU, Article 101 of the Treaty on the Functioning of the European Union (TFEU) proscribes five activities (price-fixing, controlling output, market sharing, the imposition of dissimilar trading conditions to effect a competitive disadvantage, and tying). Yet two paragraphs later, the TFEU exempts some practices which, 'contribute to improving the production or distribution of goods or to promoting technical or economic progress, while allowing consumers a fair share of the resulting benefit'.[22]

In the US, the Sherman Act speaks only of 'combination[s] in the form of trust or otherwise, or conspiracy, in restraint of trade or commerce' and 'monopolize, or attempt to monopolize, or combine or conspire with any other person or persons, to monopolize any part of the trade or commerce'.[23] Similar imprecision can be found in the statutes of, *inter alia*, Canada,[24] Ireland,[25] France[26] and Germany.[27]

However, this imprecision (or indeterminacy) is not fatal to most legal exercises, and, in particular, not to ours. Assuming a statute (or other defining provision) passes appropriate initial jurisdictional or constitutional tests for lack of vagueness,[28] so-called 'grey areas' can be clarified through the use of other hard and soft law instruments such as subordinate regulation, directives, policy manuals, and the like.[29] And in the end, administrative tribunals and/or courts are positioned to make final clarifications when necessary.

With this in mind, our immediate concern is with the central areas of anti-competitive conspiracies, the so-called 'hard-core cartels', the prohibition of

[20] *US* v. *Arnold, Schwinn and Co. et al* 388 US 365, 87 S Ct 1856 (1967).

[21] *Leegin Creative Leather Products Inc* v. *PSKS Inc d b a Kay's Kloset and Kay's Shoes* 551 US 877, 127 S Ct 2705 (2007).

[22] TFEU Article 101(3). [23] Sherman Act §§1–2.

[24] Competition Act RSC 1985, s. 45. [25] Competition Act 2002, s. 4.

[26] *Code de Commerce*, Article L 420–1.

[27] *Gesetz gegen Wettbewerbsbeschränkungen (GWB)* (Act against Restraints of Competition, ARC) § 1.

[28] See, for example, *City of Chicago* v. *Morales* 527 US 41, 119 S Ct 1849 (1999) which determined that a city ordinance prohibiting 'criminal street gang members' from 'loitering' in public places was too vague to provide adequate notice of expected conduct.

[29] International Competition Network, *Defining Hard Core Cartel Conduct* 10–11.

which is an essential element of every competition regime. These practices are easily described.[30] The International Competition Network's (ICN's)[31] observations on this point are worth noting in detail:

> Reflecting the widespread consensus, the basic statutory elements that define a hard core cartel are remarkably consistent across jurisdictions. The three common components of a cartel are:
>
> 1) an agreement;
> 2) between competitors;
> 3) to restrict competition.
>
> The **agreement** that forms a cartel need not be formal or written. Cartels almost invariably involve secret conspiracies. The term **competitors** most often refers to companies at the same level of the economy (manufacturers, distributors, or retailers) in direct competition with each other to sell goods or provide services. The aspect of a **restriction on competition** distinguishes conduct that targets open competition from benign, ordinary course of business agreements between firms.
>
> Further, in describing the typical types of hard core conduct, four categories of conduct are commonly identified across jurisdictions:
>
> price fixing;
> output restrictions;
> market allocation; and
> bid rigging.
>
> In some jurisdictions, bid rigging and output restrictions are also sometimes regarded as subsets of price fixing and/or market allocation, as the impact is to affect pricing on bids or by reducing output or to assign or divide certain contracts or market share between competitors. Regardless of the specific categorization, the categories all have in common conduct whereby competitors fix an aspect of a free market.
>
> Conduct falling within the four categories can take many forms.[32]

In sum, participants in hard-core cartels agree to insulate themselves from the rigours of a competitive marketplace, substituting cooperation for competition.[33]

30 Though, to be fair, may be difficult to observe, detect or otherwise identify in the market; for methods of determining whether collusion exists, see e.g. Porter, 'Detecting Collusion' 147 and OFT, 'Predicting Cartels'.

31 The ICN is an international organisation comprised of national and international competition agencies with the mandate of assistance in the coordination of competition policy and enforcement.

32 International Competition Network (n. 29) 10, emphasis in the original.

33 See Case T-25/95 *Cimenteries CBR* v. *Commission* [2002] ECR II-491, at para. 22, where the court notes, 'The concept of a concerted practice refers to a form of coordination

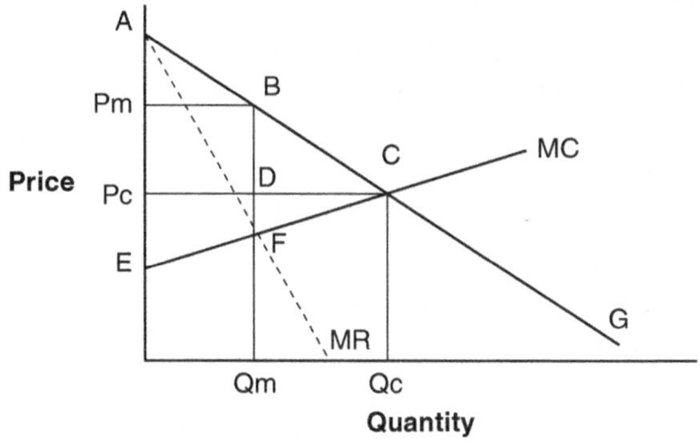

Figure 1 Welfare losses from monopoly

0.2.2 The economic effect of cartels

The effect that such cooperative agreements have is to allow the cartelists to act in the market as if they were divisions of a single monopolist, replacing competition with coordination. The classical microeconomic analysis of monopolies makes these effects apparent.

In classical economic theory, the price of a good falls as a greater quantity of the good is produced. This is graphically represented by the industry price curve (line AG) in Figure 1. The industry cost curve (MC) is represented by the line EC, through point F. In a competitive market, firms are 'price takers' (i.e. the market conditions set the price which firms are able to charge), the quantity of goods produced (Q_c) will be at the intersection of the industry price and cost curves (lines AG and MC, respectively), resulting in a competitive price (P_c).

A monopolist (or a cartel acting as a monopolist) is a 'price setter', (or 'price maker'), that is it determines the price it can obtain for its good by reducing production. Production is determined by marginal revenue (MR), and the quantity of goods produced under a monopoly (Q_m) is determined by the intersection of the marginal revenue and marginal cost curves (MR and MC, respectively) represented by point F on Figure 1. This restriction in production (i.e. $Q_m < Q_c$) entails that the price of a good under monopoly (P_m) is greater than the price under

between undertakings which, without having been taken to the stage where an agreement properly so-called has been concluded, *knowingly substitutes practical cooperation between them for the risks of competition.*' (Emphasis supplied.)

competition (P_c). Accordingly, consumers pay more for the goods under monopoly than in a competitive marketplace.

Figure 1 graphically illustrates the welfare losses from monopolies (cartels). First, there is a loss of consumer surplus. Consumer surplus is the difference between the maximum one would pay (reservation price) and the amount one actually pays for a good. Put in crude psychological terms, this entails that the greater the consumer surplus, the greater the satisfaction in 'getting a bargain'. Producer surplus is the supply side corollary of consumer surplus, i.e. the difference between price obtained by the producer and its cost. In Figure 1 this is represented by triangle P_cEC.

Since the monopoly price is greater than the competitive price, consumer surplus is reduced. This is illustrated in Figure 1, in which the triangle AP_cC represents consumer surplus under competitive conditions. By raising the price to the monopoly price, P_m, consumer surplus is reduced to the area of triangle AP_mB. The area of P_cP_mBD represents consumer surplus which under monopoly has been appropriated by the monopolist, adding to producer surplus. The producer surplus under monopoly is represented by the area of P_mBFE.

The second welfare reducing consequence of monopolies is a creation of deadweight loss. Since the monopoly price exceeds the competitive price ($P_c < P_m$), consumers whose reservation price (willingness to pay) is above the competitive price but below the monopoly price will forgo purchasing the good, leaving an otherwise unsatisfied demand. This deadweight cost to society[34] is represented by the area of triangle BCD in Figure 1.

Posner has argued that additional welfare reducing consequence of monopolies is that any additional profit obtained from monopoly will be dissipated in an attempt to realise and maintain the monopoly position.[35] Graphically put, the area represented by P_mP_cDB is the additional gain obtained by the monopolist. Accordingly, it is cost effective for the monopolist to expend this amount to acquire and maintain its position.[36] This expenditure is dissipated through lobbying efforts of governmental bodies to obtain and protect (e.g. through tariffs, lobbying efforts to ensure licences are denied to others, etc.) the exclusivity (licence, etc.) required by the monopoly. Though Posner's analysis does not consider the case of

34 It is sometimes termed the 'social cost of monopoly'.

35 Posner, 'The Social Cost of Monopolies and Regulation'.

36 In the case of a prospective monopolist, the rational expenditure is the return (the area represented by P_mP_cDB) multiplied by the probability of obtaining the monopoly.

cartels, cartels would have additional expenditures of avoiding detection and securing the compliance of their members.

In addition to these welfare losses, monopolies are a source of social loss through two sorts of productive inefficiencies.[37] The first sort, reduced product innovation, is a greater problem with cartels than monopolies. Though impossible to demonstrate graphically, the intuition behind this claim is that, due to the explicit agreement of non-competition and profit guarantees among cartelists, any incentive to improve one's product is removed. Further, given that innovation would require the expenditure of research and development costs (which would be unnecessary due to a cartel-wide agreed 'stand-still' on innovation), such investment would not be undertaken. Since the monopolist, unlike the cartelist, must be concerned with other firms developing goods which may be less expensive substitutes for its goods, the monopolist may have greater incentive for research and development expenditure. Thus, these social costs of reduced product innovation may be greater with cartels.

The second sort of social costs, those associated with reduced innovation in productive processes, have a similar intuitive explanation. Given the incentives, just as there is no incentive for cartelists to invest in research aimed at improving their product, there is a similar disincentive to make a corresponding investment in improving (i.e. more efficient) methods of production. Again, and for the same reasons, the incentives for such investment may be less for cartel participants than monopolists. (However, given that the monopolist is the sole producer of the monopolised good, it has less an incentive to develop efficiencies in the production of the good, than to prevent its customers from switching to substitute goods.)

Graphically, these costs are illustrated in Figure 2. Since the monopolist (and by extension, cartelist) operates less efficiently, its cost curve will be greater. In Figure 2, this increased cost curve is MC'. Since the monopolist sets its production so that marginal costs equals MR (marginal revenue), the intersection of MC' and MR will be 'up and to the left' of the intersection of MC and MR. Since the quantity produced determines the price, under (this inefficient) monopoly, the price will be the new P_m'. Had the monopolist acted as a 'price taker' under this new cost curve, the market price would have been P_c'. The area defined by points XBD$P_c P_c$'Y in Figure 2 illustrates this social loss.

[37] My analysis here is based on Motta, *Competition Policy* 45–51.

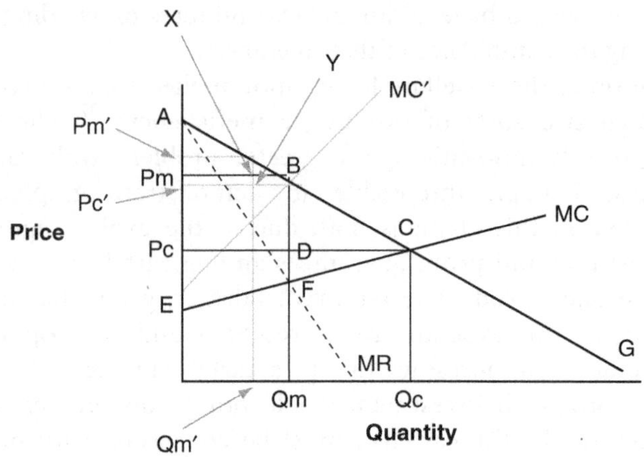

Figure 2 Loss from productive inefficiency

Productive inefficiency (of both products and processes) is related to, if not a manifestation of, Leibenstein's X-inefficiency,[38] or 'managerial slack'. This is the manifestation of a desire for a 'quiet life', removed from competitive pressures. The difference in the interests of owners (shareholders) and management gives rise to this. Motta notes:

> Shareholders care about profits, but managers care about their individual utility, determined by wage, career prospects, as well as the level of effort and time they have to put into the job. The manager might also care about profits (typically, the shareholders will write a contract where his remuneration increases with the firm's profits), but in general he will care about other things, too. As a result, when he takes decisions about technologies (or he has to take actions, which affect the firm's costs) he might not have the right incentives to adopt the most efficient ones (that is, those which maximize profits).[39]

And in collusive industry structure which guarantees a super-competitive profit, there is every incentive not to make waves.

Related to these points are two additional socio-economic concerns with monopoly (and cartels). First, though an empirical point, competitive industries are more productive.[40] Second, there is a quasi-Darwinian argument to the effect that the anti-competitive effects

[38] Leibenstein, 'Allocative Efficiency'. [39] Motta (n. 37) 47.
[40] See, ibid., 48 where Motta reviews the empirical evidence.

of monopolisation and cartels are such that they raise price to the consumer and lower social welfare.[41] In effect, though, these two points merely restate claims made above.

However described, cartels indeed do harm. The main economic harm done by cartels is in their appropriation (some have used the term 'theft'[42]) of consumer surplus, creation of a deadweight loss to the economy, and by stifling innovation in the production of new goods and design of less expensive means to produce goods. These costs are not insignificant.[43]

0.3 An outline of this work

With this description of the nature and effects of hard-core cartels in mind, we will examine the desirability of criminalising cartel conduct. We will do this from what we term a 'normative' perspective. That is to say, we will look at the moral reasons as to why such conduct should occasion the wrath of the criminal law. These moral grounds are independent from any economic or social reason for the use of criminal law to dissuade people from engaging in this sort of conduct. In many respects, the initial part of this work, in which we examine and set forth a justification for criminalising cartel conduct draws upon work

41 Ibid., 51: 'Overall, it seems that empirical studies confirm the important role played by competition in selecting the most efficient firms and thus raising productive efficiency. This also has an additional implication for competition policy: if less efficient firms were protected or subsidised, this would prevent market competition from selecting the best firms, which will actually result in higher prices and lower welfare.'

42 See, e.g., the remarks by Whish text accompanying n. 5.

43 The literature is replete with studies that attempt to estimate the costs of cartel activity. Of course, all estimates will be imprecise. However, the OECD notes: 'That the harm from cartels is large is undisputed. Quantifying it precisely, however, is difficult. Data collected through a recent OECD survey provide some additional information on the magnitude of cartels' harm. The OECD's study permits the following general, non-scientific but important conclusion: *The harm from cartels is even larger than has been previously thought, and conservatively exceeds the equivalent of billions of U.S. dollars per year*.' (OECD, *Report On The Nature And Impact of Hard Core Cartels*.) Summarising cartel overcharges, Schinkel writes:

> The majority of cartels prices within the 25 to 35% range of overcharges. The mean overcharge that the known modern international cartels for which overcharges were calculated managed to sustain is little over 28%, with a median slightly below that. Hence it is likely to be conservative to conclude that a representative cartel manages to make (annual) illegal profits of roughly 25% of total (annual) affected commerce.
>
> (Schinkel, 'Effective Cartel Enforcement' at 15.)

in the moral limits to criminal law. In effect, we return to the long-standing problem found in liberal society: given the social value emphasised by individual liberty, under what circumstances is it appropriate to restrain this freedom through the use of the criminal law?

The traditional liberal response to this conundrum has been to invoke some version of the 'harm principle', and suggest that harmful activities can be prevented. However, any sophisticated application of the principle recognises that not all harms are either amenable to, or appropriate targets for, criminalisation. Indeed, as we will argue, the usual harms which cartel activity purports to cause are not the appropriate foundations on which to justify criminally sanctioning cartel behaviour. Rather the harm lies in the pernicious effect which economically collusive activity does to the market. Our normative argument is found in Chapter 1. Here we argue that the harms identified by the micro-economic analysis of cartel activity are insufficient to serve as a foundation for the use of criminal law for their deterrence. To do this, we draw upon two strands of philosophical thought. We begin with an analysis of the moral limits to the criminal law in a liberal society. Our inspiration here is the thought of John Stuart Mill and its subsequent refinement by Joel Feinberg. The insight we glean from these ethicists is that the justification for preventing harm in society, by using society's most coercive social institution, rests in the type of harm which is sought to be prevented. We argue that only harms to our most fundamental interests (what might be regarded as welfare interests) are the proper subject for protection by the criminal law. Although we note that such welfare interests can be protected by various social institutions, we argue that none of the harms usually ascribed to cartel activity could be regarded as an interest of this sort.

We also draw on the work of John Rawls to assist us in articulating a view of the social institutions which those designing an idealised, 'just' liberal society would select. Though Rawls' perspective is an idealised one – and thus will never likely be implemented – it nevertheless provides a point of illumination: to the extent a society better reflects this ideal, the more just it can be regarded. This Rawlsian approach allows us to identify the feature that a liberal society would use as its means of distribution (or in philosophical lingo, 'its principle of distributive justice'): the market. The market provides a means of allocating goods within a society and – of the known means of distribution – it does so with the least interference with individual freedom. In this regard, it certainly dominates a command economy.

We then argue that given the fundamental role which the market has in a liberal society, as its means of distributive justice, it is justifiable to criminalise conduct which undermines this institution. Cartel activity has the effect of undermining confidence in the market, by imposing hidden rules into market activities. Thus, given the need for a civil society to ensure confidence in its most fundamental institutions, we argue that the criminalisation of this sort of market collusion is justified.

However, this conclusion contains an important caveat: it is the nature of the market within a society, and the expectations of its participants, which underlie this justification for criminalisation. If the market serves to promote goals other than those which fall under the rubric of distributive justice, then our argument is weakened. These other social goals can (and, as we will see – in the context of the European Treaty – do) include such matters as environment and employment. The significance of this caveat becomes apparent in the second part of this work.

We then turn to some additional pragmatic grounds for the criminalisation of cartel activity. A significant amount of unwanted conduct in the operation of business organisations arises from the agency model required to operate them, and the delegation of authority inherent in any agency arrangement. We argue that imposing criminal liability on business organisations for this behaviour will encourage the appropriate monitoring of corporate agents. We will note recent studies of cartel activity establish that the vast majority of such collusion has its origin in the corporate hierarchy at a level well below that of the board. Accordingly we argue that the present English *Tesco* rule of imputing liability to a corporate entity is not fit for purpose: we prefer a rule of vicarious liability. And given the nature of cartel activity, we argue that no exception to the rule (or defence) be made available for corporate 'due diligence', in other words that the rule of imposition of liability be a rule of strict vicarious liability.

Following the discussion of corporate responsibility, we turn to a further practical justification for the imposition of individual criminal liability. We use Becker's famous formula in an effort to determine the appropriate level of pecuniary sanction which must be imposed on a firm, were it to effectively deter cartel conduct. However, after further examining the typical overcharge which a firm in a cartelised industry can reap (and its consequent super-normal profit), the duration of a typical cartel, and best estimates of cartel detection, we note that such fines have to be significant. Indeed, they need to be substantially higher than those amounts imposed by, for example, the European Commission.

This leads to what we term a 'deterrence gap', where fines are essentially taxes on (or licence fees for) unwanted conduct. We argue that this gap can be closed by the imposition of additional individual sanctions of a criminal nature.

After this theoretical account, in the second part of this work we then examine the two most influential cartel control regimes in the world economy: those of the US and EU. The American system, we argue, had as its original goal the promotion of consumer welfare, although this goal was not originally phrased in that manner. This goal still remains the central goal of American anti-cartel policy. The effect of this is to assign to consumers a property interest in consumer surplus, which makes comparisons involving legal and moral inferences between theft and price-fixing (in whatever manifestation) more accurate. This property assignment supplements the initial normative consideration that undermining a regime of distributive justice is a harm to an institution of such significance that a compelling justification exists to criminalise such behaviour. As the protection of consumer surplus is the dominant, if not the exclusive, goal of American anti-cartel policy, it is clear that the conception of the market which accepts this goal regards the market as society's institution for distributive justice.

Further, the American regime imposes criminal liability vicariously, by imputing to a firm the conduct of its agent irrespective of that agent's position in the corporate hierarchy. Additionally, the Sherman Act also imposes individual criminal liability on those corporate agents who engage in cartel activity on behalf of their firm. The consequences of this are significant. The deterrence gap is closed, with the result – as we will see – recidivism in the US is currently low to non-existent.

In contrast, however, the EU's system has historically never been focused on a sole goal. We will argue that, in spite of pronouncements from individual Commissioners and interpretive discussions contained in Commission working documents, the protection of consumer welfare cannot be (nor has ever been) the exclusive goal of EU competition policy. The Treaties have always regarded a competitive market as *one of* the Union's goals. Indeed, though it may have been one among equals, it never was first among equals, and, in the post-Lisbon era, its status may have even been further downgraded. The difficulty posed by this is that with the Treaties advancing a multiplicity of goals it is difficult to regard either the protection of consumer welfare or the use of the market as exclusively a system of distributive justice as two fundamental norms of the European Union.

The consequences of this are also significant. Viewed in this way, our normative justifications for criminalisation of cartel conduct in the context of the EU as a whole are weakened. If the market is used as a means of advancing values other than distributive justice, interference with the market may be justified, particularly when those other goals are advanced. Likewise, if there is no clear assignment of property rights of consumer surplus to consumers, the supplementary justification for criminalisation is eroded. Given the multiplicity of EU Treaty goals, particularly those which bear economic relations within Europe, the EU conception of the market is more than a means of allocation of goods and services. We therefore have significant reservations about the viability of criminalising cartel conduct at the EU level. Indeed, given this very multiplicity of goals and lack of a clear assignment of a property right in consumer surplus to consumers, the arguments which we raised at the beginning of this work in support of criminalisation are seriously undermined in the case of the EU.

The significance of this conclusion for the European competition project is profound: there may be little – if any – moral force to those arguments which suggest a harmonised, EU-wide system of cartel control through the criminal justice system. Other justifications, possibly political or based upon expediency, must be proffered.

This scepticism is extended as a result of our discussion in Chapter 6, in which we consider the UK's cartel control regime. This regime is significantly different from its American cousin. Historically, since the start of the Industrial Revolution (and the attendant repeal of medieval price control and market surveillance regimes) price-fixing per se has never been viewed as a wrong which justified the intervention of the criminal law in the UK. It was always price-fixing plus some other factor which would be the foundation for criminalisation. This other factor was typically tied to fraud or some other transgression against honesty. In the context of this historical background the normative reason why 'dishonesty' was incorporated into section 188 of the Enterprise Act was evident: it merely reflected the social and commercial norms prevalent in the UK.

But, in addition to reflecting the normative content of UK commercial practice, the dishonesty element of the cartel offence was to ensure that it 'fell stillborn from the statute book', to borrow and alter a phrase from David Hume. The need to establish dishonesty before a jury would present too high a burden for a prosecution. The offence never had a chance, due to this requirement.

As the foundation of a fundamentally weak criminal regime, the UK offence lacked any credible deterrent effect. As a consequence, consultations on this offence first proposed in 2011, resulted in a reform Bill which was introduced in May of 2012. Likely to become law, the Bill amends the offence, by *inter alia*, removing the element of dishonesty, and replacing it with secrecy. The new distinguishing feature of the criminal cartel offence is a clandestine nature of the agreement to fix prices.

Again, what is clear is that the normative presupposition inherent in the UK's legal system is that the wrongness of price-fixing is not the appropriation of consumer surplus. Rather it is the existence of and reliance on (by the price-fixer) a hidden rule. To a very important extent, this dovetails very well with our normative analysis of the offence.

Ironically, as formulated, the UK's offence has this normative backing; but being unique in its dependency on secrecy (or in earlier incarnations, 'dishonesty') it was an outlier in the international community. This unique status led to profound difficulties in international cooperation, particularly when extradition was at issue. This unique position of the UK's law, we argue, provides evidence for further scepticism as to the existence of some common core of values which can be used as a foundation for international convergences. Indeed, if the US and the UK, two nations which share the 'Anglo' core of values cannot agree on what may be wrong with price-fixing, it is unlikely that a global consensus can be reached.

This scepticism is further advanced in the seventh chapter. In this chapter we look at calls for convergence. We note that convergence is both a process and a product. As a process, convergence is about how regimes harmonise their legislation. As a product, it is about a general consensus on the resulting regime. As any attempt at market regulation is inherently value laden (as we have indicated in our first chapter), convergence requires some common understanding of the values to be promoted in the marketplace, when the market is used as a means of distributive justice.

We are sceptical that there is a sufficient common normative basis to support global convergence. In our argument, we draw on the work of Geert Hofstede,[44] whose influential study of IBM employees across the globe demonstrated a number of cultural differences, which have a bearing on individual and collective responses to incentives. Hofstede's

[44] Hofstede, *Culture's Consequences*.

study analyses these values, and shows that different cultures will align differently along five axes, with different responses to matters such as:

- power distance (i.e. acceptance of unequal distribution of power and resources),
- individualism vs collectivism,
- uncertainty avoidance,
- masculinity vs femininity, and
- long-term vs short-term orientation.

As legal systems are nothing more than institutionalised incentive structures, how individuals respond to incentives should be of concern to those designing systems. To the extent that any proposed system has a cross-cultural dimension to it (as any global system will), this cultural element must be taken into account.

Once the element is taken into account, we argue that successful global convergence is a near impossible task. We suggest that a better alternative, and more effective focus for efforts, would be on convergence along regional fronts. Regional alliances and agreements are likely to be representative of (or indeed the product of) common norms, which we suggest will be a more effective means to deal with this so-viewed problem.

We are sceptical of any global solution, particularly with the development of a global system based on an American-style model, as organisations such as the OECD and UNCTAD[45] have suggested. They have had their eyes towards the American system, and with that vision in mind proposed that criminal sanctions are appropriate for hard-core cartel conduct. However, given the social and economic structures in which the American system was born and out of which it evolved, with the resulting values it protects, it is rather incongruous (if not naïve) to assume that it is appropriate to transplant it into other systems with their own (and differing) conceptions of the values served by the marketplace.

[45] See UNCTAD Model Law on Competition, Part I, Chapter XI (II) (ii).

1

A normative approach to the criminalisation of cartel activity

1.1 Liberalism and the harm to others justification of the criminal law

1.1.1 Harm (generally) and criminalisation

Although hard-core cartel activities can be readily described, and their social costs made apparent and estimated, further argument is needed to justify the control of these activities through criminal sanctions. Not all costly or harmful activities should be illegal. For instance, both tobacco use and binge drinking impose extensive economic costs and social harm in the UK,[1] yet it would be a daunting task to argue in favour of the *criminalisation* (as opposed to other methods of regulatory control) of either activity on the basis of these costs or harms.

Accordingly, to focus upon a certain activity, even if such activity is admittedly harmful and costly, and single it out as requiring criminal sanctions to eradicate it, requires an additional argument. This is not a legal matter, we are not describing what a law does or does not do; nor is it a sociological or anthropological matter, as we are not describing social or cultural attitudes towards certain practices. It is a normative matter, we are advocating what *ought* (or *should*) be the case. That is, we make the claim that cartel participants *should* occasion the wrath of the criminal law *because* X, where X provides the normative (i.e. 'principled' or 'ethical') reason for the use of criminal sanctions.

As such, our task in this chapter is quite specific: we seek a moral principle which can justify the criminalisation of those anti-competitive

[1] Allender et al., 'The Burden of Smoking-Related Ill Health in the UK' estimating that in 2005–6 the direct effects of smoking were responsible for 109,164 deaths with a cost to the National Health Service of £5.2 billion in the UK. The National Health Services estimates that in 2005 there were 14,982 deaths attributable to alcohol abuse, with an estimated cost to the NHS in England in 2004 of £2.7 billion: NHS Information Centre, *Lifestyles Statistics, Statistics on Alcohol: England*, 2010.

practices characteristic of hard-core cartels. Discussion of anti-competitive practices can only make sense within the context of a market-based economy. Indeed, legislation regulating and criminalising such practices is only found in that context. It makes no sense to discuss anti-competitive practices of the sort mentioned earlier in the context of, say, a Soviet-style centrally planned and controlled economy. Market-based economies are a hallmark of a liberal society, in which individuals are permitted to order their own lives, and determine this ordering from the choices with which they are presented. Our task, therefore, becomes that of providing a normative justification for the criminalisation of hard-core cartel activities within the context of a liberal economy or – at minimum – within the context of a liberalised society, i.e. one which adopts market-based institutions for the distribution of goods and services (as a principle of distributive justice).

Briefly put, the liberal conception of society is that of a group of individuals who are varied in their abilities, strengths and tastes, all of whom are in pursuit their individual wellbeing. Civil society is organised to permit its members the greatest opportunities to achieve those goals conducive to their individual wellbeing. If there were a genus-species taxonomy of liberalism, the foregoing would constitute a rough definition of the genus. As there are numerous conceptions of how this organisation comes about, and the role of social (governmental) constraints to the individual, these would roughly define species of liberal theories of the state. But common to all species of liberalism is the recognition of the value of freedom of individuals to enable them to make those choices crucial for the pursuit of individual wellbeing, i.e. self-determination. Accordingly, a reoccurring theme in liberal thought concerns legitimate bounds to the state's constraints on an individual's exercise of his liberty.

1.1.2 Mill and the harm to others principle

John Stuart Mill's *On Liberty* represents perhaps the first comprehensive, if not the best known, discussion of this matter. Mill's thesis is quite simple:

> that the sole end for which mankind are warranted, individually or collectively, in interfering with the liberty of action of any of their number, is self-protection. That the only purpose for which power can be rightfully exercised over any member of a civilized community,

> against his will, is to prevent harm to others. His own good, either physical or moral, is not a sufficient warrant.[2]

His argument is more complex. He moves from an analysis of the importance of freedom of opinion to its bearing on human conduct.

Mill argues free thought and speech are instrumental for at least two reasons. First, they are the cornerstones of the defence against a tyranny or corrupt government.[3] By exposing an idea openly, any truth contained in an idea will become apparent due to challenge. In a nineteenth-century manner, it is the veracity contained in an idea which guarantees the idea's survival in the world of ideas, just as fitness of an individual guarantees survival in the world of nature.

Additionally, diverse opinions have utility producing value. By acting on these different opinions, members of society can develop their individuality, experiment in their ways of living, thereby enhancing their own (and hence overall) happiness (or utility). As a person is their own best judge of what fulfils them,[4] permitting a person to act on their own opinions allows that person to pursue what is best for them. In Mill's mind, such freedom of action not only allows the individual to maximise her wellbeing; but if that action is indeed productive of wellbeing, it can provide an example for others to emulate (and potentially bring them happiness).[5]

Yet the expression of opinions and freedom of action is not unfettered. There is a legitimate social interest in restricting liberty of opinion and action when such expression or action may harm another. Mill's well-known treatment of this is worth quoting:

> No one pretends that actions should be as free as opinions. On the contrary, even opinions lose their immunity, when the circumstances in which they are expressed are such as to constitute their expression a positive instigation to some mischievous act. An opinion that corn-dealers are starvers of the poor ... may justly incur punishment when delivered orally to an excited mob assembled before the house of a corn-dealer, or when handed about among the same mob in the form of a placard ... The liberty of the individual must be thus far limited; he must not make himself a nuisance to other people.[6]

Yet Mill recognises that we are to not be protected from all harms. Every zero-sum activity has 'winners' and 'losers', and any 'loss' is a fortiori harm. However, some such activities may themselves be useful (or

[2] Mill, *On Liberty* 223–4 [3] Ibid., 228. [4] Ibid., 277. [5] Ibid., 269–70.
[6] Ibid., 260 and 267.

productive of general happiness), and thus it is counter-productive to the advancement of general happiness to prohibit these activities on the ground that they cause harm.

Other, supplementary, principles for limiting such activities must be elucidated. Mill comments:

> In many cases, an individual, in pursuing a legitimate object, necessarily and therefore legitimately causes pain or loss to others, or intercepts a good which they had a reasonable hope of obtaining. Such oppositions of interest between individuals often arise from bad social institutions, but are unavoidable while those institutions last; and some would be unavoidable under any institutions. Whoever succeeds in an overcrowded profession, or in a competitive examination; . . . reaps benefit from the loss of others, from their wasted exertion and their disappointment. But it is, by common admission, better for the general interest of mankind, that persons should pursue their objects undeterred by this sort of consequences. In other words, society admits no right, either legal or moral, in the disappointed competitors, to immunity from this kind of suffering; and feels called on to interfere, only when means of success have been employed which it is contrary to the general interest to permit – namely, fraud or treachery, and force.[7]

Though fraud, treachery and force are the most obvious criteria, it is certainly a mistake to interpret Mill as intending this list to be an exhaustive enumeration, as – for instance – he recognises that extremely offensive conduct can have the same effect as harmful conduct and thus may legitimately be prohibited.[8]

Thus outlined, Mill's views provide a strong starting point for the analysis of the limits of criminal law (and other coercive state action) within a liberal society. Harm to others, with recognition that not all harms are sufficiently vital for protection and that certain forms of offensive conduct are tantamount to harmful conduct, serves as the skeleton for the legitimate use of criminal sanctions. This skeleton must be fleshed out by a need for supplementary principles to separate protected harms from more trivial harms.

Mill's very brief account requires the expansion of two points for our purposes. First, as his account of the nature of protected harm is imprecise, further amplification of the concept of harm and why certain harms should be prevented using the threat of criminal sanctions is required. Second, Mill's justification for the narrow legitimate limits to criminal law is ultimately utilitarian. However, as utilitarianism is itself a

[7] Ibid., 292–3. [8] Ibid., 295.

contentious position, it is appropriate to offer an alternative position (either as a supplement or a substitute) for a position similar to Mill's. The following two sub-sections develop these points.

1.1.3 Protected harms

Any adequate system of criminal law must prevent some activities on the basis that they do harm to others, thus it is fundamental to secure the precise meaning of 'harm'. To proceed without this concept being clarified may yield improper results. Too wide a notion of what properly constitutes harm (and thus ought to be criminalised) will lead to overbroad legislation: too many activities will be prohibited, leading to unnecessary loss of liberty. Too narrow a concept of harm may lead to inadequate protection of the citizen.

As Feinberg notes, the word 'harm' and the concepts described by it are both vague and imprecise.[9] If we look at a standard dictionary definition, say as found in an *Oxford English Dictionary*, we note that the word 'harm' has three related meanings: (1) physical injury, (2) material damage and (3) actual or potential ill effect.[10] Likewise, as Feinberg also notes, the term is used in three different senses: first, the sense in which we say that a non-human thing is hurt by something else (e.g. 'frost does harm to the crops'[11]); second, a sense in which an interest is thwarted or set back;[12] and third, a sense in which someone has wronged (or treated unjustly) another.[13] The third sense is a subset of the second, and the first sense – as Feinberg also notes – stretches the concept: 'damaged', 'mangled', 'killed' and similar terms better describe what transpired.[14] Hence, the first sense can be set aside for our purposes.

The second sense (a setback to an interest) captures the core of the concept of harm, and is exemplified by each of the three dictionary meanings. Thus, it is appropriate to use this sense of harm as the starting point of analysis. But this sense, as it relies on the concept of interest, is also vague and imprecise. Our dictionary lists five separate meanings for the word 'interest':[15] (1) the state of wanting to know about something or someone, (2) money paid for the use of money lent, or for delaying the repayment of a debt, (3) the advantage or benefit of someone, (4) a share

[9] Feinberg, *Harm to Others* 31–4. [10] See *Concise Oxford English Dictionary*, s.v.
[11] Feinberg, *Harm to Others* (n. 9) 32–3. [12] Ibid., 33–4. [13] Ibid., 34–5.
[14] Ibid., 32–3. [15] See *Concise Oxford English Dictionary*, s.v.

or involvement in an undertaking, and (5) a group having a common concern, especially in politics or business. However, it is only the third, 'the advantage or benefit of someone', which can illuminate what is meant by the principle of 'harm to others'.

'Harm to others', in the sense that Mill or any legislator would intend, involves a setback to an individual's interests, with 'interests' taken in the sense of advantages or benefits. However, when the nature of human (and quite likely – at least higher – animal) interests is examined, we see that we have a number of types or kinds of interests. For instance, on a hot day we may wish for an ice cream. We wish to engage in physical exercise so that we become or remain fit, as we also wish to be in a state of health. And we have longer term wants – e.g. to raise our children, to build our dream home.

From this brief illustration of types of interests (ranging from immediate wants to long-term goals), two things become immediately apparent: first, the types of interests greatly differ from each other; and, second, not all of these types of interests are worthy of legal protection (particularly via the criminal law). No one could credibly maintain that hindering another's ability to exercise or build a dream house merits criminal sanctions,[16] yet at the same time deliberately worsening someone's health could well be legitimately criminalised.

The above analysis shows that we have roughly four types of interests. Following Feinberg,[17] and using his terminology, they can be cogently grouped as follows:

- Passing Wants, e.g. an ice cream on a hot day;
- Instrumental Wants, e.g. get exercise;
- Welfare Interests, e.g. be in physical health and vigour; and,
- Focal Aims, e.g. build a dream house.

The third type, welfare interests, is of central importance to the legislator.

Welfare interests are the minimum foundations on which our other goals are based, and without which our survival becomes difficult (if not impossible). A non-exhaustive list of examples includes health, freedom from pain, economic wellbeing, and personal security. Feinberg emphasises their indispensability:

[16] However, if it is through kidnapping or theft that these interests are hindered, it is the kidnapping or theft which should be criminalised.

[17] Feinberg, *Harm to Others* (n. 9) 55–64 and in particular 60.

> Our interest in welfare, speaking quite generally, is an interest in achieving and maintaining that minimum level of physical and mental health, material resources, economic assets, and political liberty that is necessary if we are to have any chance at all of achieving our higher good or well-being, as determined by our more ulterior goals. Personal welfare, as the term is used here, is an indispensably necessary condition for the achievement of ultimate well-being, but by no means a sufficient condition. One cannot get anything else if one does not have it, but one does not usually have much when one has only it. On the other hand, while one cannot live on bread alone, without bread one cannot live at all.[18]

Welfare interests are fundamental but are only as strong as their weakest link: 'All of the money in the world won't help you if you have a fatal disease.'[19] These are the sorts of interests which are deserving of legal protection, particularly by criminal law.

The satisfaction of focal aims may result in the feelings of wellbeing that one has strived for throughout one's life, and serve as a motivating factor in how one chooses to live one's life. But the protection of focal aims is not directly the realm of the law.[20] As Feinberg notes, I have my liberty, my health, my economic adequacy, personal security and the like, but 'the rest is entirely up to me'.[21] Focal aims are more complex and more individuated than welfare interests. One person's ideal of a restful life of semi-retirement in their dream house will not necessarily coincide with that of another. Accordingly, these interests are too complex and too varied to merit direct legal protection.

Likewise, passing and instrumental wants are also inappropriate candidates for legal protection. Passing wants, e.g. the ice cream on a hot day, are fleeting. It is rarely a significant setback to someone if these go unsatisfied. Instrumental wants are, as their name suggests, instrumental. We satisfy these wants as a means to achieve something. We want to exercise so that we might be healthy. Although satisfying instrumental wants is important, their importance is solely in obtaining the goal of the want. In the example, it is health which is served by the want, not the exercise. And, we note, health is a welfare interest. So, in the end, passing wants are too trivial for legal protection, and the importance of instrumental wants lies in their goals. It is the *states achieved* by instrumental wants where the borders of legal protection begin, and these states are, or are directed through, welfare interests.

[18] Ibid., 57. [19] Ibid. [20] Ibid., 61–4. [21] Ibid., 62.

The analysis of welfare interests also shows another dimension to the scope of legal protection. Most welfare interests require some form of institutional structure to protect them.[22] Economic wellbeing requires well-defined property entitlements along with a means to ensure that others respect the interests. Personal security also requires some sort of protection and enforcement apparatus. Our health interests require some safeguard mechanisms: e.g. public health, food and water inspections.

These institutional interests (our term) serve to safeguard and protect our welfare interests. For instance, tax collecting provides revenue to finance other activities – courts, defence, police and security – which in turn protect our individual welfare. As such, Feinberg notes, these institutional interests in the end belong to individuals.[23] For our purposes, it is only necessary to conclude that, in virtue of their importance, we have a stake in protecting both sorts of these sorts of institutions through legal coercion, if necessary.

Although welfare interests are the sort of interests suited to legal protection, there are limitations to their protection. These limitations are of two sorts, which we can conveniently term first and second degree limitations. First degree limitations are cases in which the interest is entirely excluded from consideration of protection, notwithstanding its status as a welfare interest of purported importance. The legal maxims *volenti non fit injuria* and *de minimis non curat lex* govern first degree limitations. Second degree limitations are cases of two (or more) sufficiently important interests conflicting in a manner which force a legislature to determine which (and by what means) one interest is to be preferred (protected) over another. These latter limitations involve the legislative task of balancing competing interests.

The preceding discussion thus shows the following. At minimum, any system of criminal law must incorporate a harm to others principle. In a liberal society, there is little room for other principles to extend the grasp of criminal sanctions. Profound offence to others may *perhaps* be one such minimal extension.[24] Not all harms are to be prevented: only those to which one does not consent, extend beyond a *de minimis* threshold, and affect our welfare interests ought to be secured by the use of criminal measures. Further, and very importantly for our purposes, although individuals may be the bearers of interests in the final analysis, institutional interests (so-called public, community, governmental interests)

[22] Ibid., 63–4. [23] Ibid., 63.

[24] Risk of harm may also provide another extension: see Feinberg, *Harm to Others* (n. 9) 11.

which serve to protect our welfare interests, can also be deserving of protection via the criminal law.

What the discussion above has not shown, however, is a reason that this liberal conception to the limit of criminal law is to be preferred over other, more far-reaching systems of legal restraint on social conduct. Mill's views (though a paradigm of liberal thinking) are ultimately based on utilitarian principles. Utilitarianism is not a self-evident truth. A further defence of the narrow bounds preferred by the liberal (and preferably based on non-utilitarian foundations) is thus essential. In the following sub-section, we outline such a defence, based on the work of John Rawls.

1.1.4 Rawls' 'veil of ignorance' and the choice of social institutions

Rawls' task, in his *A Theory of Justice*, is to provide an explicitly anti-utilitarian account of a conception of justice, one which he sees as the philosophical underpinning of any constitutional democracy.[25] Given this anti-utilitarianism,[26] it provides a useful complement to Mill's argument. If Mill's reasoning for the restriction of legal coercion to only cases of harms to others is rejected *due to its utilitarian foundation*, then Rawls' position can provide an alternative justification for the principle. Accordingly, this limitation of the legitimate exercise of criminal power can be viewed as having an alternative foundation, if not being a more universal principle underlying the moral limits of legislation within a liberal society.

The foundation of Rawls' conception of justice is based on the contractarian insights of the liberal tradition. Rawls views the social contract as a thought experiment to determine those social principles which would be selected by rational persons who have been placed under conditions which precluded them from bargaining (or reasoning) to their peculiar advantage. The Kantian (and thus anti-utilitarian) presupposition of Rawls' position is apparent: these conditions preclude individuals from bargaining to a self-exception to a general social rule (e.g. 'everyone – except myself – should do/refrain from doing X').[27]

Rawls' reasoning begins by considering a hypothetical, pre-moral situation. In this original position (his analogue of the traditional state

[25] Rawls, *A Theory of Justice*, xi. [26] See his remarks at, e.g., ibid., 130.

[27] Ibid., 157, 221–27; see also Kant, *Groundwork of the Metaphysic of Morals*, Book I, Chapter 2 (the first and third formulations of the Categorical Imperative).

of nature) human beings are taken as roughly equal, rational, self-interested,[28] risk adverse,[29] with differing conceptions of the good in life.[30] The original position is characterised by conditions of moderate scarcity,[31] and in it those reasoning to moral principles are deprived (or placed behind a metaphorical 'veil of ignorance') of any knowledge which may lead them to seek a particular preference based upon their own characteristics. Rawls points out, '[t]his explains the propriety of the name "justice as fairness": it conveys the idea that the principles of justice are agreed to in an initial situation that is fair'.[32] In addition to ignorance of our own peculiar circumstances, the veil of ignorance shields one from knowledge of the economic and political circumstances of their society and the generation to which one belongs.[33]

From this original position, Rawls argues that two principles of justice would be agreed upon and ranked in order (so as to avoid conflicts between competing applications of the principles) with priority given to the first principle. These principles are:

> First Principle
> Each person is to have an equal right to the most extensive total system of equal basic liberties compatible with a similar system of liberties for all.
> Second Principle
> Social and economic liberties are to be arranged so that they are both:
>
> (a) to the greatest benefit of the least advantaged, consistent with the just savings principle, and
> (b) attached to offices and positions open to all under conditions of fair equality of opportunity.[34]

We are primarily concerned with the first principle.

We make two interpretive points: first, Rawls notes that there are two priority rules (to which those in the original position would agree) which govern the application of the principles. The first such rule states:

> The principles of justice are to be ranked in lexical order and therefore the basic liberties can be restricted only for the sake of liberty. There are two cases:
>
> (a) a less extensive liberty must strengthen the total system of liberties shared by all;
> (b) a less equal liberty must be acceptable to those with lesser liberty.[35]

[28] Rawls (n. 25), 124–5. [29] Ibid., 131–4. [30] Ibid., 118–120, 131–2.
[31] Ibid., 109–10. [32] Ibid., 111, see also 118–23. [33] Ibid., 118. [34] Ibid., 266.
[35] Ibid.

The second rule puts priority on justice over considerations of welfare and efficiency, and is not germane to the present discussion.

Our second point concerns the so-called 'basic liberties', described in the first principle. These interests closely correlate with Feinberg's welfare interests. Rawls describes them:

> Now it is essential to observe that the basic liberties are given by a list of such liberties. Important among them are political liberty (the right to vote and to hold public office) and freedom of speech and assembly; liberty of conscience and freedom of thought; freedom of the person, which includes freedom from psychological oppression and physical assault and dismemberment (integrity of the person); the right to hold personal property and freedom from arbitrary arrest and seizure as defined by the concept of the rule of law. These liberties are to be equal by the first principle.[36]

As basic liberties are viewed as essential to a rational being's ability to order their interests so that they can achieve their own conception of the good in life (or in Feinberg's term, a 'focal aim'). And given that in the circumstances of the original position one has no concept of what their own good is, Rawls suggests that those in the original position would agree to the greatest possible set of liberties in order for those in the original position to facilitate their own pursuit of the good.[37]

Rawls opines that (1) rationality, (2) self-interest, (3) ignorance of contingent information about ourselves, and (4) knowledge of the existence of ultimate goals (though given the veil of ignorance there is unawareness of what their content and how they coincide with ultimate goals of others) of those in the original position compel them to select the two principles of justice.

He argues in the original position, stripped of all knowledge of irrelevant contingencies of oneself and others, one would immediately recognise that one could not secure any special advantages for oneself.[38] Accordingly, the initial agreement would be one in which liberties, incomes, wealth and opportunities are equally distributed. This initial equality need not be a permanent situation. If inequalities can make all people better off (including those least advantaged by the inequalities), then those in the initial position would agree to permit such inequalities.[39] Accordingly, Rawls concludes, the two principles of justice would be agreed upon.

[36] Ibid., 53. [37] Ibid., 160, see also 131–2. [38] Ibid., 130. [39] Ibid., 130–1.

Two complementary considerations lead to the ranking of the principles. As a rational person in the original position one knows one will have focal aims in life, but one is to be ignorant of what these may be and how they relate to the focal ends of one's fellow citizens. Hence, by giving priority to liberty one guarantees the ability to pursue these aims, possibly over the objections of one's fellow citizens.[40]

The second consideration is a slightly more formal approach to the first. Under the veil of ignorance, the limited knowledge which an individual possesses requires that – save for the most basic choices – any choices would be made under conditions of extreme uncertainty. The maximin rule of choice under uncertainty[41] provides an effective guide to choice. Since the relatively unfettered pursuit (i.e. subject only to like fetters imposed on others) of one's own focal aims is of paramount importance to us, that unfettered ability to pursue one's concept of the good serves as a minimum acceptable beginning position for moral society. As those in the original position would be unwilling to gamble with liberty (given the dire consequences of its loss) and that the veil of ignorance also precludes knowledge of the factual basis of any probabilities on which an expected gain/utility calculation could be based,[42] the first principle of justice would be chosen and given priority.

Once these principles are selected, those in the original position can begin the creation of a moral society, through the construction of just social, economic and political institutions. This is accomplished through a metaphorical 'lifting' of the veil of ignorance in a gradual manner, so that institutions are designed to take into account the actual circumstances in which individuals as members of a society find themselves. In accord with the conception of justice as fairness, the institutions are designed prior to the revelation to the designers of any particular (morally irrelevant) information which could be used by a particular designer to construct an institution to that designer's advantage.

Although the details of Rawls' project[43] are well beyond the scope of this text, we must identify two general features which would be contained in any social and political structure designed by those under the veil of ignorance. These are: first, the rule of law (in particular how

40 Ibid., 131.

41 See Dresher, *Games of Strategy* 21–35. This is a rule of choice when those choosing have no information about the probabilities of future events. It tells one to rank all possible outcomes, and select the least worse of them, i.e. 'maximise the minimum'.

42 Rawls (n. 25), 148–53 (particularly 149) and 160.

43 His argument occupies Part Two (171–343) of *A Theory of Justice*.

liberty limiting laws can be justified, given the first principle of justice) in such a society. And, second, the social and political institutions of distributive justice (which may have a tendency to inequalities which may be contrary to a prima facie application of the second principle of justice) in such a society.

Those developing a social system must develop certain sets of public rules to guide social conduct. When these rules construct a coercive system to regulate conduct, they become a legal system. What distinguishes a legal system from other social institutions is its monopoly on certain forms of coercion, and that law 'defines the basic structure within which the pursuit of all other activities takes place'.[44] As such, legal systems incorporate the precepts of the rule of law to varying degrees, and to the extent that a particular system better incorporates these precepts, it can be regarded as more just.[45]

The precepts impose a structure upon a legal system to permit rational individuals an opportunity to formulate reasonable expectations as to their and others' conduct.[46] They are quite minimal, and based upon Fuller's insights.[47] Because of this minimalism, their relationship which the precepts have to the first principle of justice (priority of liberty) is immediately apparent: the precepts ensure that the bounds of one's liberty are clearly demarcated so one can exercise one's liberties to the fullest with confidence and without fear.[48]

Related to the principle of liberty is the need for the existence (and occasional use) of coercive governmental power to ensure the stability of social institutions. Although we recognise the advantages of adhering to a common conception of justice and reaping the resulting benefits, under certain circumstances there may be an incentive to cheat.[49] Though we do our part, we may have suspicions that others do not, which can in turn lead to the erosion of these institutions.[50] Rawls uses the example of income taxation:

> even under reasonably ideal conditions, it is hard to imagine, for example, a successful income tax scheme on a voluntary basis. Such an arrangement is unstable. The role of an authorized public interpretation of rules supported by collective sanctions is precisely to overcome this instability. By enforcing a public system of penalties government

44 Ibid., 207. 45 Ibid., 208. 46 Ibid., 207.

47 Rawls' discussion is contained in ibid., 207–10. As Rawls notes, his analysis is based on Fuller, *The Morality of Law* and *Anatomy of Law*.

48 Rawls (n. 25), 210–11. 49 This is the social version of the prisoners' dilemma.

50 Rawls (n. 25), 211.

> removes the ground for thinking that others are not complying with the rules. For this reason, alone, a coercive sovereign is presumably always necessary, even though in a well-ordered society sanctions are not severe and may never need to be imposed. Rather, the existence of effective penal machinery serves as men's security to one another. This proposition and the reasoning behind it we may think of as Hobbes's thesis.[51]

The coercive power of the state (the Hobbesian thesis) is thus our guarantee that political and economic structures set up according to the first principle of justice are maintained. Indeed, in Kantian terms, the use of this social coercion prevents (and punishes[52]) self-exceptions to general social rules.

It is evident that there can be no universal recipe for the Hobbesian thesis. The extent of the need for, and the precise forms that state coercion takes, is dependent upon a number of social and developmental factors most of which will only be revealed as the veil of ignorance is lifted and society's social and economic circumstance become known. For instance, *ceteris paribus*, conditions of moderate prosperity will call for a different regime of property protection than will conditions of even moderate scarcity. Accordingly, the design of the coercive apparatus of the state is a balancing act performed by its architects.

Rawls' second principle of justice is ultimately a principle of distributive justice: in short, an equal distribution is to be preferred, unless an unequal distribution is to the greatest benefit of the least preferred. To extend the principles of justice to the basic structure of society a system of social institutions must be developed to tease out the content of the principles. As was the case with chosen system of legal coercion, the social principles of justice will be dependent upon the particular economic, social and developmental circumstances of the society for which the institutions are designed. Again, these are revealed as the veil of ignorance is lifted, but again – in accord with the maxim of justice as fairness – the institutions must be designed prior to the revelation of any special information which those designing the institutions can use to their own advantage.

Although the precise details of the broad-ranging system of distributive justice are contingent upon the particular circumstances of society, Rawls suggests that two elements must necessarily be found in any

[51] Ibid., Rawls' footnote omitted.

[52] On Kant's views of the necessity of punishment, see Kant, *The Metaphysic of Morals*, 'On the right to punish and grant clemency' (The doctrine of right, part five).

system of distributive justice. These are (1) a means for the distribution of goods (and services); and (2) an institutional structure to ensure that resulting distributions continue to be just, correcting injustices if and when necessary. The market (of one form or another) is the appropriate means for distribution, and appropriately designed governmental institutions are the appropriate means for ensuring the continuation of distributive justice.

Rawls' preference in the choice of the former is that of a market-based system of distribution which allows private ownership of capital and natural resources.[53] Given the evaluative purpose (comparing an existing with an ideal system for evaluation) that his theory has, Rawls' emphasis on capitalism makes sense. Further, this emphasis is also appropriate for our task, the examination of the legitimacy of the criminalisation of hard-core cartel conduct, since that conduct occurs primarily in a market-based system characteristic of a private-property regime.

A market-based system of distribution has such clear advantages over its alternative, a command-based system, that it – in some form or another – would be an obvious choice. The most significant advantage of the market system is its tendency to further liberty interests. Rawls observes:

> A further and more significant advantage of the market system is that, given the requisite background institutions, it is consistent with equal liberties and fair equality of opportunity. Citizens have a free choice of careers and occupations. There is no reason at all for the forced and central direction of labor ... There is no necessity for comprehensive direct planning. Individual households and firms are free to make their decisions independently, subject to the general conditions of the economy.[54]

In preference to a command system, a market-based system of allocation has the additional virtues of efficiency and administrative simplicity.[55]

However, in spite of the liberty enhancing features of market-based distribution systems, actual markets will fall short of the ideal. Hence they call for correction to restore both equality, and particularly the very liberty which justifies the institution of the market. Rawls remarks that market failure, in the sense of '[m]onopolistic restrictions, lack of information, external economies and diseconomies, and the like must be recognized and corrected'.[56] He continues, '[a]nd the market fails

[53] Rawls (n. 25), 243. [54] Ibid., 240–1. [55] Ibid., 239.

[56] Ibid., 240: by 'monopolistic restrictions', Rawls appears to mean 'abuse of a dominant position', see e.g. his remarks on competition, ibid., 241 and 244.

altogether in the case of public goods'.[57] We examine the implications of this for a system of distributive justice below.

1.2 An outline of a liberal theory of the limits to criminal law

The starting point for any replication of Rawls' thought experiment aimed at eliciting the legitimate frontiers of criminal law in an ideal state lies with individuals under the veil of ignorance. For the reasons provided by Rawls, those so positioned will adopt the two principles of justice and their priority rules. They will see that the precepts of the rule of law are an essential means of protecting the network of liberties advanced by the first principle of justice. Additionally, those in the original position will also recognise the superiority of a market-based system of a distributive justice over a command-based system of distribution, insofar as a market-based system is more conducive to permitting individuals to realise those ends which they strive.

Likewise, as the veil is lifted, the initial parameters of the criminal law can be established. In this state of affairs, although one is ignorant of the social conditions in which one will ultimately live, one is nonetheless aware of some of one's features. In particular, those in the original position know two aspects of their psychological make-up: they have a set of interests of varying types – though they are unaware of what precisely they may be; and, they are risk adverse, so they are unwilling to gamble in an effort to improve their situation. This risk aversion is particularly influential in their choice of a network of liberties. This network will accordingly be designed in order that they may pursue their focal aims in a manner which is as unfettered as possible.

From this awareness of their psychological make-up, and upon reflection on the types of desires they have, they would recognise that these desires would fall into a continuum (or perhaps into a number of different sets of desires), identified by the type of interest underlying a particular desire. While they would not know what they desire, they would know the sorts of desires which they are capable of having. Whether or not those in the original position would choose to organise these interests into Feinberg's four-fold classification, they would nevertheless recognise that not all interests can be protected by legal institutions in a manner which is consistent with like liberty for all.

[57] Ibid., 240.

Those in the original position would also have some other general knowledge of interests and their protection. They would know that protecting one interest entails preferring that interest at the expense of another (or another's) interest. They would also know that given the nature of focal aims, they are not susceptible of protection without infringing on the liberties of other parties, and such infringements could not be justified by parties in the original position. Thus, in the original position, the parties would know that they have focal aims, but not what these were. Since protecting one aim or one sort of aims can exclude others, and those in the original position will not be aware of their own aims (and indeed they would be unwilling to gamble with any structure which may inhibit their own attainment of these aims), they would reason that it would be irrational to protect focal aims. It would be similarly irrational to protect fleeting interests or wants. Even if these could be protected in a manner consistent with like liberty for all, such wants are too trivial to merit protection. To protect interests has a cost, not only financially and administratively, but also to liberty. Protecting such wants hinders a programme of extensive liberty.

The sorts of interests that would be protected are those fundamental interests which are essential to social life. These were termed 'basic liberties' by Rawls,[58] and – as noted above – correlate well with Feinberg's welfare interests. However, when these interests are considered carefully, not all are amenable to the protection through criminal sanctions. While those interests surrounding bodily integrity (e.g. freedom from assault) and protection of property (e.g. freedom from theft) are well suited to such protection, other interests (e.g. freedom from arbitrary arrest and detention) are better suited to protection by appropriate design of legal institutions (with the precepts of law in mind), and most political and social interests (e.g. freedom of expression and conscience) are ill-suited to protection through the criminal law.

Those in the original position would also choose to protect the institutions which have as their mandate the promotion of distributive justice through regulatory or redistributive means. We make three observations about these institutions. First, these measures are primarily regulatory, but backed up with a threat of coercion to ensure compliance and resolve the instability associated with the perception that others may be cheating. This is the immediate implication of the Hobbesian thesis mentioned by Rawls in his example of income taxation.[59] The threat (and

[58] See above text to n. 36. [59] See above text to n. 51.

use) of coercion solves many of the prisoner's dilemma-like problems associated with cooperation in social organisations. We explore this in further detail below.

Second, the exact content of the regulations underlying the institutions of distributive justice is contingent upon the economic circumstances of the society. These will become known to the parties during the metaphorical 'lifting' of the veil. Generalities will be known first, prior to individuals knowing their place and lot within society. At the stage of awareness of generalities the parties will agree upon the design and content of the regulatory institutions, so they are unable to use any specific (or morally arbitrary) information to their advantage.

Third, the completion of the content of regulatory institutions of distributive justice will parallel the completion of the coercive apparatus necessary to guarantee the general application of the first principle of justice. As noted above, protection of our interests of bodily integrity and property are most amenable to protection by the criminal law. The protection of most of the key interests in bodily integrity as well as the rudiments of the protection of property can begin under the full covering of the veil. One only requires the most minimum knowledge (i.e. the sort possessed under the full covering of the veil) to recognise that network of liberty is enhanced when coercive mechanisms to prevent, e.g. murder, assault and theft are in place.

Beyond this, however, the veil must be lifted in order that information regarding the society's state of development can be obtained. This information is essential to an assessment of the nature and scope of the property regime to be put in place, as well as to the less minimal (but nevertheless important) rights surrounding bodily integrity. Two examples illustrate this point: those drafting the Statute of Anne had no conception of digital media; and the crime of insider trading takes place only in reasonably well-developed economic circumstances. In both cases, the level of economic wealth and technological development of a society in which a particular legal system is found drives the nature and extent of the rights protected by that legal system.

This application of the Rawlsian thought experiment to the development of an ideal criminal law shows five features of interest to our task. Those designing the institutions which protect and promote the two principles of justice will design the institutions in a manner which gives priority to liberty. This entails that liberty can only be restricted for the sake of extending or promoting liberty. The immediate implication of this is, first, that the set of interests protected by criminal law will be small, covering a subset of so-called welfare interests, limited to the integrity of the person and property, and the institutions which protect those interests. A harm to others principle, perhaps extended only by an offence to others principle (if the offensive behaviour is sufficiently severe) would be the sole justification for criminal sanctions. Any other justification, e.g. moralism, paternalism, and prevention of harm to self, severely restricts a subject's liberty. Given the fundamentally risk adverse nature of those in the original position, it would be irrational for them to consent to such justifications, as by so doing, they may restrict their own liberty, and ultimately frustrate the pursuit of their own focal ends.

Second, to provide an additional guarantee of liberty, those designing legal prohibitions and sanctions will design them in accord with the precepts of the rule of law, as these provide a measure of certainty upon which members of society can rely in organising their lives. They provide a structural means of protecting the subject's liberty.

Third, it is clear that institutions (and in particular those legal structures designed to advance the principles of justice) are protected by the legal system. The interests protected by protecting institutions ultimately belong to individuals, as Feinberg correctly argues. Since the principles of justice are foundational, in the sense that all other institutions and practices are built upon and justified by them, the interests protected by the institutions of distributive justice belong to all. Indeed, in as much as the two principles of justice are formulated immediately at the start of the thought experiment, those institutions later designed to advance those principles are entitled increased protection.

Fourth, the institutions which are developed in accord with the two principles of justice will be designed to prevent and correct imbalances of liberty and equality among people. The goal of those institutions which stem from the first principle is to ensure that the web of liberty is as extensive as possible, or, in other words, that the liberties of some are not compromised to advance the interests of others. Likewise, the goals of the second principle's institutions are to ensure fair equality of opportunity for all, and not better opportunities for some at the expense of others.

Fifth, and fundamental for our purposes, is that the institutions developed on the two principles of justice which would be agreed upon are contingent in their make-up. The degree of social, economic, and technological development of a given society will determine the appropriate institutions for that society. In terms of the institutions of distributive justice, a market-based system is preferred, given its liberty enhancing effects. However, the market can take any form. As a result, the forms of impairment of the market (and its related institutions of distributive justice) will be dependent upon the particular institutions chosen, and the particular goals underlying that choice of institution. This serves to draw to our attention that the remedies viewed to be appropriate to correct (or prevent) failure in one institutional structure, may be inappropriate for use in another structure.

In the end, however, Rawls' thought experiment is just that: a thought experiment. It is neither an account of how societies develop nor a plan for a utopia. Rather, its purpose is to illustrate an ideal, just society, based on a refined notion of fairness, to which actual and proposed social institutions can be compared in order to determine how well those institutions approximate the ideal. It is with this in mind that in the next section we examine the contentions made about hard-core cartel conduct, to determine whether and how criminal sanctions can be justified from this perspective.

1.3 Cartel harms: an analysis

The economic harms caused by hard-core cartel activity have been previously enumerated.[60] Although each of these consequences of monopolies (and cartels) is harmful, not all harms to others are of the sorts which require prevention through criminal sanctions. In what follows, we argue that none of *the above enumerated* harms caused by cartels justifies intervention by the criminal law.

1.3.1 Raising the price of goods as a prohibited harm

That cartelists charge more than what otherwise would be the market price for their goods is an indisputable fact of elementary microeconomics. The prospect of earning a super-normal profit is a prime consideration in cartel formation and membership. The result of this behaviour is that the consumer pays more than what they would have otherwise paid for their good and they have less money to spend on other goods. The crux of this objection to cartel activity rests in two related notions: (1) that this behaviour involves the appropriation of consumer surplus

[60] See Introduction, section 0.2.2.

to the producers (i.e. creating additional producer surplus) which is tantamount to theft; and (2) as market prices are fair, departure from them (to the detriment of the consumer) must therefore be unfair. This objection must be met with scepticism.

The main difficulty with this objection is that it relies upon the market to define property rights. This is a reverse from the norm. In the normal course of events, property rights are well defined prior to individuals engaging in market transactions to augment their existing holdings. This prior definition of the property right is a *legal process*. In place of legal concepts defining property rights, the objection relies on *market concepts* to define those rights. This is evident in the concepts of producer and consumer surplus which rely on market price for their definition. Consumer surplus is defined as the difference between an individual's reservation price (i.e. the maximum they would pay for a good) and the (competitive) market price; producer surplus is the difference between (marginal) cost of production and the market price. To suggest that in a monopoly a producer is appropriating consumer surplus in a manner which resembles theft presupposes an inappropriate (or inapplicable) property rights regime. This presupposition is magnified by the terms 'consumer' and 'producer surplus', which connote ownership. From this connotation it is an easy, but fallacious, inference to an accusation of theft.

This inference is also bolstered by the underlying assumption that market prices are always fair, in some *normative* sense. That assumption is also dubious. Though market prices may be fair in the sense that they are the outcome of a fair process of production and exchange, two examples serve to illustrate that the mantra 'market prices are fair prices' is not a universal principle of justice. First, some goods impose externalities which are not reflected in their market price. Alcohol, tobacco and handguns come to mind as examples of such goods.[61]

Second, consider goods (particularly essential goods and staples) sold shortly before an anticipated (or just after a) natural disaster. The prices of these goods rise significantly. In the world of the basic microeconomics text, the reason for this is clear. If a market price were always viewed as fair, discussion would immediately end. However, those selling at

[61] See above, n. 1, and Cook and Ludwig, 'The Social Costs of Gun Ownership', who estimate that in the US the average marginal social cost of handgun ownership per handgun-owning household is in the range of $600–1,800.

'inflated' prices are viewed as 'profiteers', who unscrupulously take advantage of the victims of these natural disasters by charging an unfair price for basic goods. Irrespective of the economic effect,[62] our sense of fairness demands a downward adjustment of the market price to result in a 'fair' price.

An additional, and very important, concern with the objection is that, unlike in the case of theft, buying products from a cartelist is (in most cases) a voluntary exchange. The transaction occurs because the consumer wants the good and it is offered at a price below the consumer's reservation price. It is in virtue of this voluntary nature[63] that some commentators regard cartel 'overcharges' to be less morally reprehensible than other consequences of cartel activity.[64]

With these comments in mind, we turn to an evaluation of the objection in order to determine the extent to which it serves to justify the criminalisation of this sort of cartel practice. In doing so, we must consider three – related – issues. First, we must determine whether cartel overcharges are harms; second, if so, whether these harms are of the sort (i.e. of sufficient importance) to merit the intervention of the criminal law in their prevention; and, third, how a society based upon the maxim 'justice as fairness' would regard this practice.

Consumers who overpay are harmed. They have less money after the transaction than they would have, had the transaction been conducted in a more competitive market. However, it is far from clear that, merely because someone has less money 'left over' after a transaction, they should properly be viewed as being a victim of crime. As noted above, the transaction is in a very real sense voluntary. The harm done, however, is less like being a victim of theft, than the feeling of walking out of an estate agent's office or a car dealership thinking that one could have

62 Montgomery, Baron and Weisskopf, 'Potential Effects of Proposed Price Gouging Legislation', Carden, '"Beliefs", Bias, and Regime Uncertainty', and Culpepper and Block, 'Price Gouging in the Katrina Aftermath'.

63 Admittedly, some transactions may not be voluntary: the purchase of essential medicines (for which there may be no substitute) comes immediately to mind. As we briefly suggest in the conclusion of this chapter, it may be the case that some forms of extracting consumer surplus in these circumstances could merit criminalisation due to, *inter alia*, the involuntary nature of the transaction. However, a discussion of the issues involved in the balancing of intellectual property rights (and the need to reward risk-taking in the development of new medications) and the allocation of medical resources in a liberal society are well beyond the scope of this present text.

64 See, e.g., Bishop and Walker, *Economics of EC Competition Law* 166–7.

done better in the pre-purchase bargaining process. The harm is more of a feeling of 'I didn't get as good a bargain as I probably could have', than the feeling (perhaps including a very real feeling of violation) which one has after being a victim of theft.

These intuitions correlate well with the vague nature of our interests in retaining our consumer surplus. As noted above, the competitive market price sets one bound for consumer surplus; our willingness to pay sets the other. This description of our intuitions towards consumer surplus shows that a consumer's interest in retaining as much of it as possible is perhaps too fleeting of an interest to be an appropriate candidate for protection via the criminal law. Its boundaries are vague, one rising and falling with the market, the other dependent on our immediate wants and wealth. The harm-based analysis suggests that scepticism is an appropriate response to the claims that criminal sanctions should be used to protect our interest in maximising our consumer surplus. The vague and instrumental nature of the interests tells against such protection.

1.3.2 Creating deadweight loss as a prohibited harm

The harm created by a deadweight loss is very similar to the harm occasioned by overcharges. Consumers are unable to purchase a wanted good because the price charged by the cartelist exceeds their reservation price. Rather than paying more for the good, the good is simply too expensive to buy. Although the difference in the harm occasioned to the overcharged consumer and frustrated non-consumer of the good may be relevant for the determination of damages in a civil antitrust action (where this category of damages is allowed), these differences are irrelevant for our present purpose.

The notion of deadweight loss, like consumer surplus, relies upon the relationship of market price and willingness to pay for its definition. As argued in the above section, the protection of consumer surplus is (on a harm to others basis) not the sort of interest which merits protection through criminal sanctions. It is simply too vague a concept to qualify as the sort of harm which merits criminal protection. This conclusion applies not just to cases where the consumer 'overpays' but must also apply to cases where consumption is frustrated because the price for the good exceeds the consumer's reservation price (or, otherwise put, willingness to pay). Accordingly, this objection merely reduces to the previous objection.

1.3.3 *Creation of social waste as a prohibited harm*

This objection is based upon Posner's argument[65] that it is not only rational for monopolists (and cartelists) to expend any sum up to and equal to their expected return from their activity, but that they in fact so do in an attempt to gain and preserve their position. The assumptions on which Posner develops his model are questionable.[66] However, though the contentious nature of the assumptions may lead us to reject that the *entire gain* from a cartel or monopoly is dissipated in the enterprise of obtaining and maintaining that market position, it is safe to assume that there is *some cost* to the acquisition and preservation of a monopoly position, and similar costs are incurred by members of cartels.

In the case of a monopoly, these costs include the expenditures to acquire licences, lobbying costs to establish and preserve trade barriers, expenditures in advertising in an effort to maintain customer loyalty, and perhaps out and out bribes. There is some empirical evidence which indicates that wages in industries which enjoy a cartel are above what would otherwise be expected.[67] In the case of cartels, there may be the additional expenditures of policing the agreement and avoiding detection; but due to the nature of the cartel agreement, members may not incur those costs associated with licensing and promoting trade barriers to the extent incurred by the monopolist.

However, these expenditures need not be viewed as waste; rather they can be (and by some are) viewed as something of the nature of wealth transfers.[68] Lobbying costs[69] are transfers to the political class; payment of higher than expected wages is a wealth transfer to management and

[65] Posner, 'The Social Costs of Monopolies', 821.

[66] See, e.g., Fisher, 'The Social Costs of Monopoly and Regulation', Motta, *Competition Policy*, 44–5, and Viscusi, Harrington and Vernon, *The Economics of Regulation and Antitrust*, 88–9.

[67] Karier, 'Unions and Monopoly Profits', 41 and Salinger, 'Tobin's *q*, Unionization and the Concentration-Profits Relationship'.

[68] Viscusi et al. (n. 66), 88–90.

[69] Note, however, the dividing line between a 'lobbying cost' and a bribe may not be entirely clear. It is unlikely that precise distinctions among (legitimate) corporate hospitality, (illegal) 'facilitation payments' and outright bribes can be drawn. (See, e.g., Raphael, *Blackstone's Guide to the Bribery Act*, 71–6.) Nevertheless, bribery is correctly viewed as wrong (hence criminalised) precisely because it involves 'playing outside' the ostensive institutional (and market) rules and thus casting the institution or market (and their fairness) into disrepute. This is identical to our analysis of the wrong done by the cartelist: see section 1.4. Likewise, the harm done by most so-called 'white collar crime' (e.g. insider trading, securities disclosure offences) is identical.

workers; costs of acquiring a licence are a transfer to those dealing with regulation (e.g. lawyers); and advertising expenditures are wealth transfers to other industries.[70] Viewed in this manner, it is difficult to characterise this objection to cartel activity as either causing the sort of harm which calls out for criminalisation; or being of the sort of side effect of the means of distributive justice that those under a veil of ignorance would seek to control (particularly through prior legal prohibitions of the most liberty limiting sort). Further, given that those under the veil of ignorance would be unaware of their social role once the veil is lifted, it would not be rational for them to exclude the opportunity for being the beneficiaries of such wealth transfers.

1.3.4 Stunting the development of new products and processes as a prohibited harm

As illustrated above, neither the monopolist nor the cartelist has any incentive to produce new products, or develop new processes to produce existing products in a more cost-effective manner. The economic consequence of inefficient production is that the price for the good is higher than it would otherwise be, so there is a consequent capture of consumer surplus by producers along with a creation of additional deadweight loss. These purported harms caused by inefficient production reduce to the cases of the harms occasioned by cartel overcharges and creation of deadweight losses. As the latter would not be the concern of the criminal law, the same conclusion follows for harms occasioned by productive inefficiency.

The objection regarding failure to develop new products is likely incoherent. In its final analysis, the complaint that one is harmed by one's inability to obtain a good which has yet to be developed appears nonsensical. One may be harmed by having a desire which is unfulfilled. But the harm one suffers rests in the unfulfilled nature of that desire. The harm does not rest in the desire's inability to be fulfilled by a non-existent good, which is what the objection asserts. Further, even if the objection can be coherently rephrased, these harms caused by the failure to produce novel goods are hardly the sort to be of the business of criminal law.

Even if, by some stretch, the claim could be made to be coherent, the sorts of interests advanced by obtaining a particular good seem to be our

[70] The leading article is Tullock, 'The Welfare Costs of Tariffs, Monopolies, and Theft'.

more immediate interests, and not our welfare interests. It is these welfare interests which are the proper subjects of protection through criminal sanction. Given these features, those under the veil of ignorance would not pay heed to that claim. If any claim merited the response of *de minimis non curat lex*, it would be this claim.

1.3.5 Exacerbation of X-inefficiency as a prohibited harm

X-inefficiency is managerial (or productive) slack. By insulating themselves from the pressures of competition, those running cartels can live the quiet life and their divisions (or companies) can enjoy a secure return, at the expense of increased costs (but not necessarily diminished return) to the company. The harm occasioned by X-inefficiency can be viewed as being of two sorts. First, it can be viewed as a restatement of the 'inefficiencies' (i.e. costs of the creation of economic deadweight by certain productive processes). Indeed, Leibenstein's own discussion at times focuses on the relationship of this sort of inefficiency to factory workers' output.[71] So to the extent that X-inefficiency is enhanced (or another word for) productive inefficiency, it reduces to that case.

Alternatively, the harm done by X-inefficiency can be viewed as a decrease in return to owners, by virtue of increased costs. A compromised return on investment harms an owner. But preventing such losses is certainly not within the proper ambit of criminal law. To attempt to correct it through the means of criminal law entails a significant cost to liberty. In effect, and to use the vernacular, 'slacking off' would otherwise become criminalised. As the problem of X-inefficiency arises from the divergent interests of ownership and management, its solution lies in attempting to better align those interests. As a realignment of interests is the least liberty limiting option which rectifies the problem, we suggest it would be along these lines that those under the veil of ignorance would seek a solution.

1.4 Harm to the institution of distributive justice as the justification for criminalising cartel activity

To examine each of the harms which hard-core cartel activity causes and show them to be inappropriate subjects of protection through the criminal law, and then to conclude that therefore hard-core cartel activity

[71] Leibenstein, 'Allocative Efficiency', 398–403.

ought not to be criminalised is a fallacious inference. It is some species of the so-called fallacy of composition, a fallacy in which it is (falsely) inferred that what is characteristic of the whole must also be characteristic of its parts (or vice versa).

The harm done by hard-core cartel activity is to institutions, not to individuals. The cartelist's primary harm is the effect it has on the market as an institution used by society to distribute goods and services, i.e. as its means of distributive justice. The cartelist's harm is therefore not the harm it occasions to any participant in the market. As Feinberg shows, it is perfectly coherent to speak of institutional harms in this way, as in the last analysis the interests developed and protected by the institutions belong to individuals. This is particularly so when we speak of harms to the market, as the market is that institution by which individuals distribute and acquire those goods used in their pursuit of the goals which are the focal ends in people's lives.

The above Rawlsian analysis demonstrated the fundamental role played by the market in a liberal society. The market is the institution of distributive justice. Rawls' thought experiment shows that the market would be chosen by those placed under conditions of fairness (i.e. the veil of ignorance), precisely because it protects and promotes the liberty of those participating in it. Those under the veil of ignorance will reason that no alternative ordering of the means of distribution can be achieved without significant interference in citizens' lives.

However, those under the veil will realise that there is a parallel between justice in the legal system and justice in the means of distribution. As seen above, the legal system incorporates precepts of the rule of law to permit people to formulate reasonable expectations as to (their and others') conduct. Likewise, society's means of distributive justice, the market, will possess similar content so that individuals participating in the market can have reasonable expectations of how transactions will occur: at minimum we expect them to occur in a fair manner.

The substantial harm done by cartel activity to the market and to those active in the market is that it erodes confidence in the fairness of the market as a system of transfer and distribution. We, as participants in the market, have expectations of how market transactions will be conducted. These expectations are of two sorts: we have expectations of how *particular exchanges* should take place, and expectations of how *exchanges generally* should take place. We expect that particular exchanges will occur, *inter alia*, voluntarily, with relevant information being disclosed, with reasonable certainty about the object of exchange, and the like.

These principles serve to establish rules or principles for fairness in an exchange. This regulation of particular exchanges is a fundamental part of contract law and related fields.

But we also expect these individual exchanges to take place in an environment which facilitates these sorts of exchanges, which is one of fairness. At minimum, fairness dictates that we be aware of, and agree to, the rules in advance. Fairness, whether in law, the market, a game or in any other aspect of our life, precludes the existence of hidden rules, known only to some yet expected to be adhered to by all. The regulation of the environment of exchange is a fundamental part of those laws which regulate markets, whether they are of wide application (e.g. consumer protection law) or more narrowly focused (e.g. securities law).

The conduct of the hard-core cartelist strikes at our expectations for a fair environment for exchange. By agreeing on prices, quantities and markets with illusory 'competitors', the cartelists have created hidden rules, known only to themselves, but by which all are expected to play. The presence of such activities in the marketplace undermines our confidence in the fairness of the market. An often heard analogy here is that the cartelist plays 'with a marked deck'. This may not be the best analogy, as in a fixed card game the harm is unilaterally caused and is directed at the other participants. Though cartels do direct harm of this sort, their effect is also more diffuse with an impact both on actual and potential participants, calling the very enterprise into question.

A better analogy may be the harm done to a sport when its events are fixed. A spectator observing a sporting event, say, a cricket match,[72] a sumo tournament[73] or a baseball game,[74] expects to see the event determined by the skills of the participants (and perhaps with a little luck of the day). The

[72] See 'ICC tribunal bans Pakistan Test captain Salman Butt for 10 years'.

[73] See 'Japanese sumo wrestling tournament cancelled over bout-fixing allegations'.

[74] The 1919 World Series was haunted by allegations of fixed games by the Chicago White Sox players. In an effort to restore the image of the game, team owners hired a US Federal Judge, Kenesaw Mountain Landis, to become the commissioner of baseball and he was provided with a wide mandate to clean up the sport. Commissioner Landis imposed a lifetime ban on eight players who were alleged to have participated in this activity, notwithstanding their acquittals on criminal charges stemming from the purported game fixing. As a federal judge, Landis is also noted for being the trial judge who, in 1907, imposed a $29,240,000 fine (the maximum possible) on Standard Oil for antitrust violations. See *US* v. *Standard Oil Co. of Indiana* (1907) 155 F 305 (ND Ill Aug 03, 1907), reversed *Standard Oil Co. of Indiana* v. *US* (1908) 164 F 376, 90 CCA 364 (CCA7 (Ill) Jul 22, 1908) *certiorari* denied *US* v. *Standard Oil Co.* (1909) 212 US 579, 29 S Ct 689, 53 L Ed 659 (Jan 04, 1909). In reversing Judge Landis' ruling, the Seventh Circuit Court of Appeal remarked:

spectator does not expect the result to be predetermined, and such arrangements bring the credibility and integrity of the sport into question.[75] In a similar manner, by predetermining the market in the way that they do, cartelists bring the credibility and integrity of the market into question. This is their real harm. In Kantian terms, the cartelist carves out a self-exception to the expected rules of market behaviour. These rules presuppose a certain standard of conduct to which everyone is expected to adhere, but to which the cartelist will not.[76]

Thus viewed, our next task is to determine the extent that the Rawlsian idealised society would display concern for these harms. As seen above, those under the veil of ignorance have selected two principles of justice, and ordered them, so that liberty trumps (in)equality. Additionally, they would have chosen a market-based system of distributive justice, with means to correct undesirable features, namely their tendency towards inequality; and their intermittent need for a means to secure compliance. The second feature, involving the problems of isolation and compliance,

> Put into execution, this maximum sentence would add to the liabilities of defendant to its creditors, (and, according to a petition of the government on the matter of supersede as there were current liabilities of from three to five million dollars) an additional liability of twenty-nine million, two hundred and forty thousand dollars; resulting without doubt in a condition of bankruptcy that would deduct from every creditor's share of the assets to be divided a sum running from fifty to nearly one hundred per cent. of the money that such creditors had advanced. Is the defendant, by way of regulative punishments, to be thus punished? Are the creditors to be thus punished?
>
> (164 F. 376 at 387).

See H. L. Wilgus, 'The Standard Oil Fine' (1907) 6 *Michigan LR* 118 for a discussion of the commercial context in which Standard Oil's business practices occurred. On antitrust and baseball generally, see Jerold J. Duquette, *Regulating the National Pastime: Baseball and Antitrust*.

75 See Cooke J's sentencing remarks in the cricket match fixing case referred to above (n. 72):

> It is the insidious effect of your actions on professional cricket and the followers of it which make the offences so serious. The image and integrity of what was once a game, but is now a business is damaged in the eyes of all . . . Now, whenever people look back on a surprising event in a game or a surprising result or whenever in the future there are surprising events or results, followers of the game who have paid good money to watch it live or to watch it on TV, . . . will be led to wonder whether there has been a fix and whether what they have been watching is a genuine contest between bat and ball. What ought to be honest sporting competition may not be such at all. (*R* v. *Majeed, et al.*)

76 See the argument above, text to notes 72 and 73.

is an application of the Hobbesian thesis. Institutions which require cooperation for their function are inherently unstable, particularly when it is advantageous for an individual (or a small group of individuals) not to cooperate in the face of everyone else's cooperation. This is merely a multi-person version of the prisoners' dilemma.[77]

The dilemma involves two problems: an isolation problem, and an assurance problem. The isolation problem arises when each person's pursuit of their own preferred strategy results in a state in which everyone is worse off than they would have been had each person pursued their second-best strategy.[78] The solution to the isolation problem is the assurance problem: given that we can agree that the pursuit of the second-best strategy by all results in the optimal outcome for all, we need a means to assure us that everyone complies with the agreement. In the ideal state, where the citizenry is motivated to do the right thing and hence all were confident in their compatriots' willingness to do the right thing, the compliance problem would be solved without coercive enforcement.[79] But in the 'real world' things are different.

The provision of public goods is a clear case where the market fails due to the two problems.[80] By their very nature, public goods are goods which have the features of non-excludability and non-rivalry. That is to say, once provided, no one can be excluded from benefiting from a public good; and the consumption of the good by one person does not affect another's ability to also consume that good.[81] National defence and lighthouses[82] are the two classical examples.

Once citizens come to an understanding of which goods are best provided by (or that they want provided by) the state, they need to realise that they must all pay for these goods (in spite of the fact that freeriding is their preferred option). And, they must be assured that all will pay their share for these goods.[83] To assure compliance with the agreement, some coercive measures must exist. These measures are the application of the Hobbesian thesis. In the ideal state, these measures would be quite nebulous, far in the background, and never used. However, as we move further from a utopia, the measures will out of necessity become more concrete and present in society. And, from time to time, these measures will be used. This is the stuff of the criminal law.

[77] Sen, 'Isolation, Assurance and the Social Rate of Discount,' 112–14.

[78] Ibid., 122 and Rawls (n. 25), 237–8. [79] See Sen, ibid., 114–15.

[80] See Rawls (n. 25), 235–9. [81] Samuelson, 'The Pure Theory of Public Expenditure'.

[82] Coase, 'The Lighthouse in Economics'. [83] See Rawls (n. 25), 236.

Confidence in the integrity of the marketplace shares some key characteristics of public goods. Indeed it may be a public good, albeit using 'good' in a somewhat extended sense.[84] It is non-excludable and non-rivalous. Though one may self-exclude themselves from a general sense of confidence in the market, one cannot be excluded (by others having the same confidence) from possessing this view. Similarly, on its own, one person's confidence in the integrity of the market will not prevent another person from adopting the same attitude. Further, and more important for our purposes, we gain confidence in the integrity of the market by conforming to and expecting others to conform to certain standards, patterns of conduct, and other rules of the market which we explicitly or implicitly adopt.

These rules of the market exhibit the same isolation and assurance problems as the prisoners' dilemma and public goods. The dominant strategy in the marketplace is to engage in opportunistic behaviour, i.e. to cheat. However, those in the marketplace immediately realise the consequences of all engaging in their dominant strategy. But if everyone 'plays by the rules' (i.e. our second-best strategy), we avoid these consequences. The need for an assurance mechanism is thus necessary to ensure general compliance with these rules: this is the justification for the use of criminal sanctions.

The use of the criminal law to solve the assurance problem in the marketplace is further legitimised by the fundamental role which the market has as an instrument of justice. The market is a liberal society's main means of distributive justice, chosen precisely because of its liberty-producing effects. The cartelist, by manipulating the market in an opportunistic manner, undermines public confidence in the integrity of this instrument of distributive justice. It is precisely through the existence (and use) of such coercive means that citizens can have the necessary assurance in the proper and just functioning of the market. Criminal sanctions for hard-core cartel activity are thus a normatively legitimate means of ensuring the well-functioning of our society.

1.5 Conclusion: an extension and two caveats

The argument of this chapter has shown a normative justification for the criminalisation of cartel competition offences, on the basis that the cartelist fails to 'play by the rules' of the marketplace, or (in Kantian

[84] See Elzinga and Brett, *The Antitrust Penalties*, 3–16 who note this.

terms) carves out a self-exception to the general social rules governing distributive justice. We suggest that this conclusion could be extended to other non-cartel anti-competitive conduct which also does not play by the rules (or manifests a self-exception).

The phenomenon of 'pay for delay' in the pharmaceutical industry could be considered to fall under this rubric of creating a self-exception (and thus not 'playing by' the expected rules). Under a 'pay for delay' arrangement the holder of a patent which is about to expire pays a generic drug manufacturer not to produce the medicine. The patent holder thereby extends the length of time during which it can charge a monopoly price for the drug, hence earning a super-competitive return beyond that period of time permitted by the relevant legislation.[85] In effect, the patent holder 'buys' an exemption from the rules. The rules, however, were designed to reward patent holders with an appropriate return for the risks (and costs) associated with pharmaceutical innovation, and the expiration of a patent is designed to serve as a limit to the return.[86]

Unlike the purchase of almost all consumer goods, the purchase of most medicine is not something which can be forgone, or even postponed for a period of time. Depending on the medical concern, a drug purchaser's reservation price may approach that individual's wealth. As such, these purchases lack the element of volition characteristic of the vast majority of market transactions in which the consumer is 'overcharged'. It is precisely this lack of volition which distinguishes the pharmaceutical transactions from other transactions in which the consumer pays a 'higher' (yet consented to) price. But, in addition to causing harm to particular consumers by forced transactions at a super-competitive price, 'pay for delay' more importantly must be viewed as affecting the institution of limited monopolies. Time-limited monopolies have the aim, as their underlying justification, that upon the expiry of time, an adequate return (for cost and risk involved) has been received. This justification is incorporated into the legal rules which establish the patent system that provides for the time-limited super-competitive return. The 'payer for delay' accepts these rules to the extent that they

[85] Although 'pay for delay' has elements of both cartel and abuse of dominance (involving a horizontal market-sharing arrangement and an exploitation of a dominant position obtained by a patent), the abuse of dominance is logically prior to the cartel activity: without the monopoly/patent, the agreement could not occur.

[86] On this point, see, e.g., European Commission, 'Antitrust: Commission opens proceedings against Johnson & Johnson and Novartis', 21 October 2011 IP/11/1228.

benefit only it; however, when an additional benefit can accrue outside of the system, the 'payer' will buy that advantage irrespective of the rules.

Two caveats must be added to the conclusion of this chapter. First, our argument is that in as much as cartels inflict harm on an important social institution, namely the market, cartel activity can legitimately (from a normative perspective) be criminalised. In a similar vein, our argument may be able to be extended to other cases in which harm is inflicted upon other means of distributive justice adopted by a society. This is the limit of our argument: it extends only to the market as a means of fair distribution. Our argument does not support the additional inference that harms to all social institutions (or even to every important social institution) can legitimately be made the subject of criminal sanctions.[87] To immediately draw inferences of this latter sort fails to recognise that the market, as the instrument of distributive justice, would be among the first (if not the first) social institutions agreed upon by those completely under the veil.

The second caveat is the fact that criminal sanctions are legitimate methods of controlling hard-core cartel activity, says nothing about the nature and extent of those sanctions. To the extent that a society approaches the ideal, such sanctions will be milder and less frequently used. Indeed, the ideal society would not require such sanctions. The precise details of the regime chosen to enforce the rules of the market will not (and cannot) be determined until the social and economic conditions in which the market activity takes place are known. In Rawlsian terms, the veil of ignorance must first be at least partially lifted. Related to this, is that as social and economic conditions may vary so, too, must the rules and how the rules are enforced. This is not merely related to a difference in levels of economic development, but also to other social factors regarded as important by the citizens, which are manifested as part of the marketplace rules.

This latter point is of significance to anyone who in seeking a solution to the problem of cartels casts their eyes to other jurisdictions. Though there may be much to be gained from examining others' experiences, and learning from their mistakes, wholesale transplantation may not be the appropriate solution. The conditions – whether economic, cultural, or social – which give rise to a solution in one jurisdiction, may be

87 The argument here (to which this caveat is directed) would be along the lines espoused by Devlin, *Enforcement* and Stephen, *Liberty, Equality, Fraternity*.

significantly different elsewhere.[88] This is vividly so when we consider the extent to which a society has adopted the market as a (sole) means of distributive justice. In Rawlsian terms, the veil must be partially lifted before the institutions can be designed, in order that social and economic contingencies can be adequately taken into account.

For example, where there are non-market considerations in distribution (perhaps considerations of readjustment for regional disparity), transplantation of a legal regime from jurisdictions where such considerations are irrelevant may well be inappropriate. Similar considerations may also apply to societies which have recently become 'liberalised', in the sense of adopting a market-based means of distribution. Since the institutions we design receive their legitimacy from them being designed for particular conditions, failure to account for relevant differences in these conditions can deprive the institutions of their very normative legitimacy. To claim 'it worked there, so it should also work here', may be a very valid point. But it is a pragmatic point, devoid of normative force. But those designing legal (and particularly criminal) institutions need to make a normative point, one which recognises the need for relevant differences to be recognised and be taken into account in the legal response to any problem, including those associated with anti-competitive conduct.

[88] Brisimi and Ioannidou, 'Criminalizing Cartels in Greece', 173 and 175–6 make a similar point.

2

Corporate responsibility, agency and the advantages of vicarious liability

2.1 Introduction

The discussion in the previous chapter has indicated not only that hard-core cartel activity causes economic harm, but also that there are valid reasons for criminalising such behaviour. Our reasons for criminalising such behaviour, however, had initially nothing to do with the economic harm that such organisations inflicted on consumers in their discrete transactions with the cartelists; rather the morally significant harm done by these sorts of organisations rests in their undermining of the accepted rules of the market, namely that transactions occur in a situation where the 'rules' surrounding the transactions are open and clear to all participants. The cartelist, by hiding behind secret rules regarding how prices in the marketplace are established, undermines the confidence in the market which other participants have. And, as we further argued, given the fundamental role which the market serves in a liberal economy as its primary instrument of distributive justice, it is legitimate for a civil society to protect this institution with its most coercive social institution: the criminal law.

The argument of the previous chapter did not consider how the criminal law should be focused to protect the market. This concern will be the emphasis of this and the next chapter. Prima facie, there are two foci for criminal liability: the firm, and the individual member of the firm who engages in unwanted conduct for personal advantage or to advance a firm goal. We argue that both foci are appropriate targets of criminal liability. In this chapter we argue for a system of corporate liability, based on vicarious liability. In the next chapter we argue for individual criminal liability for those members of the firm responsible for the unwanted conduct. Each focus of liability has its own advantages, and – as we shall argue – given what is at stake in cartel activity, imposing both forms of criminal liability is essential to deter this activity.

The purpose of imputing criminal liability to entities such as corporations is to determine an effective means of controlling (or eliminating to the greatest extent practicable) harmful activities in which these collective entities can be said to engage. This form of collective liability is not a universal legal concept. Corporate criminal liability is unknown in German law, for instance. Likewise, a similar conception of collective responsibility, ascribing criminal wrongs to states, is unknown in International Law.[1]

Corporate criminal activity, we argue, has its origins in the principal–agent means of corporate activity. Agents are entrusted by the owners of the corporation to do its work. But the interests (and incentives) of the agents are not always aligned with those of the owners. Consequently, in corporate activity the agents are frequently presented with chances for opportunistic behaviour to advance their own interests at the firm's expense. We argue that rules of corporate criminal liability must address this problem to control this behaviour. We suggest that the English adaptation of the model of individual responsibility in an effort to impose criminal liability on corporate entities (the so-called *Tesco* rule[2]) has been counter-productive. Its anthropomorphism has obscured the actual principal–agent manner of corporate action.

A better solution in our eyes is to address this problem with a rule of vicarious liability, which does not – in the case of market collusion – include a (corporate) defence for 'adequate institutional safeguards'. Such a defence, as we argue, is only justified in cases where the activity to be controlled with a legal prohibition has some social merit. Collusion in the market is devoid of this feature. Such a rule begins to address the problem which gives rise to much corporate criminal activity. As we will argue in the next chapter, however, corporate liability must be supplemented by individual liability to completely deter the sort of collusion which leads to hard-core cartel activity.

The outline of this chapter is as follows: we first describe the nature of corporate activity, showing how the well-recognised agency problem also gives rise to criminal behaviour by corporate agents. We then consider the development of the *Tesco* rule, showing how the rule came to be. Turning to the rules of corporate criminal liability, we

1 On this point see Crawford, *International Law Commission's Articles on State Responsibility*, 16–20.

2 *Tesco Supermarkets Ltd* v. *Nattrass* [1972] AC 153.

show how the *Tesco* rule fails to adequately capture the principal–agent dynamic of the corporation. Other rules better capture this dynamic and are therefore to be preferred. To conclude, we argue that vicarious liability better solves the principal–agent dynamic which gives rise to criminal behaviour within corporate organisations, and is thus the preferred rule to use to control such crimes.

2.2 The agency problem in corporate action and control

Analysis of corporate activity shows: first, that there are a number of constituencies within the corporation; and, second, that as these constituencies will behave opportunistically towards each other, an appropriate regulatory response is to control such behaviour.[3] In effect there are (at minimum) three such constituencies: owners, managers (including employees), and creditors. Each constituency has its own incentives to engage in certain conduct in order to influence the company to behave in a manner which benefits that constituency, at the expense of other constituencies.

The owners' (shareholders') incentives are to maximise their return on investment over the time period that their investment is (or is expected to be) held. Hence, if costs can be reduced to increase returns during this time-frame, owners will promote this. Thus production may be relocated to areas in which labour costs are less, at the expense of their present employees. Likewise, the ownership has an incentive to defer (or have others pay for) costly maintenance if those maintenance costs can be pushed beyond their investment time horizon (or shifted onto other groups not necessarily within the corporation).[4]

Management's and employees' incentives are different from owners'. This is a well-discussed point in company law and management theory,[5] with the bulk of the discussion identifying the divergences in incentives,[6] suggesting legal regimes to counter the problem,[7] and identifying

[3] See, e.g., the argument contained in Kraakman et al. (eds.), *The Anatomy of Corporate Law*.

[4] An example of this might be costs involved in decommissioning nuclear power plants and the environmental 'clean-up' associated with the storage of spent fuel rods, and deferring the costs for decades (and/or offloading these costs onto the taxpayer).

[5] See, e.g., Kraakman et al. (n. 3), Cheffins, *Company Law*, 46–125, Jensen and Meckling, 'Theory of the Firm', and Alchian and Demsetz, 'Production, Information Costs, and Economic Organization'.

[6] In corporate takeovers and defences, the seminal article is Easterbrook and Fischel, 'The Proper Role of a Target's Management in Responding to a Tender Offer'.

[7] E.g. ibid., 1194–9.

incentives to realign the two constituencies' interests.[8] While they are entrusted with the management of the firm, managers (directors) will seek a remuneration package which favours their utility functions, even at the expense of firm profitability and the interests of employees and creditors. By 'utility function' is meant that pay-off which maximises managerial desire for remuneration and non-pecuniary benefits (e.g. the trade-off between work and a life outside of work).[9]

Accordingly, management (directors) may seek long-term contracts which are expensive for the company to unilaterally terminate, so as to ensure long-term employment security.[10] Additionally, in the event of impending takeover, management may act in a way that advances their interests at the expense of improving shareholder value.[11] Alternatively, management may wish to enhance their status of running a larger company, by acquiring targets at a premium not reflected in value for the shareholder of the acquiring company.[12]

Likewise, an employee's incentive is to similarly maximise their own utility function, the desired pay versus slack balance,[13] along with appropriate employment security or advancement in the company (or industry). Thus in the interests of 'slacking-off', employees may cut corners in the performance of tasks assigned to them, or in the interests of their advancing in the company (or industry) may engage in actions which could potentially compromise the firm.

Attempting to align managerial and ownership interests can also set up perverse incentives. Structuring managerial reward to performance over the previous quarter (or year), skews the managerial focus to this time-frame and not on a longer time-frame perhaps contemplated by owners (particularly if the owners are institutional investors). Likewise, tying remuneration to increased share value (e.g. via options which are triggered at a given price) can result in the board of a cash-rich company engaging in a share buy-back programme (to ensure the trigger price is met), rather than using the money for expansion or declaring a dividend.

[8] See, generally, Law Commission and the Scottish Law Commission, *Company Directors*.

[9] The pioneering study on this point is Leibenstein, 'Allocative Efficiency'.

[10] Companies Act 2006, ss. 188–189 attempt to control this by requiring that directors' long-term (i.e. greater than 2 years) contracts be approved by an ordinary resolution of members.

[11] See Easterbrook and Fischel (n. 6).

[12] See Newbould, *Management and Merger Activity*, 104 and Williamson, *The Economics of Discretionary Behavior*.

[13] Leibenstein (n. 9) also refers to employee behaviour.

Creditors, as a constituency, wish to ensure that they receive payment and in the event of insolvency will seek payment of their accounts in priority to other constituencies, particularly in priority to employees and pension funds. Likewise, in the absence of prohibitions against trading while insolvent[14] and other similar offences, management may have an incentive to continue trading in these circumstances, ultimately at the expense of the company's creditors.

In addition to the chance of facilitating opportunistic behaviour, the divergent interests among owners, management (in the sense of the directors) and employees can allow for the development of criminal behaviour. Negligence can be accurately described as an underinvestment in safety.[15] Such underinvestment can be made by management decisions to defer needed maintenance or by employee maximisation of their personal utility function by 'slacking-off' during a safety critical moment. This may well explain the circumstances which gave rise to a number of tragic accidents in recent British history.[16]

An employee's desire for advancement or a 'quiet life' is nothing more, in economic terms, than the employee desiring to maximise his own utility function, which incorporates a given reward (or work–slack balance). Such maximisation may give rise to criminal activity. A frequently mentioned motivation of those engaging in price-fixing is to isolate themselves from the rigours of competition.[17] Likewise, individuals may engage in corrupt activity (e.g. bribery) to facilitate a transaction for which they will receive credit and be appropriately rewarded in the corporate hierarchy. Accordingly, any suggestion of an effective regime to control such behaviour, particularly through the criminal law, must take these incentives into account.

2.3 Attribution rules: principles of corporate liability

Attribution rules serve to locate particular conduct and/or mental states within a collective entity (including corporations) so that the act can be regarded as the act of the collective entity. The literature identifies four

[14] Insolvency Act 1985, ss. 206–211 and 213–214; cf. *In re SGL Carbon* 200 F 3d 154 (CA3 1999).

[15] Judge Learned Hand's classic formulation of negligence in *United States* v. *Carroll Towing Co. Inc.* 159 F 2d 169, 173 (CA2 1947) explicitly relates a finding of negligence to an underinvestment in precautions.

[16] See, e.g., the investigation of the capsize of the *MV Herald of Free Enterprise* (n. 45 below).

[17] See Motta, *Competition Policy*, 47.

such rules, all of which are found as principles of corporate liability in common law jurisdictions:

- identification, i.e. the so-called *Tesco* rule;
- aggregation, in effect the summing up of the mental elements and activities of corporate employees and imputing this sum as the responsibility of the company;
- corporate fault and/or 'corporate culture', i.e. examining the corporate ethos and imputing liability if there was an attitude in the relevant corporate culture which condoned the relevant act; and,
- vicarious liability, i.e. imputing the wrongful act of a corporate employee to the corporation as a whole.

Each of these attribution rules will provide different incentives for corporate monitoring of managerial and employee behaviour. The rules of vicarious liability and aggregation provide a stronger incentive for more detailed monitoring of employee behaviour than the *Tesco* rule of identification. Corporate culture rules likely provide an incentive for an intermediate level of managerial and employee monitoring, but – as we will see below – may create a perverse incentive in expenditure on litigation costs, rather than compliance.

English criminal law is heavily reliant on the first of the above mentioned rules. In the next section, it is shown that this reliance is based on a historical mistake. It is further argued that this mistake is compounded by the ineffective nature that this rule has in aligning and controlling the divergent interests found in the modern corporation.

2.4 Identification, *Tesco* and a historical mistake

2.4.1 The development of the doctrine

The traditional common law view of corporate criminal liability holds that corporations cannot be subject to criminal liability, save perhaps for the exceptions of public nuisance, criminal libel, contempt of court, and statutory offences of absolute liability.[18] The justification for the traditional view of corporate immunity rests on variations of the argument that as the corporation neither has a mind to manifest the moral turpitude necessary to commit a criminal offence, nor can it be of the sort of

[18] See Lord Blackburn in *Pharmaceutical Society* (1879–80) LR 5 AC 857, 870 and Estey J in *Canadian Dredge and Dry Dock* [1985] 1 SCR 662, para. 32, and *Associated Newspapers* [2011] EWHC 418 (Admin).

entity subject to punishment (particularly imprisonment or execution), it thus could not be a proper subject of the criminal law. Baron Thurlow precisely expressed the central premise of this argument with the words, 'Did you ever expect a corporation to have a conscience, when it has no soul to be damned, and no body to be kicked?'[19]

The identification model serves as an attempt both (1) to construct an analogue of a mind sufficiently located within the corporate structure so that it can be deemed to be the corporate mind (and thus possess the requisite *mens rea* to establish criminal liability) and (2) to attribute acts (which ultimately are acts of individuals) to corporations so that these acts can be deemed the *actus reus* of a criminal act attributed to the corporation.[20]

The origin of identification lies in the House of Lords' 1915 decision in *Lennard's Carrying Company* v. *Asiatic Petroleum Co. Ltd*,[21] a civil case concerning the interpretation of section 502 of the Merchant Shipping Act 1894.[22] This section excluded a shipowner's liability for damage occasioned by fire on board, for which the owner was not at fault.[23] The litigation in question arose from a post-grounding fire and explosion of the cargo (benzene) carried by an oil steamer. Lennard's Carrying Company (the appellant) owned the ship, which was managed by another company, Messrs John M. Lennard and Sons. Mr Lennard was a director of both companies, and as such he took an active part in the management of the ship. Lennard's attempted to rely upon section 502; however, at the trial of this matter, no evidence was presented to rebut the presumption of negligence (i.e. failure to ensure that the vessel was seaworthy) on their part.

Viscount Haldane, LC's comments on Mr Lennard's role, and thus his ability to provide evidence to rebut the presumption of corporate negligence, are worth reproducing:

[19] Frequently quoted, and in recent times most notably in Coffee, '"No Soul to Damn"'.

[20] On the history of the doctrine, see e.g. Pinto and Evans, *Corporate Criminal Liability*, paras. 1.1–5.2, and Gobert and Punch, *Rethinking Corporate Crime*, 59–69.

[21] [1915] AC 705. [22] 57 & 58 Vict., c. 60.

[23] Section 502 of that Act reads:

> The owner of a British sea-going ship, or any share therein, shall not be liable to make good to any extent whatever any loss or damage happening without his actual fault or privity in the following cases; namely, – (i) Where any goods, merchandise, or other things whatsoever taken in or put on board his ship are lost or damaged by reason of fire on board the ship.

> Now, my Lords, did what happened take place without the actual fault or privity of the owners of the ship who were the appellants? *My Lords, a corporation is an abstraction. It has no mind of its own any more than it has a body of its own; its active and directing will must consequently be sought in the person of somebody who for some purposes may be called an agent, but who is really the directing mind and will of the corporation, the very ego and centre of the personality of the corporation.* That person may be under the direction of the shareholders in general meeting; that person may be the board of directors itself, or it may be, and in some companies it is so, that that person has an authority co-ordinate with the board of directors given to him under the articles of association, and is appointed by the general meeting of the company, and can only be removed by the general meeting of the company. My Lords, whatever is not known about Mr. Lennard's position, this is known for certain, Mr. Lennard took the active part in the management of this ship on behalf of the owners, and Mr. Lennard, as I have said, was registered as the person designated for this purpose in the ship's register. *Mr. Lennard therefore was the natural person to come on behalf of the owners and give full evidence not only about the events of which I have spoken, and which related to the seaworthiness of the ship, but about his own position and as to whether or not he was the life and soul of the company. For if Mr. Lennard was the directing mind of the company, then his action must, unless a corporation is not to be liable at all, have been an action which was the action of the company itself within the meaning of s. 502.*[24]

If anyone in the appellant company (or its sister company) had any information regarding the ship's seaworthiness, that person would have been Mr Lennard. Additionally, given his position in both companies, he could likely bind the corporations through his evidence. Alternatively, by giving evidence, Mr Lennard could have rebutted the natural inference that he was the corporation's alter ego. Yet no such evidence – one way or the other – was presented.

Ultimately, *Lennard's Carrying Company* is a case regarding evidentiary presumptions of negligence, a statutory exclusion, the appropriate witness and evidence necessary to invoke the exclusion and discharge the presumption. Viscount Haldane was merely seeking a corporate analogue of a mind which would be of the sort that possesses sufficient knowledge to provide evidence so that a court could determine whether or not a vessel was seaworthy. Unfortunately, the Lord Chancellor's words were to develop a metaphysical significance.

[24] *Lennard's* (n. 21) at 713 (emphasis supplied).

H L Bolton (Engineering) Co. Ltd v. *T J Graham & Sons Ltd*,[25] also a civil matter, is regarded to be the next in this line of cases. At issue was the extent to which a corporate landlord could intend to occupy premises, and thus be able to resist a new tenancy.[26] The landlord (Graham) was a subsidiary of a larger company, it had only an annual board meeting, and the day-to-day running of the company was delegated to management. There was no specific meeting or resolution expressing an intention to occupy the premises in question. In spite of this, the trial judge determined that the 'company, through its managers, intend[ed] to occupy the premises for their own purposes'.[27]

On appeal, counsel for the tenant maintained that this finding was incorrect, referring the court to the nineteenth-century cases holding that a corporation had no mind, and thus a corporation could not form intent. Rejecting this reasoning, Denning LJ (as he then was), remarked:

> A company may in many ways be likened to a human body. It has a brain and nerve centre which controls what it does. It also has hands which hold the tools and act in accordance with directions from the centre. Some of the people in the company are mere servants and agents who are nothing more than hands to do the work and cannot be said to represent the mind or will. Others are directors and managers who represent the directing mind and will of the company, and control what it does. The state of mind of these managers is the state of mind of the company and is treated by the law as such . . . So also in the criminal law, in cases where the law requires a guilty mind as a condition of a criminal offence, the guilty mind of the directors or the managers will render the company itself guilty.[28]

The latter sentence is ambiguous: it notes that a guilty mind of the director or manager is a sufficient condition to impose criminal liability on the company. It is not clear that the corporate officer's state is also a necessary condition.

Nevertheless, a few sentences later, he continues in a passage to which reference is less often made:

> So here, the intention of the company can be derived from the intention of its officers and agents. Whether their intention is the company's intention depends on the nature of the matter under consideration, the

[25] [1957] 1 QB 159. [26] Landlord and Tenant Act 1954, s. 30(1)(g).

[27] *Bolton (Engineering)* (n. 25) at 172.

[28] Ibid. The criminal case referred to by Denning LJ is *Rex* v. *ICR Haulage Ltd* [1944] 1 All ER 691 (CA).

> relative position of the officer or agent and the other relevant facts and circumstances of the case.[29]

This latter passage, it is submitted, presents an accurate model of corporate decision-making. Decisions are made by corporate directors and managers, who (along with agents and employees) implement these decisions. Not all decisions and actions made by those associated with a corporation should properly be regarded as the corporation's decisions and actions – that conclusion requires an investigation into the circumstances behind the decisions and actions.

The third case in this line, and the first criminal case, is *Tesco Supermarkets Ltd* v. *Nattrass*.[30] This was a prosecution under the Trade Descriptions Act 1968, section 11(2) which prohibited a product being advertised for less than the price for which it was actually on sale.[31] Section 24(1) of that Act provided a two-pronged defence to such a prosecution. The first prong required that the defendant show that the mispricing was the mistake of another person (who – pursuant to section 20 of the Act – could not be a director, manager, secretary or similar officer of the defendant corporation, if the defendant was a corporation). The second prong required the defendant to show that it 'took all reasonable precautions and exercised all due diligence to avoid the commission of such an offence by himself or any person under his control'.[32] Tesco had in place an elaborate system to ensure that its stores would offer stock at advertised, discounted, prices. But in this case, the system broke down due to the inadvertence of a shop assistant and the manager of the shop in question. The issue before the House of Lords was thus whether the shop manager was another person (than Tesco) for the purposes of section 24(1).

In the five speeches delivered in this matter, the Law Lords were unanimous in determining that the shop manager was too low in Tesco's corporate hierarchy for his actions to be attributed to the company. Lord Diplock is very clear on this point:

> In my view, therefore, the question: what natural persons are to be treated in law as being the company for the purpose of acts done in the course of

[29] *Bolton (Engineering)* (n. 25) at 173 [30] See note 2 above.

[31] Trade Descriptions Act 1968, s. 11(2) reads: 'If any person offering to supply any goods gives, by whatever means, any indication likely to be taken as an indication that the goods are being offered at a price less than that at which they are in fact being offered he shall, subject to the provisions of this Act, be guilty of an offence.'

[32] Ibid., s. 24(1)(b).

> its business, including the taking of precautions and the exercise or due diligence to avoid the commission of a criminal offence, is to be found by identifying those natural persons who by the memorandum and articles of association or as a result of action taken by the directors, or by the company in general meeting pursuant to the articles, are entrusted with the exercise of the powers of the company.[33]

Lord Diplock added that this was in fact what was meant by Denning LJ in the elaborate metaphor in *Bolton*, and that the metaphor was not to be taken as extending the class of individuals whose acts could bind a company.[34]

Lord Pearson's position was identical to Lord Diplock's, and though recognising the anthropomorphic metaphor, Lord Pearson did not become mired in the imagery:

> The magistrates' opinion that Mr. Clement [the shop manager] was not 'another person' – a person other than the company – seems to me to be clearly unsustainable. It would be immediately obvious in the case of an individual proprietor of a business and the manager of one of his shops. It is less obvious in the case of a company which can only act through servants or agents and has generally in the law of tort and sometimes in criminal law vicarious responsibility for what they do on its behalf. But vicarious responsibility is very different from identification. There are some officers of a company who may for some purposes be identified with it, as being or having its directing mind and will, its centre and ego, and its brains . . . With regard to the word 'manager' . . . the word refers to someone in the position of managing the affairs of the company, and would not extend to include a person in the position of Mr. Clement. In the present case the company has some hundreds of retail shops, and it would be far from reasonable to say that every one of its shop managers is the same person as the company.[35]

Thus, a shop manager is too low in the corporate hierarchy for their actions to be deemed to be those of the company. And this is true even if the activities in question concerned the manager's store, and were of a 'weights and measures' type offence.[36]

Viscount Dilhorne's reasoning was similar. He suggested that section 20 of the Act may be an attempt by Parliament to enumerate those sorts

[33] *Tesco* (n. 2) at 199–200. [34] Ibid. at 200.

[35] Ibid. 190–1, see also his remarks at 193: 'Mr. Clement, being the manager of one of the company's several hundreds of shops, could not be identified with the company's ego nor was he an alter ego of the company. He was an employee in a relatively subordinate post.'

[36] It should be noted that the fine in the *Tesco* case was £25, equivalent to about £320 in 2010 terms.

of individuals who may serve as the directing mind of a company, and thus whose mental states may be attributed to the company.[37] But, in any event, a shop manager could not be considered such a mind, so was a different person from the company; and the company could rely on the provisions of section 24 to avoid criminal responsibility.[38]

The Lord Morris of Borth-Y-Guest reasoned along the same premises in his speech, although he incorporated more metaphorical language. According to Lord Morris, the store manager was too far down in the corporate hierarchy to be the directing mind and will of Tesco. He was a mere cog in the machine,[39] and was controlled by the company rather than controlling it. As such, he was a different person than the company; hence the company could rely on section 24 for a defence.

The leading speech in this case, that of Lord Reid, is heavily reliant on the metaphor of a mind. In examining criminal liability in the context of a master–servant relationship, Lord Reid notes:

> Where a limited company is the employer difficult questions do arise in a wide variety of circumstances in deciding which of its officers or servants is to be identified with the company so that his guilt is the guilt of the company. I must start by considering the nature of the personality which by a fiction the law attributes to a corporation. A living person has a mind which can have knowledge or intention or be negligent and he has hands to carry out his intentions. A corporation has none of these: it must act through living persons, though not always one or the same person. Then the person who acts is not speaking or acting for the company. He is acting as the company and his mind which directs his acts is the mind of the company. There is no question of the company being vicariously liable. He is not acting as a servant, representative, agent or delegate. He is an embodiment of the company or, one could say, he hears and speaks through the persona of the company, within his appropriate sphere, and his mind is the mind of the company. If it is a guilty mind then that guilt is the guilt of the company. It must be a question of law whether, once the facts have been ascertained, a person in doing particular things is to be regarded as the company or merely as the company's servant or agent. In that case any liability of the company can only be a statutory or vicarious liability.[40]

37 *Tesco* (n. 2) at 187–8.

38 Ibid. 188: 'However this may be, shop managers in a business such as that conducted by the appellants – and their number may be of the order of eight hundred if the appellants have that number of shops – cannot properly be regarded as part of the appellants' directing mind and will and so can come within the reference to "another person" in sections 23 and 24(1)(a).'

39 Ibid. at 180–1. 40 Ibid. at 170.

After reviewing the earlier case law, and, in particular, approving the reasoning in *Lennard's* and *Bolton (Engineering)* regarding the nature of the imputed corporate mind, his lordship noted:

> I think that the true view is that the judge must direct the jury that if they find certain facts proved then as a matter of law they must find that the criminal act of the officer, servant or agent including his state of mind, intention, knowledge or belief is the act of the company. I have already dealt with the considerations to be applied in deciding when such a person can and when he cannot be identified with the company. I do not see how the nature of the charge can make any difference. If the guilty man was in law identifiable with the company then whether his offence was serious or venial his act was the act of the company but if he was not so identifiable then no act of his, serious or otherwise, was the act of the company itself.[41]

Thus, irrespective of the gravity of the offence, for the act to be deemed to be the act of the company, the actor must be identified with the company, as its directing mind or (otherwise put) as the mind of the company. The shop manager's mind certainly does not control Tesco, thus Tesco may properly avail itself of the statutory defence. The state of mind of the corporate officer is now both a necessary and sufficient condition for corporate liability.

The *Tesco* judgment is an authoritative interpretation of the Trade Descriptions Act 1968. That much is beyond doubt. But if it is the correct interpretation of that Act, then the Act is a poor piece of legislation. If the judgment is wrong, then it eviscerated an important aspect of that Act's consumer protection provisions. By placing the mental element of the offence high in the corporate structure, it creates a double standard: large organisations such as Tesco will be impossible to prosecute, but smaller, local (single owner) businesses will be easy candidates.[42]

Rightly or wrongly decided, though, *Tesco* is nonetheless the law, and particularly so when it comes to the locus of the corporate mind. Subsequent decisions have emphasised that the phrase 'directing mind and will' is primarily a rule of attribution. It is a guide to interpreting legal rules, particularly those containing *actus reus* and *mens rea* components.[43]

[41] Ibid. at 173. [42] As noted in the Crown's argument, ibid. at 166.

[43] *Meridian Global Funds Management Asia Ltd* v. *Securities Commission* [1995] 2 AC 500, 507:

> This is always a matter of interpretation: given that it [the legal rule in question] was intended to apply to a company, how was it intended to apply? Whose act (or knowledge, or state of mind) was *for this purpose*

2.4.2 *Tesco's flaw*

The identification model fails as an adequate rule for the attribution of responsibility to organisations, and fails precisely because of its anthropomorphic attributes. In seeking a directing mind and will of a corporation analogous to a mind of a human, it attempts to locate a senior decision-maker. The metaphor tends to a unique, senior decision-maker: seeking *the mind* entails seeking *a unique mind*, by analogy to a human. The seniority of the decision-maker is emphasised when the analysis focuses upon the corporate 'brain' or 'nerve centre'. And then by strict construction of the corporate constitutional documents, which is the next step in the process of attribution, the decision-maker is thus determined to be either at the corporate board level or not far removed therefrom.

This model is removed from the realities of corporate decision-making in anything but the smallest of companies. Few corporate decisions affecting the day-to-day running of a company, and particularly in larger companies, are made at the board level. Decisions at that level are mainly strategic, e.g. involving the approval of major acquisitions, dispositions, and contracts. The responsibility for other decisions, particularly those involving the medium- and short-term running of the company, is devolved down the corporate chain of command.[44]

> intended to count as the act etc. of the company? One finds the answer to this question by applying the usual canons of interpretation, taking into account the language of the rule (if it is a statute) and its content and policy.

[44] Tesco plc's description of the function and responsibilities of its board of directors is illustrative of this:

> The Board has set out a clear Schedule of Matters Reserved for Board Decision in order to ensure its overall control of the Group's affairs. These include the approval of:
>
> - the Company's strategic and operating plans;
> - annual and interim financial statements;
> - major acquisitions and disposals;
> - authority levels for expenditure;
> - treasury policies;
> - risk management and internal control systems;
> - group governance policies; and
> - succession planning for senior executives.
>
> The Board delegates to management the detailed planning and implementation of these matters in accordance with appropriate risk parameters. The Board monitors compliance with policy and achievement against objectives by holding management accountable for its activities through

This devolution of decision-making (and thus the responsibility for its consequences) isolates a larger company from criminal liability. Thus, even where a company was infected throughout with an ethos of sloppiness which resulted in many deaths,[45] when the decision-making/responsibility was sufficiently removed from the upper echelons of the hierarchy, neither the corporation nor the members of the board of directors could be successfully prosecuted for manslaughter.[46]

The removal of this model from corporate reality is further demonstrated when economic crimes are considered. Corporate bribery to facilitate a profitable arrangement is unlikely to be authorised at the board level. When these activities take place, they occur at much lower – e.g. sales and marketing – levels. Likewise, in cartel and other economic collusion cases, although there may be a few well-known exceptions,[47] those responsible for developing and participating in such collusion are generally lower in the corporate hierarchy.[48]

The consequence for the need for the criminogenic decision to be made by the directing mind of an organization (necessarily at or near the top of the corporate hierarchy) is that larger corporations, by devolving decision-making (and thus responsibility), can insulate themselves from criminal liability. As long as the board is unaware of, or otherwise avoids making decisions which may lead to corporate guilt, the company is almost certainly beyond the reach of the criminal law. As the *MV Herald of Free Enterprise* inquiry and subsequent (failure in) prosecution show us, this is so even if the corruption runs throughout the corporation.

A corollary of this ability for larger corporations to self-immunise, is that this doctrine will affect only smaller companies, typically those whose directors are intimately involved in the day-to-day running of the company's affairs. Consistent with the fact pattern of *Tesco*, this may be a small retail business, organised as a corporation, for example, for

regular updates. In addition, each substantial business within the Group is required to present to the Board on a regular basis, giving it the opportunity to understand and explore issues as deemed necessary.

45 Department of Transport, *MV Herald of Free Enterprise*, para. 14.1.

46 *R* v. *P and O Ferries (Dover) Ltd* [1991] 93 Cr App R 72 (CCC).

47 In the fine art cartel (Christie's–Sotheby's) the conspirators included the chief executive of Sotheby's and the Chairmen of both companies: see Ashenfelter and Graddy, 'Anatomy of the Rise And Fall of a Pricefixing Conspiracy', 5–6.

48 See the illuminating table contained in Stephan, 'See No Evil', which analyses forty international cartels prosecuted in the US or in the EU between 1998 and 2008. It lists the cartel and the corporate positions of the individuals involved. Although the individuals were generally quite senior corporate employees, few were board members, or in similar senior positions.

limited liability, tax or estate planning reasons. The main shareholder, director and employee, similar to what transpired in *Tesco*, may not have realised that a particular specially marked package promoted by some offer was sold out, thus leading to a customer being overcharged. Under the identification principle, that company has likely committed an offence; yet under similar circumstances, a larger company would not.

Ultimately, the identification doctrine is a less than satisfactory means of imputing criminal responsibility to an organisation. It relies upon an erroneous comparison between an individual and a group to develop a theory of criminal liability. It is somewhat uneven in its effect, singling out a narrow range of conduct, while ignoring other – morally equivalent – conduct. And, more significantly, it fails to establish any incentives to control the principal–agent issues which permit criminal behaviour to arise within a firm.

2.5 Alternative models of corporate liability

2.5.1 Aggregation

An alternative to imputing the knowledge of *an individual* who acts as the directing mind and will to an organisation, as the knowledge of the organisation, is to attribute the knowledge of *all members of the organisation* to the organisation. The American case, *US* v. *Bank of New England*[49] well illustrates the reasoning. In that case, the bank was charged with thirty-one violations of the Federal Currency Transaction Reporting Act[50] which required the reporting of cash transactions of more than $10,000. These transactions involved one of the bank's customers who would present several cheques of a total value greater than $10,000 (but each cheque worth less than $10,000) to a teller. The customer would then receive the total amount in cash. The bank failed to notify the appropriate authorities of the transactions.

In approving the trial judge's instruction on aggregation,[51] the First Circuit Court of Appeals held:

[49] 821 F 2d 844 (CA1 1987), cert denied 484 US 943 (1987). [50] 31 USCA §§ 5311–22.

[51] The trial judge's charge included the following instruction (n. 49 at 855): 'As such, its knowledge is the sum of the knowledge of all of the employees. That is, the bank's knowledge is the totality of what all of the employees know within the scope of their employment. So, if Employee A knows one facet of the currency reporting requirement, B knows another facet of it, and C a third facet of it, the bank knows them all.'

> A collective knowledge instruction is entirely appropriate in the context of corporate criminal liability . . . The acts of a corporation are, after all, simply the acts of all of its employees operating within the scope of their employment. The law on corporate criminal liability reflects this . . . Similarly, the knowledge obtained by corporate employees acting within the scope of their employment is imputed to the corporation . . . Corporations compartmentalize knowledge, subdividing the elements of specific duties and operations into smaller components. The aggregate of those components constitutes the corporation's knowledge of a particular operation. It is irrelevant whether employees administering one component of an operation know the specific activities of employees administering another aspect of the operation . . .
>
> . . . Since the Bank had the compartmentalized structure common to all large corporations, the court's collective knowledge instruction was not only proper but necessary.[52]

As one commentator notes, this model of aggregation imputes liability to a corporation in the same way the knowledge required to answer a series of questions is imputed to a quiz team.[53]

The advantage of the aggregation model of corporate knowledge is that it better reflects the realities of corporate decision-making. Particularly in large corporations, decisions of consequence are made throughout the corporation, and often well removed from the most senior levels. Indeed, the above-noted examples of corporate bribery, economic collusion and corporate manslaughter are all illustrative of circumstances in which decisions and knowledge are dispersed throughout an organisation, at levels removed from those which could be regarded as the 'corporate brain'.

The immediate consequence of this model is that corporate self-immunisation from criminal liability becomes difficult, if not impossible. Rather than proving that those at the highest corporate level had certain mental states, all the prosecution need prove is that individuals – including lower level employees – associated with the corporation (acting in the course of their duties) had the requisite mental state (or their states aggregated) for the relevant *mens rea*. Further, by regarding all members (including employees) of the corporation as contributing to the corporate mind, it is less likely to single out smaller enterprises as being particularly suitable for prosecution.

[52] Ibid. at 856, the Court's citations omitted. [53] Gobert, 'Corporate Criminality', 405.

In spite of these advantages, the aggregation model has no place in English law.[54] In a judicial review of the coroner's inquest arising out of the *MV Herald of Free Enterprise* capsize, Bingham LJ (as he then was), held:

> I do not think the aggregation argument assists the applicants. Whether the defendant is a corporation or a personal defendant, the ingredients of manslaughter must be established by proving the necessary mens rea and actus reus of manslaughter against it or him by evidence properly to be relied on against it or him. A case against a personal defendant cannot be fortified by evidence against another defendant. The case against a corporation can only be made by evidence properly addressed to showing guilt on the part of the corporation as such.[55]

It is unfortunate that the logic of Bingham LJ took a somewhat tortured turn. Aggregation has nothing to do with the proof of the prosecution's case against individual defendants; rather, it has everything to do with the case against the company who employed these individuals as its agents.

2.5.2 Corporate fault and/or corporate culture

The difficulties with the identification and aggregation models of imputing corporate liability rest in their atomistic view of corporations as collections of individuals, and seeks – through reasoning by analogy – to find a corporate mind in this structure of individuals. An alternative approach looks at corporations as social entities, not possessing a mind, but possessing a culture. It is in the corporate culture that fault and hence liability can be found.

This model is not merely a theoretical proposal.[56] It has been incorporated into the Australian (Commonwealth) Criminal Code.[57] Section 12.3(1) of that Code provides:

[54] It has been considered in the Law Commission's studies on involuntary manslaughter and on criminal liability in a regulatory context: Law Commission, *Criminal Law Involuntary Manslaughter*, *Legislating The Criminal Code Involuntary Manslaughter*, and *Criminal Liability in Regulatory Contexts*. The Law Commission sees some merits to its use in crimes of corporate manslaughter, but has reservations of its utility with other corporate crimes: *Criminal Liability in Regulatory Contexts*, paras. 5.92 – 5.110.

[55] *R* v. *H M Coroner for East Kent, ex parte Spooner* (1989) 88 Cr App R 10 (CA) at 16–17.

[56] For theoretical discussions, see Fisse, 'Corporate Criminal Responsibility', Fisse, 'Criminal Law: The Attribution of Criminal Liability to Corporations', Bucy, 'Corporate Ethos', Gobert, 'Corporate Criminality' (n. 53), Gobert and Punch, *Rethinking Corporate Crime* (n. 20) and Clarkson, 'Kicking Corporate Bodies and Damning Their Souls', 568–9.

[57] For the legislative background to the incorporation of the corporate culture model, see Allens Arthur Robinson, *Corporate Culture*, 11–17.

> If intention, knowledge or recklessness is a fault element in relation to a physical element of an offence, that fault element must be attributed to a body corporate that expressly, tacitly or impliedly authorised or permitted the commission of the offence.[58]

Subsections (2) and (4) enumerate a non-exhaustive set of evidentiary means of attributing corporate fault, and subsection (3) provides for a defence of due diligence.[59] Where the offence is one of negligence, the principle of aggregation applies.[60] Similar provisions apply, albeit for sentencing purposes, in the United States Sentencing Commission's *Guidelines Manual*.[61]

The attribution of responsibility of an offence to an organisation through its culture pragmatically avoids the need to identify any particular individual (or set of individuals) as being those who contributed to the illegal deed. This has obvious advantages in crimes such as negligence, where knowledge and decision-making are dissipated throughout the organisation's structure. Accordingly, it has the merit of not seeking the anthropomorphic mind of the organisation, thus seeking a decision-maker at an inappropriately high level in the institutional hierarchy. As expressed in the Australian version at least, it is neutral as between larger and smaller organisations. And the model makes self-immunisation from criminal liability difficult by imposing a duty to create a legally compliant corporate culture.[62]

The cultural model poses a few immediate problems. First, it may be a concern that an organisation may attempt to provide an artificial culture of compliance, by developing a 'paper' structure where 'thou shalt act legally and morally' edicts (and similar programmes) are passed down from above, only to be ignored with a wink and a nudge. This is an evidentiary issue, and where a compliance-based defence is proffered, it may be rebutted by presenting to the trier of fact evidence of the

[58] Commonwealth Criminal Code, s. 12.3(1). [59] Due diligence is not further defined.

[60] Commonwealth Criminal Code, ss. 5.5 and 12.4.

[61] United States Sentencing Commission, *Guidelines Manual*, §3E1.1 (b) - (f). See *United States* v. *Booker* 543 US 220, 125 S Ct 738 (2005), *Kimbrough* v. *United States* 552 US 85, 128 S Ct 558 (2007) and *Pepper* v. *United States* 562 US ___, 131 S Ct 1229 (2011).

[62] Commonwealth Criminal Code, s. 12.3(2)(d). Note that these provisions do not make 'corporate culture' the exclusive model of organisational liability–identification is recognised by s. 12.3(2)(a).

insincere nature of the organisation's purported ethics and legal compliance programmes.[63]

The second is far more problematic, and concerns the extent to which an extremely diverse organisation can have a single culture. It is not fanciful to suppose that in a multi-national corporation which produces multiple, differing products the ethos in its divisions will vary.[64] What, then, could be singled out as *the culture* of that organisation?

A further, less general, problem with the fault model is that it may not be necessary to combat economic crimes. As noted above, there will be someone in the corporation who forms the mental and physical elements which constitute the crimes of bribery, price-fixing, bid-rigging and the like. However, this model of fault may provide a useful component to a system of evaluating corporate responsibility, when penalties (whether criminal or otherwise) are meted out.

2.5.3 Vicarious liability

American courts have found little difficulty in attributing the criminal acts of employees to their (corporate) employers. As early as 1909, in a case involving illegal rail freight rebates, the US Supreme Court held that the attribution of criminal responsibility to an employer was merely the logical extension of the attribution of civil liability:

> Applying the principle governing civil liability, we go only a step farther in holding that the act of the agent, while exercising the authority delegated to him to make rates for transportation, may be controlled, in the interest of public policy, by imputing his act to his employer and imposing penalties upon the corporation for which he is acting in the premises.[65]

The justification for this is pragmatic:

> It is true that there are some crimes which, in their nature, cannot be committed by corporations. But there is a large class of offenses, of which rebating under the Federal statutes is one, wherein the crime consists in

[63] There may be problems obtaining this evidence as the cooperation of the organisation's members is necessary. However, a discussion of this issue is well beyond the topic of this study.

[64] This issue was noted in parliamentary hearings on the amendments which incorporated the cultural model into the Australian Criminal Code: see Allens Arthur Robinson, *Corporate Culture* (n. 57), 13.

[65] *New York Central & Hudson River Rly Co.* v. *United States* 212 US 481, 29 S Ct 304, 307 (1909).

> purposely doing the things prohibited by statute. In that class of crimes we see no good reason why corporations may not be held responsible for and charged with the knowledge and purposes of their agents, acting within the authority conferred upon them ... If it were not so, many offenses might go unpunished and acts be committed in violation of law where, as in the present case, the statute requires all persons, corporate or private, to refrain from certain practices, forbidden in the interest of public policy.[66]

This Federal rule of vicarious liability has been followed by almost every state.[67]

The Federal rule requires that the act of the agent must benefit the company to some degree, even if the agent's primary motive was to benefit themself.[68] The rule is applied even if the agent's conduct is forbidden by company policy, or other instructions. This was made clear by the Ninth Circuit Court of Appeals in the context of a Sherman Act violation. That Court held:

> For the reasons that follow, however, we think the construction of the Act that best achieves its purpose is that a corporation is liable for acts of its agents within the scope of their authority even when done against company orders.[69]

The test as to which individual may bind the company is quite broad, based upon the reasonable belief of an external observer, given the position that the agent has, has had or appears to have within the

[66] Ibid. at US 494–5, S Ct 307.

[67] Gobert and Punch (n. 20), 58–9, but note that state rules may distinguish whose actions may bind a firm for a particular class of crime, e.g. in Illinois 'A corporation can commit a misdemeanor through the acts of its agents, but it can commit a felony only through the acts of high managerial agents'. *Corpus Juris Secundum* 19 CJS Corporations § 815, citing *Morris* v. *Ameritech Illinois* 337 Ill App 3d 40, 271 Ill Dec 411, 785 NE 2d 62 (1st Dist 2003).

[68] *United States* v. *Sun-Diamond Growers Of California* 138 F 3d 961 (DC CA 1998); *United States* v. *Automated Medical Laboratories Inc.* 770 F 2d 399 (CA4 1985). The fact that the company gained no actual benefit is irrelevant: *United States* v. *Carter* 311 F 2d 934 (CA6 1963), cert denied 373 US 915, 942 (1963): 'Proof of an actual benefit to the corporation in such circumstances is not essential to its responsibility.' See also *Old Monastery Co.* v. *United States* 147 F 2d 905 (CA4 1945), cert denied 326 US 734 (1945).

[69] *United States* v. *Hilton Hotels* 467 F 2d 1000 (CA9 1972), cert denied 409 US 1125 (1973); see also *United States* v. *Twentieth Century Fox Film Corporation* 882 F 2d 656 (CA2 1989).

corporation.[70] This broad application by some courts was such that when the relevant statute provided for only imprisonment as punishment, the lack of an alternative was regarded not as a bar to the prosecution of a corporation, but as a legislative oversight.[71]

Although it is a well-entrenched doctrine of English law that the doctrine of *respondeat superior* is inapplicable in criminal matters,[72] courts will not hesitate to impute liability to corporations through the acts of their agents when the words of (or the policy behind) the relevant statute so requires. This has been so since the 1880 House of Lords decision in *The Pharmaceutical Society* v. *The London and Provincial Supply Association, Ltd.*[73]

Another Tesco case, *Tesco Stores Ltd* v. *Brent London Borough Council*,[74] illustrates this well. In that case, during a trading standards 'sting', an employee of a London Tesco store sold a copy of an '18 video' to a 14-year-old. The magistrates found that the Tesco employee who sold the video had reasonable grounds to believe that the purchaser was underage. At issue was to what degree the knowledge of the employee ought to be attributed to Tesco. After examining the wording of the relevant Act, Staughton LJ noted:

> The language here draws no distinction between the accused and those under his control. The content is concerned with knowledge and information, not due diligence. It is, as I have already suggested, absurd to suppose that those who manage a vast company would have any knowledge or any information as to the age of a casual purchaser of a video film. It is the employee that sells the film at the check-out point who will have

[70] *United States* v. *American Radiator and Standard Sanitary Corporation* 433 F 2d 173, 205 (CA3 1970): this was a Sherman Act prosecution involving price-fixing in the plumbing fixtures industry.

[71] *United States* v. *Van Schaick et al.* 134 F 592, 602 (CCY 1904):

> But it is said that no punishment can follow conviction. This is an oversight in the statute. Is it to be concluded, simply because the given punishment cannot be enforced, that Congress intended to allow corporate carriers by sea to kill their passengers through misconduct that would be a punishable offense if done by a natural person? A corporation can be guilty of causing death by its wrongful act. It can with equal propriety be punished in a civil or criminal action. It seems a more reasonable alternative that Congress inadvertently omitted to provide a suitable punishment for the offense, when committed by a corporation, than that it intended to give the owner impunity simply because it happened to be a corporation.

[72] *R* v. *Huggins* (1730) 93 ER 518, 522–3; 2 Ld Raym 1574, 1580 (KB).

[73] (1879–80) LR 5 AC 857. [74] [1993] 2 All ER 718 (QB).

> knowledge or reasonable grounds for belief. It is her knowledge or reasonable grounds that are relevant. Were it otherwise, the statute would be wholly ineffective in the case of a large company, unless by the merest chance a youthful purchaser were known to the board of directors. Yet Parliament contemplated that a company might commit the offence . . .
>
> By contrast, the single-handed shopkeeper would be less readily able to rely on the defence section, although he would fare better if he had an assistant serving at the counter while he was in the back of the shop. I cannot believe that Parliament intended the large company to be acquitted but the single-handed shopkeeper convicted.[75]

Tesco's conviction was upheld. Looking at the purpose of the Video Recordings Act 1984, the decision is almost certainly correct. But with this means of interpretation in mind, it is difficult to reconcile this case with the House of Lords' reasoning in the earlier *Tesco* case.

Likewise, in the context of an economic collusion matter, the House of Lords correctly chose to impute liability vicariously for an employee's *ultra vires* act in the 1995 case of *Ready Mixed Concrete (No. 2)*.[76] Lord Templeman's policy reasons are clear:

> Directors may give instructions, top management may exhort, middle management may question and workers may listen attentively. But if a worker makes a defective product or a lower manager accepts or rejects an order, he is the company.[77]

Lord Nolan seized upon the monitoring incentives which are provided by vicarious liability, even for an agent's *ultra vires* acts:

> Liability can only be escaped by completely effective preventive measures. How great a burden the devising of such measures will cast upon individual employers will depend upon the size and nature of the particular organisation . . . If the burden is in fact intolerable then the remedy must be for Parliament to introduce a statutory defence for those who can show that they have taken all reasonable preventive measures.[78]

The implication is that a system of vicarious liability will lead to the implementation of private monitoring programmes, which will in turn have the effect of reducing the activity which Parliament sought to curtail.

[75] Ibid. 721.

[76] Sub nom. *Director General of Fair Trading* v. *Pioneer Concrete (UK) Ltd and Another* [1995] 1 AC 456 (HL).

[77] Ibid. at 465. [78] Ibid. at 475.

Vicarious liability is thus an effective means of reinforcing legislative prohibitions. It, as noted by Staughton LJ in the second *Tesco* case, is neutral with respect to the ability of corporations to immunise themselves from criminal liability due to their size and/or organisational structure. Both large and small organisations are affected in an identical way. Further, by holding the organisation responsible for its employees, the model of responsibility through vicarious liability provides an incentive for organisations to monitor their employees, thus addressing the principal–agent problem.

2.6 The objective of corporate liability: deterrence beyond tort

The purpose of criminal law is to deter and punish unwanted activities. It shares this deterrence effect with other aspects of a legal system, particularly with tort law. But it alone has a monopoly on the direct use of the most coercive apparatus of the state, the ability to deprive persons of their liberty and property for no compensatory purposes. To the extent that a criminal law regime incorporates a punitive (i.e. retributive) element, the application of a criminal law to organisations necessarily falls short of the goals of that regime. Organisations, insofar as they act through individuals, can be deterred; but it is an error to infer that they can be punished. The individuals who constitute an organisation can be punished: the organisation cannot.

Thus the primary goal of encouraging corporate responsibility through the use of criminal sanctions is and ought therefore to deter corporate malfeasance. Tort liability has a deterrent effect, and one can (and should) use analytical lessons from tort law as an aid in the analysis of the efficacy of a deterrent regime. But we submit that it is an error to argue that since tort law (or, more specifically, negligence law) can provide this deterrent effect, the use of other regimes to control corporate malfeasance is therefore unnecessary and redundant, as some may argue.[79]

An overriding objective to a tort scheme is efficient deterrence of careless behaviour. This entails that the scheme provides optimal investment in deterrence to both avoid preventing socially useful activity by not setting up (expensive) bars to that sort of activity and to discourage harmful activity by increasing its costs, and doing so in a manner which minimises the transaction costs for all parties involved. This is best

[79] See, e.g., the arguments contained in Khanna, ‘Corporate Criminal Liability’.

illustrated with negligence. An efficient negligence scheme encourages cost-effective investment in safety, and does so with as minimal transaction costs as possible.

At the core of such analysis lie two types of rules to protect legal entitlements: property rules and liability rules.[80] When an entitlement is protected by property rules, the price of transferring that entitlement is worked out *ex ante* by the parties involved. A sale of a chattel is an example of the former rule. On the other hand, when a liability rule is used, the price or value of that which it protects is established *ex post* by a third party, independent of those involved in the relevant transaction. A judge assessing damages after a motor vehicle accident is an example of the latter rule. Under this analytical scheme, the conversion of entitlements protected by property rules into entitlements protected by liability rules by a legal system is justified to the extent that it promotes socially useful activity by reducing transaction costs.

To return to the motor vehicle example,[81] recognising the social utility of motoring, we see that it would be impossible for potential motorists to negotiate with potential accident victims to *ex ante* determine the payment to be made should an accident occur. The transaction costs would simply prevent the socially useful activity (motoring) from taking place. Accordingly, by substituting a liability rule for the property rule, the legal system will then permit the pursuit of this activity. The 'cost of accidents' can now be assessed *ex post*, in the absence of agreement (settlement) by the parties. Building on this core of legal rules protecting entitlements is a system to encourage an appropriate level of expenditure on risk prevention (or otherwise put, investment in safety) which sets the legally required standard of behaviour, falling below which will impose a duty to compensate.

To eliminate criminal liability (for either an individual or an organisation) and replace it with a tort-based model has the effect of eliminating entitlements protected by property rules and replacing them with entitlements protected by liability rules (as far as corporate actors are concerned). But, unlike when the legal system transforms property rules into liability rules, when done by a corporate malfeasor this transformation is done unilaterally and without regard to the social utility of the action requiring such a transformation. There are three objections to this.

80 Calabresi and Melamed, 'Property Rules, Liability Rules, and Inalienability'.
81 See ibid., 1108–10.

First, decriminalisation of unwanted behaviour by the use of a tort-like deterrence scheme entails that this behaviour can be engaged in for a price. In effect, licencing fees or taxes replace prohibitions for socially undesirable activity. This manner of treating undesired activity does not accord with our beliefs as to the function of fines and other court imposed sanctions for socially unacceptable behaviour. We view fines as some form of pecuniary punishment to prevent or deter bad behaviour. Except in the most trivial matters (e.g. perhaps parking) we do not view fines as some form of *ex post* permission. Indeed, we view certain activities to be of the sort that we wish to prevent their occurrence, and not permit them to be efficiently licensed or allow an efficient amount of that sort of (undesirable) behaviour.

Second, and related to the above, although this quasi-tort system of criminal liability dovetails well with social goals of ensuring optimal investment in prevention, thus ensuring neither too much nor too little is expended on preventative measures. Thereby conserving social resources, in so doing it recognises, however, that there is an optimal level of malfeasence, i.e. that which would have been too costly to avoid.[82] This may work well with regulatory regimes designed to promote appropriate expenditure for health and safety matters. However, by generalising this to all activity, the theory assumes that there is an optimal (non-zero) level of all activities, irrespective of their social cost. What is regarded as criminal activity, on the other hand, may be activity for which the optimal level is zero. In other words, we ask, what is the optimal level of corporate collusion in the marketplace; or, extended into criminal law more generally, what is or (more meaningfully put) how should society set an optimal level for theft, murder or rape?[83]

Third, this quasi-tort based system of criminal liability permits the unilateral conversion of property rules to liability rules. Yet it is possibly this very unilateral conversion which is the mark of what our educated

[82] Or, in other words, the costs of the precautions exceed the (expected) costs of the accident.

[83] See Werden and Simon, 'Why Price Fixers Should Go to Prison', 932, who comment on efficiency considerations (i.e. Becker's analysis) as follows: 'More important than any of the foregoing is that hard-core price-fixing, like many other crimes, should not be analysed within Becker's framework. Central to Becker's model is the notion that efficient offenses exist and should not be deterred. We believe that efficient hard-core price-fixing is no more likely than efficient child molestation.' See Becker, 'Crime and Punishment'.

intuitions regard as criminal behaviour. To take an example, someone may want my car. As it is protected by a property rule, if they wish to acquire it, they must bargain with me to arrive at a mutually acceptable price. They cannot merely remove it from my driveway, convert it to their use and offer me its book value in return. Yet, were the car protected merely by a liability rule, this is exactly what they could do. The difference between the two cases is between a bona fide purchaser and an apprehended thief offering restitution. By reducing corporate criminal liability to this quasi-tort system, the decriminalisation of corporate behaviour would blur this fundamental distinction.[84]

A final consideration of a non-economic nature is also relevant. In many respects criminal sanctions are productive of certain valued effects, the social utility of which is hard to quantify. The end of a criminal trial can bring closure for those affected by the wrongful conduct.[85] Additionally, criminal proceedings carry a sense of moral condemnation with them. Should corporate misfeasance be decriminalised by the adoption of a quasi-tort system of liability, these two features will – to a great extent – disappear.

The moral nature of a criminal proceeding, and the subsequent taint of a criminal conviction, is not an insignificant matter. Although the effects of such stigma may be much greater when an individual is convicted of a crime, the stigma can attach to corporations.[86] Such stigma – represented by, for example, decrease in share value after an announcement of the commencement of an investigation and/or legal proceedings – may be of significance, and is certainly an issue to be taken into consideration in the determination of any penalty.[87] Additionally, in a world where ethical considerations such as the 'greenness' of products, carbon neutrality of processes, and sustainable production of renewable resources affect consumers' purchasing decisions, it is not a hasty inference to suggest that considerations of corporate criminal malfeasance may affect these decisions.

[84] See, e.g., Posner, 'An Economic Theory of the Criminal Law', 1195.

[85] See, e.g., the sentiments expressed in 'No restorative justice for those bereaved by Potters Bar' and 'Capital punishment: an offence against victims' relatives'.

[86] See, e.g., Karpoff and Lott, 'The Reputational Penalty Firms Bear from Committing Criminal Fraud'.

[87] See ibid., 760–6; cf Bosch and Eckhart, 'The Profitability of Price Fixing: Evidence from Stock Market Reaction to Federal Indictments', 313–16.

2.7 A model corporate criminal liability regime

The foregoing considerations suggest the need for a system of criminal control of corporate behaviour above and beyond a tort-like system. As a firm is essentially an amoral entity, considerations of retribution or punishment are irrelevant to the design of such a system. Deterring socially undesirable conduct should be the primary focus of the system, along with secondary considerations of stigmatising objectionable conduct (to the extent this is coherently applied to corporate entities), and allowing victims of such conduct an opportunity for closure in the appropriate circumstances.

In addressing corporate conduct, rules of corporate criminal liability must take into account the principal–agent nature of corporate conduct, and the divergent incentives of the two corporate actors. In addition to taking into account these diverging interests, any acceptable theory of corporate liability must also pay heed to the principal's ability to effectively monitor its agents, and to set out incentives to encourage an effective level of monitoring. The goal of such a criminal liability regime is to reduce malfeasance by corporate actors to an acceptable level (or as close thereto as practicable).

The astute observer will have noticed that this recent discussion has described the ideal level of monitoring as 'effective' and the lower limit to desired criminal activity is 'acceptable'. The word 'efficient' has not been used. This is intentional. 'Efficient' describes the outcome of processes. A process is more efficient than another if it, taking the same input, produces more of the desired output (all other things being equal).

Likewise, we have referred to an 'acceptable' level of criminal activity. This, too, is intentional. It is an unfortunate fact of life that there will always be a non-zero level of criminal activity. Attempts to eradicate crime impose a cost, whether measured in money terms or in terms of liberty. The costs of crime eradication include both the financial costs of a justice (and penal) system and reduction of individual liberty. In 'combating' crime, there is a diminishing return to outlays on prevention and detection. The so-called 'wars' on drugs and terror, with their associated zero-tolerance policies, provide ample evidence of this. The costs of some crimes can be measured with some precision.[88] However, the costs of other crimes (e.g. attempts) are less subject to precise

[88] Property crimes appear to be the most amenable to the precise measurement of their costs.

measurement. Further, although the fiscal costs of crime prevention can be quantified, the costs to liberty are not subject to such easy measurement. Indeed, any scale used to measure the reduction in liberties consequent on a 'crime fighting' measure is likely to be incommensurate to a pecuniary scale. Accordingly, in establishing a goal for a level of criminal activity, we must make an explicitly normative judgment, to determine an acceptable level – with an assessment of, *inter alia*, cost and liberty considerations.

2.7.1 Agency, monitoring and liability: attribution rules

The need for rules of attributing criminal liability to corporations arises from the principal–agent relationship inherent in corporate action and the divergent interests between the parties. If the agents behaved exactly as their principals desired – because of a convergence of interests or they simply did as they were told[89] – the choice of attribution rule would be irrelevant. As the directions from the operating mind and will of the company would always and faithfully be being carried out, considerations of identification (the *Tesco* rule), corporate culture, vicarious and aggregative liability would become irrelevant. Irrespective of the rule, corporate liability would result from misdeeds of the employees/agents, precisely because they obeyed their instructions.

Once the interests of the agent and principal diverge, the choice of attribution rule has significance. The *Tesco* rule captures fewer transgressions than a rule of vicarious liability. However, the desirability of such a rule should not be determined by how wide or narrow a net it casts. Our argument is that the justification for criminal liability being imposed on corporate actors is based on their ability as principals to best monitor the conduct of their agents. Considerations of internalising the costs of activities, when these activities are done (to a non-insignificant extent) for the benefit of the corporation, lead to this conclusion. As vicarious liability is the most effective means of internalising costs, this will be shown to be the preferable attribution rule. Further, this internalisation has the additional normative advantage of not only being consistent with, but also mandated by, Kantian principles of respect for others.

[89] See Arlen and Kraakman, 'Controlling Corporate Misconduct', 690. In the following discussion of a corporate liability regime, there is heavy reliance on this analysis for its economic (but not normative) insights.

Given the principal–agent structure of corporate operations, the conduct of two parties must be considered: the conduct of the owners and that of the subordinate employees who are entrusted with carrying out decisions made in the interests of the owners. Corporate 'wrongdoing' (both civil and criminal) can emanate from the instructions or decisions of the owners (board, senior management) or can be the result of actions taken by subordinates. These two observations provide justification for a principled attribution of liability to the corporate actor: obtaining the benefits of the agent's activities and the imposition of a correlate duty to monitor the agent's activities.

Crudely put, the attribution of responsibility for an agent's actions to the principal, when the principal reaps the benefits (or at least is the intended beneficiary of some of the benefits), satisfies our intuitive moral view that 'he who gains, should pay – or at least be responsible'. This norm is consistent with (if not, is a consequence of) the basic tenets of both deontological and consequentialist ethical philosophies. A moral actor, who fails to bear the costs of their own actions thereby imposing them on others, runs afoul of the Kantian proscription not to use others as means. Likewise, the internalisation of responsibility and costs of an action to the benefiting actor underlies most of the thinking on consequentialist-based views of risk bearing and spreading.

Accordingly, an adequate and principled system of corporate criminal liability will have the effect of deterring malfeasance of both the corporate principal and the employee agents, and do so in a way such that the costs and responsibility of such deterrence falls as much as possible upon the corporate actor. To bring about such an aim, both liability and attribution rules must be examined to establish they can be used to best bring about this goal, recognising that it will be the effect of the two sets of rules taken together that achieves this outcome. Although attribution rules are the least significant of the two sets of rules, their impact on a desired liability scheme can be significant.

This can best be seen with the identification (*Tesco*) rule. Should that rule be chosen, the need for an effective means of the principal's monitoring of the agent is solved away. As this rule attributes corporate liability only for the principal's action, it creates little, if any, incentive for effective monitoring of the agents' conduct. Indeed, such an attribution rule may have the effect of encouraging an environment of corporate conduct where, although agents may be ostensively told not to participate in some activities, the particular corporate edict is given with a sufficiently subtle 'wink and a nudge'. For this reason, the identification rule should be rejected, if effective monitoring (and subsequent control) of agents' behaviour is to be regarded as a primary goal of corporate liability.

Vicarious liability, the common American attribution rule, has the advantage that when the interests of the agents are aligned with those of the principal, it induces the agents to avoid misbehaviour. This is easily seen, as in a situation when principals' and agents' interests are aligned the costs – financial or otherwise – are borne by both, hence both have an incentive to avoid these costs. Likewise, provided that the costs of monitoring are less than the costs of (prevented) misbehaviour, there is an incentive for the principal to engage in monitoring activity to avoid the costs of the agent's misbehaviour.[90] However, this cost proviso – as we will see below[91] – has significant implications for the choice of rules governing the corporate liability regime.

Aggregation, as an attribution rule, assists merely to combine elements of an offence to allow them to be deemed to be those of the principal. As such, it has utility when the offence is either care-based (e.g. negligence, manslaughter) and the conduct of no single individual falls below the duty of care (but when aggregated with others' conduct, the care standard is not met); or when the offence requires full-blown *mens rea* with an *actus* (e.g. bribery), and the various elements are found in the minds and acts of more than one agent. In these circumstances, it is a useful rule to supplement vicarious liability, ensuring that misbehaviour cannot be dissipated throughout an organisation in an attempt to avoid liability.

Corporate fault or culture, as an attribution rule, mirrors a system where vicarious liability or aggregation is used to attribute offences to corporate entities, but the corporation is provided a defence of due diligence, in that if the organisation can show it did not promote a 'culture' of a particular 'relevant conduct' (to use the Australian phrasing), it will not be held liable. However, this non-promotion of relevant conduct is nothing more than an investment in appropriate corporate compliance and employee monitoring programmes (possibly with additional investment, in e.g., safety, pollution abatement, industrial accident prevention and similar measures). Further, the defence provides an incentive for expenditure on litigation (attempting to prove there was

[90] See Arlen and Kraakman (n. 89) and Arlen, 'The Potentially Perverse Effects of Corporate Criminal Liability'.

[91] See text accompanying notes 101 to 104.

no corporate ethos of relevant conduct), rather than prevention. Thus seen, corporate fault or culture as a means of attribution of criminal liability may not be a panacea. It likely merely duplicates negligence inquiries, thereby raising the costs of enforcement.

The foregoing analysis confirms the results of our earlier discussion that the identification (*Tesco*) rule of attributing liability leaves much to be desired. It is effective only if the misdeeds can be attributable to the 'directing mind and will' of the corporation, i.e. the principal. In a regime using this rule, there is little incentive to the effective monitoring of agents by their principal. These disincentives are moderated under a system of vicarious liability, and the addition of aggregation or corporate fault/moral responsibility adds little, if anything, of additional value. A rule of vicarious liability is thus to be preferred.[92]

2.7.2 Vicarious liability: with or without a due diligence defence

The obvious weaknesses of a rule that requires full-blown *mens rea* to be imputed to a company (which would be identical to the *Tesco* rule) have resulted in the discussions of a more appropriate regime focusing on the perceived superiority of either negligence-based responsibility or strict liability over the other. There is a significant amount of literature which attempts to assess the efficacy of either of these regimes.[93] The literature demonstrates that both strict liability and a negligence-based system of responsibility have their advantages, but neither is strictly preferable over the other. The reason for this lack of dominance of one regime is that – in this view – there are two goals to be achieved by a system of corporate liability, namely an activity level goal and an enforcement goal, and the differing nature of the goals can impose demands on the chosen system of liability which can conflict.

The 'activity level goal' is to ensure that the corporate entity engages in the correct (or 'efficient') amount of any activity, which is in turn defined as the amount that would be produced in a market when the cost of the product reflected its full cost of production, including all social costs. Accordingly, in this view, the regime should seek to internalise all costs, and in particular those social costs (including costs of sanctions) of criminal activity to the product. By so doing, these costs are

92 See also the arguments in Sullivan, 'The Attribution of Culpability to Limited Companies'.

93 See the bibliography to Polinsky and Shavell, 'Public Enforcement of Law'; see also *R* v. *Sault Ste Marie* [1978] 2 SCR 1299.

reflected in the price of the product, and the optimal amount of the product will be produced.[94] A strict liability regime satisfies this goal.[95] In our view this conclusion is correct. As additional evidence of the suitability of such a solution, we note that this is consistent with a strict liability regime of product liability which forces the internalisation of all social costs to the product.[96]

The enforcement goal of this type of corporate liability regime is a rule or set of rules which seeks to minimise the costs of misconduct and enforcement (e.g. policing/monitoring costs, and all social costs of criminal activity). These enforcement means include:[97]

- private sanctioning (e.g. firing) of wrongdoers;
- the imposition of:

  'preventative measures' that deter by making misconduct more difficult or expensive for wrongdoers, or by reducing the illicit benefits of unpunished (or successful) misconduct, without affecting the probability that it is detected by enforcement officials . . . [these] rang[e] from personnel policies – for example, firing price fixers and raising the salaries of law abiding managers – to sophisticated financial controls, screening procedures, and similar mechanisms for limiting agents' opportunities to commit misconduct;[98]
- internal monitoring (policing) measures; and,
- creating a 'performance bond' that 'assur[es] the credibility of the firm's enforcement measures in the eyes of its agents'.[99]

As the means of implementing each of these measures varies from each other and the incentives which lead to an ideal outcome also vary, the resolutions to these measures do not unequivocally favour either a fault-based or a strict liability regime.[100]

[94] See Arlen and Kraakman (n. 89), 692.

[95] Ibid., citing Arlen (n. 90), Polinsky and Shavell, 'Should Employees Be Subject to Fines and Imprisonment Given the Existence of Corporate Liability?', Segerson and Tietenberg, 'The Structure of Penalties in Environmental Enforcement', Shavell, 'Strict Liability versus Negligence', and Sykes, 'The Boundaries of Vicarious Liability', 579–81.

[96] See, e.g., Burrows, 'Product Liability and the Control of Product Risk in the EC'.

[97] See Arlen and Kraakman (n. 89), 692–4. [98] Ibid., 693. [99] Ibid.

[100] Ibid., 694:

> Strict liability clearly dominates where corporate liability is deployed to encourage the private sanctioning of corporate agents, and is weakly preferable where it is a means of inducing firms to adopt preventive measures. However, duty-based liability is generally better able to induce firms to undertake optimal policing measures such as monitoring, investigating, and reporting. At the far end of the spectrum, duty-based liability is clearly superior to strict liability as a means of enhancing the internal credibility of the firm's enforcement measures.

The primary weakness of strict liability is that a strict liability based monitoring scheme creates perverse incentives, which in turn reduce its effectiveness as a performance bond. The argument for this is simple.[101] Although a firm's monitoring activities will deter (and hence reduce) misconduct, they will not completely eliminate all misconduct. Should the monitoring programme prove to be effective (as mandated by a strict liability requirement), the programme will uncover this residual wrongdoing. If, as would be the goal of the liability regime, information about this wrongdoing were placed in the hands of the government (either through a duty of self-disclosure or through the subpoena/search powers of the investigative authorities), the firm's exposure to liability would be increased. Hence, a firm will not engage in monitoring to the extent that such monitoring will enhance the firm's liability. Indeed, should the enhanced liability be significant, firms may choose to forgo an internal policing system. Furthermore, as agents (employees) become aware of the disincentives that their firm has in monitoring them, any ostensive corporate monitoring programme (either in place or proposed) will lose its credibility.

The solution to the monitoring and performance bond problem is thus to adopt a fault-based system of 'optimal' or 'efficient' monitoring. In such a system, the standard of care required is that the marginal cost of additional monitoring exceeds the marginal cost of the (undetected) and unprevented social harm. Hence firms will have the incentive to efficiently monitor their agents' activities, and their agents will comprehend that the firm has this incentive, thereby guaranteeing the credibility of the monitoring programme.[102]

However, a rule of liability which mandates that a firm only incur costs which would be efficiently expended in thwarting wrongdoing, fails to require a firm to internalise all social costs of its activities. As a fault-based system of policing requires the corporation to be responsible only in the event that it failed to detect (and prevent) wrongdoing that it could efficiently prevent, such a system recognises that the firm will not be responsible for those costs of its activities which it could not efficiently detect (and prevent). Hence, in terms of providing an incentive for sanctioning and prevention, strict liability is to be preferred.

Our solution to this conundrum is to create a system of legal liability such that the firm will be better off if it both polices its agents and reports

[101] See ibid., 707–9 and Arlen (n. 90), 842–3.
[102] See Arlen and Kraakman (n. 89), 712–17.

their misdeeds. Such a system would impose vicarious liability on the firm for its agents' misdeeds, and attribute these misdeeds to the firm on the basis of a strict liability regime. That is, irrespective of the amount of monitoring or care that the firm undertook, the firm becomes responsible for the agent's misdeed and criminal liability and consequent to this responsibility a resulting sanction attaches in the event of a misdeed. However, these sanctions will be reduced if the firm reports the agent's activities and/or is able to provide evidence of a credible monitoring programme. (Alternatively, and – from the perspective of establishing incentives – identically, an increase in sanctions will arise should the conduct not be reported or no evidence of such a programme is presented.)[103]

The use of vicarious liability for an agent's actions and absolutely attributing them to the firm provides an incentive for the firm to prevent its agents' misbehaviour. It also satisfies our intuition that the beneficiary of an activity (here, the firm) pay (or be responsible for) the costs of that activity (here, the agents' misdeeds). Likewise it begins to satisfy the desideratum that the full costs of the activity are internalised to that activity. The use of a fault-based system for monitoring and reporting establishes an inducement to monitor and report misbehaviour and thereby contribute to the credibility of the monitoring programme within the firm. Additionally, the administrative and judicial costs of determining whether or not the firm met the standard of care need not be expensive: the inquiry need only be directed at determining whether or not an obvious means of monitoring was omitted by the firm, and not – except in the hardest of cases (or 'at the margin') – directed to a cost–benefit analysis of the monitoring programme. This is a similar inquiry to the standard inquiry in a tort safety/negligence case, whereby the omission of an obvious precaution will justify a prima facie finding of negligence.[104]

One possible objection to the imposition of a duty on a firm to disclose its agents' misdeeds is that it may enhance the firm's liability for this and other matters. A firm which determines that one of its divisional

[103] The potential objection from those sympathetic to this sort of analysis is that by increasing (or not reducing) sanctions in this case, the proposed regime may over-deter the conduct by setting its price too high. The retort is obvious: as most conduct which is regarded as criminal has no social utility, over-deterrence concerns are misplaced. Such a further sanction is also justified on the grounds that it merely imposes a duty to report as part of its more general duty to monitor agents' conduct.

[104] See Arlen and Kraakman (n. 89), 732–5.

managers has been engaging in price fixing, by informing the relevant authorities of this also implicates itself, and potentially exposes itself to civil and potentially criminal liability. This enhanced liability for the firm may serve as a disincentive, resulting in a decision not to report. The retort is obvious. One fixes the sanction of not reporting at a sufficiently high level to outweigh this disincentive, or – in the alternative – one provides civil and criminal immunity to the firm (e.g. evidentiary privilege for disclosed information, and/or possible complete immunity in civil matters).

2.8 Conclusion

This chapter has shown that the principal–agent relationship inherent in corporate activity is not merely just the source of criminogenic activity at the firm level, but it is the phenomenon which must be controlled if so-called 'corporate crime' is to be deterred. We argued that the long-standing English rule that found its high-point in *Tesco* is completely inadequate to deter corporate crime. Simply and briefly put, its anthropomorphism fails to grasp the principal–agent nature of corporate activity, and it localises responsibility for such activity far too high in the corporate hierarchy to adequately provide an incentive for monitoring of the corporate agents' activities on the part of the organisation as a whole.

The proposed solution is a rule of vicarious liability, which attributes responsibility to a corporation for those activities performed by its agents. Such a rule provides incentives for the corporation to monitor the conduct of its agents (employees), thereby reducing the agents' incentives to engage in opportunistic conduct at the expense of the firm. It is argued that the incorporation of a defence of 'due diligence' for a firm, that is that the firm's engagement in suitable educational and monitoring programmes could serve as an affirmative defence for its agents' conduct, is appropriate where the activity is to be controlled within limits, and not proscribed outright. It is suggested that activities with no social utility fall within the latter category, and economic collusion is among those activities.

However, there is a limit to the extent to which sanctions can be applied to a firm, particularly for matters of collusion in an already uncompetitive or concentrated industry. Ideally, as will be explored in the next chapter, the expected sanction should exceed the expected gain from participating in the activity. However, should the reward from the participation in the activity be great and the probability that the activity will be detected be low, then the sanction must be severe. The next chapter will consider how this can lead to the bankruptcy of the offending firm and its consequent forced exit from the market. The consequences of this in an uncompetitive market may be unpalatable. Individual liability, it is argued, provides a means of supplementing corporate liability to effectively deter this sort of unwanted collusive activity within the marketplace.

3

Closing the deterrence gap: individual sanctions

3.1 Introduction

This purpose of this chapter is to argue for criminal sanctions directed towards individuals for cartel offences. Our earlier results have shown that not only is such an offence morally justified, but also that firms whose agents participate in these activities can properly (again, from a normative perspective) be subjected to criminal sanctions. In the present chapter, we extend this latter result to individuals.

The justification for such an individual criminal offence is twofold and based on the need to control opportunistic behaviour within a firm. First, and most obviously, it is the agent's conduct which is the source of the unwanted behaviour. In the context of price-fixing, it is not firms which collude; rather it is the firm's agents who do so – for whatever motive. By holding these agents personally responsible for their activities, the unwanted activity is thereby deterred. This point should be sufficiently obvious to require no further elaboration or argument.

The second justification for individual liability rests in its effect to supplement corporate criminal liability. As argued in the previous chapter, imposing liability on firms for the misdeeds of their agent establishes incentives for the firms to monitor (and control) the conduct of their agents. Indeed, in the writer's opinion, this is the underlying purpose of such liability. However, as will become apparent in this chapter, effective sanctions for failure to monitor an agent's conduct may become 'too expensive', in the sense that they may render an already uncompetitive market even less competitive, by driving a firm into bankruptcy. In effect, practical considerations pose a limit to the maximum punishment which can be meted out on a firm. These considerations, it is suggested, led to a 'deterrence gap', which arguably can be effectively filled by the imposition of individual sanctions.

This chapter is structured as follows. After sketching a theoretical model of deterrence based on the work of Becker, there is an examination of the implications of this model for cartel activity. It is noted that given the large super-normal profits which can be obtained from cartel activity, the typical duration of cartel conduct, and the (un)likelihood of detection, sanctions imposed on firms engaging in this conduct need to be substantial. But the substantial nature of such sanction – if applied – can lead to bankruptcy. The final section argues that these considerations can be avoided through the use of individual liability as a supplementary deterrent.

3.2 A model of deterrence

Firm-directed sanctions are essentially deterrent in nature. They seek to prevent certain conduct by the imposition of sanctions upon those caught engaging in the prohibited conduct. As firms are paradigms of rational, calculating, economic actors, insights from economics can assist us in predicting the behaviour of such actors. In this world of rational economic agents (assuming the return from the activity remains constant) as a good or an activity becomes more expensive, fewer agents will buy that good or participate in that activity. One can thus discourage the purchase of a good or participation in an activity by raising the price of the good or activity.

In an influential article, Becker[1] argues that crime is one such activity, and can thus be controlled by raising its price. If the price of criminal activity is sufficiently high, these activities will be eliminated. This is because, under this analysis, if the expected costs of the activity exceed its expected benefits, a rational economic actor will not engage in that activity. As applied to crime, the economically rational criminal will not offend if the expected costs of the crime exceed the expected gain, where the expected costs are the amount of the sanction (or penalty) multiplied by its probability of application.[2] The calculation is clearest when the gain from the offence is a pure monetary gain, and the sanction is expressed as a fine.[3] Cartel gains and penalties imposed on firms are of this nature.

For economic crimes committed by corporate actors, the assumptions underlying the calculation of a Beckerian fine and of economic

[1] Becker, 'Crime and Punishment: An Economic Approach'.

[2] Hence, if Fine > [1/Prob(Detection)]*Punishment, a rational agent will not offend.

[3] Illegal parking provides a clear illustration of this approach. In determining whether to park illegally, all one need do is to come to an assessment of the probability of a traffic warden issuing a ticket, multiplying that by the cost of the ticket, and comparing the result with the costs of parking legally.

rationality are not unrealistic. Unlike some crimes committed by individuals, say crimes of passion, this sort of corporate (criminal) activity is pursued for financial advantage. Becker's analysis is therefore appropriate in this case, and as such it has informed much of the recent discussion of economic crime.

Two general points need to be made regarding the Beckerian formula. First, assuming a risk neutral offender,[4] the same deterrent effect can be obtained by adjusting either (or both) component(s) of the expected costs of the crime, i.e. the probability of the application of punishment or the amount of punishment. A 95% chance of paying a £1,000 fine has the same expected cost as a 1% chance of paying a £95,000 fine; in both cases the expected cost is £950.[5] The formula says nothing about an acceptable rate of either the probability of punishment or the appropriate level of sanction. Establishing these is a policy choice, which involves both economic and other considerations.

The probability of imposing punishment can be adjusted upwards by increasing monitoring of citizens, with a commensurate increase in the fiscal costs of policing and/or a reduction in civil liberties.[6] Likewise, an extremely severe penalty can offset a low probability of imposition (perhaps arising from problems of detection). However, notwithstanding the deterrent effect of a large sentence (with low probabilities of imposition), the imposition of a severe sanction (even rarely) for matters which would otherwise be regarded as trivial raises normative concerns of proportionality between crime and punishment. These normative concerns gain an additional pragmatic dimension as administrators, judges and juries may choose to nullify laws which they view as imposing a disproportionate punishment.

Second, there is a need for a precise calculation of the Beckarian fine. If the expected cost is set too low, the result will be under-deterrence of unwanted activities. If it is set too high, there is a corresponding over-deterrence. Although it may seem counter-intuitive to speak of over-deterring criminal acts, the Beckerian formula has application to

4 If individuals are risk adverse, a lower penalty is indicated. See Polinsky and Shavell, 'The Optimal Tradeoff between the Probability and Magnitude of Fines'. However, as the focus of the present discussion is with corporate entities, the assumption of risk neutrality is appropriate.

5 Expected cost or value differ from realisation cost or value; the latter is a more subjective estimate of what the firm would actually pay or obtain.

6 E.g. by making increased surveillance easier, increasing 'stop and search' powers, relaxing exclusionary rules for improperly obtained evidence, etc.

regulation generally, and thus to the establishment of safety standards. While most criminal acts, by definition, have no social utility, those acts regulated by safety standards have some positive utility. Should over-deterrence result, socially useful activity will be forgone. Accordingly, in considering non-criminal regulated acts, over-deterrence is a legitimate consideration. However, as hard-core cartel activity has no social utility (and in this respect can be compared with criminal acts devoid of social utility[7]), considerations of over-deterrence are not particularly relevant.

3.3 Deterrence and cartel activity

When an authority imposes an optimal or Beckerian fine, that authority must have knowledge of, and apply, two variables, i.e. the probability of detection, and the gain to the offender from participation in the undesired activity.[8] Multiplying these two variables yields the lower bound of the optimal fine. However, as cartel activity is clandestine, any value obtained for either variable is necessarily imprecise.

In their study of the cartelisation of Finnish industry between 1951 and 1990, Hyytinen, Steen and Toivanen succinctly state the problematic nature of these types of studies:

> Little is known of the prevalence of cartels and, consequently, the need for competition policy. A key reason for this state of affairs is that important statistics, such as the proportion of industries (markets) that have a cartel under an existing competition policy regime, or would have a cartel if there was no competition policy, are unknown. These statistics are unknown primarily because of a lack of tools to deal with a peculiar feature of cartel data: Most of the time, it is not known whether an industry has a cartel or not. The available data depend on 1) the prevalence of cartels, 2) the probability that cartels get exposed and 3) the probability that the cartels' (non)existence in the time periods prior to their exposure can be established.[9]

[7] See, e.g., Werden and Simon, 'Why Price Fixers Should Go to Prison', 932, who argue: 'Central to Becker's model is the notion that efficient offenses exist and should not be deterred. We believe that efficient hard-core price-fixing is no more likely than efficient child molestation.'

[8] As there is a temporal aspect to the gain, the duration of cartel activity is thus an element of the gain.

[9] Hyytinen, Steen and Toivanen, 'Cartels Uncovered', 10: 'Since all the information we have about cartels is necessarily based on observations taken from specimens that were caught, the data suffers from a potentially serious sample bias. There may be a real danger that the majority of cartels that are uncovered are rather unsophisticated, whereas the smarter cartels succeed in hiding their tracks.'

That study considered cartels during a period in time in which cartel activity was legal. In an environment where such activity is forbidden, these caveats take on greater significance.

3.3.1 *Probability of cartel detection*

Recent studies of the probability of cartel detection indicate that a cartel has about a 13 to 17% chance of being discovered for each year that it is in operation. Combe, Monnier and Legal's 2008 study estimates that in the EU a cartel has an annual probability of detection of between 12.9 and 13.3%.[10] This is consistent with Bryant and Eckard's 1991 study,[11] which concluded that in the US the probability that a cartel would be prosecuted in a given year would be between 13 and 17%. Although the two studies provide remarkably consistent numbers, they are nevertheless attempts to measure clandestine activity, and are thus constrained by that consideration.[12]

3.3.2 *Cartel overcharges*

The economic analysis of cartel overcharges is also imprecise; however, it does yield a consistent (but wide) range, namely that these overcharges are between 17 and 35%. In summarising the empirical studies on cartel overcharges, Schinkel concludes:

> The majority of cartels prices within the 25 to 35% range of overcharges. The mean overcharge that the known modern international cartels for which overcharges were calculated managed to sustain is little over 28%, with a median slightly below that. Hence it is likely to be conservative to

[10] Combe, Monnier and Legal, 'Cartels: The Probability of Getting Caught in the European Union'.

[11] Bryant and Eckard, 'Price Fixing: The Probability of Getting Caught'.

[12] Bryant and Eckard, ibid., 531, admit:

> The total population of active conspiracies can be partitioned into two subpopulations, one containing conspiracies which are eventually caught and another containing those which are not. Our sample is from the first subpopulation, and therefore our statistical inferences relate directly to that population only. No data exist regarding the second population. Nevertheless, one can extrapolate to the second some information inferred regarding the first.

It is, of course, the accuracy of this extrapolation which is central.

> conclude that a representative cartel manages to make (annual) illegal profits of roughly 25% of total (annual) affected commerce.[13]

Analysing American data, Connor and Lande's 2005 study is consistent with Schinkel's analysis, and concludes:

> Our survey identified about 200 serious social-science studies of cartels which contained 674 observations of 'average' overcharges. Our primary finding is that the median cartel overcharge for all types of cartels over all time periods has been 25%: 17–19% for domestic cartels and 30–33% for international cartels. Thus, in general, international cartels have been about 75% more effective in raising prices than domestic cartels. Because the United States has historically had by far the toughest system of anticartel sanctions, this could imply that these sanctions have been having significant effects. These cartel overcharges are skewed to the high side, pushing the mean overcharge for all types of cartels over all time periods to 49%.[14]

Combining those results summarised by Schinkel with the two above-cited studies on the probability of cartel detection, one can conclude that a deterrent fine (for a particular year's activity) would need to range between (approximately) 145 and 270% of the annual affected commerce.[15]

3.3.3 *Cartel duration*

The final element which the Beckerian formula must consider in assessing optimal fines for cartel activity is the duration of the cartel, as the

[13] Schinkel, 'Effective Cartel Enforcement in Europe', 15: if fines are used to internalise the harm caused by such activity, these estimates of overcharges may well be too small to use to internalise all harm, particularly in uncompetitive downstream markets. See Bassow and Ross, 'Measuring the True Harm From Price-Fixing' 919, who conclude:

> At a most basic level, our results point to the fact that simple overcharge estimates may be gross understatements of the true harm suffered by others as a result of cartel pricing. These are errors of the first order such that simple overcharges cannot in general even be thought of as 'rough approximations' of the true harm. Just understanding how far from the true harm the simple overcharge can be, as illustrated by the examples in our tables, could be helpful to enforcement agencies and courts (and settling parties) in determining appropriate fines and damage awards.

Consequently, they argue that indirect purchasers should be able to recoup their losses.

[14] Connor and Lande, 'How High Do Cartels Raise Prices?', 559 (the authors' footnotes omitted).

[15] Assuming that the probability of detection ranges between 13 and 17% and overcharge of affected commerce is 25 to 35%, we obtain the lower bound of (100/17)*25 = 147% and (100/13)*35 = 269% as the upper bound.

damage is inflicted over a period of years, particularly with the most successful cartels. In a 2010 study analysing the duration of the 110 cartel cases which resulted in sanctions by the European Commission between 1990 and 2008, De found, 'The longest lasting cartel in the dataset is the Belgium Architect Association which lived 36 years. The average mean duration of the cartels is 8.08 years where the median life is 6 and standard deviation is 6.32.'[16] This dataset comprised only the proven duration of the lives of the cartels; in twenty of the cases the suspected duration was two-and-a-half times greater than the duration proven.[17]

3.3.4 *Implications for cartel deterrence*

Based upon the above, assuming a mean cartel life of eight years and a constant rate of annual affected commerce, the deterrent fine (for the entire cartel activity) needs to be at least in the range of 1,160 to 2,160% of an average year's affected commerce, plus any sort of top-up to account for interest and/or inflation. We also note that these figures are net of any harm which may result from the social loss of confidence in the market as an important social institution (if, indeed, that harm can be subject to any sort of accurate quantification).

3.4 Bankruptcy and the consequences of optimally deterrent fines

3.4.1 *Bankruptcy considerations*

For a firm which does not produce a diversified range of products, the consequences of an optimal fine could be dire. As there would be no reason for such a firm to retain a reserve to cover such contingent liabilities,[18] the imposition of a fine of such a magnitude could well lead to the bankruptcy of an offending firm. Though one may shed no tears for those who actively participated in the cartel activity and lost their employment as a result of their firm's bankruptcy, such bankruptcies have wider consequences.

16 De, 'Analysis of Cartel Duration', 44. 17 Ibid., 45.

18 Indeed to set aside such a charge would defeat the purpose of attempting to gain a supercompetitive rate of return which cartel activity provides; and in addition to requiring the cooperation of numerous individuals within the firm, such a charge may cause the 'wrong' questions to be asked when the firm's financial statements are examined.

Some shareholders may have relished the super-competitive return brought on by the cartel profits; innocent shareholders may have lost a substantial investment. This loss would be compounded if such holdings represent part of pension and retirement funds, whose beneficiaries have little or no incentive to monitor the activities of each investment vehicle held by their pension plan (if indeed they were aware of the contents of their plan's portfolio). Likewise, with a forced exit from the market occasioned by insolvency, innocent employees lose their incomes, creditors similarly lose, there will be a loss of tax revenue, and – assuming the firm is an employer of any significance – economic damage will be done to the community(-ies) in which it was located. But more significantly, the exit of a firm in an uncompetitive industry will lead to further concentration in the industry, thereby exacerbating the uncompetitive nature of the industry.[19]

There is a legal maximum to cartel fines. The EU caps its fines for infringements of Article 101 TFEU at 10% of 'the total turnover in the preceding business year of the undertaking or association of undertakings participating in the infringement'.[20] A similar 10% cap is found in UK law for infringements of the Competition Act 1998.[21]

Additionally, both the European Commission and American authorities recognise that bankruptcy is an unwelcome consequence of what would otherwise be an appropriate fine. The EU's Guidelines for setting fines specifically permit inability to pay to be taken into account to reduce fines for infringements of Articles 101 and 102 of the TFEU.[22] Fines have been reduced in a number of recent cases,[23] as it is apparently the Commission's policy not to put offending firms out of business.[24]

[19] On bankruptcy considerations in an anti-cartel regime, see Stephan, 'The Bankruptcy Wildcard'.

[20] Guidelines on the method of setting fines imposed pursuant to Article 23(2)(a) of Regulation No. 1/2003 [1996] OJ C210/2 (1 September 2006), Art. 32.

[21] Competition Act 1998, s. 32 and Competition Act 1998 (Determination of Turnover for Penalties) Order 2000 (as amended by the Competition Act 1998 (Determination of Turnover for Penalties) (Amendment) Order 2004 (SI 2004/1259)).

[22] Guidelines (n. 20), Art. 35.

[23] See *Bathroom Fittings* 23 June 2010, IP/10/790 (non-confidential version not yet available) in which three fines were reduced by 50% and two by 25% due to inability to pay; also *Electrical and Mechanical Carbon and Graphite Products* in which CEC had its fine reduced by 33% due to inability to pay (although this inability to pay was in part due to fines from other, contemporaneous, cartel activity).

[24] See the speech by Cecilio Madero Villarejo, 3 March 2011, 3:

> These are serious infringements and fully deserved the over €3 billion [referring to the results of antitrust enforcement in 2010] in fines we levied. Of course, and as Mr. Almunia has repeatedly said, our aim is

Likewise, the US Federal Sentencing Guidelines provide for similar treatment of organisations which are unable to pay.[25] Accordingly, antitrust fines are often reduced by American courts on the basis of inability to pay.[26]

The result is that this credible threat of bankruptcy sets an upper bound to the maximum fine that can practically be imposed on a firm. Although there may be good *economic* reasons for bankrupting an offending firm (e.g. internalization of social costs to the greatest extent possible; that the firm was inefficient and that by exiting the market upon bankruptcy its resources will be put to more efficient use and/or a more efficient entity will enter the market to replace it),[27] *non-economic* considerations (such as employment) are also germane.[28]

The 10% legal maximum, adjusted downward where bankruptcy may be a consideration, provides a limit to any fine, often precluding the imposition of an optimal fine. This limit thus results in a significant under-deterrence of cartel behaviour, leading to a deterrence gap.

3.4.2 The existing fine regime as under-deterring

That the present fining policies significantly under-deter is seen not only from the above theoretical discussion, but also in the prevalence of recidivism in both the EU[29] and internationally. Connor and Helmer's

> not to put companies out of business. This is why we have taken into account valid claims for inability to pay when calculating the fines. On 10 occasions, we reduced the fines to a level that the companies could afford to pay. But, as economic recovery picks-up, we foresee that such circumstances will be increasingly rare.

25 US Sentencing Commission, *Guidelines Manual*, §8C2.2, §8C3.3.

26 See Stephan, 'Bankruptcy Wildcard' (n. 19), 529–30, who notes that in the US this reduction is often due to plea bargains.

27 See Motta, 'On Cartel Deterrence and Fines in the European Union', at 217, who argues that in the unlikely event that a firm will have to exit the market due to a cartel activity related fine (even capped at 10% of the annual turnover), such an exit shows that such a firm was too inefficient to survive in an otherwise competitive market.

28 Although competition is one economic goal of the TEU, note that the Treaty also has a social mandate which includes employment considerations. Also note that in the American context, the political fallout from a firm's bankruptcy resulting from a Sherman Act prosecution would be significant – one could reasonably expect politicians of all levels to lobby against the imposition of such crippling sanctions. Likewise, given the current economic climate in the UK, bankrupting a firm (and inflicting the attendant economic harm on its stakeholders) would not be a politically appealing outcome to a competition investigation.

29 On recidivism and the EU's fining policy, see, e.g., Geradin and Henry, 'The EC Fining Policy for Violations of Competition Law', 447–8.

2007 study[30] shows that between 1995 and 2005, 170 firms were repeat price-fixers, of which eleven companies fixed prices between ten and twenty-six times. The leading offenders were BASF, Total SA (including TotalFina, Elf and AutoFina), and Hoffman-LaRoche (twenty-six, eighteen and seventeen offences, respectively).

In a further 2010 study of international cartel recidivism, Connor notes:

> The mean number of cartels per recidivist is 4.0, but this number is highly negatively skewed. Most of the recidivists engaged in only two cartels and two is, of course, the minimum number. At the other extreme, 52 firms were members of seven or more cartels; 26 were in ten or more cartels; and six companies engaged in 20 or more cartels . . . These top recidivists are primarily headquartered in the EU. The largest single number (eight of the 52) is French firms; indeed, three of the top six firms – each with at least 20 examples of recidivism – are French. The remaining European recidivists are mainly headquartered in Germany and other northern nations. The second largest block of leading recidivists is the seven companies from Japan and Korea. Only five U.S. companies are leading recidivists.[31]

It is fair to point out that Connor's definition of 'recidivism' is broader than the usual meaning of the term, as he includes as recidivists firms which have been charged (but not sanctioned) for an offence and deems firms which simultaneously engage in more than one hard-core cartel activity as engaging in a pattern of recidivist behaviour.[32] While his definition may be limited by its over-inclusive nature, it nevertheless illustrates patterns of behaviour by entities which are not deterred by existing legal sanctions.

Recidivistic-like behaviour in the UK is not unknown. An examination of the OFT's cartel decisions does not show evidence of true recidivism, in the sense of one party entering into a new cartel after being fined for earlier activity. This data shows, however, that in the roofing industry, a number of firms repeatedly participated in bid-rigging and cover-bidding in distinct geographic markets (north-east England, west Midlands, west central Scotland, England and Scotland generally). It is likely that the distinct geographic markets that the OFT served was the reason why these matters were not consolidated into one case. At minimum, this is evidence that that industry is corrupt.

30 Connor and Helmers, 'Statistics on Private International Cartels'.

31 Connor, 'Recidivism Revealed', 111.

32 See ibid., 103–4 and 109–10; and Connor and Helmers (n. 30), 5.

The British supermarket industry was involved in the price-fixing of tobacco,[33] and three parties involved in that matter (Asda, Safeways – prior to its acquisition by Morrisons – and Sainsbury's) subsequently admitted their involvement in the price-fixing of dairy products. As this was done by way of an 'early resolution',[34] it may be argued that there was no finding or admission of guilt in the matter.[35] Additionally, as the time period for the two conspiracies overlapped, this is not recidivist behaviour in the true sense.

Likewise, one of undertakings involved in the replica football kits matter[36] (JJB Sports) was subsequently investigated for price-fixing. Although the investigation against the firms has concluded (without bringing charges), the SFO's investigation against individuals is ongoing.[37] Again, this may show that the individuals involved have not learned a lesson. This lack of true recidivism appearing in the UK data is potentially a result of a number of factors. These include the requirement that the major cartels be dealt with by the European Commission. Additionally, cartel investigations are time intensive, requiring four to six years. This, and an approach which – due to the potential criminal nature of proceedings when individuals are involved – requires the authorities to be in possession of the most convincing evidence before a decision is made to go ahead, may slow down the accumulation of data regarding the efficacy of an Act which has been in force for under ten years.

The 2006 EU Fine Guidelines, though touted as being tougher and thus a greater deterrent than previous guidelines,[38] appear not to have a significant effect on recidivist behaviour. In examining the thirteen cartels (with seventy participants) fined under the 2006 Guidelines prior to July 2009, Connor finds that although the punishments under

[33] *Tobacco* (Case CE/2596–03), 15 April 2010.

[34] OFT Press Release 22/08, 'Lactalis McLelland agrees early resolution in dairy retail price initiatives investigation'.

[35] In other words, the claim (of unlikely truth) that 'early resolution' was offered to rapidly and cost-effectively end the matter on a without prejudice basis.

[36] *Price-fixing of Replica Football Kit* (Case CP/0871/01), 1 August 2003.

[37] SFO Press Release, 'Sports Direct plc and JJB Sports plc'.

[38] Referring to the 2006 Guidelines, Alexander Italianer (Director General for Competition, European Commission) remarked: 'We recognized that the level of our fines was clearly not deterrent beforehand, so we had to increase it in order to increase the deterrence.' Roundtable Conference with Enforcement Officials, quoted in Connor, 'Has the European Commission Become More Severe in Punishing Cartels?', 27.

the new guidelines are five times what they would have been if calculated under the former (1998) guidelines,[39] recidivist behaviour nevertheless occurs. Indeed, Connor notes nine firms were identified by the Commission as repeat offenders; however, as he also notes, several firms clearly qualified as recidivists but were not treated as such for fining purposes.[40]

The effect of these fines is primarily disgorgement, as Connor notes:

> For the first time in antitrust history, I believe we are observing fines that regularly disgorge the monopoly profits accumulated by cartelists. Applying a formula to a sample of 70 defendants that had fines imposed under the new guidelines, I find that at least 24 and possibly as many as 34 of them displayed severity above 100 per cent. Three firms in Marine Hose ranged as high as 500 per cent to 650 per cent of affected sales – possible (but rare) examples of supra-deterrence.[41]

However, disgorgement alone is an ineffective deterrent. Disgorgement merely forces the return of the ill-gain, if the offender is caught.[42] It is trite to say that were the penalties under the 2006 regime effective deterrents, recidivism – and certainly recidivism of this degree – would not occur.

The fines, at least as meted out, while appearing substantial, do not have the desired effect of deterring collusive behaviour. They are simply too small. They appear to act merely as licence fees, which may explain the amount of recidivistic behaviour observed. However, enhancing deterrence is not a simple matter of increasing the level of corporate fines, as shown by the previous discussion of maximum fines, concerns of bankruptcy and the anti-competitive effect of a firm exiting an already uncompetitive market. Further, an even larger fine would appear[43] excessive, and thus violate any notion of just punishment. In the EU

[39] Connor, ibid., 29–30 and 32.

[40] Ibid., 30, at which Connor remarks, 'One wonders whether such a severe undercounting is wilful or simply the result of poor record-keeping by the Commission.'

[41] Ibid., 31.

[42] A (potential) thief will not be deterred from stealing an item if the sole penalty were the return of the item.

[43] The key word here is 'appear'. When a deterrent fine is analysed according to the Beckerian formula, this impression vanishes. Unfortunately, even if this formula is used, all that will be seen by the public and those involved in the political lobbying process will be the final amount. Indeed, if public opinion does not view price-fixing as a serious matter, a large amount will be seen as excessive. On public attitudes towards price-fixing, see, e.g., Brisimi and Ioannidou, 'Criminalizing Cartels in Greece' and Stephan, 'Survey of Public Attitudes Towards Price-Fixing'.

where proportionality is a matter of community law, a substantial fine has the potential of being viewed as disproportionate and reduced on that ground.

3.5 Filling the deterrence gap with individual criminal liability

Using Becker's formula to capture deterrence, one sees that increasing either (or both) of the penalty or the probability of detection enhances the effect of the proposed sanction. The penalty can be increased not only by increasing the fine levied upon the firm, but through other means as well. Furthermore, the probability of detection can be increased not merely through external means (i.e. investigative agencies detecting undesirable conduct) but also through internal means (i.e. establishing incentives for offending firms to confess and turn themselves (and others) in). Adverse publicity and other reputation diminishing measures are often regarded as a means of enhancing fines.[44] But while such negative publicity can serve as a sanction, its effect is uncertain. Additionally, where the collusion involves intermediate products (a frequent feature of major international cartels), or an entire (or almost the entire) industry,[45] it is not clear how such publicity can be an additional enhancement to other sanctions meted out.

Internal means of increasing the probability of detection can be augmented by destabilising the relationships of those involved in the cartel. These relationships involve not just the relationship among the various (corporate) members of a cartel, but also the agent–principal relationship of an employee (who may possibly be facilitating the cartel's activities) and the firm involved in the cartel. Amnesty programmes of the sort practised in the US,[46] EU,[47] and UK[48] have the effect of breaking down the trust necessary to maintain the cooperation and coordination of firms' activities necessary to sustain collusive action. These

[44] See, e.g., Karpoff and Lott, 'The Reputational Penalty Firms Bear from Committing Criminal Fraud'.

[45] See, e.g., Case COMP/39406 – *Marine Hoses* (participants accounted for almost 100% of the relevant market) and Case COMP/B/37.766 – *Dutch Beer Market* (participants accounted for over 90% of the relevant market).

[46] The US programme is well described by Klawiter, 'US Corporate Leniency after the Blockbuster Cartels'.

[47] Commission Notice on Immunity from fines and reduction of fines in cartel cases.

[48] Enterprise Act 2002, s. 190(4).

programmes are reasonably effective in flushing out hard-core cartel activity,[49] but could be supplemented with other means.

It is suggested that individual criminal liability is the solution not only to increasing the probability of detection, but also to enhance the sanction variable in Becker's formula to provide an effective deterrent. Corporations do not sit around tables allocating markets or fixing prices; rather individuals do, on behalf of corporations. The imposition of individual criminal liability for such activities imparts an additional cost to those individuals participating in these activities.

Additionally, it is further suggested that this criminal liability also includes incarceration, or at least the *credible* threat thereof. Pecuniary sanctions against an individual can be indemnified, either explicitly or through wage premiums to compensate for that risk.[50] Director disqualification[51] is perhaps a useful adjunct to a system of individual criminal liability. But, on its own, it is an indeterminate sanction as its efficacy is dependent upon the particular circumstances of the director. To an individual nearing (or able to afford) retirement such disqualification is less of a deterrent than to someone differently situated, and the potential for indemnification dilutes the deterrent effect of disqualification.

The personal nature of a prison sentence and that such a measure is not in practice[52] easily indemnified, entails that such a penalty is a qualitatively different sanction from any pecuniary sanction. It is precisely this qualitative difference which makes individual criminal liability an effective supplement to any system of corporate liability. As shown above, additional deterrence cannot be obtained by increasing fines on corporate entities above a certain threshold, due to insolvency concerns. Yet, even at or near this threshold level, fines alone insufficiently deter.

[49] For a discussion of the efficacy of such programmes, see Connor, 'Cartel Amnesties Granted'.

[50] On this problem, see Bucy, 'Indemnification of Corporate Executives'.

[51] Enterprise Act 2002, s. 204 amends the Company Directors Disqualification Act 1986 to provide for a maximum 15-year directors disqualification order for individual directors who have committed certain breaches of either the Competition Act 1998 or the TFEU Articles 101 and 102. See the Company Directors Disqualification Act 1986, s. 9B; and Whish, *Competition Law*, 422–3.

[52] In theory, a wage/risk premium could be paid to the corporate 'vice-president responsible for going to jail' (this fanciful title originates with Braithwaite, *Corporate Crime* (at 328). However, given the socio-economic group from which such an executive would likely be drawn, it is not clear how high this premium would be, or whether in fact such a premium would be accepted.

Likewise, as indemnified personal sanctions merely add to the level of the fine imposed on the firm, their deterrent effect is limited.

Focusing the sanction on those who actually engage in the collusive activity for the benefit of their employer, directs a sanction to the participants thereby focusing a part of the punishment on those who actively engaged in the illegal activity. As Stephan notes, in a regime in which the consequences of illegal activity are directed only at the firm, the firm bears the entire risk of its employees activities;[53] this is so even when the employees' actions were contrary to the firm's express policies. Individual liability, in addition to any incremental deterrent effect it may have, also has the normative advantage of attributing responsibility to those who in fact were responsible for the misdeed.

In addition to the increased deterrent effect, thereby increasing the penalty variable of Becker's formula, individual criminal liability further destabilises cartels, by exploiting the divergent interests in the principal–agent relationship of firm and employee. Where an individual is not subject to sanctions, there is every incentive for an individual to 'go with the flow'. There is no personal cost to doing so, and indeed there may be a cost to one's career and/or remuneration from breaking rank. On the other hand, if a cost to 'going with the flow' is imposed, the firm's and employee's interests diverge. Faced with a dilemma of credible threat of incarceration versus being a corporate team player, it will be the rarest of employees who will not favour their own interests. This destabilising effect thus enhances the probability of detection (and eventual successful prosecution – which is the goal of detection), as with the cooperation of individuals involved (albeit under an immunity arrangement) much of the evidence necessary to secure convictions can be more readily obtained.

3.6 Conclusion

In this chapter, we have argued that individual criminal liability has the practical advantage of being able to upwardly adjust the punishment and detection variables in a version of Becker's formula,[54] thereby enhancing

[53] Stephan, 'See No Evil', 239.

[54] The original Beckerian formula merely represents a cost–benefit analysis to the firm, weighing the expected costs from the activity against its expected gain. Once individual liability is incorporated into the system of deterrence, the formula becomes mathematically (but not intuitively) more complex. At minimum, the new formula would aggregate a number of individuals' own cost–benefit analyses into the formula, plus possibly – *inter*

the deterrent effect of anti-cartel measures which incorporate it. Additional individual liability serves as a 'top-up' to any liability imposed on the firm, thereby closing any deterrence gap which so-called sub-optimal fines have on organisations. Since, as noted above, an effective deterrent fine may well exceed 2,000% of the annual affected commerce, a firm which is ill diversified in its products may well be bankrupted by such a fine. As such a bankruptcy will likely impose costs upon innocent parties, political and social considerations tell against the imposition of such penalties, irrespective of any economic advantages or efficiencies which can be gained by the imposition of such fines. The gap necessitated by these non-economic considerations can be filled by individual liability.

Further, by exploiting the divergence of interests which pre-exist in the employee–firm relationship, individual criminal liability can be used to further destabilise cartels. A leniency programme in which the winner of the 'race to the courthouse door' (or possibly, more accurately, to the prosecutor's office's fax machine) receives complete immunity introduces distrust among those participating in a collusive organisation. The distrust originates from the opposing interests among the participants when apprehension becomes more than a remote possibility. As similar distrust originates between an employee and the firm in similar circumstances, this addition of individual criminal liability adds a further dimension of instability to collusive arrangements. In addition to the corporate race for leniency, individuals will join in – racing not only against their own firms but also against other individuals representing their firms.

An additional pragmatic justification for individual criminal liability rests in the destabilising influence inherent in the threat of its imposition. The origin of much corporate crime rests in the divergence of interests of the firm and its employees. Save in the (rare, it is to be hoped) circumstances of a corporate culture which condones or promotes its employees engaging in hard-core cartel activity, criminal economic collusion occurs as a result of mid- to upper-level employees establishing conditions which benefit themselves (by insulating themselves from the rigours of competition) and their employer (again by insulating it from competitive forces). This activity may be well tolerated when the cartel is stable and operating as it 'should'. However, as the

alia – additional variables to represent increase in the probability of detection due to increased instability occasioned by the introduction of individual liability. On this point, see Polinsky and Shavell, 'Should Employees Be Subject to Fines and Imprisonment?'.

cartel approaches the end of its life the symbiosis between employer's and employees' interests wanes.

In such circumstances, particularly when there may be the impending threat of a criminal investigation in which there is a risk of a period of incarceration for an individual, a rational individual will act to advance their own interest, above all other interests. Where immunity from prosecution is offered in exchange for cooperation, the rational decision is to cooperate with the investigation. In such circumstances, the incentives faced by the agent are in opposition to those faced by the principal. The introduction of individual criminal liability and an associated immunity programme, adds a further destabilising element in addition to any similar destabilising influence resulting from immunity programmes offered to firms.

Although imposing individual criminal liability in hard-core cartel matters is justified on normative grounds, and is supported by pragmatic justifications, the addition of individual liability into a cartel control programme is not without costs. These costs are not merely financial, and therefore quantifiable with some purported degree of precision. Rather, the costs are more subtle, and less susceptible to quantification. These are the costs involved in developing an intrusive and perhaps heavy-handed system which will impose punishment of a *sui generis* nature on individuals. These costs involve an always delicate balance of competing interests involved in the implementation of a legal system. These interests must balance the use of highly intrusive investigative procedures and a vastly punitive enforcement system, with the necessary respect for individual freedoms which underlies a liberal society. Given the increased international nature of cartel activity, and thus the need to coordinate the anti-cartel regime of one jurisdiction with those of other jurisdictions, assessing the costs, and thus getting the requisite balance right, becomes a very subtle process. And it is a process in which crude, ad hoc transplantation of elements of other legal regimes may not necessarily be appropriate.

4

The American experience of cartel control: values and effectiveness

4.1 Introduction

It is fair and possibly trite to say that the American is one of the most effective, if not feared, antitrust regimes in the world. There is little recidivism. Indeed, the Department of Justice's (DOJ) statistics show that:

> No company and no individual convicted in the U.S. of a cartel offense after July 23, 1999 subsequently joined a cartel prosecuted in the United States. Moreover, no company and no individual granted conditional leniency after July 23, 1999 subsequently joined a cartel prosecuted in the United States.[1]

The date 23 July 1999 signifies the day on which the first non-American received a federal sentence for price-fixing. Data from the United States Sentencing Commission[2] shows that prison sentences are not isolated events. Between 1999 and 2009, 175 individuals were sentenced for antitrust offences, of which 83 were sentenced to prison with a median sentence of 6 months. The range was 2 weeks to 4 years.[3] The DOJ's statistics indicate that during 2000–9 the average prison sentence for price-fixing was 19 months; in the years 2010 and 2011 the average rose to 24 months.[4]

Criminal fines are meted out. During 2000–9:

> the median fine for organizational antitrust offenders was $550,000; for FY 2005 through FY 2008, the median fine tripled to $1,721,000. Even though a fewer number of organizational antitrust offenders (a total of 9) were sentenced in FY 2008 than in some prior years, the largest median fines were imposed in FY 2008 . . . In FY 2008 alone, organizational

1 Werden, Hammond and Barnett, 'Recidivism Eliminated'.
2 Summarised in Howell, 'Sentencing of Antitrust Offenders'. 3 Ibid., 8–9.
4 DOJ, Antitrust Division, 'Division Update Spring 2012'.

> antitrust offenders were fined an average amount of $56,100,000, with the median value at $42,000,000.[5]

These latter sums, too, are significant: in 2010, fines totalled $550 million; the 2011 figure was $524 million.[6]

Further, hundreds of millions of dollars are paid annually to those harmed by anti-competitive activity. Between 1990 and 2007, over $18 billion was recovered by those affected by cartel activity.[7] We note that this latter figure represents *civil* compensation; it does not include any criminal or administrative penalty. Additionally, there is evidence to suggest that organisers of international cartels will avoid affecting the American market, so as to not draw the ire of the American authorities (and the penal consequences thereof).[8]

In looking at these figures, it is fair to ask not only how this situation came to be, but also to consider if this situation can serve as a useful lesson from which other jurisdictions may draw. This is the purpose of the present chapter. Its structure is as follows. The next two sections examine the intellectual background to the Sherman Act which served as the starting point for *Federal* antitrust enforcement in the US. This Federal Act did not arise in 1890 from a proverbial vacuum. Rather, it emerged out of a rich nineteenth-century background of social thought regarding the relationship of individual freedom and the marketplace. This social thought had significant influence on the development of state antitrust law, which not only pre-dated the Sherman Act but also served to shape congressional attitudes in developing an approach to restrain harmful, anti-competitive activity. In the third section we focus on these aspects of state antitrust regimes and their influence on the congressional history of the Sherman Act.

In the fourth section, we examine how the Sherman Act was subsequently interpreted by the courts, particularly the Supreme Court, to develop clear boundaries which distinguish permitted from prohibited conduct. This development was essential, if the regime were to contain a criminal component. Considerations of certainty draw a line in the sand, and facilitate the prosecution of those who may cross the line. But legal certainty, or 'a clear line', is only one aspect of the enforcement of any regulatory regime. Other strands of the regime must be present and operate harmoniously with this sense of certainty to result in an effective

[5] Howell (n. 2), 11. [6] DOJ, Antitrust Division, 'Division Update Spring 2012' (n. 4).

[7] Lande and Davis, 'Benefits from Private Enforcement', 891–3.

[8] See, e.g., *United States* v. *Andreas* 216 F 3d 645, 651 (CA 7 2000).

regulatory scheme. These strands in the American system, namely the civil enforcement regime, certainty with respect to potential penalties and a developed leniency programme are quite diverse but are nevertheless well integrated into an effective cartel control regime. In the fifth section to this chapter, we briefly outline these other strands of the American cartel control regime, to show not only their interaction, but also to demonstrate how their effective integration contributes to an effective cartel control system.

This chapter concludes with a distillation of the American regime. This enables us to identify how it came to be that the values protected by the regime are protected in the manner in which they are protected today. As these themes will be elaborated on in the conclusion to this work, this chapter's account will necessarily be brief. Consumer welfare is the good protected, and the Americans are not unique in protecting this economic asset. However, as we shall show, the particular means by which it is protected is somewhat unique to the United States and arose out of a particular historical and cultural background. And it is against this background that the chapter ends, with some sceptical thoughts about the transplantability of the American programme.

4.2 Natural law and morality: the nineteenth-century background

The predominant set of beliefs possessed by the nineteenth-century American legal community was a vision of nature shaped by natural law, mixed with strands of individualistic, liberal (if not libertarian) views regarding individual freedom.[9] As our ensuing discussion will make clear, the interaction of these two intellectual threads would often lead to tensions. These tensions would rise to the fore when legislatures and then courts were called upon to assess the appropriateness of regulating individual behaviour, in relation to other social or 'common' goods.

The most influential exponent of natural law to or within the legal community was Joseph Story, associate justice of the US Supreme Court from 1811 and (later and simultaneously) professor of law at Harvard University, a post which he held from 1829 until his death in 1845. Publishing text and reference books on almost every area of the law,

[9] This section draws upon some of my earlier research, subsequently published as 'From Natural Law to Legal Realism'.

Story was unquestionably the widest read, and most influential, American jurist of the nineteenth century.[10] The core of Story's thought on natural law can be found in an 1836 article, 'Natural Law', written for the *Encyclopaedia Americana*.[11] He describes it thus:

> Natural Law, or as it is commonly called, the law of nature, is that system of principles, which as human reason has discovered to regulate the conduct of man in all his various relations. Doctor Paley defines it to be the science, which teaches men their duty and the reasons of it.[12]

The reference to 'Doctor Paley' is of course a reference to William Paley, the English theologian and natural philosopher, and in particular his 1795 work, *The Principles of Moral and Political Philosophy*.[13] This later work proved highly influential throughout the nineteenth century on both sides of the Atlantic, cited in debate in both the Parliament at Westminster[14] and in the American Congress.

In the natural law systems of both Story and Paley, there are sets of duties and their correlative sets of rights. The former are duties towards God (consisting of piety and devotion),[15] self-regarding ('offences against our faculties', i.e. the duty of self-preservation including the avoidance of drunkenness and suicide),[16] and other regarding (duties to family and society).[17] Correlated to these duties, are sets of natural rights. Although this latter set is not exhaustively enumerated by either Paley[18] or Story,[19] both concur that among these are rights to 'life, limbs and liberty'. Paley remarks:

> Rights, when applied to persons, are
> Natural or adventitious:
> Alienable or unalienable:
> Perfect or imperfect.

[10] Indeed, anecdotal evidence suggests that in the 1840s he was making over $10,000 a year from royalties, in contrast to his salary $4,500 annual as an associate judge of the Supreme Court.

[11] See Wardhaugh (n. 9), 308–15.

[12] Story, 'Natural Law'.

[13] Paley, *The Principles of Moral and Political Philosophy*.

[14] Hansard, HC Debates, 26 June 1844, cc. 1452–549.

[15] See Story (n. 12), also quoted in Wardhaugh (n. 9), 309 and Paley (n. 13), 198–228.

[16] Story, ibid., Paley, ibid., 187–97.

[17] Story, ibid., Paley, ibid., 151–86.

[18] Book III of *Principles* discusses the various relative duties and their correlative rights, yet no exhaustive enumeration is provided.

[19] Story (n. 12): 'It is difficult to take any exact enumeration of what may be deemed the general rights of mankind, which may not admit of some exceptions, or which may not be deemed capable of modification under peculiar circumstances.'

I. Rights are natural or adventitious.
Natural rights are such as would belong to a man, although there subsisted in the world no civil government whatever.
Adventitious rights are such as would not.
Natural rights are, a man's right to his life, limbs, and liberty; his right to the produce of his personal labour; to the use, in common with others, of air, light, water. If a thousand different persons, from a thousand different corners of the world, were cast together upon a desert island, they would from the first be every one entitled to these rights.[20]

Story adopts Paley's account of natural rights in a near verbatim manner.[21]

In the mind of both, the right to and the value of property is based on labour. In explicitly Lockian fashion,[22] although previously unappropriated land and its fruits may be there for the taking,[23] the value of a thing results from the labour or effort which goes into its appropriation or production. Thus Paley:

> Another [account of property rights] says, that each man's limbs and labour are his own exclusively; that, by occupying a piece of ground, a man inseparably mixes his labour with it; by which means the piece of ground becomes thenceforward his own, as you cannot take it from him without depriving him at the same time of something which is indisputably *his*.

[20] Paley (n. 13), 63.
[21] Story (n. 12), also quoted in Wardhaugh (n. 9), 310:

> Rights are usually divided into such as are natural or adventitious, alienable or inalienable, perfect or imperfect. We call those rights natural, which belong to all mankind, and result from our very nature and condition; such are a man's right to life, limbs and liberty, to the produce of his personal labor, at least to the extent of his present wants, and to the use, in common with the rest of mankind, of air, light, water, and the common means of subsistence.

[22] Locke, *Second Treatise on Government*, Bk II, ch. 5.
[23] See Paley (n. 13), 76:

> Another, and in my opinion a better, account of the first right of ownership, is the following: that, as God has provided these things for the use of all, he has of consequence given each leave to take of them what he wants: by virtue therefore of this leave, a man may appropriate what he stands in need of to his own use, without asking, or waiting for, the consent of others;. . .

> This is Mr. Locke's solution; and seems indeed a fair reason, where the value of the labour bears a considerable proportion to the value of the thing; or where the thing derives its chief use and value from the labour.[24]

A corollary of the right to possess property is a right of exchange or contract. Both Paley and Story recognise such rights of exchange, which at natural law are based on duties stemming from promise.[25] In a civil society, such natural rights are protected by the operation of law,[26] and such protection is among the central reasons for entering into civil society.[27]

This view of the natural order of things shaped not only nineteenth-century American economic thought, but helped shape the political and economic libertarianism which was to become characteristic of American legal thinking of that century and the early part of the next. In addition to being contained in the legal philosophy of that era, this thinking was contained in the widely read economics texts of the time.

Although nineteenth-century scholars were familiar with the texts of Adam Smith and David Ricardo,[28] nineteenth-century American economics texts read more like what we would presently term treatises on public policy. It was not until the 1870s that marginal analysis of utility was independently developed by Jevons, Menger and Walras. Marshall was not to publish his influential *Principles of Economics* until 1890, and developed mathematical analysis was not used as a tool until the late twentieth century. Rather, the leading economics text was Francis Wayland's *The Elements of Political Economy*,[29] first published in 1837, and revised and reprinted throughout the nineteenth century.[30] Other influential texts included Amasa Walker's *The Science of Wealth: A Manual of Political Economy – The Laws of Trade, Currency, and Finance*[31] and Francis Bowen's *The Principles of Political Economy Applied to the Conditions, Resources and Institutions of the American People*.[32]

Each of these works stressed a labour theory of value,[33] mutual gain through exchange,[34] and the idea that if individuals were given the

[24] Ibid., 75. [25] Ibid., 78–81 and 86. [26] Ibid., 82–5. [27] Ibid., 227–35.
[28] See, e.g., Bowen (n. 32). [29] New York: Leavitt Lord and Company, 1837.
[30] May, 'Antitrust in the Formative Era', 270: the argument of this article has significantly influenced my thinking.
[31] Boston: Little Brown, 1866. [32] 2nd edn, Boston: Little Brown, 1859.
[33] Wayland, 5–8; Walker, 8–9; and Bowen, 28–62.
[34] Wayland, 119; Walker, ibid.; and Bowen, 55–62.

opportunity to compete freely, entry to the market would prevent super-competitive returns.[35] Bowen blends these thoughts well:

> But competition is the general rule; and the effect of unrestrained competition is to distribute the value of a product equally among its various producers, leaving neither to any of them, nor to the consumer, any ground of complaint. Each receives in exact proportion to the labor which he has bestowed; the labor of all was equally necessary to present the article in its finished state; and he who finally consumes it, therefore, justly pays all by rendering an equivalent amount of labor. I place stress upon this point, because the effect of sharp competition is, in some measure to blind our eyes to the fact, that we are all indebted to the friendly coöperation of labor for all the necessaries, all the comforts, all the luxuries, which we enjoy. This coöperation and mutual dependence of all the arts and trades, all the branches of industry, all ranks and professions, is one of the most valuable lessons of Political Economy; and the fair rivalry which causes the distribution of values among them, in proportion to their respective industry and skill, ought not to create feelings of mutual jealousy and dislike, – ought not to give rise to the cry, that one class is taking more than its due share of the common product.[36]

This natural order ensured that, in May's words:

> all individuals tended to receive for their own services or goods an equivalent, proportional return per relevant unit of contributed effort, measured in terms not only of time but also of comparative productivity. As a result, economic writers concluded, consumers, owners of capital and providers of labor all gained the benefit of prices and returns that not only were natural, but also just.[37]

In the absence of artificial (or unnatural) influences in the market, competition would ensure a fair return on capital and an appropriate (if not fair) wage for labour. If the returns on capital in a particular industry or area were greater than in others, capital would naturally flow to these areas or industries, thereby restoring the natural rate of return; and where the return was less, capital would similarly flee. In a world that was seen to be the product of natural ordering and where the effect of sunk costs was yet to be fully understood, such reasoning made sense.[38]

[35] See May, 'Antitrust in the Formative Era' (n. 30), 271–2.
[36] Bowen, at 52; see also Wayland (n. 29), 172–3.
[37] May, 'Antitrust in the Formative Era' (n. 30), 273, footnotes omitted.
[38] The work of William Stanley Jevons on this point, in particular his *The Coal Question*, was neither widely circulated nor well understood in nineteenth-century America.

Such ordering additionally presupposed the need for individual liberty, in particular the ability to freely enter into contracts. Without this freedom, one's ability to trade one's labour for products is constrained; and the owner of capital would be unable to productively engage workers to obtain a return on their capital.

Monopolies were thus seen to be a threat to this natural order. By restricting who could provide a good or service not only do they prevent the free flow of capital to productive use, but they also injure the consumer (or worker) by artificially inflating the price that he must pay. Wayland succinctly makes this point:

> We see what must be the effect of monopolies. A monopoly is an exclusive right granted to a man, or to a company of men, to employ their labor or capital in some particular manner. Such was the exclusive right granted to the East India Company . . . The result of this exclusion was to prevent all other persons, except those thus favoured, from the right of investing their capital in this manner; and hence, to reduce the value of their capital, by precisely the amount of this effect. The tendency of this system may be easily seen; for, were all the modes of employing capital thus restricted, the additional capital that might be accumulated, would be utterly worthless. Nor is this all. Those who hold this exclusive privilege, being liable to no competition, may charge for their commodities whatever they choose. Here is, therefore, a two-fold injustice; first, the means of the consumer are diminished; and secondly, the price which he must pay, is enhanced at the mere will of his oppressor.[39]

Patents are an exception.[40] They allowed for the inventor to exploit his invention in order to 'enter into a mutually advantageous agreement'[41] with members of the community. If the price demanded were too high, the patented product would not be purchased. But, more significantly, after the expiry of the patent the community would 'have the use of the improvement for nothing'.[42] Economics thus not only served as a descriptive science, but also as a source of normative value.[43]

39 Wayland (n. 29), 119–20.
40 On the relationship of patents and antitrust in nineteenth-century America, see Khan, 'Antitrust and Innovation'.
41 Wayland (n. 29), 120. 42 Ibid.
43 On this point, see May, 'Antitrust in the Formative Era' (n. 30), 271–2, Hofstadter, 'What Happened to the Antitrust Movement', 195–97, and Kennedy, 'The Role of Law in Economic Thought'.

4.3 Pre-Sherman Act values: the states and Congress

4.3.1 Nineteenth-century public policy

In light of this normative background, it is no surprise that American courts and legislatures showed hostility to arrangements which restricted trade. In the courts, the 1866 Massachusetts case of *Taylor* v. *Blanchard*[44] is illustrative of this. In that case, that state's Supreme Court held that a contract which prohibited Blanchard from carrying on the business of a shoe-cutter in the Commonwealth of Massachusetts was contrary to public policy and void. In a short (nine paragraph) judgment, the court reasoned:

> The law has always regarded monopolies as hostile to the rights and interests of the public.
>
> One method of obtaining them in early times was by a grant from the sovereign to a particular individual of the sole right to exercise a particular trade. The mischief arising from these monopolies became so intolerable that the practice was suppressed by a clause in *Magna Charta* [sic]. This clause does not, however, apply to grants for the sole use of a new invention for a limited period . . .
>
> Another method by which monopolies were sought to be obtained was by private contracts, in which one of the parties agreed not to engage in some specified trade or business . . .
>
> The disposition to obtain monopolies which formerly prevailed is by no means extinct at the present day, nor is it confined to corporations. Combinations of men in business sometimes accomplish such an object, and they often succeed in obtaining exorbitant profits from the public.
>
> In the present contract the court can see nothing beneficial to the public, and are of opinion that it is contrary to the well established policy of the law, and void.[45]

As the regulation of inter-state commerce was exclusively a Federal power, prior to 1890 all regulation of monopolies and combinations could only be achieved at the state level and therefore necessarily directed only towards intra-state commerce.

4.3.2 Early state antitrust regimes

State legislatures were equally as hostile to such anti-competitive practices. Of the forty-two states of the Union prior to 2 July 1890 (the date

[44] 13 Allen 370, 95 Mass 370, 1866 WL 6386 (Mass SC 1866). [45] At paras. 2, 3, 8 and 9.

on which the Sherman Act came into force[46]) 'fourteen states had constitutional prohibitions against trusts and monopolies while thirteen had statutory regulations'.[47] These statutory regulations prohibited 'monopoly, restraint of trade, restraint of competition, pooling, price fixing, output limitations, territorial divisions, resale restraints, exclusive dealing, refusals to deal, local price discrimination, and predatory pricing'.[48] The penalty provisions were varied, and, in most cases, more severe than the $5,000 fine and one-year maximum period of imprisonment provided for by the Sherman Act when passed in 1890. May notes:

> Statutes in at least thirty-five states authorized fines, imprisonment, . . . Statutes in North Carolina, South Carolina, Oklahoma, Tennessee, and Texas authorized the longest prison terms for antitrust violations, each allowing a maximum sentence of ten years. Authorized fines ranged up to $25,000, and at least ten states declared each day of violation a separate offense. Iowa provided that corporate violators could be fined in an amount equal to twenty percent of the violator's capital stock. Nine states expressly allowed private parties injured by antitrust violations to recover actual damages, two others authorized double damages, and another nine permitted treble damage recovery. In addition, at least thirty states provided that corporate charters and intrastate business privileges could be revoked in response to violations of state antitrust laws, and at least four states declared that anyone purchasing from a seller doing business in violation of antitrust law would be freed from any obligation to pay for the purchased goods.[49]

The fines and civil penalties imposed could be severe.

In a Texas case, *Waters-Pierce Oil Co.* v. *State*,[50] after hearing evidence, the State Supreme Court described it thus:

> It is sufficient, we think, to show that from the date of its permit to do business in this state, May 31, 1900, appellant has been a party to an agreement or understanding with the Standard Oil Company of New Jersey, one object of which was to create a monopoly and control the price of petroleum oil and prevent competition in its sale in a large and specified territory, including the state of Texas, and that to a large extent such object has been accomplished. In so far as that agreement related to this state, appellant, acting by its agents, performed it within this state; and such performance within the limits of the state constitutes violations of Texas laws and renders appellant amenable to such laws, although the

[46] Idaho joined the Union on 3 July 1890. [47] Note, 'Legislation', 347.
[48] May, 'Antitrust Practice and Procedure in the Formative Era', 499; see also ibid., 374.
[49] Ibid., 499–500. [50] 48 Tex Civ App 162, 106 SW 918 (1907 Tex Civ App).

> agreement between it and the Standard Oil Company may not have been made in this state. To a large extent the case rests upon circumstantial evidence; but we cannot say that the jury were not warranted in the conclusions drawn from it.[51]

The jury imposed a civil penalty of $1,623,900 and cancelled the defendant's licence to do business within the state of Texas.[52] On appeal to the US Supreme Court,[53] the court held that the penalties assessed by the jury were not excessive. This was particularly so, given the defendant's financial position: it owned more than $40 million in property, and had paid dividends as high as 700%.[54]

While *Waters-Pierce Oil* may be at an extreme, it is certainly representative of a tendency at the state level to use state police powers to prohibit such practices. In *Standard Oil Company of Indiana* v. *Missouri*,[55] the Missouri State Supreme Court upheld ouster and a $50,000 fine against each of the three corporate defendants (including Waters-Pierce Oil). Again, the US Supreme Court[56] refused to interfere with the penalty. Oil companies were not the only targets: in *Grenada Lumber Co. et al.* v. *State ex re Attorney General*,[57] after an appeal to the US Supreme Court challenging the amount of the penalties,[58] the Mississippi Supreme Court upheld fines in a finished lumber cartel totalling $14,184,000. The meat packing, sugar and tobacco industries were also targets of state enforcement.

In fining one such meat packer, Judge Marshall of the Missouri Supreme Court expressed the commonly held antipathy regarding trusts and their pernicious effects:

> 'Competition is the life of trade.' Pools, trusts, and conspiracies to fix or maintain the prices of the necessaries of life strike at the foundations of government; instill a destructive poison into the life of the body politic; wither the energies of competitors; blight individual investments in legitimate business; drive small and honest dealers out of business for themselves, and make them mere 'hewers of wood and drawers of water' for the trust; raise the cost of living and lower the price of wages; take from the average American freeman the ability to supply his family with necessary, adequate, and wholesome food; force the boys away from school, and into the various branches of trade and labor, and the girls into workshops and other avenues of business, and make them

[51] Ibid. Tex Civ App 187, SW 930. [52] Ibid. Tex Civ App 178, SW 924.
[53] 212 US 86, 29 S Ct 220 (1909). [54] US 111–2, S Ct 227.
[55] 218 Mo 1, 116 SW 902 (1908). [56] 224 US 270, 32 S Ct 406 (1911).
[57] 98 Miss 536, 54 So 8 (1911). [58] 217 US 433, 30 S Ct 535 (1910).

> breadwinners while they are yet almost infants, because the head of the house cannot earn enough to feed and clothe his family. The people are helpless to protect themselves. The powers that be must protect them, . . .[59]

Such legislation and consequent penalties were routinely upheld by the federal courts. Indeed, interference by the US Supreme Court with either state exercises of police power to prohibit this conduct (so long as such police power was applied across all industries) or with amount of civil or criminal penalties imposed under such powers was the exception.[60]

Constitutional challenges alleging violations of the Fourteenth Amendment's equal protection clause would be more likely to be successful, particularly when the impugned legislation exempted certain industries from its scope.[61] The typical exemption was to the agricultural sector, on the premise that the evil sought to be prevented by the Act could not be caused by producers or raisers of agricultural products or livestock. The Tennessee Antitrust statute of 1897[62] was typical. Section 1 provided a wide-ranging prohibition against trusts.[63] However, section 4 provided a limited exception for the agricultural sector thus: 'the provisions of this act shall not apply to agricultural products or live stock while in the possession of the producer or raiser'.

In holding that this exemption did not run afoul of the Federal Constitution's equal protection clause, Judge Cadwell's (of that state's Supreme Court) reasoning is worth considering in detail:

> Class legislation is of two kinds, namely, that in which the classification is natural and reasonable, and that in which the classification is arbitrary

[59] *State ex inf Crow* v. *Armour Packing Co.* 173 Mo 356, 73 SW 645, 652 (1903): this was part of the same combination which was attacked in *United States* v. *Swift and Co.* 196 US 375, 25 S Ct 276 (1905).

[60] See May, 'Antitrust Practice' (n. 48), 521, 535–42.

[61] See May, ibid., 521–9.

[62] Tennessee Acts 1897, Chapter 94.

[63] Section 1 provided:

> . . . all arrangements, contracts, agreements, trusts or combinations between persons or corporations, made with the view to lessen, or which tend to lessen, full and free competition in the importation or sale of articles imported into this state, or in the manufacture or sale of articles of domestic growth or of domestic raw material, and all arrangements, contracts, agreements, trusts or combinations between persons or corporations designed, or which tend, to advance, reduce, or control the price or cost to the producer or to the consumer of any such product or article, are hereby declared to be against public policy, unlawful and void.

> and capricious. Enactments of the former kind are uniformly recognized by the supreme court of the United States and by this court as constitutional and valid, while those of the latter kind are by the same courts, and with equal uniformity, condemned as unconstitutional and invalid … Farmers and stock raisers constitute the excepted class, and they are excepted from the penalties of the act only in respect of those transactions which relate to farm products or live stock while yet in the possession of the producer or raiser. Even they are not excepted when they enter into other lines of business, or when they have transactions in relation to agricultural products or live stock which have passed out of the possession of the original owner. This classification is not arbitrary and capricious, but natural and reasonable … Obviously those transactions that are excepted from the penalties of this act rarely if ever result in evil to the public, while those upon which the penalties are imposed are believed to have that effect generally … The difference between the two classes can be well and fairly emphasized, though not fully illustrated, by contrasting the position and influence of farmers, in the disposition of their wheat, corn, hops, sugar cane, and cotton seed, with those of the milling trust, the whisky trust, the beer trust, the sugar trust, and the Standard Oil Company, in their dealings in relation to the same commodities, respectively.[64]

Similar provisions were found in the antitrust statutes of, *inter alia*, Texas, Georgia, Montana, Missouri, Oklahoma, Nebraska and Illinois.[65] The purpose of the state statutes was to focus state enforcement on those sectors of the economy which were locally felt to pose the greatest danger to the public.

In 1902 the US Supreme Court struck down a similarly worded Illinois statute on equal protection grounds in *Connolly* v. *Union Sewer Pipe Co.*[66] In that case, Connolly, who purchased pipe, disputed his liability for payment of the agreed purchase price, and sought additional damages for Union's anti-competitive conduct.[67] The Court struck down that statute in its entirety. Seizing on the point that the statute made criminals

[64] *State ex rel Astor* v. *Schlitz Brewing Co.* 104 Tenn 715, 59 SW 1033, 1036–7 (Tenn SC 1909).

[65] See May, 'Antitrust Practice' (n. 48), 521–9.

[66] 184 US 540, 22 S Ct 431 (1902).

[67] Ibid. US 543, S Ct 433:

> The set-offs claimed by Connolly were: Treble the amount of the actual damages sustained and allowed by the act of Congress of July 2d, 1890, chap. 647, known as the Sherman anti-trust act, $56,970.44; actual damages sustained by reason of the violation by the plaintiff of the provisions of the Illinois statute of July 1st, 1893, $17,323.48; and for money had and received by plaintiff of defendant contrary to law, $17,323.48.

of all who engaged in anti-competitive behaviour with the exception of some of those in the agricultural sector,[68] the court held in no uncertain terms that this was a denial of equal protection:

> We conclude this part of the discussion by saying that to declare that some of the class engaged in domestic trade or commerce shall be deemed criminals if they violate the regulations prescribed by the state for the purpose of protecting the public against illegal combinations formed to destroy competition and to control prices, and that others of the same class shall not be bound to regard those regulations, but may combine their capital, skill, or acts to destroy competition and to control prices for their special benefit, is so manifestly a denial of the equal protection of the laws that further or extended argument to establish that position would seem to be unnecessary.[69]

As a consequence Mr Connolly was denied the windfall he sought.

In spite of immediate approval from the business community,[70] the *Connolly* decision was to have limited effect. In both Federal and state courts it would be construed narrowly and distinguished, so by 1914, the US Supreme Court would hold, in *International Harvester Co.* v. *Missouri*,[71] a case which exempted providers of services from a Missouri antitrust statute, that in creating this exemption, the legislature did not act arbitrarily but made a policy decision. And it was not the purview of the court to second-guess such a decision.[72] Accordingly, similarities with *Connolly* could readily be dismissed: 'It is said that the statute as construed by the supreme court of the state comes within our ruling in *Connolly v Union Sewer Pipe Co.* . . ., but we do not think so. If it did, we should, of course, apply that ruling here.'[73] *Connolly* was finally overruled in 1940.[74]

[68] Ibid. US 560, S Ct 439:

> We have seen that under that statute *all* except producers of agricultural commodities and raisers of live stock, who combine their capital, skill, or acts for any of the purposes named in the act, may be punished as criminals, while agriculturalists and live-stock raisers, in respect of their products or live stock in hand, are exempted from the operation of the statute, and may combine and do that which, if done by others, would be a crime against the state.

[69] Ibid. US 564, S Ct 441. [70] On this point see May, 'Antitrust Practice' (n. 48), 526–8.

[71] 234 US 199, 34 S Ct 859 (1914). [72] Ibid. US 215, S Ct 865.

[73] Ibid.; cf *Connolly* at US 571, S Ct 444.

[74] *Tigner* v. *Texas* 310 US 141, 149, 60 S Ct 879, 883 (1940).

4.3.3 *The Congressional background*

In addition to this legal and moral background, public opinion, particularly as voiced in the *New York Times* and *Chicago Tribune* (the two most influential papers of the day) was strongly opposed to the trusts. For example, with the exception of 6 February 1888, the *New York Times* ran articles or editorials on trusts every day that month.[75] Likewise, during the *first week* of that month, the *Chicago Tribune* published no less than twenty-three articles on that topic.[76] Such journalistic discussion was neither isolated to those two papers nor to that month.[77]

However, trusts were not the only matters of popular concern facing the American Congress in the 1880s. The 1888 Presidential election had been fought over tariffs; with the Republicans and their candidate Benjamin Harrison supporting higher tariffs, while the Democrats, and their candidate Grover Cleveland, argued that such a policy ultimately harmed consumers and entrenched economic inefficiency. In many respects, this issue had priority in the newspapers and in Congress.[78] In addition to tariffs and trusts were the related issues of labour unions, railway pools and farm income, all of which related to the trust question. If sellers of goods could not agree to raise the prices of their goods, then it appeared inequitable that sellers of labour could so combine.[79] Likewise, lack of competition in the railway industry,[80] driven by reasons of natural monopoly[81] and considerations of Federalism,[82] raised concerns that that the consumer was being disadvantaged by the manner in which this industry set its rate.

[75] Letwin, 'Congress and The Sherman Antitrust Law', 224. [76] Ibid. [77] Ibid.

[78] Ibid., 225. [79] Ibid.

[80] On regulation of the railway industry in this era, see Hovenkamp, 'Regulatory Conflict'.

[81] Competition between railroads would require the duplication of the costs of land, track and other facilities, with the reduction of traffic over each competitor's lines. The increase in costs, and the decrease in revenue, would lead to higher rates. This economic insight was not lost in the nineteenth century: see ibid., 1037–8 and 1043–4 and the references cited therein.

[82] In particular, states could only regulate intra-state activity and the Federal government was restricted to inter-state activity. Prior to the passage of the Interstate Commerce Act in 1887 these Federalist considerations led to a legislative vacuum in which intra-state railway regulation was provided for by a multitude of differing state laws, and there was no federal regulation, as Congress had passed no such law and inter-state regulation was beyond the competence of the states. (This vacuum was made explicit with the US Supreme Court's decision in *Wabash, St Louis and Pacific Railway* v. *Illinois* 118 US 557, 7 S Ct 4 (1886), which prompted the passage of the Interstate Commerce Act.)

These concerns were exacerbated by, *inter alia*, the difference in long-haul and short-haul rates, differing rates for preferred products, and lower rates for preferred customers.[83] Three factors aggravated the popular perception of the difference in rates: first, the trusts, particularly Standard Oil, were the beneficiary of much of the discriminatory rates.[84] Second, given the vertical integration of the transportation sector, railways were viewed as preferring themselves (or their related companies) at the expense of others.[85] Finally, discriminatory pricing often formed part of a secret pricing or secret (but openly known) rebate strategy.[86] Although there may have been an argument for discounting and rebates to larger customers based on economies of scale, this was not the public perception. Further, the historical evidence shows that this perception was correct, and that the discounts exceeded the benefits of scale.[87]

Concerns over farming income were inextricably linked with the trust and railway issues, particularly in the Midwest. The latter part of the nineteenth century witnessed the growth of the Granger Movement, a populist group of farmers' organisations. The movement's objectives included, *inter alia*, agricultural education, and political lobbying to improve the economic wellbeing of farmers. Such lobby efforts included persuading state legislatures to set maximum rail transportation rates and grain elevator fees.[88] Although the four Granger States were in the Midwest (Iowa, Minnesota, Wisconsin and Illinois), concerns over farmers' income and poverty extended beyond the Midwest. Letwin succinctly makes this point:

> The low income of farmers, for which remedies were constantly being considered, was often said to be aggravated by various trusts, such as those that sold farmers bags and bought their linseed and cotton-seed. The general problem of poverty, a great concern of the time, was regularly said to be accentuated by the trusts, which were accused of dividing the country into two classes, the very rich and the very poor.[89]

The ideas which gave rise to the Granger laws and to trust-busting on the whole were to improve the economic lot not just of farmers and rural communities,[90] but also of consumers generally.

83 See Hovenkamp, 'Regulatory Conflict' (n. 80), 1044–67. 84 Ibid., 1046–8.
85 Ibid., 1047–8. 86 Ibid. 87 See ibid., 1047.
88 Ibid., 1027; these laws were the focus of the US Supreme Court's judgments in *Munn* v. *Illinois* 94 US 113, 4 Otto 113 (1876) and *Wabash* (n. 82).
89 Letwin (n. 75), 225.
90 See Hovenkamp, 'Regulatory Conflict' (n. 80), 1027, who remarks that the purpose of Granger laws was 'to improve the economic welfare of resident farmers'.

It was this confluence of ideas and opinion outside Congress that it faced in its own attempts to address the trust question. And Congress needed to act, as although states could act, they were unable to regulate entities engaged in inter-state commerce, which – of course – included some of the largest trusts like Standard Oil.[91]

Inside Congress, there was a different, but also forceful, confluence of needs which facilitated its consideration and eventual passage of anti-trust legislation. First, in light of the populist sentiment against these combinations, both major parties had their own motivations to attack the trusts. The Democrats campaigned in 1880 and 1884 against monopolies. Their 1888 platform declared: 'Judged by Democratic principles, the interests of the people are betrayed when, by unnecessary taxation, trusts and combinations are permitted to exist, which, while unduly enriching the few that combine, rob the body of our citizens'.[92] The Republicans, seen as the party of the wealthy and of big business, needed to condemn trusts, out of at minimum self-defence.[93] Their 1888 platform contained the following plank:

> We declare our opposition to all combinations of capital organized in trusts or otherwise to control arbitrarily the condition of trade among our citizens; and we recommend to Congress and the State Legislatures in their respective jurisdictions such legislation as will prevent the execution of all schemes to oppress the people by undue charges on their supplies, or by unjust rates for the transportation of their products to market.[94]

As the Republicans won the 1888 election, they were to take the lead in stewarding the legislation through Congress.[95]

The Republican Senator John Sherman was to be standard bearer for the new legislation. Although Sherman had taken an interest in antitrust legislation prior to that election, his interest increased after it. After failing to obtain the Republican nomination for President in 1888, a loss which he in part blamed on General Russel Alger's bribery of delegates,[96] Sherman needed to build a final monument to himself. An

[91] Letwin (n. 75), 246–7: 'the states lacked authority to regulate corporations engaged in interstate commerce. It seemed therefore that if antitrust legislation were needed, and if it were to be effective against the largest and most powerful trusts, it must be passed by Congress.'

[92] Quoted ibid., 248. [93] Ibid., 248.

[94] American Presidency Project: Republican Party Platforms.

[95] See Letwin (n. 75), 248.

[96] See, e.g., ibid., at 253. Alger was involved with the Diamond Match Company and its monopoly. See *Richardson* v. *Buhl* 43 NW 1102 (1889 Mich SC).

Act which would not only please populist sentiment, but also provide for an element of revenge,[97] could thus serve as an appropriate monument. One historian describes Sherman's outlook thus:

> The antitrust bill was brought to the floor of Congress by Senator John Sherman because he wanted to leave one more monument to himself. By 1888 he was aging, at times impatient and confused, but still the most prominent and esteemed Republican in Congress. He had served as representative for eight years, senator for over twenty-five, and had been Secretary of the Treasury under Hayes. He had been a candidate for the presidential nomination since 1880, and seemed finally to be winning it at the convention of 1888 until Harrison took the lead during the seventh ballot. Soon after this defeat he began to take serious interest in the trust question. His seniority and experience gave him great authority on financial questions and his recent disappointment gave him the urge to do something memorable. He began by establishing personal jurisdiction over the antitrust problem.[98]

The 50th Congress (1887–89) saw Sherman, as a ranking member of the Senate's Finance Committee, attempting to seize stewardship of antitrust legislation by introducing a successful resolution to have that committee (rather than the Commerce Committee) investigate the antitrust Bills before the Senate, on the grounds that trusts and tariffs went hand in hand.[99] Of the Bills that were considered by the committee, one – Sherman's – was returned to the floor for consideration by the full Senate.

Sherman's Bill was briefly debated in January 1889. The criticisms of the Bill concerned two aspects. First, it was potentially over-inclusive: by prohibiting 'all arrangements, contracts, agreements, trusts or combinations . . .' could render illegal not just boycotts (such as those which arose against the jute-bag trust), but also arrangements whereby labourers sought to raise their wages, and (potentially) temperance organisations whose members pledged not to consume alcohol.[100] Second, having ostensively obtained its Constitutional authority from

[97] In the debate which culminated in the passage of the Bill which was to become the Sherman Act, Sherman read into the Congressional Record the Michigan Supreme Court's judgment in *Buhl* in its entirety. Among other things it brands Alger a 'monopolist'.

[98] Letwin (n. 75), 249.

[99] On the legislative history which gave rise to the Sherman Act, see Letwin (n. 75), 247–58 and Peritz, *Competition Policy in America*, 13–26.

[100] Letwin (n. 75), 250.

the commerce clause, the critics attacked the Bill as worthless, since it then could only punish goods that had been imported (unlikely, due to tariffs) or that may be in inter-state trade (hence, too narrow an application). The Bill died on the Senate floor when Congress disbanded in March of that year.

The 51st Congress began its first session on 2 December 1889. On 4 December, Senator Sherman reintroduced his Bill from the previous Congress. It is notable that this Bill, like the previous Bill, focused on conduct which was harmful to the consumer. Section 1 of the Bill stated:

> That all arrangements, contracts, agreements, trusts, or combinations between persons or corporations made with a view, or which tend, to prevent full and free competition in the importation, transportation, or sale of articles imported into the United States, or in the production, manufacture, or sale of articles of domestic growth or production, . . . and all arrangements, contracts, agreements, trusts, or combinations between persons or corporations *designed, or which tend, to advance the cost to the consumer of any such articles*, are hereby declared to be against public policy, unlawful, and void.[101]

Indeed, in later debate, Senator Sherman was adamant that this was the purpose of his Bill. He remarked that its purpose was not 'to cripple combinations of capital and labor, the formation of partnerships or of corporations, but only to prevent and control combinations made with a view to prevent competition, or for the restraint of trade, or to increase the profits of the producer at the cost of the consumer'.[102]

Between 21 and 27 March, Sherman's Bill was debated on the Senate floor. Among the concerns of the committee of the whole was the fear that the Bill could be used to prevent labour organisation. This fear was motivated by the language sought to prevent increase of the cost to the consumer, which would be the result of an increased wage through labour organisation.[103] In spite of Senator Sherman's reassurances that such was not the Bill's intent,[104] he nevertheless proposed an

[101] Emphasis supplied, see Cong Rec S 1, 51st Cong 1st Sess (March 18, 1890) reprinted in Greenslade, 'Labor Unions and the Sherman Act', 154.

[102] 21 Cong Rec 2457 (1890), quoted in Greenslade, ibid.

[103] See Greenslade, ibid., at 154–5.

[104] 21 Cong Rec 2562 (1890), quoted ibid., 155: '[C]ombinations of workingmen to promote their interests, promote their welfare, and increase their pay . . . are not affected in the slightest degree, nor can they be included in the words or intent of the bill . . .'

amendment specifically exempting such conduct from the Bill.[105] The Amendment was adopted, and the Bill was sent to the Judiciary Committee for its consideration.

The Judiciary Committee redrafted Sherman's Bill, removing the labour exemption, and redrafting Section 2 to omit reference to raising prices. The final version of the Bill therefore focused on inter-state or international restraint of trade, ironically conceding to Senator Sherman not only that his original Constitutional justification of the Bill was indeed correct; but also that, thus justified, the Bill would be effectual. Although the labour exemption was removed, the evidence suggests that this was due to the Committee's view (as well as the view of the Senate as a whole) that the Bill was never designed to apply to these sorts of organisations.[106] The redrafted Bill passed the Senate on 8 April. It went before the House and was passed on 1 May. The House withdrew its amendment and passed the Senate Bill on 20 June, and it was signed into law by President Harrison on 2 July 1890. The resulting Act was entitled, 'An act to protect trade and commerce against unlawful restraints and monopolies'. This title would have significance for its initial interpretation.

4.4 Protection of consumer surplus: judicial interpretation of the Sherman Act

4.4.1 Early days: literalism or realism

The statute was first considered by the US Supreme Court in the 1895 case of *US* v. *E C Knight Co.*[107] which involved the Federal government's challenge to the sugar trust. At issue was whether or not that trust's acquisition (hence monopolisation) of a sugar refinery in Pennsylvania could be said to affect inter-state commerce. The Court held that although sugar was manufactured and sold in Pennsylvania, as a result of which it was likely that the sugar would be transported to other states, there was no attempt to monopolise inter-state commerce as the product was not distributed in inter-state commerce.[108] Although this decision

[105] 21 Cong Rec 2611–12 (1890), quoted ibid., 155–6. The amendment read: '*Provided*, That this act shall not be construed to apply to any arrangements, agreements, or combinations between laborers, made with the view of lessening the number or hours of their labor or of increasing their wages . . . '

[106] See ibid., 157–65. [107] 156 US 1, 15 S Ct 249 (1895). [108] Ibid. at US 17, S Ct 255.

has never been unequivocally overruled, it was almost immediately distinguished,[109] and it is now regarded as having doubtful value as precedent.[110]

The second case considered by the Supreme Court, *US* v. *Trans Missouri Freight Association*,[111] was to divide the Supreme Court 5–4, with the point on which the court divided to forever shape discussion of antitrust policy. At issue in this case was an agreement among eighteen railway companies[112] to form an association 'for the purpose of mutual protection, by establishing and maintaining reasonable rates, rules, and regulations on all freight traffic, both through and local, . . .'.[113] The defendants argued that the Act did not prohibit all agreements between competitors; rather it only prohibited agreements which unreasonably restricted trade.

The District and Circuit Court of Appeals were broadly sympathetic to the defendants' argument. The focus of the District Court was on the nature of the competitive processes, or at least that process as the court perceived it. The public were entitled to the benefit of healthy competition, and not to unrestricted competition.[114] Healthy competition permitted reasonable prosperity[115] and a fair return on capital.[116] Accordingly such an arrangement was appropriate, particularly since the court found the rates to be reasonable.[117]

109 *Pennsylvania Sugar Refining Co.* v. *American Sugar Refining Co.* 166 F 254, 92 CCA 318 (CA2 1908).

110 See, e.g., *United States* v. *Lopez* 514 US 549, 115 S Ct 1624 (1995) and *Abbott Laboratories* v. *Durrett* 746 So 2d 316, 1999–1 Trade Cases P 72, 559 (Ala 1999).

111 166 US 290, 17 S Ct 540 (1897).

112 Fifteen admitted their involvement; three others (who denied their involvement) were alleged on the bill of indictment to be members.

113 The Association's Memorandum of Agreement is quoted in full in the opinion of the Court of Appeals 58 F 58, 60–4 (CA8 1893), the District Court's judgment 53 F 440 at 456–9 (1892), and excerpts appear in the Supreme Court's judgment at US 293–8, S Ct 541–2.

114 53 F 440, 453 (CA8 1892).

115 Ibid. 451:

> Undoubtedly all contracts which have a direct tendency to prevent healthy competition are detrimental to the public, and, therefore, to be condemned; but when contracts go to the extent only of preventing unhealthy competition, and yet at the same time furnish the public with adequate facilities at fixed and reasonable prices, and are made only for the purpose of averting personal ruin, the contract is lawful. The rule of law which recognizes the rights of the public to have the benefit of fair and healthy competition, . . .

116 Ibid. 452. 117 Ibid.

The majority of the Court of Appeals for the Eighth Circuit (Judges Sanborn and Thayer) was sympathetic to this approach. The starting point of their reasoning was with well-settled rules of construction of statutes, particularly that general statutes must be read with similar general statutes, and when words using common law terms are used in a statute, courts may turn to the common law to discover the intent behind and meaning of the statute. Accordingly, the majority's initial premise was:

> Thus we are brought to a consideration of the statutes in force and the decisions that had been rendered when this act was passed to determine what contracts in restraint of trade were then illegal, for it is clear both from the rules to which we have referred and from the title of the act, viz. 'An act to protect trade and commerce against unlawful restraints and monopolies,' that it was such contracts, and such contracts only, that congress intended to declare unlawful and criminal in interstate commerce.
>
> Under the common law, the ground on which contracts in restraint of trade were declared unlawful was that they were against public policy.[118]

In spite of its clear wording, the body of the statute was interpreted using its title, thus reading into the Act a purpose of combating a common law problem and not the problem as defined by the words of the statute.

After an examination of English and American common law authorities on contractual restraints to competition, the majority concluded:

> From a review of these and other authorities, it clearly appears that when the anti-trust act was passed the rule had become firmly established in the jurisprudence of England and the United States that the validity of contracts restricting competition was to be determined by the reasonableness of the restriction.[119]

Thus:

> But contracts made for a lawful purpose, which were not unreasonably injurious to the public welfare, and which imposed no heavier restraint upon trade than the interest of the favored party required, had been uniformly sustained, notwithstanding their tendency to some extent to check competition.[120]

And, the majority opined that, in all respects, the Memorandum of Association was reasonable. It harmonised rules and regulations, freight classification and enabled the shipping and handling of freight.[121] As the majority remarked, 'The plain object of this provision was to prevent

[118] 58 F 58, 67–8 (CA8 1893). [119] Ibid. 72. [120] Ibid. 73. [121] Ibid. 79–80.

competitors from resorting to secret, unfair, and ruinous methods of warfare, to make competition fair and open, and to enable shippers to modify their action to suit the coming changes.'[122]

Presumably without realising the implications of their remarks, the majority held that allowing the freight carriers to organise themselves in this way, only permitted them to do what everyone else was doing. The majority remarked:

> In other of its features, also, the contract is not subject to criticism. In these days, when persons engaged in many other callings and avocations are in the habit of meeting at intervals, as associations, for the purpose of cultivating more friendly relations and establishing regulations conducive to the general welfare of the trade, it is difficult to see upon what just grounds representatives of railway companies can be denied the right of forming associations for the purpose of friendly conference and to formulate rules and regulations to govern railway traffic.[123]

Arguably, had this interpretation stood, the Sherman Act would have become a licence to cartelise industry.

The minority, in the form of Judge Oliver Shiras, seized upon a dissimilarity between the authorities used by the majority to justify their claim that at common law only unreasonable restraints were prohibited. All authorities which the majority considered involved only private parties agreeing to restrict their conduct vis-à-vis each other. The present case involved corporations who were discharging a public function – transporting freight as common carriers, using land granted them by a right of eminent domain.[124]

The Supreme Court divided over the appeal.[125] Mr Justice Peckham, writing for the majority, noted that the strict language of the Act drew *all* contracts, trusts and combinations into its ambit. He remarked:

> The language of the act includes every contract, combination in the form of trust or otherwise, or conspiracy, in restraint of trade or commerce among the several states or with foreign nations. So far as the very terms of the statute go, they apply to any contract of the nature described. A contract, therefore, that is in restraint of trade or commerce is, by the strict language of the act, prohibited, even though such contract is entered into between competing common carriers by railroad, and only for the purposes of thereby affecting traffic rates for the transportation of persons and property. If such an agreement restrain trade or commerce, it is prohibited by the statute, unless it can be said that an agreement, no

[122] Ibid. 80. [123] Ibid. 79. [124] Ibid. 84–90. [125] 166 US 290, 17 S Ct 540 (1897).

> matter what its terms, relating only to transportation, cannot restrain trade or commerce.[126]

The majority then noted that, unlike the case of manufacture (and hence the result in *E C Knight*), the transportation of goods is intimately tied up with their inter-state transport:[127] hence the Sherman Act must apply to the present situation.

Further, the majority noted, considerations of reasonableness in the assessment of contractual restrictions are imprecise – if not subjective – in their evaluation. The majority noted:

> If only that kind of contract which is in unreasonable restraint of trade be within the meaning of the statute, and declared therein to be illegal, it is at once apparent that the subject of what is a reasonable rate is attended with great uncertainty. What is a proper standard by which to judge the fact of reasonable rates? Must the rate be so high as to enable the return for the whole business done to amount to a sum sufficient to afford the shareholder a fair and reasonable profit upon his investment? If so, what is a fair and reasonable profit? That depends sometimes upon the risk incurred, and the rate itself differs in different localities.[128]

In dismissing considerations of reasonableness, the majority phrased its opinion in terms which were strikingly similar to – if not verbatim from – the minority opinion of Judge Oliver Shiras in the Circuit Court of Appeals.[129]

The irony of this rejection of a reasonableness standard is apparent. The minority opinion of the Supreme Court (which was to itself accept such a standard), authored by Mr Justice White, was concurred in by Mr Justice George Shiras, the elder brother of Oliver.

The minority seized upon their view of the purpose of the Act, the nature of the agreement in question, and the potential consequences of the majority's expansive reading of that section. Mr Justice White began the minority's opinion:

> I commence, then, with these two conceded propositions, one of law and the other of fact: First, that only such contracts as unreasonably restrain trade are violative of the general law; and, second, that the particular

126 Ibid. US 312, S Ct 547–8.

127 Ibid. US 312, S Ct 548: 'Railroad companies are instruments of commerce, and their business is commerce itself.' See also US 313, S Ct 548.

128 Ibid. US 331, S Ct 555.

129 Compare 58 F 91–9 with US 333–42, S Ct 555–9.

> contract here under consideration is reasonable, and therefore not unlawful, if the general principles of law are to be applied to it.[130]

In light of the findings which went into the District Court's decision, the latter proposition is unassailable.

The former point is an accurate statement of the 'general' or common law. After demonstrating this point[131] the minority turned to consider the purpose of the Act. The Act's title was determinative, as the minority rhetorically reasoned:

> Its title is, 'An act to protect trade and commerce against unlawful restraints and monopolies.' The word 'unlawful' clearly distinguishes between contracts in restraint of trade which are lawful and those which are not; in other words, between those which are unreasonably in restraint of trade, and consequently invalid, and those which are reasonable and hence lawful. When, therefore, in the very title of the act, the well-settled distinction between lawful and unlawful contracts is broadly marked, how can an interpretation be correct which holds that all contracts, whether lawful or not, are included in its provisions?[132]

The Act's title is indicative of the vice which it seeks to prevent, which is to prohibit only unreasonable restraints. To go beyond the notion of reasonableness would be to impede the liberty of contract and freedom of trade which the Act sought to promote.[133] And, foreshadowing of disputes yet to come, the minority pointed out:

> But conceding, for the sake of argument, that the words 'every contract in restraint of trade,' as used in the act of congress in question, prohibit all such contracts, however reasonable they may be, and therefore that all that great body of contracts which are commonly entered into between individuals or corporations, and which promote and develop trade, and which have been heretofore considered as lawful, are no longer such; and conceding also that agreements entered into by associations of workingmen to peaceably better their condition, either by obtaining an increase or preventing a decrease of wages, or by securing a reduction in the hours of labor, or for mutually protecting each other from unjust discharge, or for other reasonable purposes, have become unlawful, . . .[134]

In the view of the minority, construing the Act by its literal terms casts its net too wide, ensnaring useful restraints on conduct, thus frustrating its original purpose – the promotion of freedom of trade and individual liberty.

[130] US 344, S Ct 560. [131] Ibid. US 344–6, S Ct 560–1. [132] Ibid. US 352, S Ct 568.
[133] Ibid. US 355, S Ct 564. [134] Ibid. US 356–7, S Ct 565.

A year later, the Supreme Court had an opportunity to reconsider *Trans-Missouri Freight*, in *US* v. *Joint Traffic Association.*[135] The fact pattern of the latter case was almost identical to *Trans-Missouri:* a combination of railroads companies entered into an agreement to control, *inter alia*, rates, fares and traffic. The majority resisted calls to either distinguish the two cases[136] or reconsider *Trans-Missouri.*[137] The court divided along the same lines in *Joint Traffic,*[138] with the minority dissenting without reasons.

However, less than fourteen months after *Joint Traffic* had been decided, the Supreme Court was to take a substantial step away from the strict, literal interpretation of section 1 of the Sherman Act which characterised the reasoning in the previous two cases. In *US* v. *Addyston Pipe and Steel Co.*[139] the court was confronted by a cartel of six cast iron pipe manufacturers which allocated customers by territory and engaged in bid-rigging (with subsequent sharing of the profits) for unallocated customers. If the arrangements in the two earlier railroad cases had any social utility, the agreement in this case had none. Indeed, as the court noted,[140] in the absence of the cartel arrangement, pipe which could have been manufactured in Chattanooga and delivered to St Louis for $17 to $18, was instead delivered at $24.[141] Although the court did not use the terms, it saw this arrangement as a blatant appropriation of consumer surplus by the manufacturers. Hence its illegality was evident to both the literalists who formed the majority in the railway cases, and to the minority, who would have permitted 'reasonable restraints'.[142]

In a unanimous decision (which was to be the way in which the Supreme Court disposed of cartel cases in the two decades overlapping the turn of the last century[143]) the Court affirmed the Sixth Circuit Court of Appeals' judgment, authored by Judge William H. Taft. Judge Taft's decision was carefully crafted and proceeded by noting that the parties and their arrangements in *Addyston Pipe* were purely private, unlike in the railway cases where some public, or quasi-public function necessitating greater scrutiny governed the applicability of the Sherman Act to the arrangement in question.[144] The Appeals Court noted that even if such a

[135] 171 US 505, 19 S Ct 25 (1898). [136] Ibid. US 574, S Ct 33.
[137] Ibid. US 577–8, S Ct 35.
[138] On the relationship between these two cases, see Peritz (n. 99), 29–35.
[139] 175 US 211, 20 S Ct 96 (1899). [140] Ibid. US 210, S Ct 99–100.
[141] A similar calculation of delivery to Atlanta was made by Judge Taft in the Court of Appeals: 85 F 271, 293 (1898).
[142] On this point, see Peritz (n. 99), 37. [143] Ibid. [144] See notes 141, 278.

distinction could not just be drawn but also had significance (conclusions which the court found it did not need to make), if the contract were an unreasonable restraint of trade, it would be captured by the Act.[145] Noting that certain restraints on trade were necessary and socially useful insofar as they permitted 'the free purchase and sale of property',[146] Judge Taft recognised that these exceptions obtained their utility from facilitating another transaction which was the primary object of the agreement, or – in his words – 'necessary to protect the covenantee in the full enjoyment of the legitimate fruits of the contract, or to protect him from the dangers of an unjust use of those fruits by the other party'.[147]

The majority's judgment in *Addyston* was to concentrate on the interstate nature of the handling of the pipe in question, thus bringing the conduct in question into the ambit of the Sherman Act.[148] As the defendants not only manufactured the pipe but also contracted for its sale and transport across state borders,[149] the present situation was distinguishable from *E C Knight*, which involved only the manufacture of the product. As the contract in question fell within a literal reading of section 1 and served no useful purpose, the Court only needed to consider the implications of the commerce clause in any detail. Although alluded to,[150] Judge Taft's distinction between direct and ancillary restraints was to remain nascent in the jurisprudence of the Supreme Court.

4.4.2 Standard Oil: *per se and the rule of reason*

The birth of this doctrine was to occur in 1911 in *Standard Oil*,[151] a decision one text calls 'an antitrust classic'.[152] That case involved the Rockefeller oil trust, a group of thirty-seven companies, all controlled by a common holding company.[153] As Sullivan and Grimes note, although in many respects this trust raised issues which in their economic effect more closely resembled a merger, the trust operated in a clandestine manner, and used, *inter alia*, industrial espionage, predatory pricing and

145 Ibid. 278–9. 146 Ibid. 281. 147 Ibid. 282.
148 Indeed the Court of Appeals' judgment and order was limited to that 'portion or the combination or agreement which was interstate in its character'. (Note 139, US 248, S Ct 110.)
149 Ibid. US 240, S Ct 107. 150 Ibid. US 244–5, S Ct 108–9.
151 *Standard Oil Co. of New Jersey* v. *United States* 221 US 1, 31 S Ct 504 (1911).
152 Sullivan and Grimes, *Law of Antitrust*, 217. 153 Ibid., 218.

secret rebates to ensure the trust's constituents' success. The trust's collusive and concealed manner of operating gave it the flavour of the worst cartels. Accordingly, the federal government sued Standard under both sections 1 and 2 of the Sherman Act[154] seeking that the holding company be dissolved.

In construing section 1 of the Sherman Act, the Court – after considering its legislative history – concluded that the purpose of the Act was:

> under [the] view [of the court] evidenced the intent not to restrain the right to make and enforce contracts, whether resulting from combinations or otherwise, which did not unduly restrain interstate or foreign commerce, but to protect that commerce from being restrained by methods, whether old or new, which would constitute an *interference*, – that is, an *undue restraint*.[155]

Since any contractual obligation is a fortiori a restraint of trade, to rely on the literal terms of the Act would necessarily draw all contracts into its ambit, or be void for uncertainty.[156]

With this in the background, the Court announced the rule of reason, in a passage worth quoting at length:

> If the criterion by which it is to be determined in all cases whether every contract, combination, etc., is a restraint of trade within the intendment of the law, is the direct or indirect effect of the acts involved, then of course the rule of reason becomes the guide, and the construction which we have given the statute, instead of being refuted by the cases relied upon, is by those cases demonstrated to be correct. This is true, because the construction which we have deduced from the history of the act and the analysis of its text is simply that in every case where it is claimed that an act or acts are in violation of the statute, the rule of reason, in the light of the principles of law and the public policy which the act embodies, must be applied. From this it follows, since that rule and the result of the test as to direct or indirect, in their ultimate aspect, come to one and the same thing, that the difference between the two is therefore only that which obtains between things which do not differ at all.[157]

Henceforth, all and only undue restraints on trade (irrespective of the novelty or antiquity of the method) would be brought within section 1 of the Sherman Act.

However, by announcing a rule of reason to exempt certain activities from the purview of the Act, the Court simultaneously carved out a rule

154 Ibid.

155 (Emphasis supplied.) *Standard Oil* (n. 151) US 60, S Ct 515; see also US 63, S Ct 517.

156 Ibid. US 63, S Ct 517. 157 Ibid. US 65, S Ct 517–18.

for determining which activities were prohibited per se, albeit in more developed form than in *Joint Traffic*.[158] As the Court reasoned, an advantage of a per se rule is that it pre-empts any need for inquiry into the social or economic utility of an arrangement, once a violation has been established:

> That in the cases relied upon, it having been found that the acts complained of were within the statute, and operated to produce the injuries which the statute forbade, that resort to reason was not permissible in order to allow that to be done which the statute prohibited. This being true, the rulings in the case relied upon, when rightly appreciated, were therefore this, and nothing more: That as considering the contracts and agreements, their necessary effect, and the character of the parties by whom they were made, they were clearly restraints of trade within the purview of the statute, they could not be taken out of that category by indulging in general reasoning as to the expediency or nonexpediency of having made the contracts, or the wisdom or want of wisdom of the statute which prohibited their being made. That is to say, the cases but decided that the nature and character of the contracts, creating, as they did, a conclusive presumption which brought them within the statute, such result was not to be disregarded by the substitution of a judicial appreciation of what the law ought to be for the plain judicial duty of enforcing the law as it was made.[159]

The *Standard Oil* case was reargued on 12, 13, 16 and 17 January 1911, and decided on 15 May that year. Another case to also become an antitrust classic, *Dr Miles Medical Company* v. *John D. Park and Sons Co.*,[160] was argued the week before, and decided six weeks prior to *Standard Oil*.

Dr Miles involved a vertical restraint (minimum price) imposed upon retailers by the manufacturer of propriety medicines. The Court held that neither the propriety nature of the product,[161] nor the vertical nature of the restraint[162] was sufficient to distinguish that case from previous cases. After briefly discussing the common law doctrine of restraint of trade, the Court noted:

> The present case is not analogous to that of a sale of good will, or of an interest in a business, or of the grant of a right to use a process of manufacture. The complainant has not parted with any interest in its business or instrumentalities of production ... The agreements are

[158] See *Joint Traffic* (n. 135) US 568, S Ct 31.
[159] *Standard Oil* (n. 151) US 65, S Ct 517–18. [160] 220 US 373, 31 S Ct 370 (1911).
[161] Ibid. US 402, S Ct 382; see also US 408–9, S Ct 385. [162] Ibid. US 404–5, S Ct 383.

> designed to maintain prices after the complainant has parted with the title to the articles, and to prevent competition among those who trade in them.[163]

In short:

> But agreements or combinations between dealers, having for their sole purpose the destruction of competition and the fixing of prices, are injurious to the public interest and void. They are not saved by the advantages which the participants expect to derive from the enhanced price to the consumer.[164]

The prohibition against vertical restraints in the form of retail price maintenance was to remain law for the next ninety-six years.[165]

With the exception of the 1918 case involving the Chicago Board of Trade and a Depression-era coal case, the most pernicious forms of horizontal restraints were regarded by the Supreme Court as per se illegal. In *Chicago Board of Trade* v. *US*[166] the court provided what would become a classic statement of the application of the rule of reason:

> Every agreement concerning trade, every regulation of trade, restrains . . . The true test of legality is whether the restraint imposed is such as merely regulates and perhaps thereby promotes competition or whether it is such as may suppress or even destroy competition. To determine that question the court must ordinarily consider the facts peculiar to the business to which the restraint is applied; its condition before and after the restraint was imposed; the nature of the restraint and its effect, actual or probable. The history of the restraint, the evil believed to exist, the reason for adopting the particular remedy, the purpose or end sought to be attained, are all relevant facts. This is not because a good intention will save an otherwise objectionable regulation or the reverse; but because knowledge of intent may help the court to interpret facts and to predict consequences.[167]

At issue in the case was the legality of the Board's rule which severely restricted the afterhours trading of grain, and required that grain sold after closing hours be sold at the closing price: hence fixing the price of grain for afterhours transactions. The Court's analysis considered countervailing social considerations, particularly those which supported

[163] Ibid. US 407, S Ct 384. [164] Ibid. US 408, S Ct 384–5.

[165] *Dr Miles* was overturned by *Leegin Creative Leather Products Inc.* v. *PSKS Inc.* 551 US 877, 127 S Ct 2705 (2007).

[166] *Board of Trade of the City of Chicago* v. *United States* 246 U S 231, 38 S Ct 242 (1918).

[167] Ibid. US 238, S Ct 244.

improved working conditions.[168] The Board's restrictions were regarded as reasonable.

While the social benefits may have been worthy social goals, it is not clear that their pursuit through a competition agenda is the most appropriate means to advance them. Likewise, in considering the effects on competition which the Board's rules had, the Court's analysis is sparse, and is exacerbated by the lack of published findings of the trial court. As such, it is not clear – for instance – whether the underlying motivation for discouraging off hours trading was in fact to provide for additional rest or to prevent trades at night which may have been at a reduced commission (thereby enforcing a cartel on commissions).[169] While later commentators are critical of the Court's furtherance of social goals based on such sparse analysis,[170] subsequent treatment[171] of similar horizontal arrangements indicated that the consideration of social goals in competition policy was an aberration.

4.4.3 Appalachian Coals*: a Depression-era outlier*

The Depression-era case of *Appalachian Coals Inc.* v. *US*[172] represents an outlier in terms of its deference to non-competition goals in assessing the reasonableness of restraints on competition. This case, it is submitted, can only sensibly be viewed as a crisis cartel which was permitted as a result of the extreme economic circumstances facing that area (and indeed the nation) during the late 1920s and early 30s.

The case involved an ad hoc arraignment by 137 Appalachian coal producers who created an exclusive selling agency, Appalachian Coals,[173] which was tasked 'to sell all the coal of its principals at the best prices obtainable and, if all cannot be sold, to apportion orders upon a stated basis'.[174] The government contended, rightly, that this arrangement restricted competition and increased the market power of the coal

[168] Ibid. US 241, S Ct 245: 'Every Board of Trade and nearly every trade organization imposes some restraints upon the conduct of business by its members. Those relating to the hours in which business may be done are common; and they make a special appeal where, as here, they tend to shorten the working day or, at least, limit the period of most exacting activity.'

[169] See Sullivan and Grimes (n. 152), 221, who suggest this as a possible motivation.

[170] E.g. ibid. [171] With the exception of *Appalachian Coals* discussed below.

[172] 288 US 344, 53 S Ct 471 (1933). [173] Ibid. US 357–8, S Ct 473.

[174] Ibid. US 358, S Ct 473.

producers. In response, the producers raised a number of facts about the state of the industry, which included:

- resulting from the contraction of demand subsequent to the First World War, mining capacity was at 700 million tons, with a demand of less than 500 million tons;[175]
- the oversupply was exacerbated by increased production of (and competition with) petroleum, gas and hydroelectric power;[176]
- the mining process led to production of coal of varying sizes – when only coal of a certain size is wanted (and contracted for), the resulting waste coal is placed on the market as 'distressed coal', thereby forcing down prices;[177]
- there was a lack of standardisation of coal sizes and an endemic of misrepresentation of coal size by sellers;[178]
- because of the glut of coal on the market, when a single lot of coal was put on the market by multiple dealers it had the effect of causing the lot to 'bid against itself', thereby depressing the market further.[179]

The court was to approve of the arrangement (though leaving an opportunity for a re-examination if the anti-competitive effects proved to be worse than expected[180]). In so doing, the court reasoned thus:

> With respect to defendants' purposes, we find no warrant for determining that they were other than those they declared. Good intentions will not save a plan otherwise objectionable, but knowledge of actual intent is an aid in the interpretation of facts and prediction of consequences ... The evidence leaves no doubt of the existence of the evils at which defendants' plan was aimed. The industry was in distress. It suffered from overexpansion and from a serious relative decline through the growing use of substitute fuels. It was afflicted by injurious practices within itself – practices which demanded correction. If evil conditions could not be entirely cured, they at least might be alleviated. The unfortunate state of the industry would not justify any attempt unduly to restrain competition or to monopolize, but the existing situation prompted defendants to make, and the statute did not preclude them from making, an honest effort to remove abuses, to make competition fairer, and thus to promote the essential interests of commerce. The interests of producers and consumers are interlinked. When industry is greviously hurt, when producing concerns fail, when unemployment mounts and

175 Ibid. US 361, S Ct 474. 176 Ibid. 177 Ibid. US 362–3, S Ct 475.
178 Ibid. US 363, S Ct 475.
179 Ibid.; however, this argument makes no economic sense.
180 Ibid. US 378, S Ct 480–1.

> communities dependent upon profitable production are prostrated, the wells of commerce go dry. So far as actual purposes are concerned, the conclusion of the court below was amply supported that defendants were engaged in a fair and open endeavor to aid the industry in a measurable recovery from its plight. The inquiry then, must be whether despite this objective the inherent nature of their plan was such as to create an undue restraint upon interstate commerce.[181]

As the economic situation varied between industries and changed over time, *Appalachian Coals* was almost immediately distinguished in the lower courts[182] and in the Supreme Court.[183] It was ultimately overruled in 1984.[184]

4.4.4 *Per se rules against price-fixing*

An alternate line of cases, commencing with *US* v. *Trenton Potteries Co.*[185] was to determine how the Sherman Act was to be applied to naked-price fixing (and practices with similar economic effect). Trenton Potteries involved a criminal prosecution arising from an agreement among twenty-three corporate manufactures of toilet and bathroom pottery (aided by twenty individuals) to fix the prices of their product and to permit only such sales of pottery through so-called 'legitimate jobbers'. Those involved in this combination manufactured or distributed 82% of such fixtures in the US.[186] At trial, the District Court Judge's charge told the jury that if they found the defendants fixed the prices of these fittings, they were to convict, irrespective of the reasonableness of the (fixed) prices.[187]

The Second Circuit Court of Appeals held the charge to be erroneous. In reversing the Court of Appeals, a majority[188] of the Supreme Court made two significant observations, relating reasonableness to price-fixing. First, the concept of 'reasonableness' is variable:

181 Ibid. US 372, S Ct 478.

182 *Straight Side Basket Corporation* v. *Webster Basket Co.* 4 F Supp 644 (WDNY, 14 August 1933), five months after *Appalachian Coals* was decided.

183 *Fashion Originators' Guild of America* v. *Federal Trade Commission* 312 US 457, 312 US 668, 61 S Ct 703 (1941).

184 *Coperweld Corp.* v. *Independence Tube Corp.* 467 US 752, 104 S Ct 2731 (1984).

185 273 US 392, 47 S Ct 377 (1927).

186 Ibid. US 394, S Ct 378.

187 Ibid. US 395, S Ct 378–9.

188 Three judges (Van Devanter, Sutherland and Butler) dissented without an opinion; Justice Brandeis took no part in the hearing of the matter.

> Reasonableness is not a concept of definite and unchanging content. Its meaning necessarily varies in the different fields of the law, because it is used as a convenient summary of the dominant considerations which control in the application of legal doctrines. Our view of what is a reasonable restraint of commerce is controlled by the recognized purpose of the Sherman Law itself.[189]

As the purpose of the Sherman Act is to protect the public from monopolies and anti-competitive practices,[190] the elimination of competition by price-fixing is not a reasonable restraint. The majority noted:

> The aim and result of every price-fixing agreement, if effective, is the elimination of one form of competition. The power to fix prices, whether reasonably exercised or not, involves power to control the market and to fix arbitrary and unreasonable prices. The reasonable price fixed today may through economic and business changes become the unreasonable price of tomorrow. Once established, it may be maintained unchanged because of the absence of competition secured by the agreement for a price reasonable when fixed. Agreements which create such potential power may well be held to be in themselves unreasonable or unlawful restraints, without the necessity of minute inquiry whether a particular price is reasonable or unreasonable as fixed and without placing on the government in enforcing the Sherman Law the burden of ascertaining from day to day whether it has become unreasonable through the mere variation of economic conditions. Moreover, in the absence of express legislation requiring it, we should hesitate to adopt a construction making the difference between legal and illegal conduct in the field of business relations depend upon so uncertain a test as whether prices are reasonable – a determination which can be satisfactorily made only after a complete survey of our economic organization and a choice between rival philosophies.[191]

Although the Court did not explicitly state in *Trenton Potteries* that the price-fixing arrangement was per se illegal, it was sufficient for the court to note the price-making effect that the arrangement in question had, namely the 'power to control the market and to fix arbitrary and unreasonable prices'. The Court left it open as to whether market power was a necessary or a sufficient condition for the agreement to come within the

[189] Ibid. US 397, S Ct 379.

[190] Ibid.: 'Whether this type of restraint is reasonable or not must be judged in part at least, in the light of its effect on competition, for, . . . it cannot be doubted that the Sherman Law and the judicial decisions interpreting it are based upon the assumption that the public interest is best protected from the evils of monopoly and price control by the maintenance of competition.'

[191] Ibid. US 397–8, S Ct 379.

scope of the Sherman Act. However, the Court did make it clear that in such circumstances, economic analysis is not required. By eliminating the necessity of considering such evidence, the task of prosecuting an antitrust violation is simplified.

Yet, in answering questions the Court did, it left a significant question unanswered. As the agreement in *Trenton Potteries* involved companies which controlled approximately 82% of the market, it was not clear if a violation of section 1 of the Act required effective control of the market (e.g. 'monopoly') or something less. This question was to be answered some thirteen years later, in *US* v. *Socony-Vacuum Oil.*[192]

The price-fixing arrangement in *Socony* at least superficially resembled that of *Appalachian Coals*, and arouse out of identical Depression-era economic circumstances in the energy sector. *Socony* involved a group of large, vertically integrated, refineries with storage facilities and retail outlets agreeing on a mechanism to stabilise gasoline prices. The competitive pressure (or, otherwise put, threat to price stability) came from independent refiners, who had little storage capacity.

Beginning in about 1926, the oil industry was characterised by significant overproduction resulting from the need to keep wells (and hence refineries) open not only to maintain a connection to petroleum pipelines and also to avoid the need to abandon a closed well. (If a well were shut down, due to sub-surface geological changes, the well would soon have to be abandoned.) As a result gasoline needed to be continuously produced, irrespective of the price for which it could be sold. The larger refineries could insulate themselves from most of the effects of oversupply by resorting to their ability to store unsold gasoline. Smaller, un-integrated refineries had no such storage capacity and were forced to sell their gasoline ('distress gasoline') on the spot market, thus depressing the price. By the spring of 1933, the wholesale price of gasoline was below its cost to manufacture.[193]

Although the administration was to enact measures[194] (later held unconstitutional[195]) to prevent the shipment of oil and gasoline from areas of overproduction in an attempt to stabilise the price in other areas, these measures were honoured more in the breach. By 1935 the oil industry, in the form of twenty-seven companies,[196] entered into an arrangement whereby they would coordinate purchases of distress

[192] 310 US 150, 60 S Ct 811 (1940). [193] Ibid. US 170–2, S Ct 820–1.
[194] National Industrial Recovery Act (1933).
[195] *Panama Refining Co.* v. *Ryan* 293 US 388, 55 S Ct 241 (1935).
[196] *Socony* (n. 192) US 165, S Ct 818.

gasoline from the independents, store it and sell it at 'stable' prices as the market price would not be depressed by a sudden flood of gasoline.[197] Although there was no formal agreement[198] underlying the actions, there were frequent meetings among members of the self-styled 'General Stabilization Committee' at which the purchases of distress gasoline would be discussed.[199] Relying upon *Appalachian Coals*, the defence was reasonableness.

The Court promptly distinguished *Appalachian Coals*,[200] reasoning that the effect of the arrangement in Appalachian Coals was not to directly fix the price of coal. The Court noted:

> In that case certain producers of bituminous coal created an exclusive selling agency for their coal. The agency was to establish standard classifications and sell the coal of its principals at the best prices obtainable. The occasion for the formation of the agency was the existence of certain so-called injurious practices and conditions in the industry. One of these was the problem of 'distress coal' – coal shipped to the market which was unsold at the time of delivery and therefore dumped on the market irrespective of demand.
>
> . . .
>
> That agency was also to sell all the coal of its principals at the best prices obtainable and, if all could not be sold, to apportion orders upon a stated basis. And, save for certain stated exceptions, it was to determine the prices at which sales would be made without consultation with its principals. This Court concluded that so far as actual purpose was concerned, the defendant producers were engaged in a 'fair and open endeavor to aid the industry in a measurable recovery from its plight' . . . And it observed that the plan did not either contemplate or involve 'the fixing of market prices'; that defendants would not be able to fix the price of coal in the consuming markets; that their coal would continue to be subject to 'active competition'.[201]

According to the Court's reasoning, the only similarity between the two cases lay in the depressed nature of the industry.[202]

197 Ibid. US 170–210, S Ct 820–38. 198 Ibid. US 177, S Ct 824.

199 Ibid. US 178–190, S Ct 824–9.

200 Ibid. US 214, S Ct 840: 'And we are of the opinion that Appalachian Coals, Inc., v. United States, . . . , is not in point.'

201 Ibid. US 214–15, S Ct 840.

202 Ibid. US 216, S Ct 841: 'Thus in reality the only essential thing in common between the instant case and the Appalachian Coals case is the presence in each of so-called demoralizing or injurious practices. The methods of dealing with them were quite divergent.'

In *Socony*, there was an active plan to raise and fix the price the consumer paid, whereas the plan in *Appalachian* was not designed to effect the market in this manner. Further, the Court noted the possible effects that that plan had on the consumer were conjectural, as the plan had not been put into place.[203] Indeed, in remanding the *Appalachian Coals* matter back to the District Court, that court was ordered to take further action if the plan did in fact have a pernicious effect on inter-state commerce.[204]

In its clearest statement to that date, the Court declared that price-fixing arrangements, as they contain no countervailing social benefits, are per se illegal.[205] The Court dismissed the defendant's claims to the contrary rather swiftly:

> The elimination of so-called competitive evils is no legal justification for such buying programs. The elimination of such conditions was sought primarily for its effect on the price structures. Fairer competitive prices, it is claimed, resulted when distress gasoline was removed from the market. But such defense is typical of the protestations usually made in price-fixing cases. Ruinous competition, financial disaster, evils of price cutting and the like appear throughout our history as ostensible justifications for price-fixing.[206]

The 'reasonableness' of the prices is irrelevant, as today's 'reasonable' price may not be tomorrow's.[207]

Additionally, it is the tampering with market structures which leads to a violation of section 1 of the Sherman Act:

203 Ibid. US 216, S Ct 841: 'Unlike the plan in the instant case, the plan in the Appalachian Coals case was not designed to operate vis a vis the general consuming market and to fix the prices on that market. Furthermore, the effect, if any, of that plan on prices was not only wholly incidental but also highly conjectural. For the plan had not then been put into operation.'

204 Ibid. US 378, S Ct 481.

205 Ibid. US 218, S Ct 842: 'Thus for over forty years this Court has consistently and without deviation adhered to the principle that price-fixing agreements are unlawful *per se* under the Sherman Act and that no showing of so-called competitive abuses or evils which those agreements were designed to eliminate or alleviate may be interposed as a defense.' And US 223, S Ct 844: 'Under the Sherman Act a combination formed for the purpose and with the effect of raising, depressing, fixing, pegging, or stabilizing the price of a commodity in interstate or foreign commerce is illegal *per se*.'

206 Ibid. US 220–1, S Ct 843.

207 Ibid. US 221, S Ct 843: 'Those who fixed reasonable prices today would perpetuate unreasonable prices tomorrow, since those prices would not be subject to continuous administrative supervision and readjustment in light of changed conditions. Those who controlled the prices would control or effectively dominate the market.'

> Any combination which tampers with price structures is engaged in an unlawful activity. Even though the members of the price-fixing group were in no position to control the market, to the extent that they raised, lowered, or stabilized prices they would be directly interfering with the free play of market forces. The Act places all such schemes beyond the pale and protects that vital part of our economy against any degree of interference. Congress has not left with us the determination of whether or not particular price-fixing schemes are wise or unwise, healthy or destructive.[208]

Given that it is the tampering with market forces which is the gravamen of the offence, it is not necessary for those participating in the price-fixing arrangement to have monopoly power or domination in the market.[209] All that is required to establish the offence is proof that the agreement was formed for or contributed to price-fixing.[210]

It is difficult to reconcile *Appalachian Coals* with *Socony*. Arguably, in the former case, there was no intent to fix the prices which the purchaser paid (though the result is that they would pay an inflated price), and that the arrangement had yet to be put into place (hence its effects had yet to become evident, or were – at the time of the litigation – only hypothetical). That said, it is probably best to regard *Appalachian Coals* as a Depression-era outlier, and to regard *Socony* as 'a classic opinion which stands in relation to the *per se* doctrine as *Standard Oil* stands to the rule of reason'.[211]

In the following year, the Court was to consider the legality of group boycotts[212] and reject them as per se violations of the Sherman and Clayton Acts, thus obviating the need for an inquiry into reasonableness of the arrangement.[213]

208 Ibid. US 221, S Ct 843. 209 Ibid. US 224, S Ct 844.

210 Ibid. US 224, S Ct 844–5:

> Price-fixing agreements may have utility to members of the group though the power possessed or exerted falls far short of domination and control. Monopoly power . . . not the only power which the Act strikes down, as we have said. Proof that a combination was formed for the purpose of fixing prices and that it caused them to be fixed or contributed to that result is proof of the completion of a price-fixing conspiracy under s 1 of the Act.

211 Sullivan and Grimes (n. 152), 226.

212 *Fashion Originators' Guild* v. *Federal Trade Commission* 312 US 457, 312 US 668, 61 S Ct 703 (1941): although the scheme in that matter was contrary to s. 14 of the Clayton Act, the facts found by the FTC brought the 'petitioners' combination in its entirety well within the inhibition of the policies declared by the Sherman Act itself' (US 465, S Ct 706–7).

213 Ibid. US 467–8, S Ct 708.

Tying arrangements were initially considered under the rubric of the Clayton Act[214] in the context of which the Court considered whether they had (and rejected) countervailing benefits:

> Tying agreements serve hardly any purpose beyond the suppression of competition. The justification most often advanced in their defense – the protection of the good will of the manufacturer of the tying device – fails in the usual situation because specification of the type and quality of the product to be used in connection with the tying device is protection enough. If the manufacturer's brand of the tied product is in fact superior to that of competitors, the buyer will presumably choose it anyway.[215]

Although these conclusions regarding tying arrangements may rightly be subject to criticism,[216] they served as a basis for extending the per se prohibitions which the Court read into the Sherman Act to include tying.

In *Northern Pacific Railway Co.* v. *US*,[217] in extending the Sherman Act's per se prohibitions, the Court provided succinct explanations of what it then viewed to be the policy considerations underlying that Act, and the rationale for the certain practices to be regarded as per se illegal. The purpose behind the Act is to advance competition:

> The Sherman Act was designed to be a comprehensive charter of economic liberty aimed at preserving free and unfettered competition as the rule of trade. It rests on the premise that the unrestrained interaction of competitive forces will yield the best allocation of our economic resources, the lowest prices, the highest quality and the greatest material progress, while at the same time providing an environment conductive to the preservation of our democratic political and social institutions. But even were that premise open to question, the policy unequivocally laid down by the Act is competition.[218]

With this in mind, the Court noted that although the Sherman Act provided for a general provision restricting all restraints on trade, the Court has read this as prohibiting only unreasonable ones.

Yet, the Court notes, there are certain arrangements which have no redeeming value, and therefore can be conclusively regarded as illegal, and no inquiry need to be made weighing their benefits against their harms:

[214] *International Salt Co.* v. *United States* 332 US 392, 68 S Ct 12 (1947) and *Standard Oil Co. of California* v. *United States* (1949) 337 US 293, 69 S Ct 1051 (1949).

[215] *Standard Oil of California* (ibid.) US 305–306, S Ct 1058.

[216] *Eastman Kodak Co.* v. *Image Technical Services Inc.* 504 US 451, 112 S Ct 2072 (1992); see also Bork, *The Antitrust Paradox*, 365–81.

[217] 356 US 1, 78 S Ct 514 (1958). [218] Ibid. US 4, S Ct 517.

> However, there are certain agreements or practices which because of their pernicious effect on competition and lack of any redeeming virtue are conclusively presumed to be unreasonable and therefore illegal without elaborate inquiry as to the precise harm they have caused or the business excuse for their use. This principle of *per se* unreasonableness not only makes the type of restraints which are proscribed by the Sherman Act more certain to the benefit of everyone concerned, but it also avoids the necessity for an incredibly complicated and prolonged economic investigation into the entire history of the industry involved, as well as related industries, in an effort to determine at large whether a particular restraint has been unreasonable – an inquiry so often wholly fruitless when undertaken.[219]

Price-fixing, group boycotts and tying arrangements fall into this category.

Based upon *Addyston Pipe*, the Court held that market division was a per se infringement.[220] However, as the 1899 decision of *Addyston* predated the rule or reason/per se distinction of *Standard Oil* by about 12 years, and strictly speaking the incorporation of market division into the per se category was dicta in *Northern Pacific Railway*, the issue was not resolved until 1972. *US* v. *Topco Associates Inc.*[221] proved to be the logical conclusion of two other cases (*Timken Roller Bearing*[222] and *Sealy*[223]) which, while both included an element of market division, also included other anti-competitive practices that could have potentially complicated the Court's analysis or subsequent interpretations of that analysis.[224]

The issue in *Topco* was horizontal market division of private-label goods among members (themselves chains of stores) of a grocery retailers' association. The association felt that such market division was necessary in order for their members to compete effectively against the three major supermarket chains.[225] In holding that such market division is a per se violation of section 1 of the Sherman Act, *Topco* provides its reader with not only a valuable lesson in the goals of the Sherman Act, as viewed through a lens some eighty-two years after its passage, but also another lesson of the role of courts, congress and private parties in assessing the competitive merits of particular economic arrangements.

[219] Ibid. US 5, S Ct 518. [220] Ibid., see *Addyston Pipe* (n. 139) US 244–5, S Ct 108–9.
[221] 405 US 596, 92 S Ct 1126 (1972).
[222] *Timken Roller Bearing Co.* v. *United States* 341 US 593, 71 S Ct 971 (1951).
[223] *United States* v. *Sealy Inc.* 388 US 350, 87 S Ct 1847 (1967).
[224] *Timken* involved an element of extra-territoriality and *Sealy* also involved price-fixing.
[225] *Topco* (n. 221) US 598–600, S Ct 1128–30.

In *Topco*, the Court reasoned that antitrust laws serve as an economic 'Bill of Rights' ensuring the liberty to compete in the economic arena. Justice Marshall, for the majority,[226] wrote:

> Antitrust laws in general, and the Sherman Act in particular, are the Magna Carta of free enterprise. They are as important to the preservation of economic freedom and our free-enterprise system as the Bill of Rights is to the protection of our fundamental personal freedoms. And the freedom guaranteed each and every business, no matter how small, is the freedom to compete – to assert with vigor, imagination, devotion, and ingenuity whatever economic muscle it can muster. Implicit in such freedom is the notion that it cannot be foreclosed with respect to one sector of the economy because certain private citizens or groups believe that such foreclosure might promote greater competition in a more important sector of the economy.[227]

The freedom to compete is guaranteed to each potential competitor, and such freedom cannot be foreclosed in the name of 'the greater good' by others.[228]

To foreclose competition in order to advance other social goals is a judgment properly made by a democratic Congress:

> There have been tremendous departures from the notion of a free-enterprise system as it was originally conceived in this country. These departures have been the product of congressional action and the will of the people. If a decision is to be made to sacrifice competition in one portion of the economy for greater competition in another portion this too is a decision that must be made by Congress and not by private forces or by the courts. Private forces are too keenly aware of their own interests in making such decisions and courts are ill-equipped and ill-situated for such decision making. To analyze, interpret, and evaluate the myriad of competing interests and the endless data that would surely be brought to bear on such decisions, and to make the delicate judgment on the relative

226 Justices Powell and Rehnquist took no part in the decision, Mr Justice Blackmun concurred on the basis that the per se rule was too well ensconced into the Courts' jurisprudence, and the lone dissent, Chief Justice Burger, felt that this restraint on competition was fully reasonable in allowing these smaller chains to compete effectively against the big three.

227 *Topco* (n. 221) US 610, S Ct 1135.

228 Ibid. US 610–11, S Ct 1135: 'The District Court determined that by limiting the freedom of its individual members to compete with each other, Topco was doing a greater good by fostering competition between members and other large supermarket chains. But, the fallacy in this is that Topco has no authority under the Sherman Act to determine the respective values of competition in various sectors of the economy.'

> values to society of competitive areas of the economy, the judgment of the elected representatives of the people is required.[229]

To a very large extent, the court's reasoning in *Topco* represents a rejection of, or at minimum, a distancing from, the principle announced in *Chicago Board of Trade* that non-economic considerations are relevant to the assessment of restrictions on competition, and may constitute an effective countervailing consideration to the economic losses occasioned by the agreed restrictions on competition.

4.4.5 *Sensitivity to economic reality*

Countervailing economic considerations were decisive to the majority when the Supreme Court next faced the determination of the per se legality of an agreement among competitors to license copyrighted music for public use. At issue in *Broadcast Music* v. *Columbia Broadcasting Systems*[230] was an arrangement between Broadcast Music (BMI) and the American Society of Composers, Authors and Publishers (ASCAP) to provide non-exclusive licences for the public performances of copyrighted music. BMI and ASCAP (the second petitioner) were not-for-profit organisations. The latter was originally founded by members of the recording and broadcasting industry. The two organisations controlled, between them, 'almost every domestic copyrighted composition'[231] and operated by the use of blanket licences, permitting the licensee the use of all compositions in the relevant catalogue.[232] The largest users of such licences were radio and television broadcasters (of which Columbia Broadcasting Systems (CBS) was one of, if not the, largest user[233]).

The Court of Appeals held the arrangement to be price-fixing in a literal sense: the copyright holders, ASCAP and BMI have collectively agreed on the prices they would charge for the use of the music. Both the majority and Justice Stevens in dissent in the Supreme Court felt that more detailed analysis was appropriate. Their reasoning indicated that to

229 Ibid. US 611–12, S Ct 1135. 230 441 US 1, 99 S Ct 1551 (1979).

231 Ibid. US 6, S Ct 1555.

232 Ibid. The fees charged for the licences typically depended on the user's revenues, or were sold for a fixed amount, and did not distinguish among the types or amount of music used (ibid.).

233 Ibid. US 4, S Ct 1554. CBS was a founder of BMI; however, in 1959 it divested its interests in BMI (ibid. at US 5, S Ct 1555).

merely categorise a given practice as 'price-fixing' without any other analysis is a form of *petitio principii*. The majority remarked:

> To the Court of Appeals and CBS, the blanket license involved 'price fixing' in the literal sense: the composers and publishing houses have joined together with an organization that sets its price for the blanket license it sells. But this is not a question simply of determining whether two or more potential competitors have literally 'fixed' a 'price.' As generally used in the antitrust field, 'price fixing' is a shorthand way of describing certain categories of business behavior to which the *per se* rule has been held applicable. The Court of Appeals' literal approach does not alone establish that this particular practice is one of those types or that it is 'plainly anticompetitive' and very likely without 'redeeming virtue.' Literalness is overly simplistic and often overbroad. When two partners set the price of their goods or services they are literally 'price fixing,' but they are not *per se* in violation of the Sherman Act.[234]

To draw the conclusion of a per se violation, the Court noted, one cannot reason from price-fixing to a violation, but an intermediate determination of the effects of the agreement is necessary.

If the effect is to restrict competition, then the agreement is a per se violation; if the agreement has other efficiencies making markets more competitive, then further analysis is required.[235] The efficiencies found in the contracts in question involved a significant reduction in the transaction costs which would be required were a potential user of music required to negotiate for rights, in advance, before each use of a particular piece.[236] Such individual prior bargaining would be prohibitively expensive to negotiate and enforce, and would reduce, if not eliminate, the spontaneity desirable for radio and nightclub audiences.[237] The licensee obtains 'immediate use of covered compositions, without the delay of prior individual negotiations and great flexibility in the choice of musical material'.[238] Additionally, as the blanket licensing system in place neither precluded copyright owners from negotiating separate licences (outside the BMI/ASCAP regime) nor masked a price-fixing effect on other markets,[239] its pernicious effects (if any)

[234] Ibid. US 8–9, S Ct 1556–7. [235] Ibid. US 20, S Ct 1562.

[236] Ibid. US 20, S Ct 1563: 'A middleman with a blanket license was an obvious necessity if the thousands of individual negotiations, a virtual impossibility, were to be avoided. Also, individual fees for the use of individual compositions would presuppose an intricate schedule of fees and uses, as well as a difficult and expensive reporting problem for the user and policing task for the copyright owner.'

[237] Ibid. [238] Ibid. US 22, S Ct 1563. [239] Ibid. US 24, S Ct 1564.

were well outweighed by the positive efficiencies in reduction of transaction costs.[240]

Accordingly, the Court reasoned the appropriate analytic framework for analysis of this agreement was via a rule of reason approach. The majority concluded that as that sort of analytic was not before the Court on that occasion, it was not necessary to determine the legality of the arrangements under the rule of reason. Justice Stevens dissented on this point.

Justice Stevens examined the structure of the market which resulted from the operation of the contracts. The licensing provisions resulted in two features which Justice Stevens regarded as indicative of an unreasonable restraint on competition: the consequence that particular licensees would likely be required to buy more music than they required (as a result of blanket licensing), and that there were no opportunities for artists to compete on price.[241] As a less restrictive means was available, namely a selective licensing system whereby a licensee could obtain rights to part of BMI and ASCAP's catalogues, this arraignment could not survive the rule of reason analysis.

The significance of the Court's appeal to economic efficiencies in BMI was soon to be blunted in two cases decided in the early 1980s: *Arizona* v. *Maricopa County Medical Association*[242] and *National Collegiate Athletic Association* v. *Board of Regents of the University of Oklahoma*.[243] The former case involved horizontal price-fixing of maximum prices by an association of physicians who were members of the Maricopa Foundation for Medical Care.[244] The foundation was established to, *inter alia*, provide an alternative to other health insurance plans.[245] The Court described its functions as follows:

> It establishes the schedule of maximum fees that participating doctors agree to accept as payment in full for services performed for patients

[240] This use of efficiencies in antitrust was obviously not novel with this case. Williamson's analysis, which appeared in the academic literature in the 1960s, was seminal in this regards. See, e.g., Williamson, 'Economies as an Antitrust Defense', using the analysis in a merger context.

[241] Ibid. US 32–3, S Ct 1569: '. . . but the blanket license does not present a new songwriter with any opportunity to try to break into the market by offering his product for sale at an unusually low price. The absence of that opportunity, however unlikely it may be, is characteristic of a cartelized rather than a competitive market.'

[242] 457 US 332, 102 S Ct 2466 (1982). [243] 468 US 85, 104 S Ct 2948 (1984).

[244] Some 70% of the physicians in the relevant area were foundation members: *Maricopa* (n. 242) US 339, S Ct 2470.

[245] Ibid. US 339, S Ct 2470.

> insured under plans approved by the foundation. It reviews the medical necessity and appropriateness of treatment provided by its members to such insured persons. It is authorized to draw checks on insurance company accounts to pay doctors for services performed for covered patients. In performing these functions, the foundation is considered an 'insurance administrator' by the Director of the Arizona Department of Insurance. Its participating doctors, however, have no financial interest in the operation of the foundation.[246]

A 'foundation-approved' insurance plan will pay a participating physician up to the maximum set by the foundation's fee schedule. A patient covered by a 'foundation-approved' insurance plan will therefore have their medical expenses fully covered when treatment is provided by a participating physician. Participating physicians may charge more than the foundation's maximum fee to those not covered by 'foundation-approved' plans, and a patient covered by a 'foundation-approved' plan may receive treatment from a non-participating physician provided that the patient pays any excess fee.[247] And the physician-foundation members would establish the fee schedule by a majority vote of themselves.

In its defence, the foundation argued that the maximum fees permitted those insurance companies which provided 'foundation-approved' coverage to better account for their risk and exposure, thereby providing cost savings which would ultimately be passed on to the consumer.[248] As a consequence of these savings, and that the arraignments were horizontal among members of a profession in an industry with which the courts had little experience in considering antitrust implications, the foundation argued that the per se rule was inapplicable.[249]

Starting from the position that price-fixing of maximum prices had been earlier held by the Court to be per se violation of the Sherman Act,[250] the Supreme Court returned to the position articulated in *Trenton Potteries*, *Socony-Vacuum* and *Northern Pacific Railway*. The Court noted that to indicate that the price-fixing arrangement had pro-competitive effects is tantamount to saying that prices were fixed, but at a reasonable rate:

[246] Ibid. US 339–40, S Ct 2470. [247] Ibid. US 341, S Ct 2471.
[248] Ibid. US 342, S Ct 2472. [249] Ibid. US 342, S Ct 2472.
[250] *Kiefer-Stewart Co* v. *Joseph E Seagram & Sons Inc.* 340 US 211, 71 S Ct 259 (1951) and *Albrecht* v. *Herald Co.* 390 US 145, 88 S Ct 869 (1968).

> The argument indicates a misunderstanding of the *per se* concept. The anticompetitive potential inherent in all price-fixing agreements justifies their facial invalidation even if procompetitive justifications are offered for some. Those claims of enhanced competition are so unlikely to prove significant in any particular case that we adhere to the rule of law that is justified in its general application. Even when the respondents are given every benefit of the doubt, the limited record in this case is not inconsistent with the presumption that the respondents' agreements will not significantly enhance competition.[251]

Further, reiterating the point made in *Topco*, the Court noted that its deference to the per se rule is based on the proper role of the judiciary in regulating the market: the exceptions should be made by Congress, and not carved out by the courts.[252] *BMI* was relatively rapidly distinguished by the majority due to the requirement that in a blanket licensing system a price must be set, and, in *BMI*, the price was not set by the particular copyright owners.[253] The dissent, however, stressed the novelty of the method of providing medical services and suggested that the appropriate means of determining the questions involved required the evidence elicited in a full trial. One wonders, had this matter been heard thirty years later, if the outcome would have been the same.

But for the fact that it involves a sports organisation whose product is watched by tens of millions of people, *National Collegiate Athletic Association* v. *Oklahoma* is remarkable only for the fact that the Court recognised that for some products to be supplied, such as those of a sports league, some degree of horizontal cooperation is needed. Accordingly, in those cases a rule of reason analysis is the appropriate tool to use for assessing the legality of the arrangement.

The National Collegiate Athletic Association (NCAA) governs American university intra-mural sports, regulating matters such as eligibility (e.g. amateur status, academic and otherwise), squad size, recruitment, and

[251] *Maricopa* (n. 242) US 351, S Ct 2476–7, the Court's footnote (referencing *Socony-Vacuum*) omitted.

[252] Ibid. US 354–5, S Ct 2478:

> Our adherence to the *per se* rule is grounded not only on economic prediction, judicial convenience, and business certainty, but also on a recognition of the respective roles of the Judiciary and the Congress in regulating the economy . . . The respondents' arguments against application of the *per se* rule in this case therefore are better directed to the Legislature. Congress may consider the exception that we are not free to read into the statute.

[253] Ibid. US 355–6, S Ct 2479.

on-field rules. Since 1951, it regulated the televising of football and in doing so limited the exposure each team could be given.[254] Historically, the television limits were imposed out of a concern that televised games would draw ticket-buying audiences away from live games. As a result of the restricted exposure, the Universities whose teams were more popular formed the College Football Association (CFA) to promote their interests within the structure of the NCAA. The interest of the CFA's members was to seek greater television exposure (and hence revenue). This was furthered by the negotiation of a separate television contract.[255] When the NCAA announced that it would take disciplinary action and apply sanctions against any institution which violated the NCAA's restrictions on television coverage, CFA members were unwilling to commit to the alternative television arrangement, and the Universities of Oklahoma and Georgia filed suit alleging a Sherman Act violation. The court noted about the NCAA's television regime:

> It limits the total amount of televised intercollegiate football and the number of games that any one team may televise. No member is permitted to make any sale of television rights except in accordance with the basic plan.[256]

This clearly is an output restriction, which the NCAA attempted to justify on the basis of preserving attendance at live football games. The Court of Appeals held the output restriction to be illegal per se price-fixing, and further rejected the NCAA's other claims that such a television restriction was justified on the basis of balancing athletic competition and a need to 'compete effectively with other types of television programming'.[257]

Although the majority of the Supreme Court had little difficulty in rejecting the latter two arguments,[258] the majority concluded that per se analysis was inapplicable to the 'industry' in the case. Relying on Bork's[259] analysis, the court reasoned certain industries, particularly sports leagues, require a great deal of horizontal cooperation if the product is to be produced.[260] Coordination on the rules, standards for

[254] Note 243 at US 88–9, S Ct 2953–4; see Sigfried and Burba, 'The College Football Association Television Cartel'.

[255] Ibid. US 89, 95–6, S Ct 2954, 2956. [256] Ibid. US 94, S Ct 2956–7.

[257] Ibid. US 97, S Ct 2958. [258] Ibid. US 109–20, S Ct 2964–70.

[259] Bork, *Antitrust Paradox* (n. 216), 278.

[260] *NCAA* (n. 243) US 101, S Ct 2960: 'Rather, what is critical is that this case involves an industry in which horizontal restraints on competition are essential if the product is to be available at all.'

participants, and creating a niche in the market (in this case the image of the 'scholar-athlete') are all central to the provision of the product. On the basis of this essential need for horizontal cooperation, the majority reasoned that a rule of reason analysis is appropriate.

As the respondent Universities accurately conceded that the 'great majority' of the NCAA's restrictions enhanced competition,[261] the focus of the analysis must be placed on the television restrictions which formed the issue of the case to determine their justification. The Court noted that the use of a rule of reason approach does not 'change the ultimate focus of our inquiry. Both *per se* rules and the Rule of Reason are employed "to form a judgment about the competitive significance of the restraint"'.[262] And in explanation, the Court continued:

> *Per se* rules are invoked when surrounding circumstances make the likelihood of anticompetitive conduct so great as to render unjustified further examination of the challenged conduct. But whether the ultimate finding is the product of a presumption or actual market analysis, the essential inquiry remains the same – whether or not the challenged restraint enhances competition. Under the Sherman Act the criterion to be used in judging the validity of a restraint on trade is its impact on competition.[263]

The all-important footnote 26 to this noted:

> Indeed, there is often no bright line separating *per se* from Rule of Reason analysis. *Per se* rules may require considerable inquiry into market conditions before the evidence justifies a presumption of anticompetitive conduct. For example, while the Court has spoken of a '*per se*' rule against tying arrangements, it has also recognized that tying may have procompetitive justifications that make it inappropriate to condemn without considerable market analysis.[264]

The consequences of the NCAA's restrictions were clear: individual universities could not sell rights to their games, output (measured by number of games televised) was restricted, prices were higher than they would otherwise be, and the market was unresponsive to consumer preference.[265]

[261] Ibid. US 103, S Ct 2961.

[262] Ibid., quoting *National Society of Professional Engineers* v. *United States* 435 US 679, 692, 98 S Ct 1355, 1365 (1978).

[263] Ibid. US 103–4, S Ct 2961–2, footnotes omitted.

[264] Ibid.; the Court refers to *Jefferson Parish Hospital District No. 2* v. *Hyde* 466 US 2,11–12, 104 S Ct 1551, 1558 (1984).

[265] Ibid. US 104–8, S Ct 2962–4.

This latter point was key: relying on reasoning present in the Court's judgments since *Standard Oil*, the Court emphasised the fundamental role of consumer preference in antitrust law. It reasoned thus:

> Price is higher and output lower than they would otherwise be, and both are unresponsive to consumer preference. This latter point is perhaps the most significant, since 'Congress designed the Sherman Act as a "consumer welfare prescription."' A restraint that has the effect of reducing the importance of consumer preference in setting price and output is not consistent with this fundamental goal of antitrust law. Restrictions on price and output are the paradigmatic example of restraints of trade that the Sherman Act was intended to prohibit.[266]

Thus a heavy burden was placed on the NCAA to justify these restrictions.[267]

The majority had little difficulty disposing of the NCAA's proffered justifications for its restrictions: protection of attendance at 'live' football games and the maintenance of a competitive balance among (amateur) athletic teams. The evidence flew in the face of the latter point.[268] The former point was seen to be what it patently was: an output restriction to insulate ticket sales from market forces. In no uncertain terms, the Court reasoned:

> At bottom the NCAA's position is that ticket sales for most college games are unable to compete in a free market. The television plan protects ticket sales by limiting output – just as any monopolist increases revenues by reducing output. By seeking to insulate live ticket sales from the full spectrum of competition because of its assumption that the product itself is insufficiently attractive to consumers, petitioner forwards a justification that is inconsistent with the basic policy of the Sherman Act. '[T]he

266 Ibid. at US 107–8, S Ct 2963–4, quoting *Reiter* v. *Sonotone Corp.* (1979) 442 US 330, 343, 99 S Ct 2326, 2333 (1979), referring to *Standard Oil* (n. 151) US 52–60, S Ct 512–15, the majority's footnotes omitted.

267 Ibid. US 113, S Ct 2966:

> Thus, the NCAA television plan on its face constitutes a restraint upon the operation of a free market, and the findings of the District Court establish that it has operated to raise prices and reduce output. Under the Rule of Reason, these hallmarks of anticompetitive behavior place upon petitioner a heavy burden of establishing an affirmative defense which competitively justifies this apparent deviation from the operations of a free market.

268 Ibid. US 117–20, S Ct 2968–70.

> Rule of Reason does not support a defense based on the assumption that competition itself is unreasonable.'[269]

The brief analysis of the justification and effects of the restrictions was sufficient to demonstrate their anti-competitive effects.

It would be incorrect to read *NCAA* as a dramatic erosion of the per se/ rule of reason distinction. Rather, *NCAA* is properly read as being among the first in a line of cases which recognised that given the market structure of a particular industry, where either some form of horizontal cooperation is necessary for the product to be provided, or the industry possesses other characteristics which involve some horizontal cooperation of a sort different from naked price-fixing, the application of an abbreviated or 'quick-look' analysis under the rule of reason is appropriate. Examples of the former type of industries include sport leagues;[270] the latter type includes professional associations (whose activities may include a Code of Ethics)[271] and (somewhat controversially) Universities in their coordinated assessment and distribution of financial aid.[272]

The Supreme Court describes, albeit somewhat vaguely, this process in *California Dental Association* as where 'an observer with even a rudimentary understanding of economics could conclude that the arrangements in question would have an anticompetitive effect on customers and markets'.[273] Justice Breyer, in his dissent[274] notes that in making this 'quick-look' four points should be addressed:

> I would not simply ask whether the restraints at issue are anticompetitive overall. Rather . . . I would break that question down into four classical, subsidiary antitrust questions: (1) What is the specific restraint at issue? (2) What are its likely anticompetitive effects? (3) Are there offsetting

[269] Ibid. US 116–7, S Ct 2968, quoting *National Society of Professional Engineers* v. *US* (1978) 435 US 679, 696, 98 S Ct 1355, 1368 (1978), footnote omitted.

[270] See, e.g. *NCAA* (n. 243), *Law* v. *National Collegiate Athletic Association* 134 F 3d 1010 (CA 10 1998), *Chicago Professional Sports Limited Partnership* v. *National Basketball Association* 961 F 2d 667 (CA7 1992), and *American Needle, Inc.* v. *National Football League et al.* 560 US 183, 130 S Ct 2201 (2010).

[271] See, e.g., *FTC* v. *Indiana Federation of Dentists* 476 US 447, 98 S Ct 2009 (1986) and *California Dental Association* v. *FTC* 526 US 756, 119 S Ct 1604 (1999).

[272] *United States* v. *Brown University* 5 F 3d 658 (CA3 1993); see Sullivan and Grimes, *Law of Antitrust* (n. 152), 241–2.

[273] *California Dental* (n. 271) US 770, S Ct 1612.

[274] The point of dissent was whether a more complete analysis was needed. The majority decided so. In dissent, Justices Breyer, Stevens, Kennedy and Ginsburg felt that the FTC's analysis was sufficient.

> procompetitive justifications? (4) Do the parties have sufficient market power to make a difference?[275]

As Hovenkamp notes, the quick look requires us to listen to the defendant's justification for the restraint, and 'If that justification seems both plausible and sufficient to suggest that the restraint is profitable without regard to any power that the defendants might have, then a rule of reason inquiry will be necessary.'[276] If the quick look shows the restraint to be naked, then the restraint can be dealt with as a per se prohibition.

The foregoing analysis indicates the central position played by consumer welfare as a value protected by section 1 of the Sherman Act. The central focus of Sherman's original Bill, prohibiting practices which 'tend to advance the cost to the consumer of any article'[277] continues to remain the core value protected by that section, in spite of the evolution in judicial interpretation. The concern of the early, pre-*Standard Oil*, cases was to elicit the extent which agreements among members of an industry (or related industries) fell under the prohibitions of that section.

The early judicial discussion and disagreement focused on determining whether the Act prohibited 'all restraints' or merely 'unreasonable' ones. By 1911, the Court determined that only undue or unreasonable restraints on trade were prohibited by the Act. The consequence of this carving out exceptions for reasonable restraints, the Court simultaneously drew 'unreasonable' restraints within the ambit of the Act. Price-fixing was immediately seen as the paradigm of an unreasonable restraint. This conclusion, announced in *Dr Miles* (some six weeks before *Standard Oil*), continues to remain the central tenet of American antitrust law.

Yet as the Court came to recognise, price-fixing is just one example of practices which have a pernicious effect on consumer welfare. As early as 1940, in *Soconoy-Vacuum Oil*, the Court recognised that any practice which tampered with price structures had that effect.[278] Accordingly, group boycotts, market division and (somewhat controversially) tying arrangements were soon brought within the scope of the per se prohibition. In spite of the development of the quick-look approach to the rule of reason and some judicial tinkering (particularly in the case of

[275] *California Dental* (n. 271) US 782, S Ct 1618.
[276] Hovenkamp, *Antitrust Policy*, 285. [277] See text above between notes 99 and 106.
[278] See text notes 207 to 216 above.

tying[279]), all of these activities remain unequivocal violations of the Sherman Act.

4.5 Efficacy and enforcement: other strands to the American system

Yet the efficacy of a regulatory scheme, whether involving criminal or other sanctions, is only as good as its enforcement. The American regime permits dual enforcement: criminal and civil sanctions can be used; and if the matter is pursued civilly, both the federal government and aggrieved individuals[280] have standing to bring an action. The significance of this dual approach is its enhanced ability to effectively ferret out and control collusive activity which may be harmful to a consumer.

Criminal enforcement of the Sherman Act was to remain in the background in the first decades after the enactment of Senator Sherman's Act. But notwithstanding this 'secondary' role played by the criminal process, such prosecutions were brought from time to time. Perhaps the most notable of these early prosecutions was the 1927 matter of *Trenton Potteries*.[281] As noted above, this case involved naked price-fixing among twenty-three corporate manufacturers of bathroom fittings (who were in turn aided by twenty individuals, and they were also criminally charged). Their defence, rejected by the Supreme Court, was that their practice was legal, because the prices were reasonable.[282] In resolving the guilt of those indicted, the Supreme Court made significant movement towards establishing the per se illegality of certain practices.[283]

By 1940, price-fixing was determined to be per se illegal.[284] Such a determination was instrumental in the shift towards a cartel control policy which incorporated criminal sanctions. The Supreme Court had spoken: price-fixing was illegal, period. There could be no defence based on countervailing economic benefits or other social or distributive

[279] See Hovenkamp, *Antitrust Policy* (n. 276), 324–36.

[280] This can also include state and local governments.

[281] 273 US 392, 47 S Ct 377 (1927), on appeal from 300 F 550 (CA2 1924).

[282] Ibid. US 397–8, S Ct 379.

[283] The Court did not explicitly state in *Trenton Potteries* that the price-fixing arrangement was per se illegal (*Trenton Potteries* (n. 185) US 397, S Ct 379). It was not until 1940 in *Socony-Vacuum Oil* (n. 192) US 220–1, S Ct 843 that the Supreme Court unequivocally held that price-fixing was per se illegal.

[284] Ibid. US 221, S Ct 843.

concerns. A proverbial line in the sand was drawn, and all a conviction required was for a jury to be convinced that the line was crossed. The jury did not need to consider the merits of a company which crossed it.[285]

Once the legal boundaries of permissible coordinated action among competitors had been clarified, the government could begin criminal prosecutions. The late 1950s marked the prosecution of the Heavy Electrical cartel, in which the Department of Justice obtained the first prison sentences. The 1960s and 1970s saw prosecution of bid-rigging in the defence industry. The 1980s saw the prosecution of the school milk cartels.[286] The first major international cartels, lysine[287] and vitamins,[288] were unearthed and prosecuted in the 1990s. The lysine cartel was significant for its Hollywood-esque publicity value,[289] and the vitamins cartel was significant in that it saw, for the first time, a number of foreign executives receiving American jail time.[290] These individual sanctions were in addition to the then record corporate (criminal) fines.[291] In effect, this announced to the world that those whose price-fixing activities impacted on the American market could expect to feel the full wrath of US Federal criminal law, and (if an individual) would face a term of imprisonment. The result is that there has been no recidivistic behaviour of this sort.[292] This development in criminal enforcement shows the severity and effectiveness of antitrust sanctions.

4.5.1 Private (civil) enforcement

The 1914 Clayton Act, by permitting the recovery of treble damages, provided a significant incentive for aggrieved parties to seek compensation for anti-competitive harms done to them. The Congressional debates on this provision of the antitrust laws focused on two key points relating to potential plaintiffs' incentives. First, without some kind of

[285] Indeed, this advantage of per se rules was noted by the Supreme Court the 1958 case of *Northern Pacific Railway Co.* v. *United States* 356 US 1, 5, 78 S Ct 514, 518 (1958).

[286] See Robert F. Lanzillotti, 'The Great School Milk Conspiracies of the 1980's'.

[287] Connor, 'Global Cartels Redux', 300–28.

[288] See Werden, Hammond and Barnett (n. 1), 4–5.

[289] See Eichenwald, *The Informant*, on which the movie of the same name was based.

[290] See Werden, Hammond and Barnett (n. 1), 4.

[291] 'Hoffmann-La Roche agreed to pay $500 million in fines, almost five times the previous record antitrust fine. BASF paid $225 million. These fines were roughly proportional to each company's U.S. and global markets shares'. Connor, 'The Great Global Vitamins Conspiracies', 112; see Connor, *Global Price Fixing*.

[292] See text accompanying n. 1.

reward for success, those harmed would unlikely have sufficient resources to tackle the trusts; and, second, the reward would serve to incentivise 'Private Attorneys-General' to facilitate the enforcement of the antitrust regime in the face of under-resourced, unwilling, or otherwise reluctant public officials. Page describes the results thus:

> Yet, despite trebling, private antitrust suits were rare over the first several decades of the Sherman Act, and only proliferated after the electrical equipment conspiracies of the late 1950s and early 1960s. The number of private federal antitrust suits spiked from 378 in 1961 to over 2,000 in 1962. The number returned to 380, but then rose through the 1960s, reaching 1,528 in 1977. Over the following ten years, however, the number dwindled to below 1,000, and has remained between 500 and 800 since then. Indirect purchaser class actions in state courts in recent years have added to the yearly totals, although exact data on those actions are not available.
>
> This history confirms the obvious point that providing a damage remedy, even with mandatory trebling, is insufficient to stimulate private enforcement; there must also be some reasonable prospect of recovering damages to be trebled.[293]

Whether or not treble damages are in fact treble (and thus overcompensate injured Plaintiffs) is a different issue,[294] and not relevant to our present discussion. However, the fact remains that a significant amount of money is shifted towards harmed individuals.

According to figures provided by Lande and Davis,[295] between 1990 and 2007, antitrust plaintiffs recovered over $18 billion in damages. Indeed, in one 1999 case, the *NASDAQ Market-Makers Litigation*,[296] the recovery amounted to about $1.027 billion.[297] This amount, an 'out of court' settlement, represented full recovery for each of the one million parties affected and was obtained with attorney's fees of less than 14 per cent.[298] In 2010, 610 civil antitrust suits were commenced in Federal District Courts;[299] this number decreased to 507 in 2011.[300] Even if many of these are unmeritorious or settle for pennies on the dollar, these

293 Page, 'Background Note Policy Choices', 49.
294 See Lande, 'Are Antitrust "Treble" Damages Really Single Damages?'.
295 Lande and Davis, 'Benefits from Private Enforcement' (n. 7), 891–3.
296 *In re NASDAQ Market-Makers Antitrust Litigation* 184 FRD 506 (SDNY 1999).
297 Camatsos and Foer, 'Cartel Investigations in the USA', 19.
298 *In re NASDAQ Market-Makers Antitrust Litigation* (n. 296); see also ibid., 17–19.
299 US Court Service, 'U.S. District Courts – Civil Cases Commenced, 2009–2010'.
300 US Court Service, 'U.S. District Courts – Civil Cases Commenced, 2010–2011'.

numbers are indicative of a system which encourages private compensation for antitrust harm.

Three observations can be made regarding the American system. As powerful as it may be, it is far from clear that it is ideal. The controversies over the ability of indirect purchasers to recover damages and the status of the passing-on defence, originating from *Hannover Shoe* and *Brunswick*[301] and subsequent suggestions to legislatively repeal these doctrines[302] well illustrate this point. However, it is well beyond the scope of this work to either address this doctrine or suggest how other private enforcement systems should (or should not) react given the American experience.[303]

Second, a consequence – almost certainly unintended – of the treble damage regime is that it encourages out-of-court settlements of antitrust actions. Few such claims go to a jury trial,[304] as risks of a jury's determination of loss multiplied by three may by far exceed an acceptable settlement. As such, the expected cost of a settlement can likely be calculated with greater precision than a jury verdict. Additionally, such settlements represent a saving in transactions costs borne by the parties or by society (in the form of the administrative costs of the court system). Similarly, settlements have the advantage of plaintiffs receiving compensation sooner, avoiding the costs and delay (with consequent risks) of trial, appeal and (if necessary) retrial.

Third, and most significant, are procedural rules which enhance the ability of plaintiffs' recovery: in particular the use of contingency fees and class actions. Contingency fees permit plaintiffs who would be otherwise unwilling or unable to pursue actions. The risk-sharing nature of such claims can entail that the less meritorious matters will not proceed, and Federal Rules of Civil Procedure require judicial approval of the settlement and fee,[305] which provides a check on the possible opportunism which may be present in the principal–agent relationship found in the class action attorney's representation of the class.

301 *Hannover Shoe* v. *United Shoe Machinery Corporation* 392 US 481, 88 S Ct 2224 (1968), *Brunswick Corporation* v. *Pueblo Bowl-O-Mat Inc. et al.* 429 US 477, 97 S Ct 690 (1977) and *Illinois Brick Co.* v. *Illinois* 431 US 720, 97 S Ct 2061 (1977).

302 See, e.g., US Antitrust Modernization Commission, *Report and Recommendations* 267.

303 On the latter point, see Cengiz, 'Passing-On Defense'.

304 See Connor and Helmers, 'Statistics on Modern Private International Cartels, 1990–2005', which reports that less than 15% of US federal antitrust matters go to trial.

305 US Federal Rules of Civil Procedure, rule 23(e) and *In re Corrugated Container Antitrust Litigation* 643 F 2d 195, 207 (CA5 1981); on the agency problems in class action matters, see Dam, 'Class Actions'.

Class actions though oft-criticised[306] (likely unfairly[307]) as enabling the pursuit of unjustified claims (i.e. 'shaking down' deep-pocketed Defendants), are nevertheless effective means of ensuring that large groups of plaintiffs, each of which suffered only 'small' damages, are effectively compensated. Justice Breyer, dissenting in a recent case regarding class proceedings (albeit in arbitration matters), remarked:

> But class proceedings have countervailing advantages. In general agreements that forbid the consolidation of claims can lead small dollar claimants to abandon their claims rather than to litigate . . .
>
> What rational lawyer would have signed on to represent the [plaintiffs] in litigation for the possibility of fees stemming from a $30.22 claim? See, e.g., *Carnegie v. Household Int'l, Inc* . . . ('The realistic alternative to a class action is not 17 million individual suits, but zero individual suits, as only a lunatic or a fanatic sues for $30').[308]

It would be interesting to speculate what the outcome of the *NASDAQ Market-Makers* litigation would have been in the absence of class action provisions in a system where the general rule is that litigants are responsible for their own costs, irrespective of the outcome of the litigation. We suggest that not many of the one million claims would have been pursued; and even if legal fees were recoverable, the 'hassle factor' of attempting to recover would still act as a disincentive in a great deal of cases.

It is also worth noting that class actions are not a new phenomenon to American jurisprudence. The Federal Rules of Civil Procedure have always provided for class litigation. As early as 1820, courts recognised an existing equitable exception to the legal doctrine that all interested parties must be before the court.[309] This exception was later formalised as Rule 48 of the 1842 Federal Equity Rules. Additionally, other jurisdictions' experiences with class actions (particularly Canada[310])

[306] See, e.g., the majority opinion in *AT&T Mobility LLC* v. *Concepcion et ux.* 563 US ____, 131 S Ct 1740 (2011) slip opinion 15–16.

[307] On the class action attorneys as 'Private Attorneys General' and the agency problem, see Rubenstein, 'On What A "Private Attorney General" Is', and Hittinger and Bona, 'The Diminishing Role'.

[308] *Concepcion* (n. 306), slip opinion 9.

[309] *West* v. *Randall* 2 Mason 181, 29 Fed Cas 718 (CCDRI 1820), per Story J.

[310] Ontario became the first province to permit such actions in 1992 (Class Proceedings Act 1992, SO 1992 c. 6). The availability of this means of prosecuting civil actions has permitted a significant number of successful claims: see *Irving Paper Limited* v. *Atofina Chemicals Inc.* (2009) 99 OR (3d) 358 (Ont SC); see also Connor, 'Effectiveness of Antitrust Sanctions', 197 n. 11.

show that such actions are effective in permitting those suffering relatively small harms to seek recompense.

4.5.2 Certainty of punishment

As a result of perceived inequities and disparities in sentencing of federal offenders, the Comprehensive Crime Control Act of 1984,[311] *inter alia*, contained the enabling provisions for the United States Sentencing Commission and its Federal Sentencing Guidelines. Recent Supreme Court cases have held that the Guidelines are to be viewed as advisory (rather than mandatory).[312] While the effect has been making the guidelines somewhat more discretionary, judges typically will not deviate from the Guidelines.[313] Accordingly, the essence of plea bargaining (which ends 97 per cent of federal criminal matters[314]) is seeking an agreement as to which aggravating and mitigating factors will (or will not) be presented to the sentencing judge, along with an agreed sentence, so that it will be imposed.

While the Sentencing Guidelines may do an injustice to a particular offender by mandating a sentence which is inappropriate to that offender's unique circumstances (which was the reason behind the Supreme Court's holding that the Guidelines are to be regarded as advisory), they clearly establish the penal consequences for a conviction. Faced with tables, multiplying factors, and similar criteria, a potential defendant (whether corporate or individual) will be aware of the likely outcome of a guilty verdict at trial.

4.5.3 Leniency programmes

Antitrust leniency programmes are an American invention, and an American export. Since being established in 1978,[315] the DOJ's Corporate Leniency programme has been extended to individuals, and enhanced – most recently as a result of the Antitrust Criminal Penalty

[311] Pub L 98–473, 98 Stat 1976, S 1762.

[312] *United States* v. *Booker* 543 US 220, 125 S Ct 738 (2005) and *Pepper* v. *United States* 562 US___ (2011).

[313] Connor, 'Effectiveness of Antitrust Sanctions' (n. 310), 195 n. 1.

[314] *Missouri* v. *Frye* 566 US ___ (2012) slip opinion 7: 'Ninety-seven percent of federal convictions and ninety-four percent of state convictions are the result of guilty pleas.'

[315] Hammond, 'The Evolution of Criminal Antitrust Enforcement'.

Enhancement and Reform Act of 2004[316] (ACPERA) – over time. It is worth noting that as a result of its effectiveness, similar leniency programmes have been adopted in other jurisdictions: Canada adopted a leniency programme in 1991,[317] the European Commission introduced its first leniency notice in 1996,[318] and at present, over fifty jurisdictions have such programmes.[319]

The hallmarks of the American system include:

- the requirement of an admission of criminal conduct,
- the requirement for full, frank and ongoing cooperation, and
- in the case of a corporate applicant, the obligation to provide restitution to those affected.[320]

In return, the successful leniency applicant can expect that it (and its employees) will not be prosecuted, that any civil damage claims are de-trebled and that its joint and several liability with other members of the cartel is decoupled.[321]

The reduction in civil liability for a successful applicant was a feature of ACPERA, which was brought in to alleviate the legitimate concern that although the criminal consequences of successfully applying for leniency result in a savings to the corporation, the civil consequences could be considerable. Without de-trebling and decoupling, a leniency applicant is in effect handing significant evidence to the aggressive, contingency fee-seeking plaintiff's Bar.

Corporate leniency is available only to the first company which provides information in circumstances where the Antitrust Division is unaware of illegal activity. Leniency is not available to ringleaders of or coercers in cartels.[322] Our unreflective views of justice seem to indicate that such programmes allow 'bad guys' to 'get off', which may not be optimal from a deontological (or retributivist) perspective; and allowing the worst of the bad guys – the ringleaders or enforcers – to escape justice

316 Public Law 108–237: the sunset of this Act was extended to 22 June 2015.

317 See Competition Bureau (Canada) *Immunity Program under the Competition Act.*

318 Commission notice on the non-imposition or reduction of fines in cartel cases, and Commission notice on immunity from fines and reduction of fines in cartel cases.

319 Hammond (n. 315), 1 and 3.

320 See Hammond and Barnett, 'Frequently Asked Questions Regarding the Antitrust Division's Leniency Program', Question 20.

321 ACPERA (n. 316), § 213.

322 See Hammond and Barnett, 'Frequently Asked Questions' (n. 320), Question 13.

is an even less appealing situation. And it is of course to these possessing unreflective views of justice, as opposed to positions shaped by an understanding of game and decision theory, that leniency programmes and their fruits must be 'sold'.

Leniency programmes of the American sort provide an element of certainty which can be used by prospective applicants to gauge the advantages of making (an early) request for leniency. Further, this certainty is enhanced by the programme setting up a system whereby the expected costs of cooperation (i.e. successfully applying for leniency) are less than the costs of non-cooperation (although there may be potential uncertainty in their amount, there is no uncertainty that the costs of non-cooperation will exceed the costs of a successful application). Additionally, the game theoretic analysis indicates that the rewards that a successful leniency applicant can obtain act as a means to destabilise cartels. To a very real extent, such programmes compel cartel participants to play an ongoing prisoners' dilemma game.

But of significantly more importance is the relationship which individual criminal liability has in the content of these programmes. Although corporations can be said to act, the real actors are individuals, who may or may not be pursuing their own interests in such action. The agency problem in corporate activity is well-researched. The focus of a significant amount of this is in regard to management enriching itself at the expense of the owners;[323] it is also fair to state that a significant amount of corporate criminal activity has its origin in this problem.[324] A leniency programme of the American sort recognises that although crime may have its genesis in such agency relationships, the relationship can also be exploited to combat corporate crime, through the imposition of individual criminal liability. The imposition of criminal liability on corporate members, given the unique (and unindemnifiable) nature of criminal sanctions, provides a means of sharply pitting an individual employee's interests against that of his or her employer, thereby cooperating in an investigation and/or potentially providing evidence of theretofore unknown activity (whistleblowing).

323 See, e.g., the argument contained Kraakman et al. (eds.), *The Anatomy of Corporate Law*, Cheffins, *Company Law*, 46–125, Jensen and Meckling, 'Theory of the Firm', and Alchian and Demsetz, 'Production, Information Costs, and Economic Organization'.

324 See the argument in Chapter 2.

4.6 Conclusions: American values

The American anti-cartel regime is a sophisticated mix of legislation which has been interpreted to demarcate a clear line dividing prohibited from permitted conduct. It operates within a system in which private enforcement is an adjunct to public enforcement, and wherein the consequences of legal violations are clearly known and can readily be calculated. The evidence suggests that the system works well: there has been no criminal recidivism in the past thirteen years.

The core value protected is consumer surplus. This was the original justification for the Act, found in the values which pre-dated Senator Sherman's Bills. Indeed, it can be accurately suggested that the Sherman Act as subsequently interpreted assigns to consumers a property right in this surplus, which is protected both civilly and criminally. It is accordingly protected by the same means as every other property right is protected in a market economy. It therefore takes no great leap to see the reasons why consumer surplus is protected in the manner in which it is.

The description of what was protected changed over time, primarily as a consequence of the increased use of economic analysis to identify the effects exhibited by particular practices. In *Socony Oil*, the protected entity was 'price structures'.[325] In *Northern Pacific Railway*, the Court spoke of the Act's purpose as protecting 'economic liberty'.[326] And in *Sonotone*, the Sherman Act was described as a 'consumer welfare prescription'.[327] Once the Court had interpreted the Sherman Act to identify and prevent those forms of restraints which were suppressive of competition, as it did in *Board of Trade*,[328] horizontal price-fixing became identified as and has always remained the 'supreme evil of antitrust'.[329] Practices having apparently the same effect, such as market division and output restrictions, were treated similarly. And it is worthy to note that in spite of the initial similarities which the Court felt that horizontal and vertical price-fixing had with each other, the Court – when presented with economic evidence and academic argument questioning these similarities[330] – was willing to yield, and regard that the

325 *Socony Oil* (n. 192) US 221, S Ct 843.

326 *Northern Pacific Railway* (n. 217) US 4, S Ct 517.

327 *Sonotone* (n. 266) US 343, S Ct 2333.

328 See text accompanying notes 167 to 187.

329 *Verizon Communications* v. *Law Offices of Curtis V Trinko* 540 US 398, 408, 124 S Ct 872, 879 (2004).

330 See, e.g., the references contained in the Court's opinions in *Leegin* (n. 165).

appropriate analytic tool to judge vertical price-fixing was a rule of reason, not a per se prohibition.[331] Similar sensitivity to economic reality was seen in the Court's consideration of industries where a degree of horizontal cooperation was needed for the product to be produced.[332] Doctrine was (and is) to yield to economic reality.

But the protection of consumer surplus, although felt as such, was not originally phrased as such, since the term was unknown to those possessing the economic background which American jurists and legislators had in the nineteenth century. The economic concepts which serve as a foundation for the sort of economic analysis used in the latter half of the twentieth century were neither well developed nor (as a consequence) widely known in nineteenth-century America. Rather, the need for protection against anti-competitive practices was phrased in terms of protection of property and labour rights of individuals and of individuals to subsequently exchange their labour and property for fair value.

This focus on the individual and the potential threats to the individual's ability to participate in mutually beneficial exchanges was the early preoccupation of those developing state and federal antitrust laws. Paramount among these views was a suspicion of, if not outright hostility towards, large commercial enterprises which were viewed as a threat to the economic freedom of the 'little guy'. Strong penalties and criminal sanctions were the natural means of dealing with such threats. However, it is to a great extent because of these views of the relationship which the individual has to the market that the American system developed in the manner in which it did. A question that we must therefore ask, and will later in this study turn to answering, is whether the elements of the American regime are sufficiently independent of these values, in order to permit a successful transplant.

This focus on the independence of values is essential, given the efficacy of the American regime. The lack of recidivism and the anecdotal evidence which suggests that international cartel organisers arrange their affairs to avoid violating American law, indicate the deterrent effect of the American regime. This effect is a result of the manner in which that regime addresses the agency problem inherent in corporate activity and which gives rise to the formation of cartels. A corporate liability regime of vicarious liability – with no 'due diligence' type defence – with

[331] Ibid. [332] See text accompanying notes 230 to 243.

significant fines establishes significant incentives for firms to monitor their agents. To supplement this a regime of individual liability where imprisonment is a likely consequence, provides an additional deterrent effect. But the lesson, from our consideration of those values which are protected by the American antitrust regime, is that this is not punishment for the sake of punishment; rather it is punishment to protect consumer welfare.

5

The European experience

> Much of the law relating to cartels is responsive in nature, and is not encapsulated in a system designed from scratch, with a clearly enunciated purpose and complete and logically structured set of principles. Rather it is a system characterized by historical jumps, shifting boundaries, multi-level enforcement, and ambiguity of purpose. Underlying this observation are major, worrying questions: 'What is it all about, why has it come about, and where is it leading?'[1]

5.1 Introduction

In the context of the current EU anti-cartel regime, Harding and Joshua's words are certainly true. This present regime is certainly a result of its historical antecedents, of European history more generally, and a shift in European enforcement priorities over time. An analysis of the history of European competition law (or any legal regime, for that matter) will have its use in demonstrating to us the reasons this regime developed in the way it did, and how it was adapted to resolve the problems which its political masters presented to it. But a historical analysis or explanation has its limits. While such an account may tell us why we have arrived at a particular juncture with a particular legal regime, it may not inform us as to the utility, efficacy or moral merits of the resulting regime. Such analysis is the responsibility of other disciplines.

The goal of this present chapter is to examine the present European system of cartel control, viewing the initial motivations behind incorporating anti-cartel provisions in the European Treaties and then considering the case law to determine what these provisions in fact protect. In light of this, the discussion will go on to ask (and answer) an important question: given the interests which the Treaty provisions protect, can the

[1] Harding and Joshua, *Regulating Cartels in Europe*, 256.

calls to enhance these provisions with criminal sanctions be legitimate from a normative perspective?

The structure of this chapter is as follows. The next section will look at the history of European cartel control. The facts that such a history must explain are simple: prior to the Second World War, cartelisation was a welcomed feature of national industrial policy, allowing a 'rationalised' approach to the production of goods in perhaps uncertain – if not turbulent – economic times. With the ratification of the European Coal and Steel Treaty and the Treaty of Rome, an administrative-based anti-cartel regime was born. And this regime has, in the first part of the twenty-first century, developed into one which metes out apparently substantial fines on price-fixers. Typically, those explaining this history tell one of two stories: one of which has its origins in Washington DC; the other's origins are in the Black Forest. Outlining these two canonical stories is the task of that part of the chapter.

It is suggested that neither story contains the 'whole truth', though both provide part of the explanation for the thinking behind the prohibitions found in the two original (post-World War Two) European Treaties, and their early interpretation by administrative agencies (particularly the Commission) and the European Court.[2] The remainder of the 'truth', it is argued, consists first in the Commission's and Court's initial pursuit of economic integration and the reduction of intra-European barriers to trade; and, second, in subsequent years, the development of a competition policy which served to explicitly promote consumer welfare, rather than serving as a handmaiden to market integration. This aspect of the development of European competition policy is examined in the third section of this chapter.

The results of the third section set the stage for the fourth, and concluding, section of this chapter. It is argued that a system which is characterised by having its origin in these differing goals, and conjoined with a legal and executive structure that can only rely on administrative measures for enforcement, is not amenable to the use (or even importation) of a strong, criminally based, system of sanctions. Indeed, this is apparent in the attitudes found in various Member States of the EU regarding the appropriateness of this sort of use of criminal sanctions. Given this result, the chapter concludes with some pessimistic conclusions for a European cartel criminalisation project.

[2] Prior to 1 January 1989, there was only one European Court.

5.2 A tale of two cities: Washington and Freiburg

The prevalence of cartels in pre-World War Two Europe – particularly in post-Unification Germany – is well known,[3] and thus need not be discussed in any great detail here. According to Djelic's figures[4] in 1923 about 1,500 cartels were operating within the German economy. This was an increase from four economy-wide cartels in 1887. By 1923, '50% of raw steel production, 82% of coal, and 90% of paper was regulated through cartels or other types of interfirm networks and agreements'.[5] Although it was almost certainly more cartelised than other European countries at the time, Germany was not alone in its use of cartels and other types of coordinated cooperation as a means of industrial policy. Edwards notes:

> When the Second World War began, restrictive business programs sponsored by governments were pervasive in Germany, Italy, and Japan, were broadly authorized by law in Belgium, the Netherlands, Latvia and New Zealand, and were in effect in important industries in the United Kingdom and France.[6]

In addition to the industrial and economic goals furthered by cartelisation, concentration of industrial and economic power furthered the important idea of German nationhood, a powerful – and necessary – political message in post-Unification Germany.[7]

While Germany had cartel control legislation at this time, most notably in the form of the 1869 *Gewerbeordnung* (Trade Regulation) and the subsequent 1923 *Verordnung gegen Mißbrauch wirtschaftlicher Machtstellungen* (Order against the Abuse of Economic Power),[8] these legal structures were to be weakened by judicial and political means. The important 1897 decision in the *Saxon Wood Pulp Case*[9] weakened the

[3] Germany was unified in 1871. On the prevalence of cartels in pre-World War Two Germany, see, e.g., Harding and Joshua (n. 1), 65–90 and Gerber, *Law and Competition*, 16–164.

[4] Djelic, 'Does Europe Mean Americanization?', 236–7 (and table 1), and see also numbers cited in Harding and Joshua (n. 1), 68.

[5] Djelic (n. 4), 236, citing Pietri, *Evolution Economique de l'Allemagne*.

[6] Edwards, *Control of Cartels and Monopolies*, 6, quoted in Harding and Joshua (n. 1), 87.

[7] See Harding and Joshua (n. 1), 69–73 and Gerber, *Law and Competition* (n. 3), 69–91.

[8] For a summary of the latter's provisions, see Harding and Joshua, ibid., 75.

[9] *Reichgericht, Urtile von 4. Febuar* 1897 (*Sächlischen Holzstoff Fabrikanten Verband*) 38 *RGZ* 155. See Harding and Joshua, ibid., 72–3, and Gerber, *Law and Competition* (n. 3), 91–5 for a discussion of this case.

former regulation by reading into its prohibition a quasi-rule of reason.[10] At issue was the enforceability of a joint sales arrangement by the Saxon Wood Pulp producers, put in place to avoid 'economic ruin'.[11] In determining the enforceability of the agreement, the court engaged in wholesale cost–benefit analysis, balancing the advantages of an orderly economic regime against individual economic freedom.[12] While recognising that in 'a few cases arising from special circumstances' monopolies can be exploitative to consumers,[13] however, in this case the wider considerations of avoiding economic catastrophe were to prevail. As Harding and Joshua note, this was likely due to the perception that the cartel (and cartelisation, generally) was benign.[14]

The 1923 Order, while creating a Cartel Court which had the power to oversee and dissolve cartels, had very little influence on German industrial policy. Indeed, due to both the need to produce significant quantities of goods (the economical production of which was possible only by large economies of scale) for export (in order to finance the reparations required by the Treaty of Versailles) and the resulting economic crisis, the Order was seldom used. The use it had was limited to regulating the relationship that cartel members had with each other, in particular the validity of their agreements and enforceability of their coercive measures.[15]

In spite of the damaging effects of the Depression of the 1930s and the harm done to the economy through industrial cartelisation, the German National Socialist Government began a policy of increased industrial cartelisation as part of its policy of a state controlled, planned economy. Cartel practices were supplemented (both before and after 1933) by mergers of large industrial concerns, such as that merger which created I G Farben out of, *inter alia*, Hoechst, Agfa, BASF and Bayer.

In the aftermath of the Second World War, the heavy reliance by the Axis governments on cartelisation and concentration of economic power as a matter of industrial policy would serve as a point of reflection for those seeking the rebuilding of the European economy. As Harding and Joshua note:

[10] See Harding and Joshua, ibid., 72, who use the term in this context.
[11] *Holzstoff* (n. 9) 157:'*wirtschaftliche Ruin*'. [12] Ibid. 157–60.
[13] Ibid. 158: '. . . *wenn sich im Einzelnen Falle aus besonderen Umständen bedenten ergeben, namentlich wenn es ersichtlich auf die herbeiführung eines thatsächlichen Mońopoles und die wuncherilche Ausbeutung der Konsumenten abgesehen ist* . . .'
[14] Harding and Joshua (n. 1), 73.
[15] See ibid., 75–77 and Gerber, *Law and Competition* (n. 3), 123–48.

> The incorporation of the business cartel as a device of totalitarian governance in Germany, Italy, and Japan inevitably influenced perceptions of such arrangements in the immediate post-war period. The potential for political abuse of concentrated and collusive power brought home to Europeans the earlier American fears and perhaps for the first time gave rise to a significant political will in a European context for a legal control of cartelization on ideological grounds. In occupied Germany, for example, policies of decartelization were applied alongside programmes of denatzification.[16]

There are two stories as to how this political will manifested itself in cartel control regimes found in the European Treaties. We next turn to these stories.

5.2.1 *The influence of Washington*

This is the story, versions of which are told by, for example, Thorelli,[17] Lovett[18] and Djelic,[19] and told in Gerber, and Harding and Joshua.[20] Thorelli, writing in the autumn of 1958, opens his version of this post-war story in the following terms:

> While there may be other underlying causes of the new and somewhat relativistic liberalism, two potent factors deserve mention: the enormous needs involved in reconstructing war-ravaged nations, needs which obviously could not be met by old-style restrictionism, and the education supplied by the United States under various aspects of the Marshall Plan. Direct pressure was applied to recipient nations to do away with the cartel mentality as at least a formal condition of obtaining American aid. In addition, most of the European productivity teams of business, labor, and government leaders sent to this country under the Plan were greatly impressed with the achievements of the American system.[21]

By 'liberalism' Thorelli means increased international trade and a reduction of domestic cartelisation.

Related to the enhanced liberalisation of the European, and particularly German, economy, was an American driven desire to 'deconcentrate' German industry. 'Deconcentration', of course, was merely a euphemism

[16] Harding and Joshua, ibid., 87. [17] Thorelli, 'Antitrust Policy in Europe'.

[18] Lovett, 'The United States and the Schuman Plan'.

[19] Djelic, 'Does Europe Mean Americanization?' (n. 4) and 'From Local Legislation to Global Structuring Frame'.

[20] Gerber (n. 3), 166–73, 268–96 and Harding and Joshua (n. 1), 87–98; by 'told in' what I mean is that they describe (without necessarily accepting as authoritative).

[21] Thorelli (n. 17), 223.

for reducing Germany's ability to employ its industrial strength to wage war.[22] Among the foundations of this deconcentration programme was a desire to interlink the economies of Europe, thus providing a buffer against bellicose nationalistic aspirations. To the French, such integration had the advantage that since appropriation of the German coal and steel industry was out of the question, and the resurrected German industries could soon put similar French industries at a competitive disadvantage, France could maintain its influence in an integrated pan-European industry.[23]

Although such pooling (or, euphemistically, 'integration of resources') would stimulate European industry, aiding in the post-war recovery, the coordinated nature of these industries led to American fears of recartelisation of the coal and steel industries; and, as the story goes, the Americans insisted on some guarantees that such cartelisation would not occur. Djelic describes this as follows:

> While the USA were encouraging or imposing bilateral transfers of their antitrust tradition, they were also pressing for initiatives with a cross-national dimension. In Western Europe, France led the way with the proposal, in May 1950, to pool European coal and steel industries. Jean Monnet and the French Planning Council insisted that the goal was to create a competitive space to stimulate production and productivity.

[22] Lovett (n. 18), 433:

> The policy of deconcentration was a euphemism. It meant reducing Germany's capacity to dominate its neighbours or to wage war; and it could be traced back to the decisions taken by the wartime allies at their last conference, held in Berlin (Potsdam) . . . The victors enunciated the principle that 'at the earliest practicable date, the German economy shall be decentralized for the purpose of eliminating the present excessive concentration of economic power as exemplified in particular by cartels, syndicates, trusts and other monopolistic arrangements.

Citing US Department of State, *Decade of American Foreign Policy*, 38.

[23] Lovett, ibid., 430:

> By the end of 1948, perhaps earlier, French diplomats accepted that German energy resources could not be annexed, expropriated or even internationalized. France could only influence German coal and steel through a partnership. France must play a trump card, a European card, by offering to pool its coal and steel reserves with those of its neighbours. For a time such daring speculations remained confined to policy advisers within the Quai d'Orsay. Gradually the circle widened. In September, 1949, the French foreign minister, Robert Schuman visited Washington to discuss problems of mutual interest with his American and British counterparts.

Lovett's footnotes omitted.

> They wanted to alleviate American fears that this project might lead to the emergence of a European wide cartel and hence they brought in American experts to prepare antitrust provisions. The key figure was Robert Bowie, Harvard antitrust lawyer and General Counsel to John McCloy, the US High Commissioner in Germany. Bowie was already involved in the drafting of a German antitrust law when he came to Paris in June 1950 – 'on loan' from McCloy to his friend Monnet. In Paris, he wrote the provisions that would become articles 65 and 66 of the European Coal and Steel Community (ECSC) Treaty.
>
> As in Germany, resistance proved strong, notably among French, Belgian and German business communities. But the final ECSC treaty endorsed anticartel and antitrust objectives and articles 65 and 66 were incorporated as a major dimension of that treaty. Article 65 dealt with cartels and loose agreements, prohibiting them in principle. However, the European enforcement agency, the High Authority, was granted some leeway to authorize, in times of crisis, a number of exceptions. In particular, it could allow national States to grant aid to individual undertakings or industries or even to accept certain types of agreements. Article 66 of the ECSC treaty dealt with abuses of market power through concentration. In line with American antitrust tradition, only 'unreasonable' concentration was prohibited. Mergers that could be shown to increase efficiency and productivity without representing a threat to competition could be authorized.[24]

Articles 65 and 66 of the ECSC Treaty were incorporated as Articles 85 and 86 of the Treaty of Rome, and to this day still remain the primary law regarding competition in the EU.

Thus the essence of this story, at least in its outline form,[25] involves three related propositions: the need to reindustrialise Europe to alleviate the effects of war, a desire to interlink European economies and industrial bases to both facilitate the reindustrialisation process and (equally as importantly) ensure a lasting peace on the Continent; and, the reliance on an American-written and American-style antitrust policy to prevent the recartelisation of European industry (particularly in the coal and iron and steel industries). This story contains an element of the truth, as, of course, McCloy's friendship with Jean Monnet is well known, and the work of Bowie in drafting the ECSC Treaty is undisputed. However, this story is not the whole truth.

[24] Djelic, 'From Local Legislation' (n. 19), 60, references omitted.

[25] More elaborate versions of the story can be told by adding subplots involving the American promotion of the International Trading Organization, and the General Agreement on Tariffs and Trade (GATT). See, e.g., Harding and Joshua (n. 1), 90–8.

5.2.2 *The influence of Freiburg*

That the above story needs supplementing should immediately be apparent from the fact that Germany was a signatory to the ECSC Treaty. Although one story recounts, 'On April 9, 1951 when the treaty was finally about to be signed, the German Minister of Economic Affairs, Ludwig Erhard, reminded the Chancellor Konrad Adenauer that the final German decision had been "influenced by the American negotiating partners in a fashion which amounted almost to an ultimatum"',[26] this is probably not the whole truth. While there may have been a sense of victor's justice in encouraging Germany's participation in the ECSC Treaty, it is a mistake to overemphasise this subplot in the telling of the story.

The leading German negotiators of the ECSC Treaty were adherents to the ordoliberal school of economic thought. Giocoli describes this background as follows:

> The leading figure in the German delegation at the ECSC negotiation was in fact Walter Hallstein, a keen supporter of ordoliberal ideas and, later, the first President of the European Commission. Moreover, Germany's Economics Minister at the time was Ludwig Erhard, who also headed an informal group of lawyers and economists – the so-called 'social market economy group' – who largely shared ordoliberal views on several issues, including competition policy. Just one year before the beginning of ECSC talks, Erhard had been presented the first draft of Germany's competition law, which largely reflected the ordoliberal approach to antitrust. It seems therefore legitimate to argue that Germany's official position on the Treaty of Paris was, at least with respect to competition issues, significantly influenced by Ordoliberalism. It is to this school of thought that we must direct our attention in order to grasp the entire picture of the events and motivations leading to EEC antitrust law.[27]

The ordoliberal approach to the relationship of the individual and the market economy would shape the German acceptance of the ECSC Treaty's provisions, and, insofar as Hallstein was later to become the first Commissioner (indeed his Commission lasted from 1958 to 1967), the Commission's own economic thinking.

Ordoliberalism, as a school of economic thought, arose at the University of Freiburg during the Weimar Republic. It was clearly a product of its

[26] Djelic, 'Does Europe Mean Americanization' (n. 4), 245, quoting Berghahn, *The Americanization of West German Industry*, 153.

[27] Giocoli, 'Competition versus Property Rights: American Antitrust Law', 767 (Giocoli's reference to Gerber, *Law and Competition* (n. 3), 271–3 omitted). This article has influenced my thinking on the post-war development of European competition policy.

turbulent times.[28] The connection with Freiburg was fortuitous, as a confluence of independent thinking at that University, and Freiburg's general isolation from the centres of political power would provide appropriate insulation to permit heterodoxical ideas to develop and promulgate.[29] It is not the purpose of this chapter either to outline the history or to provide a detailed account of ordoliberal thinking. We can, however, adopt Giocoli's description:

> [Ordoliberalism] was a school of thought that agreed with earlier conceptions of liberalism by considering a competitive economic system necessary for a prosperous, free, and equitable society. Yet its members were also convinced that such a society could only come into existence if a 'constitutional' framework aimed at protecting the process of competition from distortions and abuses, at the equitable distribution of the benefits of the market, and at minimizing government intervention in the economy constrained the market. This mixture of legal and economic arguments was indeed typical of the Freiburg School of law and economics, from which Ordoliberalism originated.[30]

The abuse in the market which the ordoliberals feared could arise from two forces.

The primary force is the inordinate concentration of economic power in private hands; the other (and related) force consists in government grants of special privileges to economic actors, or – in contemporary terms – rent-seeking behaviour.[31] Gerber's exposition of this is worth quoting in detail:

> For [ordoliberals], it was not sufficient to protect the individual from the power of government, because governments were not the only threats to individual freedom. Powerful economic institutions could also destroy or limit freedom, especially economic freedom. Having witnessed the use of private economic power during the Weimar period to destroy political and social institutions, the ordoliberals emphasized the need to protect individuals from misuses of such power. This meant that the state had to

[28] Bonefeld, 'Freedom and the Strong State', who writes in the introduction:

> It originated in the late 1920s–early 1930s in a context of financial crisis and economic depression, political violence and austerity, conditions of ungovernability and entrenched class positions. The founding thinkers of ordoliberalism were Walter Eucken, Franz Böhm, Alexander Rüstow, Wilhelm Röpke and Alfred Müller-Armack. In the context of the Weimar crisis, they developed a particular account on how to make capitalism work as a liberal economy, . . .

[29] Gerber, 'Constitutionalizing the Economy', 25. [30] Giocoli (n. 27), 769.

[31] See Vanberg, 'The Freiburg School', 14.

> be strong enough to resist the influence of private power groups. In order for government officials to be in a position to create the structures of the new society, the government of which they were a part would have to be able to protect them against private influences.
>
> The Weimar experience led ordoliberals to demand the dispersion of not only political power, but economic power as well. For most, this meant the elimination of monopolies.[32]

To ensure this aspect of economic freedom, a strong state with appropriate, constitutionally grounded, legal institutions must govern the market order.[33] This shaping of the constitutional political-socio-economic order would be known in German as '*Ordnungspolitik*'.[34] As Vanberg remarks, '*Ordnungspolitik* in the Freiburg sense is formost [sic] competition policy, a policy that aims at securing a competitive process with desirable working properties, one that works to the benefit of consumer interests.'[35] Consumer interests (or sometimes 'consumer sovereignty') should not be identified with the economist's 'consumer welfare', but rather with a more abstract notion of freedom in the marketplace.

To protect consumer sovereignty, competition law would serve as a central feature in the ordoliberal project. As Giocoli notes:

> It is hardly surprising that competition law was the keystone of the ordoliberal program toward a transaction order. History had taught ordoliberals that economic freedom tended to be self-destructive: competition collapsed, first, because firms always preferred the private, that is, contractual, regulation of business to the market, that is competitive, one, and second, because firms were able to gain so much economic power that they could eliminate competition. In both cases, the problem was *private economic power* and the primary goal of competition law had to be the elimination of such power or, at least, the prevention of its harmful effects.[36]

[32] Gerber, 'Constitutionalizing the Economy' (n. 29), 36–7. Regarding the prohibition of monopolies, Gerber also notes (at 51):

> The monopoly prohibition was directed primarily at cartels and other agreements between competitors. Such agreements created the very power that threatened the competitive process and, therefore, had to be prohibited. The ordoliberals had witnessed the destructive influence of cartels on the German economy, polity and society during the Weimar period, and they considered a prohibition of cartel agreements to be necessary for the maintenance of a competitive economy.
>
> (Gerber's footnote omitted.)

[33] See, e.g., Vanberg (n. 31), 5 and Gerber, 'Constitutionalizing the Economy', ibid., 47–9.

[34] Vanberg, (n. 31) at 6. [35] Ibid., 13. [36] Giocoli (n. 27), 773.

The ordoliberal competition regime would give effect to the economic constitution, thereby ensuring individual freedom (or consumer sovereignty) within the market. The substantive elements would include cartel control, as such combinations were anathematic to the individual interest,[37] and requirements for firms to divest should they *behave as* a monopolist. This latter provision, in a very real sense, very much resembled a rule of reason: were the divesture to cause economic waste, it would not be required.[38]

To ensure the application of these substantive principles, the ordoliberal programme envisioned by Walter Eucken contained novel procedural and administrative provisions. Gerber's description, although not brief, provides the essential details of these provisions:

> The most original procedural component of the ordoliberal model was the enforcement of competition law by an autonomous monopoly office. This concept was new, deriving neither from prior European experience nor from U.S. antitrust law. According to Eucken, 'In the situation of the modern industrial state this great, central figure of the monopoly office had to appear. Without it the competitive order and with it the modern "*Rechtsstaat*" is threatened. The monopoly office is as indispensable as the highest court.'
>
> The monopoly office would have sole responsibility for enforcing this new type of law. It would both investigate alleged violations of the statute and initiate investigations on its own. When it found violations, it would have the authority to take certain enforcement actions. These included,

[37] Gerber, 'Constutionalizing the Economy' (n. 29), 51 writes: 'A monopoly prohibition was designed to prevent or eliminate the economic power that by its very existence distorted the competitive order. A firm or group of firms that had power over price or the power to hinder the performance of its rivals was structurally inconsistent with the complete competition standard.'

[38] Gerber, ibid., 52 remarks:

> Divestiture would not be required in cases of natural monopoly or monopoly based on a legally protected right (for example, a patent or copyright), or when divestiture would otherwise be impractical or entail economic waste. In such cases, competition law was to provide a standard of conduct for the firms involved. This standard was arrestingly simple. It required that economically powerful firms act as if they were subject to competition – i.e., as if they did not have monopoly power.
>
> The idea was appealing. It promised – through a single objective legal mechanism – to limit the harms associated with both private economic power and state intervention. Application of the as-if standard required that firms refrain from conduct that would be unavailable to them as if they had no monopoly power.

> for example, invalidating cartel contracts and ordering the termination of particular conduct, in some cases with the threat of fines for failure to comply. The actions of the office were subject to review by the regular courts for conformity to the economic constitution.
>
> The most important – and most controversial – characteristic of this office was its autonomy. It was not intended merely to be a part of the state bureaucracy and hence subject to political influence. The ordoliberals had witnessed during the Weimar period the ability of cartels and large corporations to eviscerate attempts at control by putting political pressure on the executive branch, and they were convinced that this new office had to be autonomous in order to avoid such influences. They envisioned it as a quasi-judicial office, guided not by political considerations, but by the application of judicial methods to authoritative texts.[39]

The independence of the Cartel Office would ensure its autonomy from capture by rent-seeking interests, thereby avoiding one of the principal potential market abuses of concern to the ordoliberals. It is hard not to see the origins of the Directorate General for Competition (and its antecedents) in Euken's description of an idealised Cartel Office.

In the absence of additional concrete evidence it is almost always a mistake to examine two positions, identify that they are consistent with each other, and then conclude that the earlier necessarily influenced the other. We can conclude, based on the public evidence which surrounded the debate on the adoption of the 1957 German competition law (*Gesetz gegen Wettbewerbeschränkungen (GWB)* – Law Against Restraints on Competition), that there was an ordoliberal influence on the framework established by this statute, in spite of the compromises[40] won by industry. Gerber describes the results of this influence:

> In 1956 the two sides reached a compromise that led to the enactment of the Law Against Restraints on Competition ... The basic structures and the vocabulary of the act – which is still in effect – reflect strong ordoliberal influence. The GWB calls for a prohibition of cartels, as had been so vigorously demanded by the ordoliberals for so long. It also includes a variety of measures aimed at preventing the abuse of economic power, including a variant of the quintessentially ordoliberal 'as-if' standard of conduct. The law's procedural mechanism is also ordoliberal (and far from U.S. ideas) in that it creates a relatively autonomous office – the Bundeskartellamt or Federal Cartel Office (FCO) – to enforce the law and virtually excludes private antitrust suits.[41]

[39] Gerber, ibid., 54–5; Euken's quotation is taken from his *Grundsätze*, 294.
[40] On the compromises, see Gerber, ibid., 64. [41] Ibid., 65.

The compromises won by industry included exceptions for crisis cartels and standardisation agreements. However, in the light of subsequent developments in EU law the significance of these exceptions has diminished, and conditions for private antitrust suits have become more favourable.[42]

We cannot draw similar conclusions about either the ordoliberal or American influence on the competition provisions of the Treaties of Paris or Rome. We can note that there are certain similarities. Articles 65 and 66 of the ECSC Treaty (to become Articles 85 and 86 of the Treaty of Rome) seemingly contain a per se prohibition of cartel activity. While it may be true that, as Djelic notes, 'such antitrust tradition and the oligopolistic understanding of competition that was associated with it were clearly foreign to European industrial traditions',[43] it is somewhat hyperbolic to conclude, as she does, that these had 'direct and unmistakable American origins',[44] which were imposed in Europe by a core group of 'American missionaries'.[45] It is equally as consistent to explain the novel approach to competition policy adopted in the aftermath of the war as originating from the ordoliberal tradition. And certainly the similarities between ordoliberal and American antitrust conclusions made it easier for those negotiating the content of the Treaties' competition position to compromise.

[42] On the present conditions for private antitrust actions in Germany, see Peyer, 'Private Antitrust Litigation in Germany'.

[43] Djelic, 'Does Europe Mean Americanization?' (n. 4), 245–6. [44] Ibid., 246.

[45] Ibid., 243:

> The State Department in Washington, the American Military Government in Germany or the Economic Cooperation Administration, the agency running the Marshall Plan, saw it as their mission to fight in Europe the 'communist party line' thanks to the 'American production line' . . . This meant a radical structural transformation of European economies and industries and the redefinition, in particular of trade patterns on the old continent using the American economic space as the model of reference . . . A small group of progressive American businessmen, active in Washington since the New Deal, was particularly involved in this project. In their desire to give the rest of the free world 'an opportunity to learn of the principles and advantages of free enterprise,' *these American missionaries* singled out as one of their core priorities the transfer to partner countries of American competition legislation . . . They saw the American antitrust tradition as both a key element of the American model and as a potentially powerful tool of its transfer to other countries.
>
> (Emphasis supplied; Djelic's references omitted.)

5.3 Completing the market: the early days of European competition policy

The Treaty of Rome was signed on 25 March 1957, and came into effect on 1 January the following year. Its competition provisions, Articles 85 and 86, mirrored the provisions of the ECSC Treaty, and remain the EU's primary competition legislation to this day, albeit in renumbered form. Articles 87–89 of the Treaty of Rome required the production of Regulations or Directives to give effect to Articles 85 and 86, and in particular to define the administrative framework (and judicial supervision thereof), the scope of application of the Articles, and the means of enforcement (specifically fines and periodic penalty payments) of the Treaty's provisions.[46] It took over four years before these Treaty provisions were implemented by Regulation 17/62[47] which came into force on 13 March 1962.

Regulation 17/62 established a system of notification and negative clearance, under which those undertakings participating in 'agreements, decisions or concerted practices' to which Article 85(1) may apply, were required to notify the Commission to seek a decision regarding the applicability of the exemptions contained in Article 85(3).[48] The subsequent decision of the Commission was reviewable by the Court of Justice.[49] Should the Commission decide that the agreement (etc.) was incompatible with Article 85, it could order the practices to be terminated,[50] and it had the power to enforce its decisions with fines and periodic penalty payments.[51] In addition the Commission was granted the authority to examine agreements[52] on its own initiative and make inquiries into any sector of the economy.[53]

The immediate consequence of Regulation 17/62's system of prior notification was on the Commission's workload. The Commission's resources would be primarily dedicated to the clearance of practices of which it was notified, and not with the investigation of agreements (etc.) which infringed the Treaty's competition provisions, leading in many cases to delays of several years.[54]

46 Article 87(2).

47 Regulation No. 17 First Regulation implementing Articles 85 and 86 of the Treaty.

48 Ibid., Arts. 2–8. 49 Ibid., Art. 9. 50 Ibid., Art. 3. 51 Ibid., Arts. 15–17.

52 Ibid., Art. 3. 53 Ibid., Art. 12.

54 See the House of Lords Select Committee on the European Union, *Fourth Report*, para. 96:

> There have over the years been many criticisms of the Commission's performance in enforcing the Competition Rules ... The workload

Notwithstanding the Commission's dedication of resources to the clearance procedures, it was nevertheless able to find the resources to reactively enforce Articles 85 and 86. Such enforcement activity had its naissance in the Commission's decisions (and the Court's subsequent judgments) in the market division case of *Consten and Grundig* v. *Commission*,[55] and in the two cartel cases (both of which also contained additional elements of market division) of *Quinine*[56] and *Dyestuffs*.[57]

5.3.1 *Market Integration as a goal of competition policy*

At issue in *Consten and Grindig*,[58] was an agreement between Grundig, a German electronics manufacturer, and its French distributor Consten. The latter was appointed Grundig's sole distributor in France, in exchange for which Consten undertook to provide repair facilities and aftersales service, make investments in advertising, and guarantee a certain level of purchases from Grundig. In addition, Consten was prohibited from selling goods which would compete with Grundig's products and similarly prohibited from exporting Grundig's products from France. Similar conditions on local distribution were imposed by Grundig on its other (regional) sole distributors.

Several months after the contract was concluded, to further attempt to protect its distributorship Consten registered in France the trademark

exceeded the Competition Directorate's resources, and though the Committee did not undertake a detailed inquiry into the staffing level we concluded that there was a clear possibility that the DG was understaffed. In our 1993 Report we noted that improvements had been made and that the backlog of notifications was being reduced. But the Committee again expressed concern at the lack of resources in the Commission to deal with Article 81 and 82 cases. In 2000, the overall position has improved in some respects but remains unsatisfactory. It is clear that there is pressure on the system and under the present arrangements parties to a notified agreement still have to wait for a substantial time, possibly years, for a Commission decision or, more usually, a comfort letter. There is general agreement that the system needs to be reformed though views differ as to how this might best be done.

(Footnotes omitted.)

[55] *Grundig-Consten* (IV-A/00004-03344) [1964] OJ 23/2545; Cases 56 & 58/64 *Consten and Grundig* v. *Commission* [1966] ECR 299.

[56] *Entente internationale de la quinine* (IV/26.623) [1969] OJ L192/5; Case 45/69 *Boehringer Mannheim* v. *Commission* [1970] ECR 769, Case 41/69 *ACF Chemiefarma NV* v. *Commission* [1970] ECR 661.

[57] *Matières colorantes* (IV/26.267) [1969] OJ L195/11; Case 48/69 *Imperial Chemical Industries Ltd* v. *Commission* [1972] ECR 619.

[58] *Consten and Grundig* (n. 55) OJ 2545–7, ECR 303–5.

GINT ('Grundig International'), which was used on all appliances manufactured by Grundig. In April 1961, a French Company, UNEF, imported into France and sold to French retailers Grundig appliances and did so by undercutting Consten's prices. Consten in turn sued UNEF for trademark infringement and unfair competition. During the course of this litigation, Grundig notified the Commission of the arrangements with its sole distributors, including Consten.

In spite of the suggestions made by Consten and Grundig that such territorial restrictions were necessary to eliminate free-rider problems with respect to guarantee and post-sales service,[59] the Commission saw the network of sole distributorships as nothing more than an attempt to fragment the common market and – by so doing – isolate each distributor from the forces of competition.[60] This conclusion was ratified by the Court of Justice in its analysis of the Commission's decision.

The Court considered the absolute territorial restrictions imposed by the contract, and noted that the contractual and intellectual property restrictions entailed that a third party (such as UNEF) who wished to parallel import into the territory of a sole distributor would run 'serious risks'.[61] As such, the Court held that the Commission, in its investigation of Grundig's distribution system, properly placed the network of contracts into their proper context:

> The situation as ascertained above results in the isolation of the French market and makes it possible to charge for the products in question prices which are sheltered from all effective competition. In addition, the more producers succeed in their efforts to render their own makes of product individually distinct in the eyes of the consumer, the more the effectiveness of competition between producers tends to diminish. Because of the considerable impact of distribution costs on the aggregate cost price, it seems important that competition between dealers should also be stimulated. The efforts of the dealer are stimulated by competition between distributors of products of the same make. Since the agreement thus aims at isolating the French market for Grundig products and maintaining artificially, for products of a very well-known brand, separate national markets within the community, it is therefore such as to distort competition in the Common Market.
>
> It was therefore proper for the contested decision to hold that the agreement constitutes an infringement of Article 85(1). No further considerations, whether of economic data (price differences between France and Germany,

[59] Ibid. OJ 2551. [60] Ibid. 2552. [61] Ibid. ECR 343.

> representative character of the type of appliance considered, level of overheads borne by Consten) or of the corrections of the criteria upon which the Commission relied in its comparisons between the situations of the French and German markets, and no possible favourable effects of the agreement in other respects, can in any way lead, in the face of abovementioned restrictions, to a different solution under Article 85(1).[62]

This statement can, quite fairly, be taken to entail that a market division is a per se (or at least, as close to per se as European law could come) violation of Articles 85 and 86. Further, the agreement between the two parties regarding use of the GINT trademark was nothing more than a supplementary means of enforcing the division of the market, and as such is also prohibited by the two Treaty Articles.[63]

The Quinine and Dyestuffs Cartels involved similar market division but each contained the aggravating factor of price-fixing. Quinine (produced from cinchoma bark) is used to prevent malaria and in the production of other pharmaceuticals. It was in fairly scarce supply until the years following the Second World War when both new plantations in South-East Asia were established, and a means to synthesise it was discovered. The cartel involved cooperation among manufacturers which had occurred since 1913.[64] But the cartel in the form which concerned the Commission's decision was a defensive cartel, put together in 1960 to combat the glut of not only bark but also surplus quinine on the market. (The latter glut resulted from the US Government's reduction of its stockpile by auction in 1958.) However, in the early 1960s, due to the increase in American military

[62] Ibid. 343.

[63] Ibid. 345:

> Consten's right under the contract to the exclusive user in France of the GINT trade mark, which may be used in a similar manner in other countries, is intended to make it possible to keep under surveillance and to place an obstacle in the way of parallel imports. Thus, the agreement by which Grundig, as the holder of the trade-mark by virtue of an international registration, authorized Consten to register it in France in its own name tends to restrict competition.
>
> ...
>
> That agreement therefore is one which may be caught by the prohibition in Article 85(1). The prohibition would be ineffective if Consten could continue to use the trade-mark to achieve the same object as that pursued by the agreement which has been held to be unlawful.

[64] On the background to this cartel, see Goyder and Albors-Llorens, *Goyder's EC Competition Law*, 173–4 and Harding and Joshua (n. 1), 123–4.

activity in South-East Asia, demand for quinine increased, resulting in an increase in price. The cartel ended in 1965.

The cartel agreement had a number of aggravating features described in the Court's judgment:

> This cartel was based in the first place on an agreement relating to trade with third countries (hereinafter referred to as the 'export agreement') and providing inter alia for the fixing by agreement of prices and rebates relating to exports of quinine and quinidine and the allocation of export quotas supported by a system of compensation depending on whether the export quotas were exceeded or not fulfilled.
>
> Furthermore, a gentlemen's agreement between the same parties extended the abovementioned provisions to all sales within the common market.
>
> This agreement also established the principle of the protection of domestic markets in favour of each of the producers and bound the French members of the cartel to refrain from manufacturing synthetic quinidine.[65]

The cartel members would fix a quota and the prices of products exported from the Common Market, and would bind themselves by 'Gentlemen's agreements' to protect each other's domestic markets and to base the prices in their domestic markets on the export prices.

The Commission meted out substantial fines on the participants[66] and although the Court reduced the fines slightly, it was adamant regarding its conclusion regarding the legality of market division. It noted that:

> despite the scarcity of raw materials and an increase in the demand for the products in question, . . . as the contested decision finds, a serious threat of shortage nevertheless emerged only in 1964 as a result of the interruption of Nedchem' s supplies from the American General Service Administration.
>
> . . . [S]uch a situation cannot render lawful an agreement the object of which is to restrict competition in the common market and which affects trade between the member states.[67]

A similar conclusion was to be drawn in the Commission's *Dyestuffs* decision dated eight days after the *Quinine* decision[68] (and its subsequent confirmation by the Court).[69]

[65] *Quinine* (n. 56), paras. 5–7.

[66] The fines totalled 300,000 units of account (OJ L192/22), but this total was reduced slightly by the Court.

[67] *Quinine* (n. 56), paras. 126–7. [68] Note 57.

[69] Cases 49, 51–57 *ICI* v. *Commission*, *BASF* v. *Commission*, *Bayer* v. *Commission*, *Geigy* v. *Commission*, *Sandoz* v. *Commission*, *Francolor* v. *Commission*, *Cassella* v. *Commission*, *ACNA* v. *Commission* [1972] ECR 619.

Dyestuffs involved a cartel of nine[70] of the major producers of dye within the Common Market.[71] The lasting significance of this decision lies in the Commission's view (with which the Court agreed) that strong evidence of a concerted practice can be found in parallel behaviour of participants in an anti-competitive arrangement.[72] According to the Court, the evidentiary value of the parallel conduct increases when such conduct permits the consolidation of a position which fragments the Common Market.[73] The market in dye is characterised by little elasticity of demand, hence a strategy of fragmenting the market can be profitable as there will be few (if any) arbitrage opportunities to undermine the strategy.[74]

The dye manufacturers argued before the Commission and Court that there was a need to divide up their market to concentrate on local customers, in order to provide them with technical assistance and prompt delivery.[75] However, the Court noted that this practice had other results:

[70] Cassella Farbwerke Mainkur AG, Bayer AG, Hoechst AG, Française des matières colorantes SA (Francolor), Aziende Colori Nazionali Affini SpA (ACNA), SA Ciba, J R Geigy SA, Sandoz SA, and Imperial Chemical Industries Ltd (ICI). It is interesting to note that all the five remaining members of I G Farben (BASF, Bayer, Hoechst and Cassella) participated in this cartel. One supposes that it was difficult to escape from a past culture of cooperation.

[71] The cartel involved nine of the ten producers responsible for the production of 80% of dye in the Common Market.

[72] See *ICI* (n. 69), para. 66:

> Although parallel behaviour may not by itself be identified with a concerted practice, it may however amount to strong evidence of such a practice if it leads to conditions of competition which do not correspond to the normal conditions of the market, having regard to the nature of the products, the size and number of the undertakings, and the volume of the said market.

This paragraph is repeated verbatim in the other judgments.

[73] Ibid., para. 67:

> This is especially the case if the parallel conduct is such as to enable those concerned to attempt to stabilize prices at a level different from that to which competition would have led, and to consolidate established positions to the detriment of effective freedom of movement of the products in the Common Market and of the freedom of consumers to choose their suppliers.

[74] The Commission's concerns with fragmenting the market extended beyond agreements to do so. Compare Case 27/76 *United Brands* v. *Commission* [1978] ECR 305 which involved an Article 82 prohibition.

[75] *ICI* (n. 69), para. 79.

> Although the foremost reason why producers have acted in this way is in order to adapt themselves to the special features of the market in dyestuffs and to the needs of their customers, the fact remains that the dividing-up of the market which results tends, by fragmenting the effects of competition, to isolate users in their national market, and to prevent a general confrontation between producers throughout the Common Market.[76]

Such fragmentation was taken into account by the Commission in meting out the fines to the undertakings involved,[77] and the Court did not interfere with the amount of the fines. Thus began a lengthy line of cases in which the ECJ stressed the impermissibility of market fragmentation.[78]

Although fragmentation of the market is – in the early jurisprudence of the Commission and Court – the closest legal prohibition found in European law to a per se rule, for an agreement which fragments the market to run afoul of the Article 85 prohibition, it must be captured by that Article's jurisdictional provision that the agreement 'affect trade between Member States'. Agreements which, though they divide markets, have only a *de minimis* effect on inter-state trade are thus not prohibited by that Article.[79]

This early focus on the use of the competition rules to complete the internal market is apparent from the enforcement effort made by the Commission, in spite of its limited resources. Fragmenting the market was seen as the original anti-competitive practice and was to be prosecuted, as condoning that practice would permit activity which if done by Member States would be contrary to the Treaty's provision. In this vein,

76 Ibid., para. 81. 77 See *Dyestuffs* Decision (n. 57), 14–15.

78 See, e.g., Case 48/69 *Imperial Chemical Industries Ltd* v. *Commission* [1972] ECR 619, paras. 115–16; Case 22/78 *Hugin Kassaregister AB* v. *Commission* [1979] ECR 1869, para. 17; Joined Cases 100–103/80 *Musique Diffusion Française SA* v. *Commission* [1983] ECR 1825, para. 86; Joined Cases 25 & 26/84 *Ford Werke AG* v. *Commission* [1985] ECR 2725, para. 16; Case C-185/93 *Bundesanstalt für den Güterfernverkehr* v. *Gebrüder Reiff* [1993] ECR I-5801, para. 22; Case T-62/98 *Volkswagen AG* v. *Commission* [2000] ECR II-2707, para. 174.

79 See Case 5/69 *Völk* v. *Vervaecke* [1969] ECR 295, 302, paras. 5–7:

> Consequently an agreement falls outside the prohibition in Article 85 when it has only an insignificant effect on the markets, taking into account the weak position which the persons concerned have on the market of the product in question. Thus an exclusive dealing agreement, even with absolute territorial protection, may, having regard to the weak position of the persons concerned on the market in the products in question in the area covered by the absolute protection, escape the prohibition laid down in article 85(1).

in its *First Report on Competition Policy*,[80] the Commission indicated that completing the internal market is and must be the paramount emphasis of Community competition policy. In no uncertain terms, it wrote:

> With regard to rules of competition applicable to enterprises, the Community's policy must, in the first place, prevent governmental restrictions and barriers – which have been abolished – from being replaced by similar measures of a private nature. Agreements on quotas as well as agreements for the purpose of dividing the Common Market into regions, or of dividing up or fragmenting markets by other means are in flagrant contradiction to the provisions of the Treaties. Economic integration will never be fully achieved if agreements and concerted practices of this kind are not resolutely opposed. Indeed, they could even prejudice the degree of integration already achieved.[81]

Two pages later, the Commission presented a five-point enumeration of its enforcement priorities. Two of these points deserve our attention:

> The Commission's decisions, the Court's judgments and the communications and regulations concerning the rules of competition applicable to enterprises, all point to certain features of the Community's competition policy which deserve special mention, namely:
>
> 1. Restrictions on competition and practices which jeopardize the unity of the Common Market are proceeded against with special vigour. Cases in point are agreements on market – sharing by dividing areas, agreements to allocate customers, and collective exclusive dealing agreements . . .
> 2. Enterprises engaging in restrictions on competition which are forbidden and who are thereby seriously damaging consumers' interests must expect heavy fines;. . .[82]

It is significant to observe that price-fixing is not mentioned by name, but is merely subsumed into a general category of practices which are antithetical to consumers' interests. The third through fifth priorities were abuse of dominant positions contrary to Article 86, Article 85(3) exemptions for small and medium-sized enterprises (SMEs), and a clear statement that the Commission did not pursue matters which had no appreciable effect on inter-state trade. These latter two points will be discussed below.

The importance of this observation is that the Commission's concern with price-fixing rested on its effect on inter-state trade. Unlike the

[80] Commission, *First Report on Competition Policy.* [81] Ibid., 13. [82] Ibid., 15–16.

American focus or the concerns of those engaged in the micro-economic analysis of competition policy, both of which were described in previous chapters, the Commission appeared to give little thought to the cartelists' appropriation of consumer surplus. Indeed the prefatory remarks to the price-fixing section of the First Report merely state, 'Joint price-fixing of goods sold in the Common Market is also likely to affect adversely trade between Member States and seriously restrict competition.'[83] Remarkably, that Report's discussion of Quinine and Dyestuffs did not mention the increased prices the consumers of those products paid as a result of the arrangements in question.[84] Parenthetically, we note that the only mention of harms done to consumers in that Report was in the discussion of the *Vereeniging van Cementhandelaren*[85] (Dutch Cement Dealer's Association) decision in which the Commission indicated that the elimination of price-fixing of imported and recommended price of domestically produced cement would fail to pass on any competitive advantages to consumers. The Commission made no explicit reference to increased prices paid by consumers of cement products.[86]

The necessity for a practice to have an effect on inter-state trade is a significant jurisdictional requirement of Articles 81–83. As most European enterprises were (and are) SMEs, this is significant as, a fortiori, SMEs would have a difficult time surpassing this threshold. In 1970, the Commission promulgated its first *de minimis* notice.[87] This notice was important, as approximately 90% of the undertakings operating in the Common Market during the 1960s and 1970s would hence be exempted by these provisions.[88] As Buch-Hansen and Wigger note, this was part of the Commission's policy

83 Ibid., 28. 84 Ibid.

85 *Vereeniging van Cementhandelaren* (IV/324 72/22/CEE) [1972] OJ L13/34. The Court dismissed the Association's application to annul the Commission's decision: Case 8/72 *Vereeniging van Cementhandelaren* v. *Commission* [1972] ECR 977, noting, para. 29: 'An agreement extending over the whole of the territory of a Member State by its very nature has the effect of reinforcing the compartmentalization of markets on a national basis, thereby holding up the economic interpenetration which the Treaty is designed to bring about and protecting domestic production.'

86 *First Report* (n. 80), 30: 'Indeed, so long as organized trade maintained a system of fixed prices and, to a certain extent, recommended prices, the advantages which should be passed on to the consumers from competition between manufacturers and importers on the Dutch markets were not likely to materialize.'

87 Communication de la Commission, du 27 mai 1970, concernant les accords d'importance mineure qui ne sont pas visés par les dispositions de l'article 85 paragraphe 1 du traité instituant la Communauté économique européenne [1970] OJ C64/1.

88 Buch-Hansen and Wigger, *The Politics of European Competition Regulation*, 67, citing Bright, 'EU Competition Policy', 540–1.

to promote cooperation among SMEs as a strategy to develop countervailing forces to national champions.[89] When arrangements did have the requisite effect on inter-state trade, the vast majority were cleared.[90]

5.3.2 *Economic crisis and litigation failure: a reformulation of competition policy*

Between 1975 and about 1985, the Commission somewhat altered its focus towards cartel control. The oil crisis of 1973 and the resulting (and ongoing) economic shocks led the Commission to treat crisis cartels with leniency as it noted in its 1982 *Twelfth Report on Competition Policy*.[91] Such lenient treatment was to continue until at least the mid-1990s.[92] However, the economic conditions which give rise to crisis cartels are also breeding grounds for the pernicious sort of cartel. Notwithstanding the lenient treatment accorded to crisis cartels during this time, no such leniency was extended to other types of such arrangements.

As Harding and Joshua observe, although there was little litigation on point, the Commission was nevertheless active in dealing with those pernicious arrangements. Indeed, it was at this time that the Commission developed the Dawn Raid investigative technique, which when combined with relatively unsophisticated means of cartel organisation and record keeping, made obtaining evidence of collusion an easy

[89] Ibid.

[90] Ibid:

> With regard to the agreements requiring EC scrutiny, the Commission allowed the vast majority of the notified deals, either straight away or by granting exemptions under Article 101(3). Almost a third of all cases received exemption, less than 15 per cent of the cases were held to infringe Article 101 and Article 102 of the Treaty, and, until 1970, no fines were imposed.

[91] Commission, *Twelfth Report on Competition Policy*, 45:

> Against this background, and in order to combat the structural problems of individual sectors, the Commission may be able to condone agreements in restraint of competition which relate to a sector as a whole, provided they are aimed solely at achieving a coordinated reduction of overcapacity and do not otherwise restrict free decision-making by the firms involved. The necessary structural reorganization must not be achieved by unsuitable means such as price-fixing or quota agreements, nor should it be hampered by State aids which lead to artificial preservation of surplus capacity.

[92] *Stichting Baksteen* (IV/34.456 94/296/EC) [1994] OJ L131/15.

task.[93] During this time, cartels dealing in spice, vegetable parchment, tobacco, glass, rolled zinc, aluminium, industrial chemicals, roofing felt and wood pulp were prosecuted. Although the vast majority of these were fined (the remainder were mainly ordered to or had terminated their arrangement), few of the Commission's decisions were litigated.[94]

While cartel prosecution was to continue administratively with vigour in the latter half of the 1980s,[95] the relative tranquillity in European cartel litigation was to end in the late 1980s. A series of four cases (the litigation of which would not end until 2002), which involved the Wood Pulp (litigated twice),[96] PVC,[97] Soda Ash,[98] and Italian Flat Glass[99] industries would demonstrate fault lines in the Commission's strategy. Of these four cases, only the first *Wood Pulp* case could be regarded as a victory for the Commission.

In that case, the Commission's victory consisted in establishing that the Treaty provisions had extra-territorial application, when the activities of an undertaking located outside the EC had an effect on the common market.[100] Notwithstanding this victory, the matter was returned to the Court of First Instance (CFI) for consideration of the evidence. When it reappeared before the Court of Justice some four-and-a-half years later, the Commission's evidence was found wanting.[101] A similar conclusion was drawn by the CFI in *Italian Flat Glass*.[102] The *PVC* and *Soda Ash* matters involved procedural twists resulting in defeat for the Commission. Harding and Joshua summarise the results: 'By now the Commission was feeling strongly frustrated. Most of these cases produced clear evidence of collusion, while the decisions and fines were being wholly or largely overturned on procedural grounds in a context of developing procedural law.'[103]

[93] Harding and Joshua (n. 1), 130–2. [94] See ibid.

[95] Under the direction of Commissioner Peter Southerland (1985–89), the Competition Commission was to promote trade among Member States by challenging industrial policy regarding state aid, reducing state monopolies and combating (at the administrative level) cartels: see Buch-Hansen and Wigger (n. 88), 80–1.

[96] Joined Cases C-89/85, C-104/85, C-114/85, C-116/85, C-117/85 and C-125–9/85 *Ahlström Oy et al.* v. *Commission* [1988] ECR 5193 ('*Woodpulp I*') and Joined Cases C-89/85, C-104/85, C-114/85, C-116/85, C-117/85 and C-125–9/85 *Ahlström Oy et al.* v. *Commission* [1993] ECR I-1307 ('*Woodpulp II*').

[97] Case C-137/92P *Commission* v. *BASF et al.* [1994] ECR I-2555.

[98] Case T-30/91 *Solvay et al.* v. *Commission* [1995] ECR II-1775.

[99] Case T-68/99 *Società Italiano Vetro et al.* v. *Commission* [1992] ECR II-1552.

[100] *Wood Pulp I* (n. 96) 5243. [101] *Wood Pulp II* (n. 96), paras. 126–7.

[102] *Italian Flat Glass* (n. 99) at para. 265. [103] Harding and Joshua (n. 1), 137.

Concurrently with the frustration of the final decade of the twentieth century, would be the increased reliance on (and later need for) economic analysis on the part of the Commission. At the vanguard of this was the 1996 Green Paper on Vertical Restraints,[104] which – according to Georgio Monti – was the Commission's 'first serious and sustained attempt to deploy economic analysis to competition law'.[105] The reliance on detailed economic analysis would soon become a new hallmark of Commission competition policy, due to the personal focus (and influence) of Competition Commissioners Van Miert, (Mario) Monti and Kroes, and out of necessity due to the frustration resulting from the Commission's lack of success in its litigation before the European Courts.

This frustration almost certainly reached a boiling point in June 2002, with the CFI's *Airtours*[106] decision. This case involved a challenge to the Commission's decision to prohibit a merger between two UK package holiday operators. In annulling the Commission's Decision, the court was critical of the Commission's economic evidence, and voiced this in no uncertain terms:

> In the light of all of the foregoing, the Court concludes that the Decision, far from basing its prospective analysis on cogent evidence, is vitiated by a series of errors of assessment as to factors fundamental to any assessment of whether a collective dominant position might be created. It follows that the Commission prohibited the transaction without having proved to the requisite legal standard that the concentration would give rise to a collective dominant position of the three major tour operators, of such a kind as significantly to impede effective competition in the relevant market.[107]

The CFI voiced similar criticism of the Commission's reasoning in two other cases later that summer.[108] As part of the effort to solve the lack of thoroughness of the evidence mustered before the court in cartel and merger cases, the Commission would be to turn to micro-economic analysis in an attempt to utilise that discipline's tools to provide the required rigour.

The office of Chief Competition Economist was created in July 2003. The creation of this office was not the only reform to the EC's competition

[104] Green Paper on Vertical Restraints COM (1996) 721 final (22 January 1997).
[105] Monti, *EC Competition Law*, 82.
[106] Case T-342/99 *Airtours* v. *Commission* [2002] ECR II-2585. [107] Ibid., para. 294.
[108] Case T-310/01 *Schneider Electric SA* v. *Commission* [2002] ECR II-4071 (*Schneider/Legrand*) and Cases T-502 and T-80/02 *Tetra Laval* v. *Commission* [2002] ECR II-4381 (*Tetra Laval/Sidel*).

regime during the first years of the twenty-first century. Similar reforms came with revised regulations concerning mergers[109] and rules regarding the application of (the then) Articles 81 and 82 of the Treaty.[110] It was not merely the lack of analytical rigour which led to the reform; rather it was a confluence of factors which led to such reform. These factors also included the Commission's mergers and Article 81 notification/enforcement workload, which required a reprioritisation of its administrative responsibilities, and it would be unfair to discount the personal interests and influence of Karel Van Miert and Mario Monti, the Commissioners responsible for Competition between 1993 and 2004. The accession of ten new Member States on 1 May 2004 would therefore provide a convenient terminus a quo from which a new (or 'modern' competition) regime could emerge – if not an additional reason for reform.

5.3.3 *Economic analysis, modernisation and the shift to consumer welfare*

Discussions of reform to the implementation of Articles 85 and 86 (and, in addition, the Merger Control regime) began in the late 1990s.[111] The Commission's workload considerations were cited in the discussions of potential reform[112] and the imminent expansion of the EC was also viewed to be a consideration.[113] In the White Paper on Modernisation, the Commission indicated its sensitivities towards the competition culture of countries which would soon become Member States:

> The enlargement of the Community will also make it necessary to strengthen competition policy with regard to cartels and abuses of dominant positions. Dominant positions held by undertakings which inherited state monopolies are particularly numerous in the applicant countries, and such undertakings might be tempted to abuse those positions so as to make up for their lack of economic competitiveness. The tradition of the planned economy

[109] Council Regulation (EC) No. 139/2004 of 20 January 2004 on the control of concentrations between undertakings (the EC Merger Regulation).

[110] Council Regulation (EC) No. 1/2003 of 16 December 2002 on the implementation of the rules on competition laid down in Articles 81 and 82 of the Treaty.

[111] See, e.g., European Commission, White Paper on Modernisation of the Rules Implementing Articles 85 and 86 of the EC Treaty Commission Programme No. 99/027 (Brussels, 28.04.1999) ('White Paper'); and European Commission, Green Paper on the Review of Council Regulation (EEC) No. 4064/89 COM (2001) 745 final ('Green Paper Merger').

[112] Green Paper Merger, ibid., 7, White Paper, ibid., 13–16.

[113] Green Paper Merger, ibid., White Paper, ibid., 8.

> is also a potential danger inasmuch as it encouraged agreements between 'competitors'. Any proposal to amend the competition rules of procedure must take account of the fact that those countries, with administrative structures that are still not very familiar with the concepts of market and free enterprise, will have to apply them as part of the 'acquis communautaire'. The enlargement will also have a mechanical effect in increasing the number of restrictive practices and abuses of dominant positions potentially subject to Community law. In a European Union with more than 20 Member States, the rules for implementing Articles 85 and 86 must be modernised if competition policy is to continue to operate efficiently.[114]

The Modernisation Package included reforms to merger law, and included a new Regulation 1/2003 to better enforce Articles 81 and 82.[115] The significance of this Regulation was to give direct effect to Articles 81 and 82 of the Treaty, and to remove the notification requirement replacing notification with a requirement for self-assessment by undertakings contemplating arrangements which may fall within the provisions of Article 81. Further, that Regulation also included provisions governing cooperation between the Commission and the National Competition Authorities (NCAs) and the Commission and the courts of Member States. The former would serve as the basis of the legal foundation for the European Competition Network, and both provisions were fleshed-out by subsequent Commission notices.[116]

In 2002 the Commission also promulgated revisions to its leniency policy.[117] The original 1996 policy[118] provided for leniency (a 75 to 100% reduction in fine) for the first firm to provide useful evidence (subject to certain conditions) of cartel activity.[119] Though space constraints preclude a detailed discussion of the history or development of the European leniency programme[120] it would be fair to say that the efficacy of the Commission's original programme was limited by uncertainties as

114 White Paper, ibid., 8.

115 Space considerations preclude further discussion of the development of the EU's merger rules. See, e.g., Goyder and Albors-Llorens (n. 64), 384–98 for such a discussion.

116 Commission notice on the co-operation between the Commission and the courts of the EU Member States in the application of Articles 81 and 82 EC [2004] OJ C101/54; Commission notice on cooperation within the network of competition authorities [2004] OJ C101/43.

117 Commission notice on immunity from fines and reduction of fines in cartel cases [2002] OJ C45/3.

118 Commission notice on the non-imposition or reduction of fines in cartel cases; the US DOJ takes credit for its leniency programme being the inspiration of the Commission's programme. See Hammond, 'The Evolution of Criminal Antitrust Enforcement'.

119 See ibid., Part B.

120 See, e.g., Harding and Joshua (n. 1), 241–9.

to how the Commission's fining policy would be applied in a particular case,[121] the fact that the Commission's practice was to grant reductions in (as opposed to immunity from) fines, and doubts as to the likelihood of detection.[122] Indeed, as the results of Chapter 3 indicate,[123] these fines more likely had the effect of a licensing fee, rather than a deterrent. If the objective behind a leniency programme is to exploit the prisoner's dilemma nature of the cartel members' relationship, this version was not fit for purpose.

The 2002 revisions represented little improvement, as Harding and Joshua correctly note: 'The new [2002] leniency programme therefore appeared to be as much of a playground for Prisoner's Dilemma calculations as its predecessor.'[124] While this notice offered full immunity for the first cartel member to provide the Commission with evidence that it theretofore did not possess which would provide grounds for a 'dawn raid',[125] runners-up in the leniency race to the Commission could have their fines reduced.[126] However, by couching the leniency conditions in vague terms such as 'submit evidence which in the Commission's view may enable it to carry out an investigation'[127] or 'the evidence ... represented significant added value',[128] the Commission failed to specify with the requisite degree of precision what may be expected from an undertaking seeking leniency, turning what should have been a rational calculation into a guessing game. And, again, negligible fines with a low probability of detection reduced the risk to a business expense.

[121] Although the Commission attempted to clarify the fining policy with guidelines published in January 1998 (Guidelines on the method of setting fines imposed pursuant to Article 15(2) of Regulation No. 17 and Article 65(5) of the ECSC Treaty), these standards were nevertheless vague. As such, when read alongside the leniency policy, the package of the two could hardly be viewed as coherent, contrary to the Commission's statement that 'The two instruments form a whole, which the Commission considers will make its policy in this field more effective, more coherent and more clear.' *Twenty-Seventh Report on Competition Policy*, 29–30. The fining guidelines have subsequently been revised: Guidelines on the method of setting fines imposed pursuant to Article 23(2)(a) of Regulation No. 1/2003; but again, except for fixing reference points for base amounts of fines and providing an enumeration of aggravating and mitigating factors, these revised Guidelines provide little information which could allow for a precise calculation of liability and hence a decision as to the rationality of applying for leniency.

[122] See Harding and Joshua (n. 1), 242. [123] See pp. 97–101, above.

[124] Harding and Joshua (n. 1), 243.

[125] Put formally, an investigation pursuant to Article 14(3)–(6) of Regulation 17/62.

[126] 2002 Notice (n. 117), para. 23. [127] Ibid., para. 8(a). [128] Ibid., para. 23(a).

The 2006 leniency notice[129] somewhat improved the situation by not only establishing a procedural mechanism to facilitate the application process[130] but also setting out with greater clarity the Commission's expectations from a leniency applicant.[131]

Additionally, during the last five years of the twentieth century and the first two years of the twenty-first, the Commission would be involved with the prosecution of three significant international cartels: amino-acids (lysine),[132] vitamins[133] and citric acid.[134] The Commission's investigation of these spun out the American investigations which resulted in criminal indictments of the same cartels.[135] While the Commission may not have been the first agency to unearth and prosecute such behaviour, the Commission was able to impose apparently large fines on the undertakings involved.[136]

In addition to their publicity value, its imposition of such fines in cartel cases would permit the Commission to stress the value of competition policy to consumers. In the 2001 *Report on Competition Policy* this value was explicitly stated in terms of consumer welfare: 'In 2001 a series of cartel decisions highlighted the sustained effort by the Commission to tackle flagrantly anti-competitive behaviour by undertakings in a wide range of sectors. These decisions provide evidence of the direct impact of competition policy on consumer welfare . . .'[137]

This new emphasis on hard-core cartel activity, its effect on consumers, and attempts to deter it through large fines can be seen in the rapid increase in fines meted out by the Commission in response to activity prohibited by Article 101. According to the Commission's findings regarding cartel fines, published in June 2012,[138] during the ten-year period 1990–99, cartel fines amounted to just over €832.5 million. In the following *five* years (2000–04), the amount of fines nearly quadrupled to

[129] Commission Notice on Immunity from fines and reduction of fines in cartel cases; this was based on the ECN's model leniency programme.

[130] Ibid., paras. 14–22, 27–30. [131] Ibid., paras. 8–13, 31–5.

[132] *Amino Acids* (Case COMP/36.545/F) [2000] OJ L152/24.

[133] *Vitamins* (COMP/E-1/37.512) [2003] OJ L6/1.

[134] *Citric Acid* (COMP/E-1/36 604) [2002] OJ L239/18.

[135] See, e.g., our discussion of the Commission cartel investigations, above, p. 156 but compare them with the results of American enforcement, p. 196.

[136] Indeed, as of June 2012 the total fine in the vitamin cartel (€790.5 million) remains the fourth largest fine imposed on a group of undertakings for cartel activity by the Commission, and Hoffman La Roche's fine for their participation in that cartel (€462 million) remains the second largest fine imposed on an individual undertaking for such behaviour.

[137] *Thirty-First Report on Competition Policy*, 11. [138] Above, n. 136.

€3.6 billion. In 2005–09 that amount exceeded €9.64 billion. Fines in the first two-and-a-half years of the present decade have exceeded €3.88 billion. While these figures are not adjusted to take into account reductions by the Courts, these amounts are consistent with Commissioners Monti,[139] Kroes[140] and Almunia's[141] statements regarding the pernicious effects of cartel behaviour on consumer welfare.[142]

5.3.4 *Is consumer welfare the sole standard?*

However, in spite of this recent emphasis by the Commission on consumer welfare, it is simply incorrect to regard consumer welfare as the sole standard by which EU law now weighs competitive and anti-competitive effects of an agreement. First, the practice and statements of the Commission belie this; second, the Courts' interpretation of competition policy takes account of values other than consumer welfare; and, third, the European Treaties, particularly in their most recent manifestation of the Lisbon Treaty, emphasise multiple values which must be considered alongside the Union's competition regime.[143]

First, in addition to the abovementioned consideration of consumer welfare, the Commission has repeatedly taken other criteria into account in assessing arrangements for consistency with Article 101. Considerations of employment were (in part) accepted by the Commission as part of an

[139] Monti, 'Competition enforcement and consumers': 'It is my firm conviction that when competitive forces are at play, consumers will take the main benefit. Producers make greater efforts to attract customers by offering them lower prices, higher quality and better service than when the market is controlled by a cartel, a monopolist or a handful of companies.'

[140] See her remarks quoted on p. 2, above and n. 142, below.

[141] Almunia, 'Competition policy for innovation and growth':

> Yes, I hear some voices recommending that we should go a bit softer on companies in these lean years. But I have a completely different opinion.
>
> Anti-competitive behaviour imposes a hidden cost on consumers and on the companies that play by the rules and neither can afford this extra cost during a downturn.
>
> We must strengthen our vigilance because when a company breaks competition law it undermines the efforts of regulators to build more efficient markets; it saps the energy of our economy and ultimately slows our progress towards the recovery.

[142] Neelie Kroes' statement on 15 September 2005 (European Competition day) that 'Consumer welfare is now well established as the standard the Commission applies' underscores this emphasis on consumer welfare: Kroes, 'European Competition Policy'.

[143] On this point, see Hodge, 'Compatible or Conflicting', 112–14.

orderly restructuring of the Dutch brick industry, due to its overcapacity.[144] It noted:

> A social plan for the sector has been negotiated with the trade unions, the implementation of which is to be monitored by Stichting Baksteen. The parties will endeavour to ensure that, in carrying out the restructuring operation, employees are redeployed wherever possible and in accordance with the legal and/or contractual obligations in force in the Netherlands.[145]

In exempting the restructuring under then Article 85(3), the Commission recognised the social and employment advantages of what would have otherwise been a straightforward output restriction/quota cartel.

The Commission has considered environmental concerns as countervailing concerns to possibly anti-competitive behaviour (and presumably will continue to do so). In 2000, the Commission granted an Article 81(3) exemption to the *Conseil Européen de la Construction d'Appareils Domestiques* (*CECED* – The European Association of Manufacturers of Domestic Appliances) to approve an industry-wide agreement to phase out the production of inefficient washing machines, and replace them with 'greener', more efficient (and expensive) appliances. Although consumers may recoup the additional cost of the new machines over time (in the form of reduced electrical consumption), such savings were not determinative. After a 'back of the envelope' calculation of the marginal damage resulting from electricity production (carbon dioxide and sulphur dioxide emissions), the Commission concluded:

> On the basis of reasonable assumptions, the benefits to society brought about by the CECED agreement appear to be more than seven times greater than the increased purchase costs of more energy-efficient washing machines. Such environmental results for society would adequately allow consumers a fair share of the benefits even if no benefits accrued to individual purchasers of machines.[146]

The final sentence of the Commission's remarks quoted clearly signify its willingness to take into consideration values other than consumer welfare in its assessment of agreements.

CECED should not be viewed as an anomaly; rather it is probably best viewed as an extension of (and potentially weakening the strictness of)

[144] *Stichting Baksteen* (n. 92).
[145] Ibid., para. 12. See also the Commission's statements in the *Twelfth Report on Competition Policy* (n. 91), points 38–41.
[146] *CECED* (Case IV.F.1/36.718) [2000] OJ L187/47.

the Commission's reasoning in the *Vereniging van Onafhankelijke Tankopslag Bedrijven (VOTOB)* matter in which the Commission recognised the need for industry-wide cooperation to reduce negative externalities (here chemical vapour emissions), yet was critical of a fixed, uniform 'environmental charge' imposed by the six undertakings involved, as the fixed nature of such charges went beyond 'what is necessary to achieve that goal, to the detriment of competition'.[147]

Furthermore, market integration remains an important focus of the Commission's statements, if not its energies. The 2011 *Report on Competition Policy*, in discussing the Commission's investigation of Telefónica and Portugal Telecom,[148] noted:

> The completion of the single market cannot become a reality if companies conclude agreements to share the market along national borders. Agreements which include noncompete clauses put the integration of the single market at risk. The Commission thus sent a Statement of Objections to Telefónica and to Portugal Telecom, as the companies had agreed not to compete on their respective telecommunications markets within the Iberian Peninsula.[149]

Such activities and recent statements significantly undermine the suggestion that consumer welfare is now the Commission's sole focus.

Further, even if the Commission were to focus exclusively on consumer welfare as the goal of Union competition policy (or as the exclusive underlying value protected by Article 81), such a focus runs counter to the jurisprudence of the Court of Justice. In the recent *GlaxoSmithKline* case which considered the anti-competitive nature of restrictions on parallel trade, the Court of Justice rebuked the CFI for reasoning in this manner. In no uncertain terms, the Court held:

> With respect to the Court of First Instance's statement that, while it is accepted that an agreement intended to limit parallel trade must in principle be considered to have as its object the restriction of competition, that applies in so far as it may be presumed to deprive final consumers of the advantages of effective competition in terms of supply or price, the Court notes that neither the wording of Article 81(1) EC nor the case-law lend support to such a position.

[147] *Twelfth Report on Competition Policy* (n. 91) at paras 177–86: the quotation is from para. 177.

[148] Case COMP/39839 *Telefónica and Portugal Telecom*.

[149] Communication from the Commission to the European Parliament, the Council, the European Economic and Social Committee and the Committee of the Regions, *Report on Competition Policy 2011*, 17.

> First of all, there is nothing in that provision to indicate that only those agreements which deprive consumers of certain advantages may have an anti-competitive object. Secondly, it must be borne in mind that the Court has held that, like other competition rules laid down in the Treaty, Article 81 EC aims to protect not only the interests of competitors or of consumers, but also the structure of the market and, in so doing, competition as such. Consequently, for a finding that an agreement has an anti-competitive object, it is not necessary that final consumers be deprived of the advantages of effective competition in terms of supply or price . . .
>
> It follows that, by requiring proof that the agreement entails disadvantages for final consumers as a prerequisite for a finding of anti-competitive object and by not finding that that agreement had such an object, the Court of First Instance committed an error of law.[150]

The Court noted that case law since *Consten and Grundig* requires one to view the values protected by Article 101 as extending beyond the exclusive protection of consumer welfare.

Additionally, the European Treaties set out competition as one among a number of values to be promoted by the (now) Union. Prior to the Lisbon Treaty (which came into effect on 1 December 2009) the two constituent Treaties of the EU (the Treaty Establishing the European Community (TEC) and the Treaty on European Union (TEU)) spoke obliquely about the role of competition within the Union. Although Articles 81–86 of the TEC are the Community's competition provisions, in addressing the principles of the European Community, the TEC mentions a 'high degree of competitiveness and convergence of economic performance' in Article 2. This is done in the context of other community goals which include 'a high level of employment and social protection', along with matters such as environmental protection, a 'high level of employment and social protection', and raising the standard of living. Article 3 TEC then mentions as one of twenty-one activities of the Community 'a system ensuring that competition in the internal market is not distorted'. Other such activities include environmental policy, common agricultural and fisheries policy, and coordination of employment policy.

In setting out the objectives of the Union, Article 2 of the TEU does not mention competition. Rather it discusses 'an area without internal frontiers, through the strengthening of economic and social cohesion

[150] Joined Cases C-501, C-513, C-515 and C-519/06 *GlaxoSmithKline Services* v. *Commission* [2009] ECR I-9291, [62]–[64].

and through the establishment of economic and monetary union . . .'. It is fair to state that both Treaties, then, set out a multiplicity of goals for the European enterprise, with competition policy being among them. It is a matter of academic debate, to which we need not at present enter, whether or not this multiplicity of goals sets out a hierarchy, and, if so, where in this hierarchy competition policy's place is.[151] What is clear, however, is that even if, *arguendo*, the promotion of consumer welfare is taken as the sole goal of EU competition policy, other values can and almost certainly *should* be taken into account in assessing particular arrangements for consistency under Article 81(3).

However, with the Lisbon Treaty coming into force in December 2009, it would not be unreasonable to state that this date marks a change for the goals emphasised by European competition policy. The structure of the Lisbon Treaty shows that competition policy is now (at best) 'one among equals' or more likely, a less equal value, where some values are 'more equal than others'. If anything, competition is certainly not *primus inter pares*.

The Lisbon Treaty is an amending treaty, which – in structure – necessarily piggy-backs on the existing Treaties. The two Treaties (the TEU and the former TEC, now renamed the Treaty on the Functioning of the European Union (TFEU)) are accorded equal legal value.[152] The TEU makes no reference to competition.[153] Rather, Article 3(3) provides:

> The Union shall establish an internal market. It shall work for the sustainable development of Europe based on balanced economic growth and price stability, a highly competitive social market economy, aiming at full employment and social progress, and a high level of protection and improvement of the quality of the environment. It shall promote scientific and technological advance.[154]

Additionally, the TFEU omits the twenty-one 'activities of the Community' enumerated in Article 3 of the (former) TEC, of which a system ensuring that competition is not distorted is one.[155] These new amendments are significant.

First, it is well known that the deletion of the reference to undistorted competition was done at the insistence of the French delegation[156] to (it

[151] See, e.g., Townley, *Article 81 and Public Policy*, 48, Odudu, *The Boundaries of EC Competition Law*, Monti, 'Article 81 EC and Public Policy', and Hodge (n. 143).
[152] TEU Article 1. [153] See TEU, passim, and Hodge (n. 143), 104.
[154] TEU Article 3(3). [155] TEC Article 3(1)(g).
[156] See, e.g., Van Rompuy, 'The Impact of the Lisbon Treaty', 2.

was to be hoped) rid the Treaties of an Anglo-Saxon vision of competition as an end in itself. In celebrating this achievement, the then French President Sarkozy remarked, 'We have obtained a major reorientation of the objectives of the Union. Competition is no longer an objective of the Union, or an end in itself, but a means to serve the internal market.'[157]

Second, and more significantly, Article 3(3) speaks of a 'social market economy'. This phrase is at minimum 'code' for, if not a direct reference to, an ordoliberal vision of the economy, and its resulting conception of competition and market structure. This is particularly evident when the phrase is read in the context of the other Union values detailed in that Article.

However, notwithstanding this deletion of reference to undistorted competition in the Lisbon Treaty proper, Protocol 27, appended to (and forming an integral part of) the Treaties[158] states:

> THE HIGH CONTRACTING PARTIES,
>
> CONSIDERING that the internal market as set out in Article 3 of the Treaty on European Union includes a system ensuring that competition is not distorted,
>
> HAVE AGREED that:
>
> To this end, the Union shall, if necessary, take action under the provisions of the Treaties, including under Article 352 of the Treaty on the Functioning of the European Union.[159]

As Van Rompuy notes, the reference to Article 352, *inter alia*, preserves the Union's competency in merger control.[160]

The incorporation of a reference to undistorted competition into Protocol 27 may alleviate concerns that the omission from the new TFEU of (former) Article 3(1)(g) of the TEC may eviscerate Union competition policy, or at least relegate it into the class of 'also rans'. These concerns are particularly germane given the reliance which the European Courts have placed on this provision (and its predecessors) in considering competition policy since (at least) the *Continental Can*[161] decision to (the relatively

157 Ibid. (Van Rompuy's translation). In the original: '*Nous avons obtenu une réorientation majeure des objectifs de L'Union. La concurrence n'est plus un objectif de l'Union ou un fin en soi, mais un moyen au service du marché intérieur.*'

158 TEU Article 51; see Case C-496/09 *Italy* v. *Commission* NYR (17 November 2011), para. 60.

159 Protocol No. 27 on the internal market and competition [2008] OJ C115/309.

160 Van Rompuy (n. 156), 3.

161 Case C-6/72 *Europemballage Corporation and Continental Can Company Inc.* v. *Commission* [1973] ECR 215, para. 22.

recent) *Sot. Lelos kai Sia EE* v. *GlaxoSmithKline*.[162] Further concerns about the new place of competition policy in the post-Lisbon regime arise from the new policy-linking provision of TFEU Article 7[163] and the possibility that the provisions of TFEU Article 173(1) (formerly TEC Article 157(1)) on cooperation between undertakings and (potential) favouritism of small and medium-sized enterprises may be taken to account in balancing Treaty objectives.

However, as Hodge rightly points out,[164] Article 7 is merely a codification of existing case law.[165] Further, nothing new is added to the Treaties by Article 173. So until the ECJ is faced with deciding a case which squarely pits some competition policy objective against another value enumerated in the Treaties, it would be speculative to suggest the precise role that competition plays within the post-Lisbon regime. What is not speculation, though, is that competition is merely one of the goals advanced in this new regime. It is also not speculation to suggest that it had never been a goal in itself, nor that in assessing the values protected through a vigorous competition regime, consumer welfare was (or is) primary.

A reading of the Lisbon Treaty and its predecessors demonstrates that the Union (and its predecessors) always has had multiple values: competition is merely one of these. As Townley notes, the competition provisions of the Lisbon Treaty are 'part of a web of inter-related Treaty articles',[166] which set up a 'hierarchy' among the articles mediated

[162] Cases C-468/06 to C-478/06 *Sot. Lelos kai Sia EE et al.* v. *GlaxoSmithKline AEVE* [2008] ECR I-7139, para. 49; see also, e.g., Case C-240/83 *Procureur de la République* v. *ADBHU* [1985] ECR 531, para. 9; Case T-83/91 *Tetra Pak International SA* v. *Commission* [1994] ECR II-755, para. 114; Case C-126/97 *Eco Swiss China Time Ltd* v. *Benetton International NV* [1999] ECR I-3055, para. 36; Case C-453/99 *Courage Ltd* v. *Crehan* [2001] ECR I-6297, para. 20; Case C-289/04P *Showa Denko KK* v. *Commission* [2006] ECR I-5859, para. 55; Case C-308/94 *SGL Carbon* v. *Commission* [2006] ECR I-5977, para. 31; Cases T-217/03 and T-245/03 *FNCBV et al.* v. *Commission* [2006] II-4987, para. 97; Case T-25/04 *González y Díez SA* v. *Commission* [2007] ECR II-3121, para. 55; Case T-69/04 *Schunk GmbH and Schunk Kohlenstoff-Technik GmbH* v. *Commission* [2008] ECR II-2567, para. 207.

[163] TFEU Article 7: 'The Union shall ensure consistency between its policies and activities, taking all of its objectives into account and in accordance with the principle of conferral of powers.'

[164] Hodge (n. 143), 107.

[165] Hodge, ibid., cites Case C-233/94 *Federal Republic of Germany* v. *European Parliament* [1997] ECR I-2441, para. 48 and Case C-379/99 *PreussenElektra AG on the Interpretation of Article 30 of the EC Treaty* [2001] ECR I-2159, paras. 76–81 in support of this proposition.

[166] Townley (n. 151), 48.

by policy-clauses.[167] Ultimately, this suggests – almost certainly correctly – a regime of values with some being more paramount than others. Hodge suggests – again, almost certainly correctly – that Article 3 TFEU appears to enumerate those values at the top of the pyramid.[168] If these authors are correct, a 'social market economy' (as opposed to unstrained competition) along with values such as employment, social progress and environmental quality are near the top of this hierarchy.

Likewise, the predecessors to the Lisbon Treaty were very similar webs.[169] The values which these earlier Treaties contained were similarly linked by both explicit linking clauses and by the case law of the ECJ. As Hodge notes, 'Those who believe in the sole consumer welfare goal for EU competition law must argue that Article 101 should be read in isolation from the rest of the Treaty because the TFEU insists on the inclusion of multiple goals.'[170] Hodge's point is equally as valid with regard to the Lisbon Treaty's predecessors. It can also be extended to caution against reading Article 101(3) narrowly, and in isolation, so that that Article is taken to refer only to consumer welfare and not to other values which promote 'economic progress' and confer a 'fair share to consumers'.[171] In fact, the Commission itself may be a deserving candidate for censure on this point.[172]

5.4 Conclusion

At this point, it is useful to reflect upon the quotation from Harding and Joshua with which this chapter opened. The phrase 'ambiguity of purpose' is certainly appropriate to describe the EU's competition policy since the Treaty of Rome, for it well describes the multiple goals which the Commission faced in discharging its mandate under (now) Articles 101 and 102 of the Treaty. These goals were (and are) economic – in an extended sense – and non-economic, the latter including considerations such as environment. In advancing what it viewed to be the goals inherent

[167] Ibid. [168] Hodge (n. 143), 105.

[169] The main difference is the substitution of the values listed in TFEU Article 3 for the twenty-one values found in Article 3(1) of the TEC.

[170] Hodge (n. 143), 105.

[171] These possibly include employment (viewing the consumer as a provider of labour) and environmental protection (see, e.g., the Commission's reasoning in *CECED*, n. 146). On this point, cf Hodge (n. 143), 131 and Faull and Nikpay, *EC Law of Competition*, 295.

[172] See Guidelines on the application of Article 81(3) of the Treaty, para. 34: 'The aim of the Community competition rules is to protect competition on the market as a means of enhancing consumer welfare and of ensuring an efficient allocation of resources.'

in (now) Article 101, the Commission organised its priorities to deal with those issues which it found of most pressing need, as would be the responsible choice of any agency whose resources were scarce. And, given the burdens placed on the Commission by the notification regime of Regulation 17/62, these resources as they were devoted (if not overstretched) to the notification process were scarce indeed.

To answer one of Harding and Joshua's questions, 'why has it come about?' we get little help in examining the pre-history of the Treaty of Rome, but can obtain some insight from the early days of Europe's competition enforcement scheme. If anything, the analysis of the influences which led to the Treaty of Rome results in an ambiguous conclusion. We certainly know the American authorities had the Sherman Act in mind when they looked at the cartelised nature of the inter-war industrial fabric of Europe (and particularly Germany). A strong antitrust regime, in the style of that Act, would assist in preventing the organisation of industry in a manner which could easily be evolved into a war machine. We also know that those listening to the American authorities were adherents to ordoliberal views, which viewed with grave suspicion the inordinate concentration of power – whether public or private – in the market, and viewed that as an affront to freedom of the individual. Yet, at the same time, both 'sides' were recognising the merits of integrating the economies of Europe. Not only would integration confer immediate economic benefit, but it also would facilitate a lasting peace.

If we look at the Commission's early use of its powers under Article 85 (and Regulation 17/62) we can obtain more of an answer to this latter question. Market integration was the Commission's initial focus of Article 101 (then 85) enforcement. We glean some insight from the litigation history of *Consten and Grundig*, the first significant competition decision of the European Court. The notification system disclosed the very existence of the imputed arrangement, and the Court backed the Commission in holding that as market integration was among the goals of the Treaty, it would be incongruous to permit parties to privately engage in market-dividing practices which would be prohibited if public bodies were to so do. In many respects, *Consten and Grundig* was a serendipitous discovery for the Commission: what better means to achieve the common market goal of market integration than prohibiting the arrangements in this case, then using the subsequent litigation as a test case. However, as this was a notified decision, only the legality of the private arrangements (and not a fine) was at stake in the resulting litigation.

Similarly, the first significant cartels prosecuted by the Commission – *Quinine* and *Dyestuffs* – were also, to a large extent, chance finds. The US authorities informally provided the Commission with information about the existence of the Quinine cartel, which the Commission was able to use as a foundation for its own investigation. In Dyestuffs, the preliminary information resulted from complaints from the customers' trade association. In both cases, after a protracted investigation the Commission was able to impose punitive fines which were upheld by the court (albeit with some fine tuning of the amount) after litigation.

It is unsurprising that others reported the existence of these clandestine cartels to the Commission: once only assumes that, unlike the case of *Consten and Grundig*, the Quinine producers and Dyestuffs manufacturers knew their agreements would fall afoul of Article 85. The need to rely on such sources for information is an ongoing difficulty in detecting any hidden activity, and not just this sort of collusion. The history of cartel control throughout the world shows this need for authorities to acquire this sort of information. This need is a constant in any enforcement scheme, and not just a European phenomenon. Indeed, out of this need to obtain this type of information and drawing on the successes of the US DOJ, the Commission adopted a leniency programme which since its inception has evolved into being the primary source for intelligence regarding the existence and activities of Europe's cartels.

What is also not surprising is that the early cartels tackled by the Commission, in addition to having a price-fixing (or price discrimination) effect, also involved market fragmentation. This fragmentation took the form of explicit territorial restrictions (*Consten and Grundig* and *Quinine*) and the more subtle approach of not dealing to other members' customers (*Dyestuffs* and – to a great extent – *Quinine*). In the early environment of enforcing the Treaty, completing the internal market was a priority. Given that these cartels involved price-fixing plus, their doubly offensive character made them particularly deserving targets for the Commission's enforcement activity.

Completing the internal market, and hence the eradication of practices – whether the result of public or private activity – which fragmented the market, was apparently the Commission's main goal (or at least predominant among its goals) during the early days of its anti-cartel enforcement activities. However, the recent twenty-five or so years have witnessed a subtle shift away from this goal towards a new goal of protecting consumer welfare. Any identification of the reasons for this shift is speculative. The shift could be due to viewing the internal market as completed, it could be due to adopting a more 'Chicago-style' approach to the goals of (and analytic methods used in) antitrust, it could be a means of demonstrating to European citizens (particularly in the newer Member States) the value of a strong competition regime, or it could be a result of the personalities and personal agendas of those driving the process. It is most likely that all of these factors (and possibly others) contribute to the explanation.

Protecting consumer welfare has recently become the Commission's ostensive exclusive goal of anti-cartel, if not antitrust, enforcement. While, as we have seen, statements from the Commission indicate the aim of the EU's competition rules is to protect consumer welfare, these statements are rather hyperbolic. The Commission's practice has also been, when appropriate, to consider non-consumer welfare enhancing aspects of potentially anti-competitive agreements, and to take these effects into account. The *Stichting Bakseen* and *CECED* decisions well illustrate this point. Indeed, the 'back of the envelope' reasoning found in *CECED* well demonstrates the extent to which the Commission will – should it so choose – prefer other sorts of considerations, at the expense of consumer welfare.

Further this myopic view of the Commission (and others) towards consumer welfare is neither sustained by a close reading of the Treaties nor by the case law of the ECJ. The Treaties, as we noted, set out a number of goals for the EU. Competition is merely one of these goals: and it is certainly not first among equals – and post-Lisbon, it may even be less equal than others. With these multiple Treaty goals in mind, it is difficult to fathom why the protection of consumer welfare should be viewed as the completion regime's exclusive goal. Accordingly, the ECJ was right in its rebuke of the CFI and Commission, when it recently held that it was improper to focus only on this aim of the competition rules.

The inexorable conclusion, then, is that the EU competition regime is multifaceted. However, this conclusion compels us to inquire whether, given the multiple goals of the regime, the regime is amenable to the use of criminal sanctions to achieve its goals. Specifically, we must consider whether thwarting any of the goals of the EU's competition regime is deserving of the sort of censure meted out by criminal law. An equivalent way of stating this is to ask if the harms protected by the EU's competition regime are sufficiently fundamental to deserve the protection of the criminal law.

The sceptical conclusion which we must draw is that these values are insufficiently fundamental to be protected by criminal sanctions. The two key values are market integration and protection of consumer welfare. In our initial discussion of the normative merits of criminalising cartel activity, we were sceptical regarding the merits of criminal prohibitions on cartel activity justified solely on the basis that such behaviour involved the appropriation of consumer surplus by producers. These transactions are – to a morally significant extent – voluntary. In the absence of a clear assignment of property rights in consumer surplus to consumers, it is merely rhetoric to term such collusive practices 'theft' and regard them as such. As European law makes no such assignment, consumer welfare – though a goal worthy of advancing – cannot serve as a normative basis for the criminalisation of European competition policy.

Likewise, the inhibition of effective market integration cannot serve as a moral foundation, either. Market integration is not a goal in itself; rather it is a means to a specific end. In the case of the Common Market it was, *inter alia*, to enhance European citizens' (i.e. consumers') lives by providing them access to goods from other Member States without the imposition of tariffs (if done through public means) or price discrimination (if the market is privately fragmented). By opening up the market of consumers for a product, this would have the additional effect of permitting successful producers to take advantage of economies of scale, thereby further decreasing the cost of goods to the ultimate consumer. In effect, the purpose of market integration is to enhance consumer welfare. Thus viewed, hindering the European goal of market integration merely has the potential to reduce consumer welfare; thus the case for its use as a moral justification for the criminalisation of cartel activity reduced to that of harm to the consumer welfare standard.

Two further considerations enhance our scepticism. First and foremost, as a guide to (or stipulation for) conduct, rule of law considerations inform us that substantive criminal law must be as unambiguous as possible in its prohibitions. Thus, in describing prohibited conduct, per se restrictions are to be preferred over prohibitions which admit of exceptions, particularly when the exceptions may admit to vagueness in their definition, assessment, or weighing against other potentially quantifiable economic values.

This is particularly true in an antitrust regime in which economic and non-economic values may be required to be balanced. For instance, in determining the acceptability of an industry-wide agreement to reduce output to mitigate the effects of overcapacity, while at the same time preserving regional employment to the greatest extent possible, there will be a number of elements which resist precise measurement. Accordingly, were there a per se restriction against agreements to reduce output, our hypothetical arraignment would immediately be seen as running afoul of the statute. However, were the statute to be drafted (or interpreted) to provide an exception for restraints where there are sufficient countervailing values (with, in this somewhat hypothetical case, employment and regional development considerations among the permitted exceptions), determining the legality of the scheme is no longer an easy task. This argument suggests that a competition regime which incorporates a plurality of goals and takes seriously the promotion of each of the goals, as the EU's does, will necessarily lack an important desideratum of criminal law: the need for clarity in those rules which prescribe conduct, when the sanctions for their violation are dire.

The second consideration which enhances our scepticism of the utility of criminal sanctions to enhance the EU competition regime is in criminal law as a social phenomenon. Criminal law reflects a society's values. At the outset of this work, we argued for an idealised vision of the foundations of a criminal legal system in a liberal, market-driven society. Our argument there was to show an ideal: to put forward a standard to compare existing and proposed regimes so that they may be evaluated relative to the ideal.

However, in spite of this idealised vision of what the law ought to be, we must keep in mind that law is also a social construct, receiving at least part of its normativity through its acceptance by the society that it purports to govern. If a law were to proscribe conduct which its subjects felt was benign (or they were at minimum indifferent to), much of the persuasive moral force in obeying the law would dissipate. Otherwise put, it is difficult to criminalise activities which people do not believe to be harmful or 'wrong'. As we noted in our introduction, public attitudes towards price-fixing – the most blatant and egregious form of cartel conduct – in Europe are not unanimously supportive of either viewing this activity as harmful, or for deterring it through the imposition of criminal sanctions. These attitudes being what they are casts doubt on an important normative (or at least social) underpinning of attempts at the criminal enforcement of competition law.

In short, we are not convinced that a European system of anti-cartel enforcement is amenable to enhancement through the use of criminal sanctions. There is certainly no clear assignment of a property right to consumer surplus to the citizens of Europe – which would be the minimum feature we would expect to find were we wishing to justify criminalising cartel conduct. The multifaceted nature of the goals inherent in the European Treaties further demonstrates the difficulties which the use of a criminal-based anti-cartel regime may have. The conception of the market found in the European Treaties is more than a means of distributing goods. The market of the Treaties also serves an explicit social purpose which possesses its own set of ends and may not be amenable to the use of criminal sanctions to further these ends.

Given these divergent ends, it is not surprising that the EU system of cartel control fails to address those agency problems which give rise to the phenomenon in the first place. As a result, the correspondingly higher recidivism rate (than, say, in the US) found in the EU should also not be unexpected. The results of our third chapter indicate that European fines are too low, and that there is no supplement of individual sanctions which could control the agency relationship inherent in modern corporate activity. In these circumstances, at least when governed by the minimum standards of EU law (i.e. without the possible supplement of national criminal laws), one can only expect that individual corporate agents will continue to engage in cartel activity, reaping the benefits of it, and offloading the costs of this activity onto the undertakings which employ them.

6

Cartel control in the UK: the failure of supplementary criminalisation

6.1 Introduction

We began our account of American attitudes regarding trusts (or cartels) at roughly 1880, the year in which the Sherman Act was passed by Congress. If we begin our account of the English view of cartels at the same year we see a different attitude, one which accepted – if not encouraged – economic collusion, even at the expense of consumer welfare. This late Victorian attitude, shaped by laissez-faire political and economic thought for a century, was to dominate English thought on the problem, and is still influential today. In effect, this view holds that in the absence of aggravating factors such as dishonesty, misrepresentation or violence, agreements which advance a party's commercial interests cannot be criminal, even if such agreements fix prices or otherwise restrain trade.

However, post-nineteenth-century British use of cartels was not restricted to private arrangements among ostensive competitors to advance their own economic interests. Prior to reforms to Britain's competition regime in years spanning the end of the twentieth and beginning of the twenty-first century, cartel activity was at times encouraged by the government as a means of both industrial and social policy. It is against this background of an attitude which shifted between benign indifference and active promotion of economic collusion that current British policy towards cartel activity must be viewed. This attitude is particularly apparent in the drafting of the original UK cartel offence,[1] and has shaped the avenue of reform of this offence over the past few years.

The present chapter will examine the UK's cartel offence in the context of its late Victorian background. The chapter is structured as

[1] Enterprise Act 2002, s. 188.

follows. The next section examines the British approach to cartelisation in the period between (roughly) 1880 and the Second World War. This period represents a part of history in which late-Victorian laissez-faire ideology become engrained into English law and governmental policy. As a result of this entrenched tolerance of cartel activity, cartelisation became a matter of industrial policy, particularly during the Depression. This use of cooperation was used as a means of industrial policy in declining industries such as cotton, spinning and coal. The Coal Mines Act 1930[2] is briefly examined as an illustration of this policy. This Act, which served to reorganise the British coal industry to mitigate the economic downturn of that industry since the First World War, provides an interesting point of contrast to the American private response found in the arrangements which underlay *Appalachian Coals* and *Socony-Vacuum Oil.*

The chapter moves on to examine the post-Second World War regime which commenced with the Monopolies and Restrictive Practices Act 1948 and – in one form or another – existed until the overhaul of the UK's competition regime which resulted in the Competition Act 1998 and the Enterprise Act 2002. Again the 1948 regime, though modified over time, served as a means of government policy (from both sides of the political spectrum) to organise the UK's economy, particularly in the face of competition from abroad.

The UK's competition regime was overhauled in the final decade of the twentieth century. In this overhaul, the Government introduced the UK's first cartel offence as section 188 of the Enterprise Act. The fifth section of this chapter examines the offence against the background of the difficulties which the public authorities have had in putting it to use. To date, there has been one collapsed prosecution[3] and one plea-bargain[4] under the cartel offence provisions. The plea-bargain was a result of an agreement by the defendants with American authorities in order to serve time in a UK prison, and not in an American correctional facility. These results could hardly be deemed a success. The failings of this offence are analysed.

[2] 20 & 21 Geo. V, c. 29.

[3] *R* v. *George and others* (Southwark Crown Court, May 2010); see also *IB* v. *The Queen* [2009] EWCA Crim 2575, *R* v. *George and others* [2010] EWCA Crim 1148, [2010] 1 WLR 2676.

[4] *R* v. *Whittle, Allison and Brammar* [2008] EWCA Crim 2560.

The inadequacy of the existing cartel offence was one of a number of reasons which led to the coalition Government's suggestion of improving the UK's already 'world class' competition regime. In March 2011, the Government announced a consultation[5] seeking suggestions for improvement to the regime. A Governmental response[6] was published a year later, followed soon thereafter by the introduction into Parliament of a Reform Bill.[7] The sixth section of this chapter examines the proposed reform to the cartel offence. It is argued that, from a normative and an economic perspective, the suggested improvements to the cartel offence do not accomplish their stated goals, and the revised offence is potentially less effective than the offence it replaces.

The conclusion to this chapter suggests that the failings of the former cartel offence and its replacement are intrinsically bound in a perspective of cartel activity shaped (or, indeed, shackled) by its late Victorian intellectual antecedents. An effective anti-cartel regime requires these shackles to be removed, and, indeed, there are good economic and moral reasons for so doing. The proposed reforms do go a fair way to the removal of these shackles, and put the offence on a sufficiently strong moral foundation to justify the use of the coercive apparatus of the criminal law. However, these same reforms fail to mesh with the international consensus regarding the harm occasioned by hard-core cartel activity. As such, not only is the deterrent of the redefined offence weakened, this definition of the offence, unique to the UK, turns the UK cartel control regime into an international outlier.

6.2 The UK regime: 1880–1936

6.2.1 The rise of marketplace liberalism

By 1880, medieval protectionist policies, both of industries and of price regulation, had largely disappeared. The development of mechanised and powered production processes had rendered the manual production methods favoured by the guilds obsolete. The nineteenth-century introduction of the powered loom, for instance, caused a shift of the industry from London to locations such as Manchester, where lower wages could

[5] Department for Business, Innovation and Skills, *A Competition Regime for Growth: A Consultation* (hereafter 'Consultation').

[6] Department for Business, Innovation and Skills, *Growth, Competition and the Competition Regime: Government Response* (hereafter, 'Response').

[7] 2011–12 Session, HC Bill 7.

aid in the profitable production of cloth, and particularly cotton, as a result of the increase in imports of raw cotton from the US.[8] Additionally, almost fifty years had passed since Parliament had abolished the old offences of forestalling, engrossing, regrating and related 'restraints' on trade.[9]

The law regarding restraints of trade had developed into an odd dualism. If the restraint was imposed on a party to the contract, the courts were willing to scrutinise the effects of the contract in light of public interest. As the Law Lords would state in 2008:

> By the end of the 19th century it was established that as between master and servant, principal and agent and the buyer and seller of a business covenants in restraint of trade were, in general, void and so unenforceable, unless the restrictions they contained were shown to be reasonable in the interests of the parties themselves and reasonable in the interests of the public. The House so ruled in *Nordenfelt v Maxim Nordenfelt Guns and Ammunition Co Ltd* [1894] AC 535, and that ruling continues to represent the law today.[10]

However, the law developed in a different direction in cases of restraints of trade the effects of which were not felt by the parties to the contract. In such cases, even if there was a significant anti-competitive effect to the agreement, barring fraud, coercion or other similar circumstances, the contract was – at worse – void, but certainly not criminal.

Between 1875 and 1921, a series of five cases – all still good law – were to crystallise the common law's permissive attitude towards agreements

[8] Mitchell, *British Historical Statistics*, 759–60.

[9] Each of these offences of medieval origin are some form of arbitrage. Blackstone defines forestalling as, 'be the buying or contracting for any merchandise or victual coming in the way to market or dissuading persons from bringing their goods or provisions there ; or persuading them to enhance the price when there : any of which practices make the market dearer to the fair trader'. This appears to be either a form of arbitrage or trading during the hours in which the market is closed. Regrating is defined as 'the buying of corn or other dead victual, in any market, and selling it again in the same market, or within four miles of the place. For this also enhances the price of the provisions, as every successive seller must have a successive profit.' This is merely a form of arbitrage. Engrossing consists in 'the getting into one's possession, or buying up, large quantities of corn or other dead victuals, with intent to sell them again. This must of course be injurious to the public, by putting it in the power of one or two rich men to raise the price of provisions at their own discretion.' Again, this is either a form of arbitrage or wholesaling. (Blackstone, Book IV, ch. 12, parts 6–8.) On these offences, see Letwin, 'The English Law Concerning Monopolies'.

[10] *Norris (Appellant)* v. *Government of the United States of America and others* [2008] UKHL 16 at [8].

among traders which had anti-competitive effects on other parties. All of these cases involved what would be termed 'hard-core' cartel activity: three involved price-fixing[11] and two involved big-rigging at the expense of the public purse.[12] In the laissez-faire world of late Victorian capitalism, as one was free to pursue one's own commercial advantage, one could combine with others in such a pursuit. As Lord Morris indicated in 1891:

> Again, what one trader may do in respect of competition, a body or set of traders can lawfully do; otherwise a large capitalist could do what a number of small capitalists, combining together, could not do, and thus a blow would be struck at the very principle of co-operation and joint-stock enterprise. I entertain no doubt that a body of traders, whose motive object is to promote their own trade, can combine to acquire, and thereby in so far to injure the trade of competitors, provided they do no more than is incident to such motive object, and use no unlawful means.[13]

Of course, not every means could be used in one's self-interested pursuit: activities such as fraud, misrepresentation and coercion rendered the agreement void or even actionable. However, injuries occasioned by restraint of trade were not *ejusdem generis*.

First, and foremost, the courts recognised that to the extent that competition in economic activity was a zero-sum game, the 'winner's' gain was obtained at a loss to the 'loser'. This loss, of course, represented a harm to the loser. Accordingly, to the extent that the competitive process is socially condoned or encouraged for its benefits, harm induced by competition was not actionable. Lord Coleridge CJ, in his trial judgment in *Mogul Steamship* remarked:

> It must be remembered that all trade is and must be in a sense selfish; trade not being infinite, nay, the trade of a particular place or district being possibly very limited, what one man gains another loses. In the hand to hand war of commerce, as in the conflicts of public life, whether at the bar, in Parliament, in medicine, in engineering, (I give examples only,) men fight on without much thought of others, except a desire to excel or to defeat them.[14]

Lord Coleridge's sentiments reflect the views of John Stuart Mill's analysis of competitive harms, published 29 years earlier in *On Liberty*.

[11] *The Mogul Steamship Company, Limited* v. *McGregor Gow & Co., and others* [1891] AC 25 (HL), *Attorney General of Australia* v. *Adelaide Steam Ship Co. Ltd* [1913] AC *781*, *North Western Salt Co. Ltd v. Electrolytic Alkali Co. Ltd* [1913] 3 KB 422.

[12] *Jones* v. *North* (1875) LR 19 EQ 426, *Rawlings* v. *General Trading Co.* [1921] 1 KB 635.

[13] *Mogul* (n. 11) at 50; see also Lord Halsbury LC's speech at 38 in *Mogul.*

[14] *Mogul* (1888) LR 21 QBD 544 at 553.

6.2.2 *Mill's liberal influences*

Mill, in analysing the extent that the criminal law ought to restrain harm, noted that not all harms are deserving of proscription through the use of the criminal law. Mill remarks:

> In the first place, it must by no means be supposed, because damage, or probability of damage, to the interests of others, can alone justify the interference of society, that therefore it always does justify such interference. In many cases, an individual, in pursuing a legitimate object, necessarily and therefore legitimately causes pain or loss to others, or intercepts a good which they had a reasonable hope of obtaining. Such oppositions of interest between individuals often arise from bad social institutions, but are unavoidable while those institutions last; and some would be unavoidable under any institutions. Whoever succeeds in an overcrowded profession, or in a competitive examination; whoever is preferred to another in any contest for an object which both desire, reaps benefit from the loss of others, from their wasted exertion and their disappointment. But it is, by common admission, better for the general interest of mankind, that persons should pursue their objects undeterred by this sort of consequences. In other words, society admits no right, either legal or moral, in the disappointed competitors, to immunity from this kind of suffering; and feels called on to interfere, only when means of success have been employed which it is contrary to the general interest to permit – namely, fraud or treachery, and force.[15]

And applying his analysis to trade, Mill continues:

> Again, trade is a social act. Whoever undertakes to sell any description of goods to the public, does what affects the interest of other persons, and of society in general; and thus his conduct, in principle, comes within the jurisdiction of society: accordingly, it was once held to be the duty of governments, in all cases which were considered of importance, to fix prices, and regulate the processes of manufacture. But it is now recognized, though not till after a long struggle, that both the cheapness and the good quality of commodities are most effectually provided for by leaving the producers and sellers perfectly free, under the sole check of equal freedom to the buyers for supplying themselves elsewhere. This is the so-called doctrine of Free Trade, which rests on grounds different from, though equally solid with, the principle of individual liberty asserted in this Essay. Restrictions on trade, or on production for purposes of trade, are indeed restraints; and all restraint, qua restraint, is an evil: but the restraints in question affect only that part of conduct which

[15] Mill, *On Liberty*, Book V.

> society is competent to restrain, and are wrong solely because they do not really produce the results which it is desired to produce by them.[16]

In Mill's analysis in the inherently social act of commercial trading, there are winners and losers. Additionally, as acts which constitute commerce are social, that is their effects concern more than the individual actor, there may possibly be a social justification for interference with individual action to prevent the harms. However, in true utilitarian fashion, the benefits from such intervention must be weighed against the adverse consequences of such intervention.

In Mill's mind – and indeed in the mind of the Victorian economic and social liberal – the history of social intervention in the market has demonstrated that such intervention typically fails to yield the benefits sought. In reality – in this *Weltanschauung* – history also demonstrates that the desired results (namely quality goods obtainable inexpensively) result when individuals are permitted to conduct their economic affairs as they choose. As such, counter-productive social intervention in the market is undesirable.[17]

Mill's ideas were not alien to the late Victorian judiciary. Interests which were harmed through economic competition, in the absence of fraud, coercion, misrepresentation and the like, were not legally protected. Lord Halsbury was to rhetorically ask in *Mogul Steamship*:

> I think this question is the first to be determined: what injury, if any, has been done? What legal right has been interfered with? Because if no legal right has been interfered with, and no legal injury inflicted, it is vain to say that the thing might have been done by an individual, but cannot be done by a combination of persons.[18]

16 Ibid.

17 Mill qualifies this by noting (ibid.) that certain practices such as fraud can be prohibited, but the justification for their prohibition is different from wholesale intervention in the market:

> As the principle of individual liberty is not involved in the doctrine of Free Trade so neither is it in most of the questions which arise respecting the limits of that doctrine: as for example, what amount of public control is admissible for the prevention of fraud by adulteration; how far sanitary precautions, or arrangements to protect work-people employed in dangerous occupations, should be enforced on employers. Such questions involve considerations of liberty, only in so far as leaving people to themselves is always better, caeteris [sic] paribus, than controlling them: but that they may be legitimately controlled for these ends, is in principle undeniable.

18 *Mogul* (n. 11) at 38.

Indeed, these sentiments were well expressed (and echo Mill's analysis) by the Court of Appeal by Fry LJ in the same case:

> Competition exists when two or more persons seek to possess or to enjoy the same thing: it follows that the success of one must be the failure of another, and no principle of law enables us to interfere with or to moderate that success or that failure so long as it is due to mere competition. I say mere competition, for I do not doubt that it is unlawful and actionable for one man to interfere with another's trade by fraud or misrepresentation, or by molesting his customers, or those who would be his customers, whether by physical obstruction or moral intimidation.[19]

Further, as the judiciary viewed itself as ill-suited to fabricate any new boundaries between permitted and illegitimate means of competition, this resulted in an institutional reluctance to consider the social or economic merits and effects of the arrangements in question.

This judicial reticence to create new boundaries between permitted and impermissible competition was based on the role of the judiciary in making policy decisions (which are the purview of Parliament), particularly when the anti-competitive practices at issue might have social benefits. Lord Bramwell, in his speech in *Mogul Steamship*, clearly states the former point:

> The first position of the plaintiffs is that the agreement among the defendants is illegal as being in restraint of trade, and therefore against public policy, and so illegal. 'Public policy,' said Burrough J. (I believe, quoting Hobart C. J.), 'is an unruly horse, and dangerous to ride.' I quote also another distinguished judge, more modern, Cave J.: 'Certain kinds of contracts have been held void at Common Law on the ground of public policy; a branch of the law, however, which certainly should not be extended, as judges are more to be trusted as interpreters of the law than as expounders of what is called public policy'. I think the present case is an illustration of the wisdom of these remarks. I venture to make another. No evidence is given in these public policy cases. The tribunal is to say, as matter of law, that the thing is against public policy, and void. How can the judge do that without any evidence as to its effect and consequences?[20]

Such judicial deference to Parliament was not unique to matters of economic policy.[21]

[19] (1889) LR 23 QBD 598 at 626. [20] *Mogul* (n. 11) at 45, references omitted.

[21] This deference is still present today. See, e.g., the speech of Lord Bingham in *Regina* v. *Secretary of State for Work and Pensions (Respondent), ex parte Kehoe (FC) (Appellant)* [2005] UKHL 48 at [10], [2006] AC 42 at 58.

The need for this reserved approach by the judiciary to voicing conclusions with policy implications was exacerbated by competing social considerations present in the choices. The dilemma was well put by Lord Haldane LC, some twenty-two years later:

> Unquestionably the combination in question was one the purpose of which was to regulate supply and keep up prices. But an ill-regulated supply and unremunerative prices may, in point of fact, be disadvantageous to the public. Such a state of things may, if it is not controlled, drive manufacturers out of business, or lower wages, and so cause unemployment and labour disturbance.[22]

Making a perceived choice between permitting parties to engage in practices which may restrict the opportunity of others to compete or preventing such practices and possibly stoking economic and social difficulties was viewed by nineteenth-century judges as being properly a political choice – one to be made by those in Parliament.

From time to time, cases involving price-fixing[23] and bid-rigging[24] were to come before the courts which would consistently hold that in the absence of misrepresentation, fraud or other similar aggravating elements, such restraints of trade were likely legal,[25] at worst void or unenforceable,[26] and certainly not criminal. And to the extent that these cases stand for the proposition that such conduct is not criminal under English law, they are still good law.[27]

It is easy to understand why and how this view of contractual restraints on competition not only took hold but also remained influential in the legal and political community. Victorian liberalism was based on a concept of individual freedom which embraced laissez-faire capitalism and its attendant views towards freedom of contract. Some of the views propounded by Mill in *On Liberty* may have been radical when they were first published, but by the 1880s a significant amount of these views had become accepted. This is, of course, not to say that Mill himself was responsible for the transformation of English thought on this matter, rather that he was an early exponent of positions which,

[22] *North Western Salt* (n. 11) at 469. [23] See those cases referred to in n. 11, above.
[24] See those cases referred to in n. 12, above.
[25] See, e.g., *Northwest Salt* (n. 11) at 469–71, per Viscount Haldane LC.
[26] See, e.g., Lord Bramwell's speech in *Mogul* (n. 11) at 46–7.
[27] *Norris* (n. 10) at [18], citing *British Airways Board* v. *Laker Airways Ltd* [1985] AC 58 at 79.

though at first they may have been radical, were later to become orthodox.

But in addition to being a social reformer, Mill was also influential as an early economist. His 1848 work, *The Principles of Political Economy*, was among the – if not the – most influential British works of economic theory in the nineteenth and early twentieth centuries and was *the* academic text.[28] However, as influential as it may have been, it was a product of its time: it lacked the rigour and mathematical precision which was to become characteristic of the discipline. Further, while Mill's *Principles* contains insightful analyses of issues such as labour, trade and production, its analyses of price, supply and demand are wanting. It was not until 1890 that Alfred Marshall published his *Principles of Economics*, containing the first detailed account of the concepts of consumer and producer surplus. This analysis, complete with the supply and demand graph which was to become a staple of microeconomic analysis, was used to analyse monopolies. Thus Marshall:

> The *prima facie* interest of the owner of a monopoly is clearly to adjust the supply to the demand, not in such a way that the price at which he can sell his commodity shall just cover its expenses of production, but in such a way as to afford him the greatest possible total net revenue.[29]

And Marshall was quick to see that in such a situation, a monopolist can readily appropriate what would later come to be called 'consumer surplus' (in his words, 'consumer's rent') to itself.[30] Marshall's work, though issued in eight editions between 1890 and 1920, was not to become a standard textbook in the English university curriculum until after the First World War. Given the lag in time between its adoption as a leading text and the reception of its ideas by those charged with political and legal decisions of this nature, it is not a surprise that harm to consumer welfare from monopolies was not explicitly recognised by parliamentarians until the latter half of the twentieth century.

6.3 The economic downturn of the 1930s: cartels as industrial policy

6.3.1 Economic downturn: the coal industry as an example

The start of the Great Depression is often viewed to be 29 October 1929, 'Black Tuesday', when the New York Stock Exchange's Dow Jones

[28] Ekelund and Hébert, *A History of Economic Theory and Method*, 172.
[29] Marshall, *Principles of Economics*, 477–8. [30] Ibid., 489–90.

Industrial Average continued a downward slide (which started in September of that year and was exacerbated by a sharp decline the day before). It would take until November of 1954 for the market to recover to pre-1929 levels. While 29 October 1929 may be a convenient date insofar as it provides a clear point of focus, the stock market crash was almost certainly a symptom of greater economic decline which the industrialised world faced in the decade following the First World War. A symptom of this downturn was a decrease in consumption and a resulting drop in domestic (both in the US and UK) manufacturing. As a result of this decline in industrial output, there was a corresponding decline in the need for energy to drive manufacturing. In the UK the effect was felt by the coal industry, an industry which was already suffering from a substitution of petroleum as a fuel source.

The economic downturn in the coal industries on both sides of the Atlantic was exacerbated by a decrease in demand, driven by a drop in heavy manufacturing resulting from the lack of need to produce war material. In the UK, the increased competition from foreign sources of coal caused a reduction in exports; and in the US, the development of the petroleum industry added a cheaper source of energy for use in manufacturing.

The American response to the coal problem was fought on both public and private fronts. Congress passed the National Industrial Recovery Act of 1933 which permitted the use of cartels as a means of industrial (and social) policy in an unsuccessful attempt to stimulate economic recovery. The Act, later to be ruled unconstitutional by the Supreme Court,[31] provided for a limited kerb on the application of the Sherman and Clayton Acts. Prior to this Act's entry into force, however, attempts at private means of reducing the effects of the economic downturn in the coal industry had been made, the most notable of which was the scheme put into place by the coal producers of Appalachia, later to be held as not unlawful by the US Supreme Court.[32]

A similar crisis faced the British coal industry. Lucas described the grim situation faced by that industry in 1930:

> The grim fact is that by 1929 the industry was on the verge of bankruptcy. Even before 1930 the major part of the British output of coal was being raised at an actual loss. Between 1913 and 1929 the output of British mines had declined from 287,000,000 tons to 258,000,000 tons; yet the

[31] *Schechter Poultry Corp.* v. *United States* 295 US 495 (1935).
[32] See our discussion above, pp. 136–8.

> production of the rest of the world had increased about 19 per cent. Coupled with this decline in output was an even greater relative drop in exports – from 73,000,000 in 1913 to 60,000,000 tons in 1929. Inevitably there arose a great disparity between the volume of profitable sales and productive capacity. This, in turn, added to the already high costs and led to disastrous competition within the industry. The situation was aggravated by the large number of small, independent firms. Not only did their existence add substantially to the cost of raising coal, their reluctance to enter combinations had also largely frustrated the many proposals for reorganizing the industry.[33]

In the absence of restrictions on competition, the industry's response would have been to reduce its costs even further by lowering wages – which ran contrary to promises made by Ramsey MacDonald's Labour Government.[34]

The Government's response, the Coal Mines Act 1930,[35] attempted to introduce some stability into the industry through two systems: a system of regional cartels which fixed output and prices, thereby stabilising wages; and a means by which the industry could be reorganised through amalgamation which – if necessary – could occur with the opposition of the owners of affected collieries. To achieve the first goal, Part I of that Act established a Central Council which administered seventeen district schemes. The mandate of the Central Council was to coordinate the production quotas and establish minimum prices.[36] Part II of the Act created the Coal Board Reorganisation Commission. Lucas wrote:

> This body is 'to promote and assist, by the preparation of schemes and otherwise, the amalgamation of undertakings' where 'such amalgamations appear to the Commission to be in the national interest.' If it appears that a specific amalgamation is desirable and the collieries concerned show no disposition to put it into effect, the Commission can call upon the owners to prepare a scheme and if they fail to do so, the Commission itself shall draw one up.[37]

This latter agency proved to be ineffective. Only seven mergers occurred prior to 1932, and the Commission never used its powers to require a mandatory amalgamation.[38]

The 1930 Act was underwhelming in its effect. While the Act's price control provisions had the consequences of stabilising coal prices, it is

[33] Arthur F. Lucas, 'A British Experiment in the Control of Competition: The Coal Mines Act of 1930', 419 (footnotes omitted).
[34] Ibid., 420. [35] 20 & 21 Geo. V, c. 34. [36] Lucas (n. 33), 420–1, 422–8.
[37] Ibid., 434. [38] Ibid., 435.

likely that this was a result in the halting of a drop in prices, rather than a net increase.[39] Among the most plausible explanations for this were first that the Council fixed production quotas by region, with little explicit regard to overall British production, and regional cartels could engage in undercutting each other at the national level thus driving the overall price down.[40] Second, there was evidence (even discussed in Parliamentary Debates) that although there was adherence to quota restrictions by industry, industry was less obedient to price restrictions, with cheating running rampant.[41] And third, the failure to achieve the sort of amalgamation which was envisaged to save the industry can be blamed on a lack of political will. One commentator writes:

> Finally, the policy of compulsory amalgamation raised the critical issue as to whether or not an independent Government agency should shape the organization of an industry in a direction to which its leaders were utterly opposed. It is no coincidence that failure to reorganize was one of the principal reasons advanced for the nationalization of the industry following the publication of the Reid Report in 1945. In short, reorganization of the kind envisaged by the Reorganisation Commission necessitated the removal of the industry from private hands, a step which could not be contemplated in the political circumstances of the thirties.[42]

The political will was to come several years later, manifesting itself in the Coal Act 1938[43] which mandated the Coal Commission to purchase the fee simple of British coal[44] and the Coal Industry Nationalisation Act 1946[45] which completed the nationalisation of the coal industry and established the National Coal Board as a statutory corporation to run the industry.[46]

6.3.2 Other industries

The coal industry was only one of a number of British industries which benefited from an environment which condoned or encouraged cartel activity. In her study of twentieth-Century British competition policy, Mercer writes:

[39] Ibid., 432. [40] Ibid., 438–9.
[41] Ibid., 433, citing Hansard, HC 5th Series, vol. 266, col. 1226 (1 June 1932).
[42] Kirby, 'Government Intervention on Industrial Organization: Coal Mining in the Nineteen Thirties', 173.
[43] 1 & 2 Geo. VI, c. 52. [44] Ibid., s. 3. [45] 9 & 10 Geo. VI, c. 59. [46] Ibid., s. 1.

> [During the 1930s] governmental policies created hot-house conditions for cartelisation. Not only did imperial preference, tariffs and the IDAC [Import Duties Advisory Committee] promote domestic cartels as a first step to the promotion of international agreements, but specific policies succoured them, for instance the Budget of 1935 and the Finance Act of 1936 gave tax concessions to voluntary schemes which sought to eliminate excess capacity. Governments tried to rationalise and promote amalgamations in coal, cotton and iron and steel. It was divisions among industrialists and the banks' failure to provide long-term finance when they became involved in rationalisation that meant that such schemes were transformed by the industrialists involved into cartel schemes alone.[47]

Rationalising industry through amalgamation and cooperation, hence directly and indirectly encouraging cartelisation, was seen as an effective means of industrial organisation to reduce overcapacity and alleviate the social effects of high unemployment.

It was an ironic coincidence that the Coal Act came into force on 29 July 1938. That was the same day that Japanese and Soviet troops first clashed in the Battle of Lake Khasan, a prequel to subsequent Japanese invasions of Soviet Territory in what would become the Second World War. Two months and a day later, on 30 September, Chamberlain would return to Britain with his copy of a later infamous agreement, and announce 'peace in our time'. The events of the Second World War, and the resulting need for the economy and industry to be organised with the war effort in mind, overshadowed any concerns industry or the public had regarding economic collusion. Even in the extenuating circumstances of war, where 'normal' means of economic organisation could be dispensed with, the collusive attitude prevalent in British industry meant that 'emergency' organisation did not vary far from the norm.

6.4 Post-war: the Monopolies and Restrictive Trade Practices Commission, the Restrictive Practice Acts and Court

Cartel policy in post-Second World War Britain was influenced by two different forces: the external force of an American-driven desire to

[47] Mercer, *Constructing a Competitive Order*, 49. The IDAC was established under the Import Duties Act 1932 (22 & 23 Geo. V, c.8) to consider import tariffs. The threat of the imposition of tariffs was frequently used to coerce agreements from non-British manufacturers to join the domestic, British, cartel: see Mercer, 28.

mount a unified, international attack on cartel activity as part of the Bretton Woods system, and the from time-to-time competing views of the government and business regarding the appropriateness of controlling activity which theretofore was generally tolerated. Other accounts of this history exist;[48] our goal in this section will be to demonstrate the tolerant British view towards economic collusion held during this time, which has, in the present writer's estimation, led to the present state of weak criminal control of such practices.

6.4.1 *Post-war internationalisation*

In preparation for the end of the Second World War, the 1944 conference at Bretton Woods, New York served to formulate initial plans to rebuild the world's economy, and to do so in a way which would prevent reoccurrences of the economic crises which sewed the seed of the recent war. Fixed exchange rates and financial stability would be anchored by the International Monetary Fund. This would, it was thought at the time, serve to prevent economic crises which could generate political instability. The International Bank for Reconstruction and Development (later to become a part of the World Bank) would serve to assist in post-war reconstruction, and the International Trade Organization (ITO) was proposed as the vehicle by which the rules governing international trade would be established.

Among the ITO's goals were the reduction of tariffs and elimination of domestic restrictive business practices, which included cartel activity. The former would prevent the sort of protectionist policies which exacerbated the Great Depression, and the latter would facilitate domestic consumption of imported goods, thereby complementing the former goal. Chapter V of the Havana Charter[49] provided for an obligation on each member to prevent 'on the part of private or public commercial enterprises, business practices affecting international trade which restrain competition, limit access to markets, or foster monopolistic control, whenever such practices have harmful effects on the expansion of production or trade and interfere with the achievement of any of the other objectives act [sic] forth in Article 1'.[50] Article 46(3) continues to enumerate a non-exhaustive list of restrictive business practices which

[48] See, for example, Mercer, ibid.
[49] Available at: www.wto.org/english/docs_e/legal_e/havana_e.pdf.
[50] Ibid., Article 46(1).

includes those practices which are today commonly regarded as hard-core cartel activity.

The project envisaged by the ITO was never completely realised. As a result of opposition by the American Congress, primarily due to the ITO regime being perceived as a threat to American sovereignty, President Truman withdrew the Treaty for ratification in 1951.[51] An agreement, intended at the time to be provisional, the General Agreement on Tariffs and Trade (GATT), which came into force in 1947, served to address the tariff issue. While the GATT served as the genesis of the World Trade Organization, the implementation of an agreement to combat restrictive business practices at that global scale has yet to be achieved.

Although the American failure to ratify the Havana Charter in 1951 at least temporarily derailed a global effort (albeit American-driven) to halt tolerance of such practices, prior to the Treaty's withdrawal from the Senate, there was significant American pressure applied to other governments to combat such business practices in their domestic markets. Such pressure was applied to the UK, and as the Government of the UK was in need of American financial support in the immediate aftermath of the war, the American Government applied economic pressure and attempted to link financial aid to the elimination of cartels.[52] This attempted link was more subtle than the link forged on the Continent.

However, the American attempt at a link was made somewhat difficult by circumstances peculiar to Britain. Although the British economy was in dire straits, it did not require rebuilding to the extent that the German economy (and infrastructure) did. Hence, though there was reliance on American financial assistance, there was a limit to the amount of pressure that could be applied. Second, there was no counterpart of ordoliberalism alive in the British economic, political or legal communities, which acted as an intellectual counterweight to the laissez-faire liberalism reflected in judicial decisions which preceded the war. Finally, the Attlee Government's social and economic policies (to which all parties were to some extent committed) of full employment and nationalisation of key industries would shape the response to collusive activities in the economy. However, the Government was forced to walk a tight line between the interests of labour and industry to implement these latter policies.

[51] Michael Trebilcock, Robert Howse and Antionia Eliason, *The Regulation of International Trade*, 24.

[52] See, e.g., Mercer (n. 47), 79, 91–2 and 103.

6.4.2 *The post-war UK regime*

The Monopolies and Restrictive Practices Act 1948 can be seen as an attempt to address these competing matters. That Act established the Monopolies Commission, giving it the power to investigate those industries under threat of monopolisation by a single firm or a group of firms acting in concert. The Commission had no enforcement power of its own. After its investigation, it could publish a report into the suspected practice with the intention that the Board of Trade and the appropriate government department would act upon the report's content.[53]

The Act had the effect of simultaneously appeasing American demands that something be done about restrictive business practices[54] and alleviating the business community's fear that containing restrictive practices was tantamount to importing the Sherman Act.[55] However, to accomplish these goals, the Act had to be ineffectual window dressing, which it indeed was. Between 1949 and 1956 (the year the Commission was replaced), it investigated the supply of twenty-five different products. The average length of time between commencement of the investigation and publication of the report was twenty-seven months. In only one case, that concerning dental goods and instruments,[56] was the investigated practice declared illegal. Voluntary action on the part of the investigated industry was sufficient action to resolve the dispute, if action was indeed needed as a remedy.[57] Mercer argues – quite rightly – that although business interests did not 'capture' the Commission, they certainly co-opted it;[58] and any countervailing power and hence influence which labour or consumer interests had was nominal. The Act established an administrative procedure, and failed to explicitly

[53] Mercer (ibid., 109) describes the division of responsibility as follows:

> Central to business success was the clear division of function between the Commission and the Board of Trade. The Board had the duty to identify cases for referral, which it did after consultation with the 'sponsoring' department. The Commission then conducted the enquiry, wrote the report and made recommendations. The procedure then returned to the Board of Trade and the sponsoring departments to decide whether any section of the report should be omitted on grounds of national security or business confidentiality, and then to conduct negotiations with the firms concerned with a view to carrying out the Commission's recommendations.

[54] Ibid., 96–9. [55] Ibid., 96.

[56] The report is available at: http://webarchive.nationalarchives.gov.uk/20111202195250/http://competition-commission.org.uk/rep_pub/reports/1950_1959/001dental.htm.

[57] See Mercer (n. 47), 105–7. [58] Ibid., Chapter VI passim.

recognise economic harm which stemmed from such collusion. The most significant reason this failure of the Act to address the harm caused by monopolistic activities was that the Commission was directed to determine whether or not the practices in question were contrary to 'the public interest'. Yet, at the same time, the Act provided no definition or guidance as to what the 'public interest' was.[59]

In many respects the demise of the regime established by the 1948 Act was a result of one of its only successes. That Act had proven to be unpopular both with the business community and the public. The business community was dissatisfied by the administrative nature of the hearings, and the fact that each matter was dealt with individually with no guidance or criteria to be used to assist in shaping the Commission's future decisions.[60] Further, the public had become aware of the pernicious effects of collusive activities and other restrictive practices. This culminated with the 1955 publication of the Commission's *Report on the Supply of Tyres in the Motor Vehicle Industry*.[61] However, perhaps the final straw was the June 1955 report on collective discrimination[62] which urged that such practices be made illegal.[63] As Jewkes, writing in 1958, noted:

> This forthright declaration involving, as it would have done, legislation which, for the first time, would have turned certain forms of monopolising into a criminal offence, confronted the Government with a choice. Either it must accept the recommendations of the report or it must produce some revised scheme of its own. In framing the Act of 1956 it chose the latter course.[64]

The 1956 Act would reorient the British response to collusive and restrictive business practices.

The watershed insight of the Restrictive Trade Practices Act 1956 was the recognition that cartel practices were harmful to the consumer and therefore, in the absence of proof to the contrary, not in the public interest. This was the first modern (i.e. post-Industrial Revolution) parliamentary recognition of the economic harm caused by this sort of activity. In addition to this insight, that Act also imposed a requirement

[59] Jewkes, 'British Monopoly Policy 1944–56', 6.

[60] Dennison, 'The British Restrictive Trade Practices Act of 1956', 65.

[61] Jewkes (n. 59), 4.

[62] The Monopolies and Restrictive Practices Commission, *Collective Discrimination: A Report on Exclusive Dealing, Collective Boycotts, Aggragated Rebates and other Discriminatory Trade Practices*.

[63] Jewkes (n. 59), 4–5. [64] Ibid., 5.

that parties entering into specified types of collusive agreements[65] register their agreement with the Registrar of Restrictive Trade Agreements, who would then refer the agreement to the Restrictive Practices Court. This court, having the stature of the High Court, would then determine whether the impugned agreement was in the public interest or not. The onus was on the parties to the agreement to rebut (on a balance of probabilities – given the civil nature of the court) the presumption that the agreement was contrary to the public interest.[66] By vesting this decision-making power in a court, the Act broke away from the administrative model which defined the earlier regime, and which was the source of criticism from the business community.[67]

Section 21(1) of the Act provided for seven 'gateways' (as they later came to be called[68]) by which an agreement could be shown to be not contrary to the public interest. Dennison has discussed these gateways in some detail,[69] but for our present purposes only two are of relevance: that the agreement provides 'specific and substantial benefits or advantages' to consumers which would be lost in its absence[70] and that the agreement had a beneficial effect on employment.[71] The Court did not use a light touch in applying these criteria to legalise restrictive agreements. Indeed, the Court's approach, given the benevolent treatment restrictive agreements had been given since the nineteenth century, was possibly somewhat a surprise.

Regarding this point, Wilks writes:

> After decades of a permissive approach by the judiciary to restrictive practices businesses might have expected a lax regime to be established under the Court. There is, in fact, no particularly rigorous expectation built into the legislation, which also has a range of exceptions and loopholes inserted as a result of special pleading. In fact the Court, initially under Mr Justice (later Lord) Devlin, proceeded to bowl over restrictive agreements to send shock waves through industry which transformed the cosy world of cartels and restrictive practices.[72]

Although cartel activity was not per se criminal, the Court had the power, after finding a particular agreement was contrary to the public

[65] On this point, Dennison (n. 60), 66 comments, 'The specified matters cover prices, terms and conditions of sale, quantities and descriptions of goods, processes of manufacture, and persons or classes of persons and places and areas to be supplied. Certain specific exclusions (apart from statutory agreements) refer to foreign trade, the main point being the exclusion of any agreement which covers exclusively the export of goods.'

[66] See, ibid., 66–7. [67] See Mercer (n. 47), 127–8. [68] Dennison (n. 60), 67.

[69] Ibid., 67–80. [70] Ibid., 69–75. [71] Ibid., 76–8. [72] Wilks, *In the Public Interest*, 37.

interest, to issue an injunction to compel the parties to cease and desist from engaging in the practice.[73] Disobedience of the injunction was punishable as contempt.[74] The effect of the Act, whether intended or not, was to virtually eliminate cartelisation from British industry by the mid-1960s.[75]

With a few minor enhancements related to monopolies and mergers, this regime continued well into the late 1980s. By the late 1970s, as Gerber argues, the Government recognised that the then regime was inadequate to protect the competitive process.[76] Heeding the advice of two interdepartmental committees, the Thatcher Government was to enact the Competition Act 1980. This Act was to add an additional element of institutional complexity to the UK regime. Section 2 of the 1980 Act permitted the Director General of Fair Trading to order an inquiry into the activity of any firm engaging in an anti-competitive practice.[77] If the Director (or more accurately, the OFT) determined that the practice was anti-competitive, after the requisite investigation, the Director could accept undertakings from the investigated firm in relation to the practice;[78] and if the issue was not so resolved, the matter could be referred to the Monopolies and Mergers Commission.[79] However, any non-consensual final resolution of the matter rested in the hands of the Secretary of State,[80] thus ultimately imposing a political master over this new layer of enforcement. This political mastery was somewhat surprising since 'public interest' was not a factor which the OFT needed to take into account. The OFT's mandate was distortion, restriction or prevention of competition, which are purely economic criteria.

[73] See, e.g., the result in *Re Yarn Spinners Agreement (No. 1)* [1959] 1 WLR 154, [1959] 1 All ER 299 (RTCP); see also Dennison's analysis of the Court's reasoning in determining that the agreement in this case was contrary to the public interest and his analysis of the Court's treatment of other agreements: (n. 60), 69–80.

[74] See, e.g., *Director General of Fair Trading Appellant* v. *Pioneer Concrete (UK) Ltd and another* [1994] 3 WLR 1249, [1995] 1 AC 456 (HL) discussed at p. 74, above.

[75] Wilks (n. 72), 37. [76] Gerber, *Law and Competition in Europe*, 223.

[77] Anti-competitive practices were broadly defined by s 2:

> that person pursues a course of conduct which, of itself or when taken together with a course of conduct pursued by persons associated with him, has or is intended to have or is likely to have the effect of restricting, distorting or preventing competition in connection with the production, supply or acquisition of goods in the United Kingdom or any part of it or the supply or securing of services in the United Kingdom or any part of it.

[78] Competition Act 1980, s. 4. [79] Section 5. [80] Sections 8–10.

While the Competition Act 1980 permitted the investigation of a particular firm and not an industry as a whole, it represented something of an advance. Its major effect was to supplement, by adding an additional layer of a regulatory agency, the monopolies provisions.[81] In so doing, this Act provided further evidence of an ongoing British response to problems in market regulation. A problem is identified and an ad hoc response, typically in the form of legislation, is instituted. This response is often made in isolation and without consideration of how the response interacted with other elements of the regulatory structure. This ad hoc approach continues – as we will see later in this chapter – today.

6.5 The British reception of European reform

6.5.1 Reforming the regime

By the final decade of the twentieth century, it was time to reform the British competition regime yet again. In the final years of the Conservative Government no less than eight Reports, Green and White Papers, draft Bills and similar works were produced.[82] Upon election in May 1997, the Labour Government began its reform processes, which culminated in the Competition Act 1998.[83]

The Competition Act 1998 attempted to rectify problems with the previous regime. While the pre-Competition Act regime was not inconsistent with the European regime of Regulation 17/62, insofar as both regimes required that parties to a restrictive agreement notify a public authority of the existence of the agreement and seek an exemption for it, both regimes shared the same need for the regulatory body to act reasonably quickly and accurately apply the relevant law to restrain anti-competitive practices.

As we have seen earlier,[84] the European regime's mandatory notification resulted in delays of up to three years[85] before the notified agreement was vetted by the Commission. Although the UK regime was not as slow as this, there was no means by which interim prohibitions of the notified practices could be made where such prohibitions were in the public interest. All that would result was that, after investigation, the parties would be told to cease the practice, but would not be required to disgorge their gains.

[81] Robertson, 'The Reform of UK Competition Law – Again?', 210.
[82] See Utton, 'Fifty Years of U.K. Competition Policy', at 280. [83] Ibid., 280–1.
[84] See above, pp. 181–2. [85] See ibid.

Likewise, there was significant uncertainty about which law to apply: European law, or a more domestic product.[86] The Competition Act explicitly modelled its provisions on, and mirrored the language of, the then Articles 85 and 86 of the Treaty, prohibiting agreements distorting competition (so-called 'Chapter I prohibitions')[87] and abuses of a dominant position ('Chapter II prohibitions').[88] The latter prohibition was not part of the earlier, Conservative Government's suggestions of reform, due to the perceived difficulty of defining 'abuse', and the fact that, in Utton's words, 'Article 86 had not so far been a great success'.[89] The Competition Act thus began a realignment of the UK's competition regime with that of the European law, which was to prove necessary by the coming into force of Regulation 1/2003 some three and a half years after the main provisions (Chapter I and II prohibitions) of the Competition Act came into force.

However, the most significant element of the Competition Act 1998 lay in its introduction of a substantial deterrent to anti-competitive practices. The pre-1998 regimes lacked this effect. Although penalties could be meted out for failing to heed an order of the Restrictive Practices Court, this was an infrequent event.[90] The toothless nature of the previous regime could be explained at a result of a benign, light touch approach. Robertson, writing in 1996, suggested:

> The major strength of the current UK system is its benign approach. It is also its major weakness. The strength lies in the fact that business does not run the risk of competitive behaviour being the subject of the imposition of fines or actions for damages.
>
> The weakness lies in the lack of deterrence...
>
> The Government hitherto has been convinced that the risk of competitive behaviour being condemned operates as a deterrent; ...[91]

Whether this benign approach was intentionally established to avoid deterring potentially beneficial pro-competitive arrangements, or alternatively as a further result of industry lobbying for and obtaining a regulatory agenda which suited its interests,[92] is not clear. What was clear, as was noted by these commentators, was that the pre-Competition Act regime had little to no deterrent effect.[93]

[86] Robertson (n. 81), 214–15. [87] Competition Act 1998, s. 2. [88] Ibid., s. 18.
[89] Utton (n. 82), 281. [90] Ibid., 276. [91] Robertson (n. 81), 215.
[92] As Mercer (n. 47, pp. 105–7) argues was the case with the 1948 and 1956 regimes.
[93] Robertson (n. 81), 215; Utton (n. 82), pp. 275–6.

The Competition Act permitted, for the first time in the UK, financial penalties to be imposed upon undertakings which participated in certain forms of hard-core cartel activities.[94] Section 36(8) of that Act provides that an undertaking may be penalised up to 10% of its (annual) turnover for participating in these activities. While the OFT's fine guidelines on determining the penalty have been revised over time,[95] this maximum has remained unchanged due to the operation of European law. In addition to enhancing deterrence by permitting the imposition of fines, the Competition Act also enhanced the investigatory powers of the Director of Fair Trading (now the OFT) by providing specific investigatory and enforcement powers, including the powers to enter premises with or without a warrant.[96] Additionally, again for the first time, the Director was able to impose interim measures for the purpose of 'preventing serious, irreparable damage to a particular person or category of person, or. . . protecting the public interest'.[97]

The deterrent effect of the Competition Act was to be supplemented by the Enterprise Act 2002, which – again for the first time – established a criminal cartel offence in the UK. In addition, the Enterprise Act tinkered with the institutional structure of UK competition regulation by abolishing the office of the Director of Fair Trading and replacing it with the OFT, streamlining the merger and market investigation process by allocating responsibilities between the OFT and the Competition Commission, and creating the Competition Appeal Tribunal as an appellate body. While the significance of the changes in institutional structure is profound, particularly in the light of recent proposals for

94 Section 2(2) of the Act (paralleling the European Treaties) identifies these as:

> agreements, decisions or practices which –
>
> (a) directly or indirectly fix purchase or selling prices or any other trading conditions;
> (b) limit or control production, markets, technical development or investment;
> (c) share markets or sources of supply;
> (d) apply dissimilar conditions to equivalent transactions with other trading parties, thereby placing them at a competitive disadvantage;
> (e) make the conclusion of contracts subject to acceptance by the other parties of supplementary obligations which, by their nature or according to commercial usage, have no connection with the subject of such contracts.

95 See OFT, *Guidance as to the Appropriate Amount of a Penalty* (OFT 423) and OFT, *Guidance as to the Appropriate Amount of a Penalty* (OFT 423rev).

96 Competition Act 1998, ss. 25–31.

97 Ibid., s. 35(2).

reform,[98] our concern here is with the former augmentation to the UK's cartel control regime.

6.5.2 *The attempt at criminalisation*

The Enterprise Act's cartel offence (s. 188) had its origins in a joint report of the Treasury and Department of Trade and Industry entitled *The UK's Competition Regime*,[99] a subsequent White Paper, *A World Class Competition Regime*,[100] and a report prepared by Sir Anthony Hammond and Roy Penrose for the OFT, entitled *Proposed Criminalisation of Cartels in the UK*.[101] The starting premise of these documents was that notwithstanding the enhancements to the administrative regime which now could impose substantial fines on undertakings, the UK's anti-cartel regime remained weak; consequently, further enhancing the regime's deterrent effect was necessary.

Laying the foundation for a criminal offence was the task of the White Paper. Its analysis of criminalisation began by reciting the OECD's work on hard-core cartels[102] and the then recent cases of (*inter alia*) the Lysine and Vitamins cartels. It then noted that for fines to effectively deter an undertaking from entering into cartel activity, they would need to be increased six- to ten-fold.[103] However, the White Paper, basing its reasoning on American data, immediately concluded that raising fines to this deterrent level could have the consequence of driving the undertaking into receivership. As the White Paper noted, 'This would not be fair. In many cases, the cartel will have covered one aspect of the firm's business and the real participants will have been the few executives involved. Very large fines would damage innocent employees, shareholders and creditors who have done nothing to harm consumers or break the law.'[104]

The alternative, argued the White Paper, is sanctions imposed on individuals, since personal sanctions have the immediate effect of forcing the individual to consider the consequences of his or her actions. As it notes, 'The threat of a criminal conviction and the possibility of a prison sentence means that individuals are more likely to think very

[98] See Consultation (n. 5) and Response (n. 6).
[99] Department of Trade and Industry, July 2001.
[100] Cm 5233, 30 July 2001 (hereafter, 'White Paper').
[101] OFT 365 (November 2001) (hereafter 'Hammond-Penrose Report').
[102] White Paper (n. 100), 7.4–7.7. [103] Ibid., 7.14. [104] Ibid., 7.15.

carefully before engaging in cartels.'[105] Similarly, the White Paper also argues that although imposing fines on individuals may be a useful enhancement to the cartel-control regime's deterrent effect, fines on their own are inadequate as a deterrent insofar as the possibility for their indemnification is open.[106]

The White Paper's discussion of criminalisation concluded by raising without resolving two issues: the definition of the proposed offence, and the penalties consequent on a conviction for offending. The White Paper suggested the obvious, remarking that the new offence must be carefully drafted, to catch 'only individuals actively involved in agreements which could never be exempt',[107] and noting 'The Government has no desire to criminalise involvement in benign agreements . . .'[108] Price-fixing was the paradigm case of activity which was to be prohibited,[109] but, as the same economic results could be effected by different means (customer allocation and output restrictions), the Government reasoned that these, too, should be brought into the ambit of the new offence,[110] along with bid-rigging due to the pernicious effect that has on public sector procurement.[111]

The White Paper was agnostic on whether or not to include non-EC exempted vertical restraints (particularly those involving market power abuses) within the offence, and invited further submissions on this point.[112] In the end, vertical restraints were excluded from the final definition of the offence, likely as a result of the submissions made to, and the conclusions reached by, the authors of the Hammond-Penrose Report.[113] However, in assessing the offence generally, the White Paper settled on two possible approaches to the definition of the offence, inviting responses.

> The first approach would maintain a direct link with EC law, and:
> Make it unlawful for a person to participate in an agreement whose purpose is one or more of the hard-core cartel activities identified above [i.e. price-fixing, customer allocation, output restrictions, bid-rigging], where the agreement also involves a breach of either Article 81 of the EC

[105] Ibid., 7.16.

[106] Ibid., 7.17: 'Some countries impose criminal fines against individuals involved in serious competition breaches. The Government believes that this would improve the deterrent effect of our regime, but is unlikely to provide adequate protection against cartels. In practice firms could find ways to cover the costs for individuals fined. The New Zealand Government is currently seeking to outlaw exactly this behaviour.'

[107] Ibid., 7.26. [108] Ibid. [109] Ibid., 7.19. [110] Ibid., 7.19–7.20. [111] Ibid., 7.21.

[112] Ibid., 7.23. [113] See Hammond-Penrose Report (n. 101), 2.8.

Treaty or the equivalent prohibition of the Competition Act 1998 (Chapter I).[114]

Although, as the authors of the White Paper note, such a proposal has the merit of maintaining a link with EC law, it may require a jury to assess economic arguments.[115] In addition, but not addressed by the White Paper, is that if the offence were so defined, it would clearly capture that activity commonly viewed to be harmful to the public interest: the appropriation of consumer welfare.

The second approach would have removed the link between the proposed offence and EU law, and criminalised 'the dishonest participation' in 'one or more of the specified hard-core cartel activities'.[116] The advantages to this definition of the offence – reasoned the White Paper – was that a jury need not be confronted with economic evidence; a jury would only be required to consider whether or not the accused acted dishonestly, and as a defence the accused could raise honest belief in that 'he was acting in accordance with Article 81 or Chapter I'.[117]

The White Paper invited submissions on defining the offence, noting 'it is critical that the offence is defined in a way which is both clear and easy for business and the courts to understand. It must also be actively applied so that its deterrent effect is genuinely felt'.[118] It is a shame that those deciding on the appropriate scope of the offence did not better heed these words.

A similar invitation was extended for submissions on the level of the penalty. The White Paper merely states that while Canadian and Japanese law impose penalties of five years, the American Sherman Act's maximum is three years; and, in addition, in the UK offences such as insider trading and obtaining property by deception (viewed as analogous crimes, as they have 'similar characteristics') carry penalties of seven to ten years.[119] Leaving any conclusion as to the length of potential sentence open, the White Paper reiterated the Government's positions that a strong sentence was needed, and that a fine-only regime should be avoided to avoid the possibility of indemnification by an employer.[120]

The November 2001 Hammond-Penrose Report was commissioned with the goal of reviewing the necessary legislative and procedural changes which would be required if the OFT were to be responsible for

[114] White Paper (n. 100), 7.29. [115] Ibid., 7.30. [116] Ibid., 7.31. [117] Ibid.
[118] Ibid., 7.33. [119] Ibid., 7.34. [120] Ibid., 7.36.

a regime that would prosecute individuals who engage in hard-core cartel activities.[121] This report would, in effect, establish the policy framework under which the criminal regime would be established. In addition to discussing the institutional adaptations which prosecuting this offence would require, the relationship between civil and criminal proceedings and the possibilities for extending the then existing leniency programmes in the face of criminalisation, the Report was to delineate the parameters of the offence and the penalties which ought to be imposed on those convicted of this sort of activity.

Although the Report's authors felt it was inappropriate to precisely define the cartel offence,[122] the authors came down squarely in favour of including dishonesty as an element of the offence. Not only would the incorporation of dishonesty remove the need for lay juries to be confronted by economic evidence, it had a signalling effect. It was felt that dishonesty would indicate that the offence 'was serious and should attract a substantial penalty'.[123] The authors' focus was clearly on keeping economic arguments out of court. White-listing agreements which may be exempted by Article 81 of Chapter I was rejected on the grounds that the impugned agreement might have resulted in a permitted economic benefit.[124]

The Report recommended a maximum penalty of at least five years' imprisonment and unlimited fines for those convicted of the offence.[125] Like the White Paper, the Report based its reasoning on this point primarily on comparable international standards. Canada and Japan had sentences of this range, Ireland was proposing to raise its penalty to this level,[126] and although the then American maximum penalty was three years, American law could allow for an increase in appropriate circumstances.[127] In addition, the Report noted (without further elaboration) that a five-year maximum sentence satisfies the need for the relevant investigating authorities 'to have the available powers associated with an arrestable offence'[128] pursuant to the Police and Criminal Evidence Act 1984.[129]

[121] Hammond-Penrose Report (n. 101), Foreword. [122] Ibid., 2.2. [123] Ibid., 2.5.
[124] Ibid., 2.6. [125] Ibid., 7.2 and 7.4. [126] Ibid., 7.1.
[127] Ibid., 7.2; see also 1.14, 1.22 and 4.1–4.24. [128] Ibid., 7.1; and see 7.3.
[129] Additionally, the Report recommended that investigators be granted powers under the Regulation of Investigatory Powers Act 2000 to permit not only 'directed surveillance' but also the use of 'covert human intelligence services' and wiretaps (Hammond-Penrose Report (n. 101), 1.15).

The incorporation of dishonesty as an element of the offence uses the *Ghosh*[130] test of dishonesty, which requires a jury to consider two questions: first, was the defendant's conduct dishonest by 'the ordinary standards of reasonable and honest people'?[131] If not, an acquittal ensues. If so, the jury is asked the second question: did the defendant realise what he was doing was, by the same standards of reasonable and honest people, dishonest?[132] If this latter question is answered in the affirmative, a conviction ensues; otherwise the defendant must be acquitted. Courts have subsequently determined that in directing the jury, judges should use the precise form of words contained in *Ghosh*[133] and not invite the jury to inquire, for instance, whether or not the conduct was dishonest by the standards of the reasonable and honest businessman.[134] The effect of this incorporation of the *Ghosh* test was that although juries would not have to face complicated economic evidence regarding the putative economic benefits of the arrangements in question, juries would be faced with another – potentially equally as confusing – task. They now would be required to engage in a sociological consideration of social mores and in particular those surrounding commercial practices. Although the jury will not explicitly be asked to examine the commercial context of the agreement, given the nature of the trial, it would be unrealistic to expect jurors to divorce their deliberations from the commercial context of the behaviour on trial.

However, notwithstanding this, as one Member of Standing Committee B indicated in Committee Hearings on the Bill which would later become the Enterprise Act 2002: 'I said that the concept of dishonesty was relevant. It is a perfectly common concept in English criminal law and should present no particular difficulties.'[135] In spite of suggestions that the Bill be amended to substitute 'recklessly' or some

[130] *R* v. *Ghosh* [1982] QB 1053 (CA). [131] Ibid. 1064D. [132] Ibid. 1064E.

[133] *R* v. *Hyam* [1997] Crim LR 439 (CA), stressing that it is preferable for the judge to use the words of Lord Lane.

[134] See, for instance, *R* v. *Robertson* [2006] EWCA Crim 1289 where, in spite of the admonition in *Hyam*, the Court of Appeal held (at para. 27):

> We cannot see how the complained of words in the summing-up in any way prejudiced the applicant. Reasonable and honest people engaged in business are by definition reasonable and honest people: they happen also to be in business. In our judgment nothing in the additional words detracted from the basic test for dishonesty laid down in *Ghosh*, or created a different test, or indeed caused any unfairness to this applicant.

[135] Nigel Waterson MP, Hansard, Standing Committee B, Tuesday 23 April 2002, col. 148.

similar term for dishonesty, the latter term remained as the offence's definition.[136] Dishonesty was to be an essential element of the new offence, as defined in section 188 of the Enterprise Act. That section provides:

> (1) An individual is guilty of an offence if he dishonestly agrees with one or more other persons to make or implement, or to cause to be made or implemented, arrangements of the following kind relating to at least two undertakings (A and B).

[136] In reply to proposed amendments by the Minister of State, Melanie Johnson is somewhat telling regarding the Government's reasoning on this point:

> The Bill provides for a definition based on dishonesty in order to create a tightly defined offence. We think that that is important. Although there is no legal requirement for an exact correspondence between the new criminal offence and EC or domestic competition law, we would like there to be consistency. The dishonesty test is designed to achieve both these objectives; a tightly drawn offence and consistency.
>
> Bona fide activity, or activity which would be exemptible under existing EC or domestic competition law, should not be caught in practice. This will be achieved first because the OFT will not prosecute a case where there is any real possibility that the agreement between the undertakings would be compatible with Community or domestic competition law; and secondly, because for a conviction, the court must be convinced beyond reasonable doubt that the defendant acted dishonestly.
>
> The sort of evidence that would point to dishonesty is likely to include a failure to seek legal advice, combined with attempts to disguise or hide activity. For example, holding secret meetings and the absence or destruction of records, and other such practices, would be instances of such evidence.
>
> Dishonesty would be proved according to the well-established Ghosh test, which requires the jury to consider two questions. First, was what was done dishonest by the standards of reasonable people? Secondly, did the defendant realise that this was the view of reasonable people? The conduct is only dishonest if the answer to both questions is yes. In a criminal trial the answer must be yes beyond any reasonable doubt for dishonesty to be proved.
>
> That means that the defendant must have believed his or her conduct to be wrongful in nature, in the sense of realising that reasonable people would regard it as such. For example, a defendant whose company had an exemption from the commission, or legal advice stating that the agreement would be exempt, could hardly be regarded as dishonest in concluding such an agreement. In other areas of the law juries have shown themselves to be well capable of identifying dishonesty using the test.
>
> An offence based on knowing or reckless conduct, as is proposed by the amendment, would not be focused in this way. It would cover a much wider range of anti-competitive activity than the Government intend.
>
> (Hansard, Standing Committee B, 18 April 2002, cols. 135–6.)

(2) The arrangements must be ones which, if operating as the parties to the agreement intend, would –
(a) directly or indirectly fix a price for the supply by A in the United Kingdom (otherwise than to B) of a product or service,
(b) limit or prevent supply by A in the United Kingdom of a product or service,
(c) limit or prevent production by A in the United Kingdom of a product,
(d) divide between A and B the supply in the United Kingdom of a product or service to a customer or customers,
(e) divide between A and B customers for the supply in the United Kingdom of a product or service, or
(f) be bid-rigging arrangements.

The Act made *dishonest* participation in hard-core cartel activity a criminal offence. The offence is further restricted by section 189, which exempted non-horizontal arrangements from the offence's ambit.

6.5.3 *The failure of criminalisation*

The offence, as framed, proved to be ineffective. Although in its 2011 Consultation document, the Government notes that that offence's deterrent was weaker than intended, due to 'so few completed cases to date',[137] the Report then somewhat disingenuously claims that only two matters have reached trial stage, with 'only one of them resulting in convictions'.[138] In fact, there has been only one trial, which concerned price-fixing of fuel surcharges by British Airways and Virgin Atlantic. The trial collapsed in spectacular fashion on 10 May 2010.[139]

The matter which (in the Government's words) 'resulted in convictions' involved a guilty plea before an English court by several British executives implicated in the Marine Hose cartel.[140] These guilty pleas were predicated on a plea bargain with the American authorities, under which the British executives would plead guilty in an English

[137] Consultation (n. 5), 6.5. [138] Ibid.

[139] *R* v. *George and others* (Southwark Crown Court, May 2010); see also *IB* v. *R* [2009] EWCA Crim 2575, *R* v. *George and others* [2010] EWCA Crim 1148, [2010] 1 WLR 2676, and the OFT's review of their handling of the case: OFT, 'Project Condor Board Review' (October 2010).

[140] *R* v. *Whittle, Allison and Brammar* [2008] EWCA Crim 2560.

court, seek a specified sentence, and serve it in a British prison. The plea bargain also contained the proviso that should the English court sentence them to a lesser period, they would return to the US, plead guilty to offences in an American court and serve the balance of the agreed sentence in an American prison.[141] While the Court of Appeal expressed significant discomfort with the effect of the plea bargain with American authorities and how it should be received by an English court, it nevertheless acquiesced and sentenced the offenders to the period which they had agreed with the American authorities.

It is clear that 'dishonesty' was the undoing of the cartel offence.[142] The *Ghosh* test required that the jury canvas attitudes regarding the relationship of price-fixing and dishonesty. However, as Stephan's 2008 study demonstrated, it is far from clear that the British public regard price-fixing as dishonest, or at least sufficiently dishonest to incur the wrath of a criminal sanction. He notes:

> The dishonesty test in the UK criminal offence was adopted from criminal law, yet only seven per cent of respondents would compare price-fixing to theft, and only eight per cent to fraud. Most fail to draw obvious parallels between price-fixing and more established crimes. Moreover only two in every four people strongly feel price-fixing is dishonest; suggesting that, while a social stigma against such behaviour exists, it is not strong enough to support imprisonment. This may make it hard to secure a conviction under the UK criminal offence.[143]

Faced with popular attitudes such as these it would be an uphill battle to secure a conviction before a jury.

In addition to these popular attitudes, likely prevalent in any jury, other factors would hinder the efficacy of the section 188 offence. The Hammond-Penrose Report optimistically suggested that there would be no more than 'six to ten prosecutions a year for the cartels offence' with the likely number nearer six than ten.[144] This optimism soon proved ill-founded. Had the prediction proven accurate, this amount of prosecutions could have served as a fertile training ground, allowing investigative and prosecutorial staff an opportunity to develop the

[141] Ibid. [25]–[28].
[142] On this point, see also Stephan, 'How Dishonesty Killed the Cartel Offence'.
[143] Andreas Stephan, 'Survey of Public Attitudes', at 144; see also Stephan, 'Cartel Laws Undermined'.
[144] Hammond-Penrose Report (n. 101), 3.6.

requisite expertise that such matters require.[145] In addition to training opportunities, this amount of prosecutions should also have resulted in a pool of potential matters sufficiently large from which appropriate, and winnable, prosecutions could be drawn. It is successful prosecutions which enhance deterrence. Failed (or a lack of) prosecutions invite contempt.

As Stephan argues, one of the death-knells of the cartel offence was poor case selection.[146] Poor case selection will drive a poor quality of prosecution results. And although only one case was prosecuted by the OFT, the collapse of this trial effectively undermined any deterrent effect which the cartel offence may have had. It immediately became obvious to both government and academic critics that reform to the cartel offence was needed.

6.6 The 2012 reforms

6.6.1 Calls for consultation

In the aftermath of the fiasco of section 188, reform to the cartel offence would become a centrepiece of the Coalition Government's proposals to reform the UK's competition regime. This reform, spearheaded by the 2011 consultation document published by the Department of Business, Innovation and Skills, was predicated on enhancing and improving what the Government (in its words) stated to be a 'world class'[147] competition regime. In addition to proposed reforms to the cartel offence, the consultation discussed options for a number of institutional reforms to, *inter alia*, consolidate the competition authorities (merging the OFT and Competition Commission into the Competition and Markets Authority (CMA)), modernise the markets regime, and streamline decision-making in merger and antitrust cases.

Four options to reforming the cartel offence were proposed in the consultation. In the introduction to the discussion of proposed reforms, the Consultation identifies them thus:

> Option 1: removing the 'dishonesty' element from the offence and introducing guidance for prosecutors.

[145] Indeed, developing this expertise was a concern raised in the Hammond-Penrose Report (ibid., 3.4–3.21 and 4.23), and was discussed in the OFT's inquiry into the collapse of the BA matter (*R* v. *George and others*): Project Condor Review Board, 4–7.

[146] Stephan, 'Dishonesty', (n. 142), 451–4.

[147] Consultation (n. 5), 1.5.

Option 2: removing the 'dishonesty' element from the offence and defining the offence so that it does not include a set of 'white-listed' agreements.

Option 3: replacing the 'dishonesty' element of the offence with a 'secrecy' element.

Option 4: removing the 'dishonesty' element from the offence and defining the offence so that it does not include agreements made openly.[148]

In the Consultation, the Government favoured the fourth option. This was advocated on the following grounds. First, such a definition of the offence precludes defences based on economic evidence. Second, such a definition also sufficiently differentiates the (new) offence from European law in a manner which Regulation 1/2003 would regard to be 'national competition law'.[149] This would have the consequence of preventing the Commission from pre-empting a British investigation and prosecution, were it to become involved. And, third, as defined the offence would not capture arrangements which may have countervailing benefits and, as such, are permitted by the Competition Act. The Government's position appeared to be yet again shaped by the two fears that jurors could not handle economic evidence and that too wide a definition of the offence could potentially discourage beneficial activity.

It is also significant to note that the Consultation Paper and the Government's response considered revisions to the cartel offence in abstract, independent of the relationship that a reformed offence would have to the penalties which may underlie it, a leniency programme (and the relationship which leniency in administrative matters may have to immunity in criminal matters), and the means of private enforcement. Clearly, as the recent ECJ judgment in *Pfleiderer*[150] and its fallout demonstrate,[151] modifications to any aspect of the competition enforcement regime have consequences for other aspects. The ad hoc approach which governed the 2011 Consultation failed to recognise this.[152]

148 Ibid., 61.

149 Council Regulation 1/2003/EC of 16 December 2002 on the implementation of the rules on competition laid down in Articles 81 and 82 of the Treaty ([2003] OJ L1/1).

150 C-360/09 *Pfleiderer* v. *Bundeskartellamt* NYR (14 June 2011).

151 *Pfleiderer* v. *Bundeskartellamt* 51 Gs 53/09 AG Bonn (18 January 2012) and *National Grid Electricity Transmission plc* v. *ABB Ltd et al.* [2012] EWHC 869 (Ch) (4 April 2012).

152 On this point, see Wardhaugh, 'The Cartel Offence Within A "World Class" Competition Regime'.

The Government's response settled in the fourth option. This was not without some controversy by commentators[153] and other respondents to the Consultation. The focus of most of the criticism of this option was directed at two points: first, whether or not secrecy truly captured that aspect of hard-core cartel activity which merits the condemnation of the criminal law (and the moral disapproval which a criminal prosecution brings). And second, if secrecy were the relevant aspect, to clarify the conditions under which an agreement was not made 'secretly' and its makers would therefore be exempt from prosecution.

6.6.2 *The Reform Bill*

Notwithstanding these concerns, the Government introduced the Enterprise and Regulatory Reform Bill[154] in May 2012. Its relevant provisions would amend the Enterprise Act by deleting 'dishonestly' from section 188, and adding a new section, 188A, which would read as follows:

> (1) An individual does not commit an offence under section 188(1) if, under the arrangements –
> (a) in a case where the arrangements would (operating as the parties intend) affect the supply in the United Kingdom of a product or service, customers would be given relevant information about the arrangements before they enter into agreements for the supply to them of the product or service so affected,
> (b) in the case of bid-rigging arrangements, the person requesting bids would be given relevant information about them at or before the time when a bid is made, or
> (c) in any case, relevant information about the arrangements would be published, before the arrangements are implemented, in the manner specified at the time of the making of the agreement in an order made by the Secretary of State.

153 Bailin, 'Doing Away with Dishonesty', Ioannidou, 'Reforming UK Competition Law Regime', Leppard, 'The Reform of the UK Competition Regime: What can be Learnt from France?', Patel, 'The Removal of Dishonesty from the Cartel Offense and the Publication Defense: A Panacea?', Summers, 'What Should the Dishonesty Element of the UK Cartel Offence be Replaced With?'.

154 See n. 7, above.

(2) In subsection (1), 'relevant information' means –
(a) the names of the undertakings to which the arrangements relate,
(b) a description of the nature of the arrangements which is sufficient to show why they are or might be arrangements of the kind to which section 188(1) applies,
(c) the products or services to which they relate, and
(d) such other information as may be specified in an order made by the Secretary of State.
(3) An individual does not commit an offence under section 188(1) if the agreement is made in order to comply with a legal requirement.
(4) In subsection (3), 'legal requirement' has the same meaning as in paragraph 5 of Schedule 3 to the Competition Act 1998.
(5) A power to make an order under this section –
(a) is exercisable by statutory instrument,
(b) may be exercised so as to make different provision for different cases or different purposes, and
(c) includes power to make such incidental, supplementary, consequential, transitory, transitional or saving provision as the Secretary of State considers appropriate.

The cartel offence received some debate in Parliament,[155] and in mid-October 2012, further amendments to the defences[156] were added to the

[155] By mid-November 2012, the Common's debate on the Bill represented about 1,600 pages of Hansard, of which only about 30 were devoted to the cartel offence, with little of the new defences and no discussion of BIS's fourth option. I am indebted to Peter Whelan who pointed this out in private correspondence.
[156] Clause 41(6) of the Bill provides:
(6) After section 188A . . . insert – '188B Defences to commission of cartel offence
(1) In a case where the arrangements would (operating as the parties intend) affect the supply in the United Kingdom of a product or service, it is a defence for an individual charged with an offence under section 188(1) to show that, at the time of the making of the agreement, he or she did not intend that the nature of the arrangements would be concealed from customers at all times before they enter into agreements for the supply to them of the product or service.
(2) It is a defence for an individual charged with an offence under section 188(1) to show that, at the time of the making of the agreement, he or she did not intend that the nature of the arrangements would be concealed from the CMA.
(3) It is a defence for an individual charged with an offence under section 188(1) to show that, before the making of the agreement, he or she took reasonable steps to ensure that the nature of the arrangements would be disclosed to professional legal advisers for the purposes of obtaining advice about them before their making or (as the case may be) their implementation.'

Bill, in an effort – presumably – to resolve any ambiguity as to potential defences open to those charged with cartel activity.

These last amendments to the Bill provide a defence to the accused that he or she did not intend to conceal the nature of the agreement from customers who may be affected by the arrangements or the CMA. A further and unusual defence is available to the accused, namely that he or she took legal advice on the matter. Three observations should be made about this latter defence. First, it is apparently unique, as seeking legal advice (while certainly prudent[157]) is rarely – if ever – a criminal defence.[158] Second, it is not quite clear how the defence, in practice, will function, as it appears (in the strict wording of the statute), to be available only to that person who may have sought legal advice (and not to other members of the firm), and it does not require that the advice be followed. Finally, this proposed defence appears to relate to considerations of honesty, as suggested by remarks made by the then Secretary of State during the 2002 Committee deliberations regarding the original offence:

> The sort of evidence that would point to dishonesty is likely to include a failure to seek legal advice. Combined with attempts to disguise or hide activity. For example the holding of records, and other such practices, would be instances of such evidence. Dishonesty would be proved according to [the] well established Ghosh test, which requires the jury to consider two questions . . .[159]

The motivation behind the proposed new defences is far from clear, but the defence of seeking legal advice appears to bring the consideration of secrecy full-circle back to dishonesty.

In addition, cl. 41(7) of the Bill would require the CMA to prepare and publish prosecution guidelines for the offence.

157 See, e.g., Lord Wolfe's speech in *Christian and others* v. *The Queen (Pitcairn Islands)* [2006] UKPC 47 at [41], [2007] 2 AC 400 at 417, [2007] 2 WLR 120 at 133:

> The sheer volume of the law in England, . . . , creates real problems of access even to lawyers unless they are experts in the particular field of law in question. The criminal law can only operate . . . , if the onus is firmly placed on a person, who is or ought to be on notice that conduct he is intending to embark on may contravene the criminal law, to take the action that is open to him to find out what are the provisions of that law.

158 I can find no other English statute or authority which provides such a defence.

159 Melanie Johnson, Hansard 18 April 2002, Standing Committee B, col. 138, para. 5, quoted in Lever and Pike, 'Cartel Agreements, Criminal Conspiracy and the Statutory "Cartel Offence": Part 2', at 165.

As of the writing of this chapter (November 2012), the Bill had been given second reading in the Lords, and will likely pass the Lords and be given Royal Assent in early 2013. Given the paucity of discussion of the proposed redefined offence and its defences relative to other improvements to the UK's competition regime, the embryonic version of the offence contained in the Bill will likely be born to become the UK's new criminal cartel offence.

It is premature to assess the efficacy of the proposed new offence. It will take a number of years before such an assessment can be reasonably made, as – to put matters somewhat bluntly – there needs to be a passage of time for cartelists to engage in their (now necessarily) secret activities, and their clandestine arrangements unearthed, investigated and prosecuted. To the extent that successful prosecutions establish the success of a new legal regime, it will necessarily be a matter of time before such measurement can occur. However, if the efficacy of a criminal or a regulatory regime is to be measured by its deterrent effect, time will also be necessary. But notwithstanding the need for some time to elapse to gather sufficient empirical data regarding the new cartel offence, there are nevertheless some abstract or theoretical (if not normative) considerations by which the evolution of the UK's cartel control regime and the new cartel offence can be evaluated. This is the purpose of the remainder of this chapter.

6.7 Conclusion: tolerance and ad hocery – the failure of supplementary criminalisation

As can be seen from our above discussion, the history of British cartel control law and policy has been one of half-hearted, ad hoc attempts to do something about economic collusion. This policy, which culminated in the Enterprise Act 2002's prohibition on cartel activity, was, in every respect, a supplement to the provisions of the Competition Act 1998. To date this attempt at supplementary criminalisation of cartel activity has been an abject failure. The lack of successful prosecutions under section 188 of the Enterprise Act and the need for the cartel offence to be redefined yet again in 2012 is ample evidence for this proposition. The failure of supplementary criminalisation rests, in our view, on the ad hoc manner in which it was introduced into the cartel control regime by the Enterprise Act and the underlying – and often expressed – concern that as some forms of economic collusion may be beneficial, too stringent a regulatory regime may deter useful activity.

The history of cartel control in the twentieth century shows this initially tolerant, then half-hearted, ad hoc approach to cartel control. The late-Victorian legal legacy which may well be symbolic of a quasi-libertarian 'freedom of contract' mantra, not only did not criminalise collusive behaviour, but permitted such practices, even if those practices resulted in the state (and hence the public) being placed in a detrimental position through practices such as bid-rigging.[160] Further, while the fact that Marshall's analysis of monopoly and its relationship to consumer surplus was not well known outside academic economists (and certainly not well understood by judges, legislators and governmental policy-makers) until significantly after the First World War might mitigate matters, a similar judicial and legislative attitude towards practices which in effect redistributed wealth (in the form of consumer surplus) from consumers to producers was also prevalent. In effect, not only did the common law permit such practices but there was no legislative will to alter the common law's stance.

This permissive attitude served successive governments, of all political stripes, well. Governments which tended to be friendly (if not beholden to) the business community, could bank on such cooperation within the business community. Indeed, as Mercer quite convincingly argues, this tolerant and cooperative attitude extended into co-option by business interests of the earlier bodies (in the form of the Monopolies and Restrictive Practices Commission) responsible for the enforcement of competition policy with at least the implicit support of the then government.

But this co-option and acquiescence thereto was not the exclusive prerogative of the right. The post-war Labour Government of Attlee relied upon collusive activity, albeit done visibly, as a means of industrial and social policy, to promote, among other policies, full employment. Indeed, such cooperative means of industrial organisation were used in times of national emergency, whether in the war efforts during both World Wars, or during the Depression which preceded the Second World War. Given the utility which such cooperation had for social and industrial policy, it is not difficult to understand why policy makers could fear that too stringent a control regime could deter such benefits. The perceived utility of such collusion and cooperation in enhancing employment and aligning the UK's industries for purposes of economic recovery or supporting the war efforts would serve as important benefits.

[160] See our discussion above, pp. 214–15, 219.

It was irrelevant whether or not these schemes in fact fulfilled their purported goals of actually stabilising prices, promoting full employment, or otherwise allowed their ostensive end to be achieved in the manner anticipated. Like with many other policies of a political or economic nature, it was only the short-term perception which mattered. And as illusive as the purported benefits may have been when viewed retrospectively and in the long term, these forms of cooperation provided that perception during their currency.

The longstanding aversion to deterring conduct which may prove beneficial is clearly seen in the hesitation with which criminalisation of cartel activities was approached by successive governments. The 'dishonesty' provision of section 188 of the Enterprise Act was explicitly implemented to avoid capturing otherwise beneficial activity. Unfortunately not only did the Act thus drafted not capture benign activity, it failed to capture malignant activity and – by so failing – did not provide an effective deterrent to such behaviour. The lack of prosecutorial success with this offence is strong evidence for, if not conclusive proof of, this claim.

In the reform process of 2011–12, in spite of the efforts to strengthen the offence and thereby enhance its deterrent effect, the fear that a redefined offence would cause such Type I errors was pervasive through this process. Indeed, in the discussion of the proposed options for reform of the offence, the Consultation expressed concerns that an improperly redefined offence could lead to the prohibition of arrangements which would otherwise be acceptable due to their benefits.[161] These concerns were underscored in the Government's own Response to the Consultation[162] and in committee debates on the Bill.[163] As a result, replacing dishonesty with secrecy was viewed as the option which was least likely to hinder such efficiency-producing, but collusive, agreements.

From the perspective of our normative argument with which this book began, the reforms proposed in the Enterprise and Regulatory Reform Bill squarely address what we identified as the fundamental wrong committed by those participating in hard-core cartel activity: the use of hidden rules in the marketplace, to the detriment of those participating in the market. And as we have earlier argued, given the fundamental

[161] See e.g. Consultation (n. 5), 6.28–6.29. [162] Response (n. 6), 7.28.

[163] See, e.g., comments by Norman Lamb MP (Junior Minister for Business, Innovation and Skills), Hansard, Public Bills Committee, 10 July 2012 (afternoon session), cols. 545–55.

importance which the market serves as a liberal economy's means of distributive justice, governments are entitled to protect the market from this sort of clandestine, collusive activity, and protect it using the coercive power of criminal law if necessary. Viewed this way, the proposals in the Bill sit upon a sufficiently solid normative foundation to justify the application of criminal sanctions for contravening the law.

However, the reformed offence is nevertheless an ad hoc addition to the UK's competition regime. As an ad hoc response, it attempts to resolve one difficulty with the competition regime without considering how this partial solution affects the regime as a whole by altering those incentives provided by other elements of the regime, or by considering how an alteration of the UK regime alters the relationship which the UK regime may have with comparable regimes elsewhere. These, though pragmatic considerations, are nonetheless vital considerations.

A leniency programme is put into place so that the competition authorities can obtain the sort of information which they need to prosecute (whether civilly or administratively) prohibited activity. The clandestine nature of hard-core cartel conduct requires the carrots of these programmes to be held out to potential applicants. In exchange for providing the information on the clandestine activity, the leniency applicant is provided with immunity from prosecution or a reduction in penalty. However, unless there is a realistic fear of prosecution and hence a need to be immune from a (or receive a reduced) penalty, there is no reason to believe that such programmes will be effective in gathering the needed information – as there will be no need for applicants to take advantage of them. Thus leniency and deterrence go hand in hand to elicit the sort of information needed by the authorities. It is also significant to note that the OFT published a consultation document on leniency some months after the BIS consultation closed.[164] It is unfortunate that there was no coordination between these two bodies to enable a coordinated approach to establishing the appropriate incentives to enable investigators access to needed intelligence.[165]

[164] OFT, Applications for Leniency and No-action in Cartel Cases. OFT's Detailed Guidance on the Principles and Process: A consultation on OFT Guidance (October 2011, OFT803con).

[165] Additionally, since leniency and civil enforcement regimes are interlinked, as the recent decisions of the ECJ in *Pfleiderer* (n. 150) and the High Court in *NEGT* (n. 151) demonstrate, balancing the incentives of public (i.e. criminal/administrative) enforcement and leniency with private enforcement is also of importance. On this point, see the opinion of A G Mazák in *Pfleiderer* at [38]–[40].

In redesigning the cartel offence, whether in the initial Consultation, Governmental Response, in the Bill or in Parliament, scant attention was paid to these sorts of interactions. Likewise, although the Consultation and, in particular, the Response,[166] did touch upon the need to enhance deterrence by more effective enforcement, no consideration was paid to enhancing deterrence by increasing the penalties for the offence. Such an increase in penalties, it is noted, would be consistent with the global trend of such penalty enhancements for hard-core cartel offences.[167]

Furthermore, in developing a competition regime, it would be prudent for jurisdictions such as the UK to take heed of how other regimes attack the problem, since the social and economic harm caused by hard-core cartel activity is the same in whatever jurisdiction it is found. Indeed, in the larger, international cartels, it is the same group of undertakings engaging in the same conduct, acquiring the same benefits by imposing the same economic damage in several jurisdictions throughout the globe. At minimum, other jurisdictions provide lessons as to what may work. Indeed, the successes of the American leniency programme were a sufficiently clear lesson as to an effective means for authorities to obtain information regarding this sort of activity. Its effectiveness in the US has led to similar programmes being adopted in jurisdictions around the world.

In addition to lessons of this sort, considerations of how other jurisdictions define the offence also serve a pragmatic purpose. Consistency in definition leads to a common understanding of what the offence is – it almost becomes a standard, international, 'legal language of antitrust'. This in turn facilitates international cooperation in investigation of offences, in transmittal of information and evidence, and in extraditing accused – all of which require a shared conception of what the offence is. In *Norris*, it was precisely because of this lack of a shared conception of the offence, more precisely the required 'double criminality', which led to the failure of the extradition.

A common conception of the harms caused by such activities, and a similarity in drafting the prohibitions against such activities, will enhance the international regime, and thereby enhance the deterrent effect of a particular jurisdiction's regime. Internationally, the common consensus of the harm caused by hard-core cartel activity is that such

[166] Response (n. 6), e.g. 7.39.

[167] See, e.g., my comments on this point in 'The Cartel Offence Within A "World Class" Competition Regime' (n. 152), 583–4.

arrangements reduce consumer welfare. As such, statutes are typically drafted with this in mind. The UK Government took a different approach, and deliberately so. This is the most significant weakness of the new approach: by putting the UK's offence 'out of synch' with the rest of the world, it hinders prospects for international cooperation, particularly when investigating and prosecuting the larger and most pernicious cartels, and thus reduces any deterrent effect gained by multi-jurisdictional enforcement.

In effect, the UK's approach to the criminalisation of cartel activities has been one of an ad hoc, supplementary approach. The general ad hoc approach to cartel control leads to an imbalance of incentives within the competition regime. Further, the chosen definitions of the offence have led to its failure as a deterrent. The first incarnation of the cartel offence, in the form of section 188 of the Enterprise Act 2002 was, at best, ineffective. The collapse of the BA price-fixing trial ensured its death in that form. While it may be too soon to judge the success of its resurrection form in the new Bill, the definition of the offence – unique to the UK – and its peculiar set of defences, do not bode well for a successful future. While it may adequately capture what we regard to be the most morally abhorrent aspect of cartel conduct, its unique definition of the offence makes it an outlier in, and probably an unwelcome addition to, the global antitrust community.

7

Internationalisation and transplantation

7.1 Introduction

Although the concern of the preceding chapters has been with the 'transatlantic core' of competition regimes, namely those of the US and EU (including the UK), competition regulation is a global phenomenon. This transatlantic core has traditionally provided apt illustrations of what effective regimes 'look like'. This is best seen in public statements by officials in the respective competition authorities when they publically extol the virtues (if not ferocity) of their regime. For instance, the effectiveness of these regimes is 'proven' by these advocates by appeal to how they invoked fear in potential cartel participants[1] or by the amount of fines which the regime's enforcement agency and/or courts mete out.[2] Given these public pronouncements and the indisputable fact of political, trade and economic influence possessed by both the US and the EU, this transatlantic core is viewed as a set of potential patterns for a competition regime, to be emulated and transplanted worldwide. This view of the perceived superiority of the transatlantic models is very much a call for a global convergence towards one or the other system, or – at

1 See, e.g., Werden, Hammond and Barnett, 'Recidivism Eliminated'.

2 See, e.g., Alexander Italianer, 'Trends in Cartel Enforcement and Policy':

> The successes in cartel case work, based on leniency or not, brings me to a second trend: more intensive and tougher enforcement by competition agencies.
>
> As will be developed by the panel afterwards, this is highlighted by an increase in the number of cases prosecuted and the increasing level of fines and other sanctions imposed on companies and their executives who are guilty of cartel behaviour. This holds true for anti-cartel enforcement in the European Union, both at the level of the European Commission and at the level of the EU Member States, which have increasingly considered the fight against cartels as their priority.

Former Commissioner Kroes is also well known for making such statements.

minimum – towards their common values, to the extent that such commonality exists.

This chapter is about convergence of antitrust regimes. It expresses a sceptical view about this exercise when pursued at the global level. As antitrust regimes are essentially about market regulation, and as we (will continue to and) have argued that a culture's understanding of the role of the market as a means of distributive justice is inherently value laden, one cannot expect global unanimity as to the appropriate values which ought to be advanced through market regulation. In spite of this scepticism about a globalisation project, the writer remains more optimistic about the possibility of regional convergence, as it is in regional groupings where common normative understandings are likely to be found. The discussion begins by addressing the nature of convergence: this serves as a foundation for the suggestion that regional associations and agreements are better frameworks for harmonising competition goals.

Consideration is given to the work of Geert Hofstede, whose analysis of cultural values and their implications for developing legal institutions and regimes is just becoming noticed by the competition policy community. Hofstede's insight that differing cultures possess differing values which result in differing needs for incentives points to further difficulties in 'one size fits all' strategies for cartel control via criminalisation, leniency and enhanced corporate governance regimes. A result of this work by Hofstede is that any suggestion of importing or transplanting a legal regime into another jurisdiction must take into account potentially differing cultural values between the donor and recipient regimes. In the final section of this chapter, which provides suggestions for best practice in convergence, this Hofstedian lesson is taken into account in making these suggestions.

7.2 Convergence: goals and types

7.2.1 Types of convergence

These calls for 'convergence' can be of at least two sorts. In effect, when one talks about a convergence of (in this case) legal institutions and principles, two questions arise: first, we can meaningfully ask, 'Convergence of what?'; and we can also ask, 'Convergence by what means?' Answering the former question displays one means of convergence, namely that in regard to convergence of standards, i.e. the legal rules by which certain forms of economic conduct are shaped. Such 'shaping' occurs in numerous ways. This shaping can occur in a hard fashion, where one jurisdiction adopts the legislative approach of another. For instance, in combating hard-core cartel activity, it could explicitly incorporate a cartel control regime patterned after the Sherman Act or Article 101. This is the most evident of this means.

Another form of convergence is 'soft' convergence. This sort of convergence happens through the adoption of another jurisdiction's means of interpreting statutes, or addressing the issue of harm or damages. An example of the latter is found in a recent case before the Supreme Court of Canada. The Canadian courts are facing the two (related) problems of determining whether indirect purchasers have standing in private damages claims and to what extent a passing-on defence should be available in such matters. As Canada's Competition Act[3] is silent on that matter, the Supreme Court of Canada is now tasked with deciding these points; an explicit appeal to the American position found in *Hannover Shoe* and *Illinois Brick* was made in both the lower courts and in the argument before the Supreme Court.[4]

Another form of convergence can be in the institutions adopted by a jurisdiction as part of its competition regime. This form of convergence can be as stark as a choice between a prosecutorial model and an administrative model. However, institutional convergence can also consist in less structural means. Adopting leniency programmes patterned after those introduced in another jurisdiction are clear examples of such a form of convergence.[5] In a similar fashion, the expansion of plea bargaining and negotiated settlements can similarly be viewed as an instance of this type of convergence.[6]

The process by which convergence occurs can be viewed as occurring from either the 'top down' (or hard convergence) or 'bottom up'

[3] RSC, 1985, c. C-34.

[4] On 17 October 2012, the Supreme Court of Canada heard appeals in *Pro-Sys Consultants Ltd et al.* v. *Microsoft Corporation et al.*, *Sun-Rype Products Ltd et al.* v. *Archer Daniels Midland Company et al.*, and *Samsung Electronics Co. Ltd et autres* v. *Option Consommateurs et autres* on appeal from the Court of Appeal of British Columbia (former two) and the Court of Appeal of Quebec (the latter), respectively.

[5] The US takes credit for the development of such programmes. They also take credit for promoting the success of these programmes and their being adopted throughout the world. See Hammond, 'The Evolution of Criminal Antitrust Enforcement Over the Last Two Decades'.

[6] This is well discussed by articles found in Claus-Dieter Ehlermann and Mel Marquis (eds.), *European Competition Law Annual 2008*.

(soft convergence). Typical of the former is the harmonisation (or attempted harmonisation) through international conventions and treaties. Perhaps the most prominent example of this is the European Treaties which, along with Regulation 1/2003, attempt to harmonise the content of European competition law. The North American Free Trade Agreement (NAFTA) in part seeks to establish some (albeit limited) harmonisation among the US, Canada and Mexico in their competition regimes.[7] Similar competition arrangements can be found in the Pacific Rim, in the ASEAN block, and in Africa.[8]

Soft, or perhaps 'bottom up' convergence comes to be through less formally (or legally) binding means which facilitate the reception of influences of other jurisdictions (and the lessons which those jurisdictions may have learned from them). The informality of this process entails that the means for reception are varied: such convergence can occur, for instance, through importing rules or standards from other jurisdictions, through exposure to new analytical techniques and programmes, and through the general environment facilitated by 'joining a club' such as the ICN or OECD. These means of soft convergence typically do not *require* the explicit alteration of the receiving jurisdiction's regime (whether by modification of existing provisions or adoption of new provisions) that hard convergence, 'imposed' by treaty, may entail. As such, these means may be easier politically to sell, as such changes to a jurisdiction's legal regime can be presented as emanating from within the jurisdiction, as opposed to being imposed from without, and thus devoid of any fears of a 'loss of sovereignty' which such external influences have.

At this point, two observations are made about convergence. First and foremost it is almost trite, but essential, to point out that movement towards (or repulsion from) legal convergence is not restricted merely to competition and market concerns. While the globalisation of markets and the internationalisation of commerce may suggest a need (certainly a practical one) to harmonise commercial regimes, convergence is not necessarily restricted to economic matters – to provide a few examples, food safety, environmental and human rights concerns also drive discussions of convergence.

[7] NAFTA Chapter 15, in particular Article 1501; see Collins, 'Harmonizing the Antitrust Laws of NAFTA Signatories', and Dabbah, *International and Comparative Competition Law*, at 403.

[8] See, e.g., Dabbah, ibid., 366–417 for a good discussion of regional arrangements.

Second, and potentially less trite, ultimately any talk about legal convergence, to the extent that legal rules contain a normative element, is also talk about convergence of values. Therefore, suggestions that legal regimes should adopt press protections which provide protection for statements made 'in the public interest' or that they should adopt 'American-style' sanctions on participants in hard-core cartel activity are not just appeals to the values contained in the proposed reforms (in our example, privilege and punishment, respectively) but are also (at least implicit) arguments for the superiority of those values over the values held by the presently existing regime.

7.2.2 Convergence, legal values and norms

Accordingly, to assess any calls or strategies for convergence or transplantation requires an analysis of the values inherent in both the 'donor' and 'recipient' systems to determine if the proposed 'graft' is an appropriate fit. This is particularly necessary when the calls for transplantation also include suggestions for the use of criminal sanctions. Given that criminal sanctions are the most coercive means which the state has to shape the conduct of those within its jurisdiction, and the existence and use of these sanctions indicates that society's strong moral disapproval of the legally prohibited conduct, any suggestions that one jurisdiction adopt the values of another jurisdiction should be subject to scrutiny. This scrutiny should include an analysis of the values which both the donating and receiving regimes possess to determine whether a suggested transplant might be acceptable.

While this point may have been obvious to some comparative lawyers,[9] it is a point to which competition lawyers and officials have only become sensitive within the past few years. In an important 1973 lecture, later published, Otto Kahn-Freund recognised the need for sensitivity to value and norms within calls for the use of comparative law as a means to further reform; appealing directly to Montesquieu's caution that a nation's 'political laws' ('*lois politiques*', i.e. constitutional, administrative and procedural laws) and 'civil laws' ('*lois civiles*', i.e. private law) are so inexorably grounded in the environmental and social factors in which the nation finds itself, that legal transplantation is a 'great hazard'

[9] Kahn-Freund, 'On Uses and Misuses of Comparative Law'.

(*un grand hazard*).[10] Kahn-Freund rightly points out that in the years subsequent to Montesquieu, although his enumeration of environmental factors 'has not lost its validity',[11] other – political – factors have gained prominence. His central thesis is that, since the Enlightenment, the 'process of economic, social cultural assimilation or integration among the developed countries ... has been accompanied by a process of political differentiation'.[12]

This new political element, in Kahn-Freund's opinion, represents the most serious challenge from a practical perspective to any attempt at legal transplantation. He aptly notes, 'Anyone contemplating the use of foreign legislation for law making in his country must ask himself: how far does this rule or institution owe its existence or its continued existence to a distribution of power in the foreign country which we do not share?'[13] Although we may disagree with Kahn-Freund as to the extent to which entrenched political and social power as opposed to other factors (such as what may be viewed as cultural matters[14]) may play in the ability for legal transplantation to succeed, our dispute with him is one of proportion. While we recognise the profound influence which the distribution of power has on the amenability which a system may have for legal transplantation, we do not discount the influence of other factors to the degree that he did.

Among the normative premises of the argument of the first part of this book is that a liberal society will choose a market as its principle of distributive justice. Laws proscribing hard-core cartel activity gain their moral force in virtue of their place in protecting this fundamental social institution.[15] To the extent that the institutions (and their legal foundations) which underlie society's principles of distributive justice are tied with concerns about 'getting', 'receiving', and (re)distributing, their relationship with social power is evident. And this is quite apparent whenever distributive (or redistributive) concerns are phrased in terms of zero-sum games, with 'winners' and 'losers'.

Among the purposes of the discussion of the American, European and British anti-cartel regimes has been to examine those values in the

[10] See Kahn-Freund (n .9), 6–13 and Montesquieu, *Esprit des Lois*, Book I, ch 3 (Des Lois Positives).

[11] Kahn-Freund (n. 9), 8. [12] Ibid. [13] Ibid., 12.

[14] Vaguely these can be seen as an inquisitorial versus an adversarial model, the role of lay members in the fact-finding process, a preference for an administrative or judicial procedure and the like.

[15] See the argument at pp. 43–8, above.

market which underlie those jurisdictions' approaches to cartel control; and in the case of the United States, its successful (and widely accepted) use of criminal sanctions to deter such conduct. To extend our analysis to calls for international convergence, or, alternatively, narrower calls for the transplant of one regime's legal rules into another regime, requires a similar sort of analysis. However, as we are sceptical about the viability of such convergence, our analysis can be somewhat more critical and indicate the difficulties which such convergence faces. While these difficulties are neither logically nor practically insurmountable, they present a challenge to the process, and as such need to be considered by those who suggest convergence of competition regimes or rules. At minimum such consideration is good practice.

The remainder of this chapter proposes to indicate the difficulties which convergence presents. As we will see, these difficulties surround not just the values present in the donor regimes, which may make their reception difficult, but also those in the institutional framework by which such convergence would be achieved. As we will see, there is sufficient divergence in the values found in the transatlantic core to raise scepticism that there are 'common' values which merit global dissemination, and, given this divergence, any multilateral attempt to convergence is likely to result in either failure, or – at best – a weak and ineffective regime. The chapter ends with some remarks regarding best practice for convergence, which draw upon the following discussion.

7.3 Anglo-American values of antitrust

7.3.1 Introduction

As regimes of the US and EU are not only perceived as effective competition regimes, their efficacy is such that they serve as an influence on the competition regimes of other jurisdictions which wish to develop a competition regime. The substantive provisions of the Hong Kong Competition Ordinance[16] are patterned on the model found in the European Treaties, the relevant provisions of Indonesia's competition law of 1999[17] appears patterned on those of the Sherman Act. Other examples of the transatlantic core's influence abound.

While the effectiveness of the American Sherman Act in its ability to deter hard-core cartel conduct is without doubt, as are the successes which

[16] Ordinance No. 4 of 2012. [17] Law 5 of 1999.

the EU's Competition Commission has had in meting out fines on such conduct, there is nevertheless concern about unreflective transplantation of these regimes. The difficulty in using these regimes as patterns to be emulated is that such imitation is an implicit appeal to the values contained in the transatlantic core of competition law. However, as the preceding discussion has shown, even within this core itself, there is a lack of consensus as to what values are to be protected through this form of market regulation. The key issue to be resolved prior to any proposal for transplantation is to determine the values inherent in the donor regime to insure their suitable fit in the recipient jurisdiction.

7.3.2 American values

This assessment is easiest when the American cartel control regime is considered. As our discussion in Chapter 4 indicated, that regime has consistently served to protect consumer surplus. This was indeed the primary goal of the Sherman Act, and was done by proscribing both attempts at monopolisation and the making of agreements which restrain competition. Although the term 'consumer surplus' was not a term used by those discussing or judicially elaborating on Senator Sherman's Act in its early days, the concept of what the Act protected was well understood. It protected consumers from paying more than they should as a result of the monopolistic practices – whether unilateral or as a result of collusion.

The descriptions of the purpose of the Sherman Act, whether described as protecting 'price structures',[18] 'economic liberty',[19] or as a 'consumer welfare prescription'[20] serve to underscore the focus which early legislators had on the individual and the individual's ability to meaningfully participate in commercial activity, free from the fear that larger enterprises will threaten this liberty. As we have seen, the early characterisation of this legal protection for 'the little guy' was phrased in terms of individual liberty, with the corresponding ability to exchange their labour (and its fruits) for fair value. This characterisation of anti-competitive practices as threats to the property rights of individuals made for an easy path towards the acceptance of criminal penalties for the most serious of anti-competitive activities. If what we now call consumer surplus was a form of the consumer's property, then its illicit

[18] *Socony Oil* at US 221, S Ct 843. [19] *Northern Pacific Railway* at US 4, S Ct 517.
[20] *Sonotone* at US 343, S Ct 2333.

appropriation is tantamount to theft, just as any other sort of illicit appropriation of property is.

The Sherman and Clayton Acts, as subsequently interpreted, have the consequence of an assignment of certain property rights to consumers. They entrench a property right to consumer surplus, shielding it by means of possible civil damages and criminal penalties. Judicial interpretation of these Acts can therefore be viewed as nothing more than determining matters such as the extent of the property right and the type and nature of evidence that one must provide to establish that this property right has been wrongly appropriated. As the American anti-cartel regime has recognised consumer surplus as a property right, it is not at all surprising that it protects this property with the same sanctions that it uses to protect other more tangible forms of property.

7.3.3 European values

In contrast, aside from some rhetorical flourishes in speeches of competition officials,[21] the EU's anti-cartel regime not only makes no such property claims, but any claim about the paramount nature of the role of the protection of consumer surplus must be taken with some scepticism. This is clear from our foregoing analysis of the European regime. It is fair to state that the main concern of the EU's competition regime since its inception has been to assist in the establishment of a European market which is free from internal barriers to the movement of goods, services, people and capital.

This was established by the Court of Justice in the early case of *Consten and Grundig*.[22] The central focus of that case, and the point which drove the Court to reason in the manner in which it did, was the market fragmenting effect which Grundig's proposed means of distribution would have. It would, as the Court noted, have the effect of permitting private parties to accomplish what the Treaty prohibited public authorities from implementing. This Court's reasoning is emphatic:

> Finally, an agreement between producer and distributor which might tend to restore the national divisions in trade between Member States might be such as to frustrate the most fundamental objections [sic] of the Community. The Treaty, whose preamble and content aim at abolishing

[21] See former Commissioner Kroes' speech, 'Tackling Cartels – A Never-Ending Task'.

[22] See our discussion at pp. 182–4, above.

> the barriers between States, and which in several provisions gives evidence of a stern attitude with regard to their reappearance, could not allow undertakings to reconstruct such barriers. Article 85(1) is designed to pursue this aim, even in the case of agreements between undertakings placed at different levels in the economic process.[23]

Assistance in the completion of the internal market was at least the original value of the European competition regime, and it is certainly among the regime's present values.

Further, even in a jurisdiction such as the US, which appears to have at first glance a single goal advanced by its competition regime, upon closer examination, this single goal in fact appears to be a blend of two goals which closely resemble each other. Protection of consumer surplus appears to be the paramount value of cartel control. However, in antitrust (aka 'dominance') and merger control, total welfare is often viewed as the goal which the system does (and should) advance. While this standard is often and correctly viewed as being one of Robert Bork's well-known prescriptions for shaping antitrust policy,[24] work by other scholars such as Meese[25] has shown not only that this standard has a well-established history in American antitrust law but also that, without understanding the use of this standard, one will obtain a limited understanding of the history of US merger and antitrust law. In particular, the development of the doctrines surrounding *Alcoa*[26] and *United Shoe*[27] are otherwise inexplicable.[28]

This multi-flavoured approach to both the American and European antitrust regimes can lead to the occasional divergence in result. The varying treatment of Microsoft (regarding its dominance in operating system and media player software) by the US and EU authorities may be explained by such a divergence in goals to be advanced by the competition regime.[29] Likewise, the different reception of the Boeing-McDonnell Douglas merger on both sides of the Atlantic may (at least in part) be

[23] *Consten and Grundig* at 340. [24] See *The Antitrust Paradox*, at 217–62.

[25] Meese, 'Debunking The Purchaser Welfare Account of Section 2 of The Sherman Act'.

[26] *United States* v. *Aluminum Co. of America* 148 F 2d 416 (CA2 1945).

[27] *United States* v. *United Shoe Machinery Corporation* 110 F Supp 295 (D Mass 1953), aff'd, 347 US 521 (1954) (per curiam).

[28] Meese (n. 25), 690–719.

[29] On this divergence, see De Smet, 'The Diametrically Opposed Principles of US and EU Antitrust Policy'.

similarly explained.[30] As this book was being completed, the US Federal Trade Commission has closed their investigation into Google's alleged anti-competitive practices after obtaining commitments by Google to alter some of its business practices.[31] It remains to be seen how the Commission will respond to Google's practices, and whether or not a divergence in goals will occasion a divergence of results.

However, differences of goals have yet to cause a difference in cartel enforcement between US and EU (but not the UK) authorities. Corporate members of major international cartels are fined on both sides of the Atlantic, aided by the routine cooperation of and information sharing by the two authorities. While it is true that in the EU such sanctions are viewed as 'administrative' in nature, their severity has led many a commentator to the opinion that these sanctions are of a quasi-criminal nature, and those facing them deserve appropriate legal protection.[32] In spite of the procedures chosen, whether through an initially administrative process subject to judicial review (as in the EU) or an entirely judicial process (as in the US), the same corporate misconduct is routinely sanctioned.

But this value convergence ends when individuals are concerned. While the US routinely imprisons price-fixers, the EU has no such jurisdiction. Criminal law has been left to Member States to develop and implement. In spite of calls to develop a European cartel offence or a harmonised approach to the application of individual criminal sanctions for cartel activity,[33] no such measures have been put into place. While it is fair to say that since 2008 the European Council, Commission and Parliament have had more pressing concerns, a lack of pan-European consensus on the moral nature of the cartel offence tells against the adoption of such European measures.[34]

7.3.4 British values

This divergence in values leads to difficulties in the transatlantic harmonisation of cartel enforcement using sanctions directed at individuals.

[30] On the background to this, see, e.g., Karpel, 'The European Commission's Decision on the Boeing-McDonnell Douglas Merger'.
[31] FTC Press Release, 'Google Agrees to Change Its Business Practices'.
[32] See, for instance, Andreangeli, 'Competition Law and Human Rights'.
[33] See, e.g., Wils, 'Is Criminalization of EU Competition Law the Answer?'
[34] See, for instance, Stephan, 'Survey of Public Attitudes' and Brisimi and Ioannidou, 'Criminalizing Cartels in Greece'.

This is particularly so between the US and UK authorities – differences in goals have prevented effective coordination of enforcement. The failed attempt at extraditing Ian Norris[35] on price-fixing charges is almost conclusive of this point. As the House of Lords held, price-fixing – in the absence of aggravating conduct such as dishonesty – was not a criminal offence at the time of Mr Norris's activities.[36] The criminalisation of pricing-fixing *simpliciter* in the US, and the UK's requirement that to be criminal the activity must consist of price-fixing *plus something else* demonstrates the wide gulf of values between these two jurisdictions.

The statutory offence found in section 188 of the Enterprise Act 2002 did little to facilitate an alignment of US and UK values. That section required price-fixing to be done dishonestly as a prerequisite to criminalisation. In effect, it did little more than codify the gravamen of what the House of Lords had identified as the common law offence in *Norris*. Given that dual criminality is a necessary condition for a successful extradition application, section 188 was no improvement on the past. The reforms to the offence proposed in the Enterprise and Regulatory Reform Bill will also do little to address this disharmony, as that Bill – when it becomes law, as it likely will – merely substitutes secrecy for dishonesty, as the additional factor beyond price-fixing required to make the act criminal. Again, in terms of transatlantic coordination, the added element of secrecy will prove to be a formidable barrier to extradition. In spite of two attempts to enhance the cartel offence into a deterrent regime which was fit for purpose on the world stage, the UK offence still requires some factor beyond mere price-fixing. The longevity and persistence of the requirement of this element is testimony to a transatlantic difference in values.

The values identified above are the values which surround the use of criminal sanctions. These values differ in both the content of the criminal offence and subject of the sanction. The US approach, centred on protecting consumer surplus, views attempts at cooperation among competitors with suspicion, and particularly so with horizontal arrangements, and where such activity consists in price-fixing (or economically similar activities such as output quotes and

[35] See our discussion, pp. 214–15, above.

[36] Norris was, however, eventually extradited on charges of obstruction of justice for his part in destroying documents and coaching fellow cartel members in their responses to investigators. He was sentenced to eighteen months in federal prison.

market sharing) the conduct is criminalised – whether the participant in that activity is a corporation or an individual. The European approach, by contrast, censures the same conduct through administrative sanctions, as the European Treaties provide no criminal jurisdiction. Similarly, given the Treaties' application of the prohibition against anti-competitive practices to undertakings, individuals are not the targets of sanctions. The values encapsulated in the Treaties show a condemnation of hard-core cartel conduct, but a reluctance to sanction individuals for their part in such arrangements. The UK will, at least theoretically, impose sanctions on individuals. However, for a sanction to be imposed, an additional element beyond (mere) price-fixing is required. Originally the additional element was some form of aggravating conduct such as dishonesty (as the House of Lords indicated in *Norris*). The Enterprise Act 2002 later clarified this to specifically require dishonesty, which the 2012 Bill replaced with secrecy. Price-fixing alone was not the activity which was regarded as the wrong. It was the dishonest intent, or is the secretive nature behind the activity, which is the concern. This later concern, we note, is very much akin to the concerns we raised about the wrongness of price-fixing in our own normative discussion.

7.4 Competing values at the global level

7.4.1 Hofstede's results

It is significant to note that the US, UK and the EU (albeit to a lesser degree) share common cultural traits. Geert Hofstede in his influential work[37] has identified five axes or cultural dimensions which can be used to identify and compare differences in cultural values:

- power distance (i.e. acceptance of unequal distribution of power and resources),[38]
- uncertainty avoidance,[39]
- individualism vs collectivism,[40]
- masculinity vs femininity,[41] and,
- long-term vs short-term orientation.[42]

[37] Geert Hofstede, *Culture's Consequences*. [38] Ibid., 79–143. [39] Ibid., 145–208.
[40] Ibid., 209–78. [41] Ibid., 279–350. [42] Ibid., 351–72.

Hofstede's insights have been applied to an analysis of the cross-cultural dimension of cartel policy, most prominently by Cheng[43] and Lee.[44]

Lee notes that his research results are preliminary. As procedural and institutional factors can influence competition culture and the legal responses to anti-competitive activities, he notes further inter-disciplinary work is needed to robustly demonstrate these correlations. Notwithstanding this need, Lee's preliminary insights are not only illuminating, but add strength to our argument that underlying cultural differences reflect divergent social values, precluding a 'one size fits all' approach to cartel control.

Lee summarises his preliminary results thus:

(1) nations with individualistic values are likely to have a more rigorous anti-cartel policy than those with collectivist ones;
(2) nations with high tendency to avoid uncertainty are inclined to have a relatively lax anti-cartel policy;
(3) nations that show the combination of cultural values similar to those of the US tend to have a more rigorous anti-cartel policy;
(4) Anglo cluster countries (the US, Canada, UK, Ireland, Australia and New Zealand) tend to have relatively rigorous anti-cartel policies.[45]

This should hardly be a surprise. Cultures (or nations) which emphasise collective values are not only more willing to act collectively (whether in business relations or in other aspects of life) but will also tolerate, or at least not discourage, such activity through social institutions including their legal systems.[46]

These results have greater significance when not just business practices are considered, but also when institutions such as the market are examined. Outside a command economy (in the context of which any talk about a 'competition regime' is nonsensical) the market is used – to one degree or another – as a society's means of distributive justice. Differences in risk aversion ('uncertainty avoidance'), inequality of distribution, and temporal orientation all relate to distributive outcomes. Social responses to risk aversion and inequality of distribution can be

[43] Cheng, 'How Culture May Change Assumptions in Antitrust Policy' and Cheng, 'Convergence and Its Discontents'.

[44] Lee, 'Culture and Competition: National and Regional Levels'. [45] Ibid., 39.

[46] It is also not a surprise to note that Hofstede does not consider regional associations such as the EU as entities distinct from their constituent nations. Likewise, no consideration of sub-national entities (e.g. Flanders/Wallonia, Anglophone/Francophone Canada) is provided.

implemented by the degree of 'social safety nets' or redistributive practices implemented to mitigate the perceived harshness of market outcomes. Temporal orientation, or 'thrift', can manifest itself not just in considerations of establishing incentives for individuals to make choices over their lifespan, but also through considerations of intergenerational distribution: allocating (using) resources over (sometimes extended periods of) time. Social views towards the market and how it is regulated will reflect these values. From a global perspective, significant divergence is to thus be expected.

7.4.2 Difficulties with 'top-down' convergence

As legal standards are reflective of social values, legal standards which are 'out of synch' with social values will soon become ignored, suffer from nullification or at the most extreme undermine social respect for the legal system. Accordingly, in light of the divergent social values and how they are manifested in cultural attitudes towards business practices and the market in general, it is unrealistic to assume that there can be a universal, 'one size fits all' means of addressing perceived problems with economic collusion. This has significant consequences for global coordination and convergence of competition law.

Most significantly, this recognition of the diversity of values among nations casts doubt on the utility of 'top down' convergence programmes at the global level, such as those proposed[47] to be implemented through an agreement monitored by organisations such as the WTO. The experience of the ITO shows that for any such global trade or competition organisation to be effective, the participation of the US – and now EU – is required. Given this at least implicit requirement, prima facie, one of two alternatives is likely to occur.

The first alternative is that entities such as the US and EU will attempt to ensure that their values, to the extent that common ground can be found, are reflected in this overarching agreement. In treating economic collusion, this is likely to take the form of some sort of a prohibition on hard-core cartel activity, as in spite of the divergences of the US and EU regime, the two share this common element. However, though protection of consumer surplus by prohibiting such collusion may be common to the US and EU, it is not difficult to envisage a situation where other social values could conflict with this economic goal. One can envisage a

[47] E.g. Taylor, *International Competition Law: A New Dimension for the WTO?*

situation (similar to what was alleged in the recent UK CAT matter of *Tesco*[48]) of buyers' cartels (particularly in the food sector) which have as their effect the reduction of surplus to (food) producers, yet at the same time enhancing consumer welfare or some other goal. One can extend this thought to situations where, for reasons of food security, local development or even outright (but possibly misplaced) protectionism, a nation may wish to establish a regime of 'cooperatives' in the food (or financial) sectors. Such cooperation, to be effective, may take the form of arrangements (such as fixed prices and market segregation) which are normally viewed as abusive hard-core cartel conduct.

Further, even on the assumption that widespread consensus can be found regarding the limits (or exceptions) to cartel conduct, any global competition agreement of this sort is likely to include more than just prohibitions on collusive activity: unilateral practices, procedures for investigating and controlling anti-competitive activity and sanctions are viable candidates for inclusion on the negotiating agenda. Merger control is likely not to be addressed in the first incarnation of such an agreement – as that aspect of competition policy is typically among the later developing features of a jurisdiction's competition regime.[49] However, substantive considerations of predatory pricing (clearly related to existing international commitments on dumping and subsidies) and procedural matters such as cooperation during investigations are likely to be topics for consideration. Yet, given differences in the treatment of these issues even in developed legal regimes, forging a consensus may prove difficult.[50]

The other prima facie possible outcome of a global attempt at competition regime convergence is a 'watered down' regime, which everyone can accept. To get the widest consensus possible, the standards adopted by this sort of regime are weak. In effect, this is a race to the bottom or 'lowest common denominator' regulation. While on some intuitive basis it may appear that some regulation is better than

[48] *Tesco Stores Ltd, Tesco Holdings Ltd and Tesco Plc* v. *Office of Fair Trading* [2012] CAT 31: in this case, one of the allegations made was that there was an agreement to fix prices and pass on the increase to the farmers from whom milk was purchased.

[49] This is illustrated quite well by the development of such policy in the US (by the Clayton Act of 1914, twenty-four years after the Sherman Act) and the EU (Council Regulation (EEC) 4064/89, twenty-eight years after Regulation 17/62, although European attempts at merger control were made earlier using the provisions of what is now Article 102).

[50] Note the varying treatment of resale price maintenance and predatory pricing in the US and EU, and also compare the differing standards of access to leniency applications throughout the EU.

none, it is suggested that this sentiment is misplaced. There is a danger that, over time, a minimum standard will become an accepted standard; and, as the accepted standard, it – over time – will become a standard which will be difficult to enhance. This may be exacerbated if nations treat participation in such international regimes opportunistically: as a good club to be a member of due to its reputation-enhancing effects, but at the same time unenthusiastically playing (or pretending to play) by the club's rules.[51]

These difficulties inherent in a global programme of convergence of competition laws effected by a top-down approach suggest that it is both the *global* and the *top-down* nature of such a proposal which would make its implementation difficult. Accordingly, abandoning either (or both) the top-down nature or the global aspect of such a project may yield better results. Lee suggests the latter.[52]

7.4.3 Regional agreements as an alternative

Regional competition agreements – or trade agreements containing competition provisions – stand a better chance of being more effective than their global counterparts. These sorts of agreements tend to be the products of geographic blocks whose values are more homogeneous than those found globally. Given this commonality of underlying values among the participating nations, such regional pacts also have a better chance of delivering more substantial content than a potentially watered-down global pact. Indeed, to the extent that such agreements can be interlinked with other regional projects, say free trade agreements, these competition agreements have a greater likelihood of success. Trade liberalisation agreements, insofar as they are entered into by nations seeking the benefits of free trade, contain the 'carrot' necessary to encourage the adoption of meaningful (at least in the eyes of the other parties) competition law. Additionally, depending on the terms of the dispute resolution or complaint mechanism which the agreement may include, there may be a sufficient 'stick' present in the agreement

[51] There have been some suggestions that this is occurring with the WTO's trading rules: see, e.g., 'WTO issues loom over EU–Russia summit' (*Financial Times*, 21 December 2012) and 'Trade troubles: Russia should embrace constraints of WTO membership' (*Financial Times*, 10 December 2012).

[52] Lee, 'Culture and Competition' (n. 44), 51–2.

to compel compliance with its terms, avoiding those problems (alluded to above) associated with opportunistic membership.

In many respects the North American Free Trade Agreement (NAFTA) illustrates this point well. A North American Free Trade pact became the subject of negotiations during the latter half of the 1980s, during which time Mexico had no competition law. After some years of negotiation, NAFTA was signed on 17 December 1992. NAFTA's provisions on competition are primarily found in Article 1501, which provides:

> 1. Each Party shall adopt or maintain measures to proscribe anticompetitive business conduct and take appropriate action with respect thereto, recognizing that such measures will enhance the fulfilment of the objectives of this Agreement. To this end the Parties shall consult from time to time about the effectiveness of measures undertaken by each Party.
> 2. Each Party recognizes the importance of cooperation and coordination among their authorities to further effective competition law enforcement in the free trade area. The Parties shall cooperate on issues of competition law enforcement policy, including mutual legal assistance, notification, consultation and exchange of information relating to the enforcement of competition laws and policies in the free trade area.
> 3. No Party may have recourse to dispute settlement under this Agreement for any matter arising under this Article.

The treaty does not define the content of 'appropriate action'. The Sherman Act and Canada's Competition Act served to implement this. Mexico introduced its federal law on competition[53] in June of 1993, some six months prior to NAFTA's coming into force on 1 January 1994. These legislative provisions are supplemented by a network of bilateral cooperation agreements, which, *inter alia*, resolve conflicts among the jurisdictions' competition statutes and facilitate information exchange in investigations.[54]

As a result, Mexico developed a quality competition regime. By 2004, in the context of a peer review of the Mexican regime, the Organisation

[53] Mexico, Ley Federal De Compentencia Económica (in force 23 June 1993).

[54] See OECD Directorate for Financial and Enterprise Affairs Competition Committee, Latin American Competition Forum – Session I: Competition Provisions in Regional Trade Agreements – Note by the United States 10–11 September 2008.

for Economic Co-operation and Development (OECD) was able to remark:

> The Commission has matured into a credible organisation, viewed with respect both domestically and internationally. It pursues its mission according to best principles of management and the highest standards of public service, and has mobilised its limited resources effectively to focus on the matters most relevant to promoting competition policy in Mexico. The CFC's accomplishments are remarkable given the difficult environment in which it operates.[55]

Starting from a position of nothing, to progress to this level within a decade is remarkable. The incentives of the rewards from the free trade agreement and the small number of jurisdictions involved (three) could overcome any divergence of cultural values in Hofstede's sense.

7.4.4 *Global 'bottom-up' convergence*

The other alternative to a global top-down regime is a global bottom-up system. The International Competition Network (ICN), the OECD and the United Nations Conference on Trade and Development (UNCTAD) present models of this sort of a system, in varying degrees of formality. The ICN is the least formal of these organisations.[56] As its name suggests, it is an international network of competition agencies which has as its mission the promotion of competition policy and advocacy. Although it holds an annual meeting and more frequent workshops, most of its business is conducted telephonically or electronically. Aside from facilitating networking opportunities, which are themselves conducive to cooperation, the ICN seeks to develop best practice recommendations for not just policy, but for investigative techniques and other practices. In effect, the ICN as a network serves as a forum for agencies (particularly in developing competition regimes) to obtain assistance and guidance from each other. However, in spite of it being a forum for technical development and cooperation, the ICN does not serve as a means by which information on active investigations is shared among agencies.

The OECD and UNCTAD are more formal international organisations. The OECD was the successor to the Organisation for European Economic Co-operation (OEEC) which was established to administer

[55] OECD, *Competition Law and Policy in Mexico*, 63.

[56] Dabbah (n. 7), 149–52 provides a brief introduction to the ICN's history and mandate.

the Marshall Plan (and to a lesser extent Canadian aid) in post-Second World War Europe.[57] After the winding down of the aid programme and buoyed by its success,[58] the members of the OEEC reinvented their project in 1960 (with the Convention establishing the OECD coming into force in September 1961) to promote economic development and trade at the world level, while recognising and working within the interlinkages of national economies in the global economic order. As it notes, it promotes a process whereby nations (and not necessarily OECD member nations) can 'agree on rules of the game for international co-operation'.[59]

As such, the OCED is more than just an entity devoted to competition policy and advocacy. As part of the development of international 'rules of the game', it takes a wide perspective as to this mandate, setting rules, standards and guidelines for matters as diverse as agriculture, taxation and bribery. While the OECD Council has the power to make decisions (which are legally binding to the same extent as Treaties on members who do not abstain from the decision), this power is infrequently used and has never been exercised in competition matters.

Rather, the OECD will influence competition policy through less formally binding means such as: Round-Tables – bringing together participants of many nations to discuss matters which are of common concern; Recommendations and Best Practices – which can influence future design of policy and legislation; and Peer Reviews – evaluations of a nation's competition regime, most often with some suggestion for improvement. It is through this sort of 'soft persuasion', that the OECD attempts to shape not just global competition policy but also those other regimes within its mandate.

The OECD's membership consists of thirty-four countries. It works with the BRICs (Brazil, Russia, India and China) and emerging countries such as Indonesia and South Africa. Insofar as its members account for the vast majority of the world's trade in goods and are by most measures the world's most affluent countries, the OECD is often, and perhaps unfairly, criticised as being a club of 'rich countries' in pursuit of its own interest at the expense of the 'poor'. In contrast, UNCTAD, as a UN body concerned with trade and the needs of developing countries, provides a counterpoint.

[57] Dabbah also provides a useful sketch of the OECD: ibid., 130–41.

[58] As the OECD's website hails: www.oecd.org/history

[59] www.oecd.org/about/whatwedoandhow/

Also a creation of the early 1960s,[60] UNCTAD[61] provided a counterweight for developing countries, recognising that their interests in the global trading system diverge from the developed countries. As its name suggests, the central emphasis of its work is in development, and particularly the linkage which development has to trade liberalisation. As benefits from liberalised international trade accrue more effectively within a liberalised domestic market, as Dabbah notes, 'UNCTAD's venturing into the field of competition law was nothing but a natural and short walk, which was orchestrated by its developing country members'.[62] The conference itself meets on a quadrennial basis; its Board meets annually and two to three executive sessions are held every year. Its staff, working groups and consultants perform leading work in topics within its mandate. In the competition field, recent work significant to our present focus includes a group of studies relating competition provisions in regional trade agreement and development.[63] Like the overwhelming majority of the OECD's work, UNCTAD's work is strictly speaking not binding on its members. It gains its binding nature through its persuasive effect as a UN body, and from time to time its recommendations are ratified through UN Resolutions.

The most significant of such resolutions is that ratifying 'the Set', or, formally, The United Nations Set of Principles and Rules on Competition,[64] which was adopted by the General Assembly on 5 December 1980.[65] The Set recognises the harm which restrictive business practices cause on economies (particularly developing economies), and provides a recommended framework of 'Multilaterally Agreed Equitable Principles and Rules' designed to facilitate the promotion of competitive markets. Among the conduct which the Set suggests enterprises 'should refrain from' are the common hard-core cartel activities: which include fixing prices, bid-rigging, market/customer allocation. The Set is notable in that it draws all activity which has 'adverse effects on international trade' within its ambit, thereby including export cartels.[66]

While the Set has been periodically reviewed, it has not been implemented in any formal sense. Its influence to this point is as a set of recommendations. Possibly more influential has been the UNCTAD's Model Law on Competition,[67] most recently revised in 2010. This Model

[60] 1964, to be precise. [61] Again, Dabbah provides a good sketch, ibid., 141–9.
[62] Ibid., 141–2. [63] UNCTAD, *Competition Provisions in Regional Trade Agreements.*
[64] TD/RBP/CONF/10/Rev. 2 ('The Set'). [65] Resolution 35/63.
[66] The Set (n. 64), D 3. [67] TD/RBP/CONF.7/8.

Law builds on the principles discussed in the Set, and it is designed to serve as a template with commentary to be used developing regimes in formulating their own regimes. The accompanying commentaries include descriptions of how more developed regimes have addressed the concerns raised in the Model Law's provisions. Rather than stipulating how an effective regime must address the issue, the Model Law provides appropriate responses.

The Model Law suggests that collusive behaviour (of the sort described in the Set) be prohibited. Neither the Model Law nor the Commentary indicates what sort of rules (e.g. per se, rule of reason, effects based, etc.), exceptions to rules (e.g. *de minimis* exceptions, provisions paralleling Article 101(3), etc.), how the rules are to be enforced (e.g. criminally, civically, or a combination), or what sort of body (e.g. administrative and/or judicial) should be mandated with the enforcement of this regime. By providing examples of good practice from other jurisdictions, the Model Law can be used as a sort of menu from which appropriate responses can be chosen, with attention to what may work within a given regime. As such, those developing the details of a nascent competition regime can select appropriate responses, bearing in mind any local pragmatic, institutional and normative concerns which can facilitate or hinder the implementation of the given aspect of the regime.

In addition to the Set and the related Model Law, UNCTAD is also involved with peer reviews of national competition policy and the provision of technical expertise. Further, it is currently in the process of developing an online information-sharing system, which would permit the exchange of information among competition agencies, subject to considerations of confidentiality.[68]

Also notable about the approach of UNCTAD is its recognition of not only the linkages between trade, development and competition, and its emphasis on the latter's enhancement of the former; but also of the utility of regional agreements to facilitate trade and hence development. This recognition of the link among international trade, development and competition regimes allows for the explicit treatment of export cartels as an element of its recommended measures. These cartels, while welfare producing (or appropriating) for the exporting nation, reduce consumer welfare in the importing nation.

[68] On this programme, see Ezrachi and Qaqaya, 'UNCTAD's Collaborative Information Platform'.

Since a normative justification for liberalised trade consists in its welfare enhancing effects for all nations,[69] and not just exporting nations, the control of such cartels is of twofold importance. First, the elimination of export cartels will increase consumer welfare in importing (presumably the developing) nations thereby allowing such nations a greater share of the benefits from trade, and – if the linkage between trade and development is accurate – aiding them in their development process. Second, there is something beyond a mere symbolic effect that by eliminating these restrictions, from the perspective of the importing nation, they are seen to obtain the advantages of liberalised trade: these benefits are directly felt, and not resented as accruing in the wallets of 'others abroad' at the expense of 'us here'.

UNCTAD's soft approach to convergence has its merits, and is arguably preferable to either the OECD's or a hard approach illustrated by a hypothetical WTO-based system. By emphasising linkages between trade and development and a competition culture's role in liberalising markets so the benefits of trade can accrue more generally within a nation, the benefits of a competition regime can be made apparent to those nations which are in the process of considering adopting or have recently adopted a competition regime. Similarly, by encouraging the development of competition provisions within the framework of regional trade agreements, the content of these provisions is likely to capture more of the values shared among the region's members than a pan-global treaty negotiated by numerous states from differing regions, at differing stages of development and possessing differing cultural values in Hofstede's sense. The recognition – implicit in the Set and explicit in the UNCTAD Model Law – that there are numerous effective ways to combat anti-competitive activity lends credence to the benefits of this regime's approach.

While in the writer's view, a soft approach to convergence is the preferred approach, any sort of convergence, even with the technical assistance and information-sharing capacity which associating with other agencies provides, is limited by two other factors: the resources allocated (and the expertise of) the appropriate authorities, and – in the case of controlling collusive activity – national responses to problems in corporate governance. In the subsequent two sections, these themes are developed.

69 See, e.g., Sykes, 'Comparative Advantage and the Normative Economics of International Trade Policy'.

7.5 Resource allocation, institutional credibility and national priorities

7.5.1 Resource allocation as a global problem

The recognition of a nation's fundamental values surrounding the rules of the marketplace, their incorporation into a competition regime which has teeth, and aided by international exchange of information does not guarantee an effective anti-cartel agency. To some extent, the UK experience is living proof of this proposition. Section 188 of the Enterprise Act 2002 criminalised dishonest price-fixing, which reflected the values of the common law. The OFT has been well funded, certainly so by international standards. Yet, the OFT's sole success in criminal enforcement to date has been to obtain guilty pleas motivated out of the accuseds' desire to serve their sentences in a UK prison, in place of a US prison. The OFT's one attempt at a trial spectacularly collapsed in May 2010, as a result of disclosure issues.

It is clear that part of the responsibility for the OFT's difficulties rests in the definition of the UK's cartel offence, and the need to prove 'dishonesty' – with the resulting confusion added by the *Ghosh* test of dishonesty. However, this excuse only cuts so far. In its post-mortem of the failed prosecution, the OFT noted:

> The OFT decided not to refer Project Condor [the BA price-fixing investigation] to the Serious Fraud Office (SFO) for possible investigation by the latter but instead to consult the SFO as needed. Whilst the SFO had superior criminal investigatory experience and resources, especially in relation to forensic analysis and recovery of electronic data, the SFO did not have the OFT's competition expertise. In the light of the factors outlined at the beginning of the previous section, it was considered important that the OFT should develop its own criminal enforcement capability.[70]

The picture painted is a criminal investigatory agency with no competition experience, and a competition enforcement agency with little criminal prosecutorial experience.[71] This was exacerbated by the fact that, at the relevant time, the SFO was under pressure due to its

[70] OFT, Project Condor Board Review (December 2010), 11.

[71] See Wardhaugh, 'The Cartel Offence within a "World Class" Competition Regime: An Assessment of the BIS Consultation Exercise and its Results', 584–5.

own workload.[72] This is, to a very real extent, a resources question: simply put, there were too many demands made on the same resources.

This is an example which arose in a comparatively well-funded, 'world class', respected competition agency. As a lesson it emphasises the need for an agency to be properly funded, staffed, and trained. This lesson is transferrable, particularly to nations developing their own competition culture and/or enforcement agency. In addition, independence – not a concern in the OFT's case – is also an essential element of any credible regime.

'Independence' must not be confused with non-cooperation. As Project Condor shows, there is a need for agencies to work together. This may particularly be the case in developing nations in which agencies involved with trade, development, finance and (possibly) foreign affairs may need to work with the competition authority. Rather 'independence' means freedom from external influence, which may serve to compromise agency performance. As such there are good reasons for staffing this authority with its own permanent, full-time staff. Both permanence and full-time commitment aids in avoiding any divided loyalties between the staff member's exercise of duties in the competition authority and her duties to the agency from which she was seconded (and to which she will eventually return) or at which she spends the other half of her work week.

Training is also important, and the absence of such was highlighted in the BA case. No matter how good a prosecuting authority may be, it (or more precisely put, those staffing it) will require training to develop expertise in dealing with economic evidence. This difficulty will be exacerbated to the extent that any anti-cartel provisions adopted incorporate a rule of reason formulation and/or permit efficiencies-based defences.[73] In addition to the need for the authority to become fluent in the nature of economic reasoning and analysis, there is a similar need for judges to acquire this skill. This is critical: given the need for any subsequent judicial review of the competition authority's actions (or trial after the authority's investigation), there is a need for judges to 'get it right'. Indeed, judicial unfamiliarity with economic analysis and its use

[72] Project Condor Review (n. 70), 12.

[73] With this in mind, it could conceivably be argued that a per se approach to criminalisation could reduce enforcement costs. However, the gains from such reduction would need to be measured by the potential losses by deterring otherwise beneficial cooperation. This is an empirical issue, which requires data from actual economies, and as such is beyond the scope of this work.

in competition law is a concern in developed nations,[74] leading to suggestions that specialist tribunals and/or specialised divisions of more general courts[75] be the appropriate bodies to provide oversight. But this is costly and probably not cost effective in jurisdictions where judicial and court resources may be otherwise stretched thin.

7.5.2 *Resource allocation and competing demands*

This concern about resource availability is exacerbated when the needs are those of Less Developed Countries (LDCs), and indeed those countries which, though not LDCs, are not as well resourced as the major economic superpowers. As with any government, there is only so much that can be spread around, and choices must be made. Developmental needs include matters such as public health, education and literacy programmes, infrastructure (ports, roads) improvements, improvements to the financial sector to facilitate the availability of capital, and improvements to the market to permit distribution of the benefits of trade and development, to enumerate just a few. It is a false disjunction to suggest that improvements to one of these aspects can only be done at the expense of other aspects.

However, in addressing resource allocation – and particularly within the context of development needs – some concerns we noted in our first chapter are relevant. In that chapter, in the analysis of harm, we identified a number of interests which an individual can be said to have.[76] The most fundamental of these were welfare interests, as these are the interests on which all else is built. Welfare interests consist in matters such as health, freedom from pain, security and economic wellbeing. In the individual, as we noted, these are only as strong as their weakest link; if one is in poor health, all the money in the world will not assist him.[77]

The situation within a country is somewhat different, however. The weakest link metaphor breaks down. Unlike an individual who can have

[74] Baye and Wright, 'Is Antitrust Too Complicated for Generalist Judges? The Impact of Economic Complexity and Judicial Training on Appeals' and Wright and Diveley, 'Do Expert Agencies Outperform Generalist Judges? Some Preliminary Evidence from the Federal Trade Commission'.

[75] In Sweden, for instance, all competition matters are initially heard at the Stockholm District which (de facto) acts as a specialised antitrust court.

[76] See our discussion at pp. 22–6, above.

[77] See our discussion of Feinberg's treatment of this issue: pp. 22–4, above.

it all but for one thing (e.g. wealth and security, but not health), at the national level there tends to be a correlation among development, public health and the presence of those individual democratic freedoms which tend to include liberal market values. Indeed, one epidemiological study (using China as an example) concludes:

> Democratic institutions and practices can affect human development in multiple ways, including population health and well-being. The absence of democracy, in particular, can have deleterious effects on health . . .[78]

Indeed this relationship between democratic institutions, development and social wellbeing has been the subject of an influential work by Amartya Sen,[79] which argues for a broader based approach to development, one which includes more than increasing national wealth.

If there is some truth in these theses (which we accept), then, while developing a competition culture is essential to development, a nation need not develop such a culture in preference to other liberal institutions. Thus the issue is crystallised: how to best develop these institutions with limited resources. There can be no unique answer to this – particularly given the conclusions developed by Hofstede. Nevertheless, these considerations point to the suggestion that, to enhance a nation's development, it must invest in a number of institutions, some political, some public health, some infrastructure related, to achieve this goal.

A competition authority is merely one such institution, and the extent of the funding which should be allocated to that particular agency is far from obvious, given the competing demands on a nation's resources. Indeed, an argument could be constructed that coercive response to collusion in the marketplace may not be the most appropriate initial reaction for a regime which seeks to promote freedom. Depending on the nation's history and culture, responses using the criminal law – particularly to social institutions which involve property, its use and distribution – may well not be viewed as liberty enhancing. Again, these sorts of considerations militate against the suggestion that criminal sanctions are a 'one size fits all' solution to economic collusion.

[78] Ruger, 'Democracy and Health', at 303. [79] *Development as Freedom.*

7.6 Corporate governance and cartel control

7.6.1 The nature of the problem

There is a link between how enterprises are governed, and how cartels are controlled. We explored this link earlier, in the first part of this work. Furthermore, there is a connection between business practice (and hence governance responses to firms) and the manner in which the market is viewed: the two are reflections of each other. Legal regimes, visions of the market and conduct in the market all exhibit social values inherent in a society in which the market, the legal regime and the marketplace participant operate.

Our consideration of the US, EU and UK regimes shows a similarity of approach in their attempts to control economic collusion. Corporate conduct is shaped by providing incentives, to both the corporation and to the individuals who act for the corporation, to behave in particular ways (or, at minimum, to dissuade them from acting in other ways). The underlying means used to shape conduct is a direct appeal to self-interest. Sanctions are placed on undesired corporate conduct, with the idea that sufficient sanctions will deter the unwanted conduct. A corporate entity is a rational, self-interested, wealth maximiser; and if anything will be persuaded by these sorts of incentives, a corporate entity will.

These incentives are established by rules of absolute liability. In the EU and UK, the sanctions on undertakings are meted out administratively. In the US, sanctions for cartel matters are criminal. The use of absolute liability as a means of holding the relevant undertakings responsible for the conduct of their agents can be justified on the following bases. First, that such a rule imposes a supervisory duty on the corporate entity: to ensure that it monitors the activities of those it trusts to conduct its affairs. And, second, to the extent that an undertaking has benefited by collusive activity, such sanctions serve as an attempt to, at minimum, disgorge any benefit which the undertaking has obtained from this activity.

In the US, there has been little difficulty in imposing criminal liability on corporate entities. A rule of vicarious liability – the corporation being responsible for the sins of its agents and employees – was the rule from the start. And, although the rule has its origins with an antitrust prosecution,[80] the rule of vicarious liability was not to remain the exclusive

[80] See our discussion at pp. 71–5, above.

purview of corporate liability in antitrust matters. It is used in other financial matters, as well as in environmental and safety matters.[81]

7.6.2 *Individual criminal liability*

On the other hand, the imposition of criminal sanctions directly on corporate entities in the UK and the EU is not as straightforward. The EU has no competency to impose criminal penalties, whether they are imposed on individuals or on undertakings. Indeed, if the EU were to develop competency in criminal matters, it is unlikely that such competency would immediately be used to impose criminal liability on corporate entities, and particularly so for hard-core cartel activities. While, within Europe, there may be some consensus as to what activities ought to be the source for criminal sanctions, price-fixing is not one of these activities.

Furthermore, the notion that legal entities (and not just natural persons) can be the subjects of criminal prosecution is unknown to, for instance, German criminal law[82] in spite of a general tendency in Europe to expand corporate criminal liability.[83] Additionally, the existence of EU legal doctrines such as subsidiary (which mandates that the smallest administrative unit which can act to deal with a problem should deal with the problem) would tell against the wide-ranging EU use of criminal penalties.

In the UK, the *Tesco* test imposes a high standard for the attribution of criminal liability to corporate entities. Specific statutory exceptions aside, the 'controlling mind and will' of the corporation must be involved in the activity for that activity to be attributed to the corporation. In practice, this 'mind and will' is at or near the directors' level – which is a level far above the level at which collusive activity is planned and executed.

In many respects, it is irrelevant whether the behaviour of companies qua companies is shaped by criminal or administrative sanctions. The administrative penalties imposed by the European authorities are apparently significant. The € 896,000,000 fine imposed on Saint Gobain

[81] The ongoing (at the time of writing) prosecutions arising out of the 2010 Deepwater Horizon Oil Spill in the Gulf of Mexico well illustrate this use of vicarious liability.

[82] See, e.g., Diskant, 'Comparative Corporate Criminal Liability'.

[83] See Allens Arthur Robinson, *'Corporate Culture' as a Basis for the Criminal Liability of Corporations.*

in 2008 for its participation in the car glass cartel is prima facie significant. And in virtue of this initial appearance of significance, appropriate legal (human, civil) rights protections are accorded during the investigation, hearing and judicial review processes.[84]

The significance of any sanction – whether administered criminally or administratively – is the incentive that it possesses and thus its ability to shape conduct. A criminal sanction, as applied to a corporate entity, adds nothing further than an equivalent administrative sanction. Unlike a natural person, a corporation cannot be imprisoned; liberty concerns are irrelevant to corporate bodies. Civil disqualification consequent on criminal conviction[85] is typically not a concern for corporations: as any similar disentitlements can be imposed by enhancements to the administrative sanctions. Disqualification from the participation in public procurement contracts for sanctioned bid-riggers can be made consequent on an administrative finding (if the administrative regime is so structured); such disqualification need not require a criminal conviction.

While a criminal conviction may add further stigma to a corporate entity which has been convicted of an offence, in reality this stigma is nothing more than a surcharge on the fine imposed against it. Should consumers refuse to purchase goods from an entity to which this stigma has attached, its revenue declines, hence imposing a further cost (sanction) on the entity. However, should the activity be industry-wide (as successful cartels must be), due to the lack of alternatives open to consumers, such a boycott is likely to prove ineffective.

We should also note that shaping corporate behaviour through incentives is not merely restricted to the use of sanctions. Rewards (typically tax breaks, subsidies and favourable regulatory regimes) are frequently distributed to encourage certain forms of behaviour – particularly location and expansion to a particular region, although such incentives are often used to encourage the adoption of new technologies or processes (e.g. green rebates). Sanctions and rewards are merely the sticks and carrots which a nation can use to shape the conduct of its citizens – whether corporate or natural.

[84] See, for instance, Melícias, '"*Did They Do It?*"' for a recent discussion of some of these issues.

[85] In the US this can be quite severe, with convicted felons losing the right, *inter alia*, to vote, depending upon the legal provisions of their state of residence.

Our discussion of criminal sanctions directed at individuals shows how criminal sanctions can be used to supplement those meted out to corporate entities which fail to control their agents. To be effective to deter any unwanted activity, the expected costs of the sanction must exceed the expected benefits of the activity. In the case of cartels, however, the appropriate level of sanction may well be beyond a firm's ability to pay, thereby driving it into bankruptcy. The anti-competitive effects of this are apparent: an already concentrated[86] and collusive industry will become more concentrated (and more easily subject to further collusion) by the exit of the now bankrupt firm.

The imposition of sanctions on individuals, who after all are the people who form and run cartels on behalf of companies (and quite often do so for their own, and not just the company's, benefit[87]) can serve as a supplement to the (often inadequate) fines which can be meted out on firms. As a supplement of this sort, such sanctions serve to further the goals of good corporate governance. The American figures, which show an absence of recidivism after 23 July 1999, the date on which the first non-American corporate executives were sentenced to prison for Sherman Act violations, provide strong evidence for this point.

Additionally, individual sanctions will have an additional destabilising effect on collusive organisations. When sanctions are only applied to firms, an individual has relatively little to worry about. The consequences of the cartel activity become the responsibility of the firm. And indeed – depending on the length of time required to complete the investigation – the cartel participants may no longer be employed by the firm. When some of the consequences are shifted onto individuals, the equation changes: this is particularly so when individuals are given the opportunity to avoid these adverse consequences through a leniency programme. Indeed, the proliferation of such programmes and their success in obtaining information useful to the authorities (and hence destabilising cartels) shows their efficacy.

These are the responses found in the American and British methods of dealing with economic collusion. The EU, due to the limitations imposed on its actions by the Treaties, cannot impose criminal sanctions, nor can it impose sanctions on individuals in competition matters.[88] However,

[86] As the less concentrated an industry (i.e the more players), the more difficult that industry is to cartelise.

[87] See our discussion at pp. 10, 54–6, and 79–87, above.

[88] Unless, of course, the individual in question is an 'undertaking'.

by imposing apparently significant sanctions on undertakings for their employees' misconduct, the EU adapts to the Anglo-American model to the best degree it can, given constitutional limits.

The model chosen is predicated on a vision of atomistic, self-interested individuals. The efficacy of the US's criminal leniency programme is directly built upon this pursuit of individual self-interest. The corporate leniency programmes of the US, UK and EU models are built on similar assumptions, albeit at the level of the (self-interested) corporate person. There is an attempt to set fines and sanctions to a level so that a self-interested wealth maximiser would avoid the conduct in question.

7.7 Collectivist values and individual responsibility

7.7.1 *Hofstede's insight* redux

This model of cartel control – and, indeed, to a great extent the model chosen for a significant amount of market regulation – is based upon the values advanced in the liberal market, and in particular the liberal market of the Anglo-American construction. The market model chosen by a society, as discussed in the earlier part of this work, is reflective of the principles of justice found within that society.

It is easy to understand why a society which is high in Hofstede's individualistic and certainty-seeking values (like those found in the Anglo-American axis), would accept this atomistic, conception of the market. This view of the market, and, by extension, of how participants are to behave (and, by extension, have their behaviour controlled), gives rise to not only the behaviour seen in the market (such as opportunistic price-fixing), but also the means of governing and controlling behaviour in the market.

In societies whose Hofstedian axes tilt in other directions, other sorts of conduct in the market – and measured responses to this conduct – is appropriate. This is significant where social values of cooperation enhance trust. Stephan's work on Chinese business culture shows the importance of *guanxi*, a form of trust, which manifests itself in ongoing relationships rather than self-interested, atomistic behaviour.[89] These relationships, often cemented by social and geographical connections and family ties, place an emphasis on honouring one's word.[90]

89 Stephan, 'Cartel Laws Undermined', 361–2.

90 See also Cheng, 'How Culture May Change Assumptions' (n. 43), 214.

The consequences of loss of *guanxi* are significant: ostracism of one form or another is the inevitable result.[91]

This is significant. This trust, based on longstanding ties, will lead to conditions which allow for the formation of collusive agreements. Further, the social disposition to trust and the social (and economic) consequences of breach of this trust will tend to thwart measures used elsewhere to breakdown trust and stability within collusive groups. Leniency programmes, promising a 'get out of jail free card' to those who first seek such a card, are predicated on two assumptions.

The first such assumption is that there is sufficient distrust among one's fellow cartel participants to need such a card. The prospective leniency applicant's worry is that someone else will seize the opportunity first. If, on the other hand, cartel participants have sufficient trust in each other to eliminate such concerns, no one need apply for the 'get out of jail free' card. The second assumption is that the consequences of receiving immunity (or leniency) are better than not. In other words, by 'confessing', and thereby implicating the other members of the collusive organisation, the leniency applicant is better off. If, however, the adverse consequences of 'confession' exceed its benefits, confessions will not be forthcoming. In a society which places a premium on trust and keeping one's word, and when failure to do so can result in a form of social and economic 'death', one would not expect such programmes to be successful.

7.7.2 Collectivist values and legal norms

Of more significance to the main theme of this work is the relationship which collectivist values have to legal norms. Our earlier argument entailed that legal norms, and particularly the more fundamental legal norms such as principles of distribution, are to a large extent shaped by social values and gain their legitimacy through these values. A society which values (if not rewards) atomistic conduct will be more amenable to regulation which prevents collusion – particularly if the collusion can be shown to be damaging to individuals. It is not self-evident that a similar conclusion can be drawn from a society which values collective conduct. As Cheng notes, 'Unfortunately for cartel enforcement, cultures which discourage defection are usually also tolerant of cartels and unsupportive of criminal sanctions.'[92]

[91] Ibid., 214; Stephan (n. 89), 362.

[92] Cheng, 'How Culture May Change Assumptions' (n. 43), 215.

A plausible response to this cultural tolerance of cooperation is to advocate criminalisation as a means to change behaviour. The problem, though, is that if these values of cooperation are deeply entrenched, any legislation is a candidate for nullification – by enforcement authorities who choose to turn a blind eye, or their political masters who may flaunt the law for reasons of industrial policy. Alternatively, calls for criminalisation may go unheeded.

Cheng examines the cartel control regime in China and Japan. In the latter, he notes, although Japan had criminal sanctions against cartels since the 1960s, this legislation was widely ignored by both industry and government. Not only were there few prosecutions,[93] but cartelisation was from time to time encouraged by the government as a means of aiding SMEs. China got its first competition law ('The Anti-Monopoly Law') in 2007. That law did not criminalise cartel activity: the contemporary global calls for criminalisation were ignored in China.

In addition to shaping attitudes towards business practices, social values also shape how business organisations are governed and controlled. An immediate corollary of this is that incentives which shape behaviour within an organisation may well be culturally dependent and/or, given this cultural context, redundant. A culture which promotes cooperation has a different set of options open to it to encourage its employees to act in particular ways, than a culture which emphasises individual, atomistic activity. The latter may need to adopt a reward/punishment strategy predicated on individual performance. Other alternatives are open in the former case.

7.8 Global convergence of corporate governance

To the extent that cartel control is a corporate governance problem, and can – at least in part – be addressed through appropriate governance measures, proposals to enhance governance structure must take into account the social context in which the corporation is run and operated. A similar conclusion can be drawn about the transplantation of governance regimes as was drawn about competition regimes: there is a need to take social values of the sort identified by Hofstede into account in designing effective governance regimes.

[93] Indeed Cheng notes (ibid., 216): 'Until recently, the only criminal prosecution of cartel activity was during the oil crisis in the 1970s.'

This is a point which has been given little attention, particularly among those organisations which act at the interface of competition, development and corporate governance. The OECD is illustrative of this point. Its discussions of corporate governance seen in the 2004 *OECD Principles of Corporate Governance*[94] and in the more recent 2011 publication, *OECD Guidelines for Multinational Enterprises*[95] simply do not consider the possibility of divergences in underlying social values. The 2004 *Principles* are oriented towards enterprises in developed nations. The 2011 *Guidelines* are more of a guidebook as to proper conduct for multi-nationals in the appropriate running of their subsidiaries in developing countries. While that publication begins with an enumeration of seventeen general principles suggesting what enterprises should act or what the OECD encourages enterprises to do,[96] none of these recommendations addresses (or even suggests) a responsibility to develop an awareness of cultural differences, and a correlative responsibility to adapt appropriately.

This cultural dimension is significant. It shows that a 'one-size fits all' remedy for cartel control is not only unworkable, but also unwanted and normatively suspect. Cartel control is fundamentally about regulating the market, given the expectations which all participants in the market have. But the market is more than merely a means by which goods and services are exchanged: it also serves as a principle of distributive justice within a society. As such the market often is more than just a means of exchange; it can be a means of redistribution or a form of insurance,[97] or a manifestation of other characteristics viewed as components of a 'good life'.

If a society recognises some inherent goodness in cooperation, and incorporates that into its standards for distributive justice, to attempt to transplant a system which prevents such cooperation into that society's legal regime is fraught with complications. We have identified some of these above. The primary complication is one of values. Price-fixing may either not be seen as bad in itself, or it may be seen as the price which is to be paid to advance other social goals.

The cultural dimension has significance to more than just the goals which an anti-cartel regime may wish to advance through its choice (or rejection) of sanctions. A society chooses not just what goals it wishes to advance, but also the means by which the goals are advanced. There is

[94] Paris: OECD, 2004. [95] Paris: OECD, 2011. [96] Ibid., 19–20.

[97] Perhaps collusive activities which stabilise prices in the event of oversupply is an example of this.

a cultural dimension to the latter as well. In an individualistic society, one centred on the Anglo-axis of Hofstede's values, the carrots and sticks of rewards and sanctions aimed at individuals are effective in shaping desired conduct – whether in the operation of a company or in regulating the market. In a society centred on other values identified by Hofstede, one would expect other stimuli to be more appropriate or effective, and thus a better cultural fit than criminalisation.

This brief assessment has shown that 'getting it right' when it comes to the internationalisation of cartel policy and the transplantation of legal means to control anti-competitive activity is an interdisciplinary problem. It is not the exclusive domain of competition lawyers whose views have been shaped by economic studies of industrial organisation. Whenever 'transplantation' (or similar discussions about incorporating a new method of legal controls) into a 'recipient' legal regime is proposed, the input of behavioural economists, cultural anthropologists and development economists needs to be provided. This is particularly so, the further the 'recipient's' values are from the values found in the 'donor'.

This interdisciplinary facet of the so-called cartel control problem and its solution by transplantation has only recently become noticed in the academic community.[98] It has been ignored – or more likely not seen – by international organisations which produce policy and offer advice and training to jurisdictions with nascent competition regimes. The cultural dimension and the multidisciplinary solution play no part in the exhortations by US or EU competition officials in their attempts to address the convergence of cartel control regimes. In the remainder of this chapter, it is proposed to somewhat briefly fill this lacuna, by offering suggested elements of good practice in the internationalisation or global convergence of cartel control regimes.

7.9 Cartel control, convergence and good practice

A central theme of our present discussion has been to determine and analyse the values which are advanced by existing anti-cartel regimes. The bulk of the second part of this work has been to conduct such an analysis of the US, EU and UK regimes. These regimes, particularly the former two, are seen as viable templates to be used as models for transplantation. Yet what has become evident is that there are a number of

[98] See Stephan (n. 89), Cheng (n. 43) and Lee (n. 44).

different values which each of these systems advance, and indeed such systems – particularly the EU's – may advance more than one goal. This immediately raises the questions of what goals ought to be exported and, if particular goals are selected, whether they fit well into the recipient jurisdiction's legal system.

If we start with the American cartel control system as an example, it is clear that a central premise of that regime – as stated by Justice Scalia – is that collusion is the supreme evil of antitrust.[99] As a result, the American regime has often been characterised as protective of competition as opposed to protective of competitors. Yet, since 1911, and the development of a distinction between per se prohibitions and rule of reason analysis, it is not collusion *simpliciter* which has been prohibited; rather it is collusive conduct which results in certain outcomes which is prohibited. The outcome which the cartel control regime seeks to prevent is the appropriation of consumer surplus.

As a result, the Sherman Act operates to create a statutory assignment of a property right in this form of surplus to consumers. Accordingly, the appropriation of this property – in the context of the American system – is viewed as similar to the appropriation of any other sort of property: as a form of theft. As such, it is an easy normative and legal inference to punish or deter such property appropriation in the same way that other sorts of theft are punished – by the use of the criminal law.

However, the American antitrust regime is equivocal as to whether or not the protection of consumer surplus is the sole goal. In other areas, particularly merger control, total surplus may be the goal which is (or should be) advanced. This equivocal nature of the American regime must be taken into account in any consideration of its export.

From a normative perspective, as argued earlier, calls for the criminalisation of cartel activity because it attacks consumer surplus are, without the use of an intermediate premise, normatively suspect. Our argument is that it is the surreptitious nature of cartel arrangements, which strikes at the foundation of free exchange (a fundamental element of the principle of distributive justice in a liberal, market society) that is the wrong done. In this regard, the system which would result from the UK's Enterprise and Regulatory Reform Bill captures the harm done by such activity. However, in the international community, this proposed system is an international outlier. The author predicts that, given its status as an outlier, there are likely to be significant difficulties in

[99] *Verizon* v. *Trinko* at US 408, S Ct 879.

the interaction of the future UK regime and other criminal regimes, in the likely event that the Bill becomes law. A replay of *Norris* is almost inevitable.

The values advanced by the EU's regime, we saw, are not exclusively directed at the preservation of consumer welfare. In spite of recent rhetoric directed at cartel activity, likening their results to theft, consumer welfare concerns are a relatively recent development in the EU's cartel control regime. The initial concern of the Commission and Court was completing the market: ensuring that private actors could not do, through private means, what Member States were prohibited from doing through public action. However, between this initial concern with market completion and the contemporary concern of protecting consumer welfare, EU competition policy made a bit of a brief diversion into other values, particularly environmental and social values, when it considered cartels established for environmental and industrial reorganisation purposes. In its treatment of these arrangements, the Commission at least implicitly gave consideration to values other than the protection of consumer surplus.

In assessing the appropriate 'donor' regime to transplant into an emerging regime, the metaphorical 'transplant surgeons' must explicitly recognise these 'donor' values. Further, in any transplant the recipient needs to be considered, for suitability. The values accepted by the host or recipient regime also need to be considered throughout the process. Returning briefly to Hofstede's framework, a cartel control regime which was developed by centring on Anglo-American values of individualism and intolerance for uncertainty will not find a home in cultures which place a premium on cooperation and collectivist action and are tolerant to uncertainty.

This 'home' is not just a pragmatic consideration, in the sense that a regime will bring with it incentives which shape the behaviour of those governed by the regime; and 'to work', in the pragmatic sense, the incentives need to appeal to the values of the governed. The 'home' must also have a normative fit, one where the values which are sought to be imported are consistent with the values already present in the system. This takes on added significance when criminalisation is being considered, as criminalisation is a regime's most coercive means of shaping its citizens' behaviour. And, when the values affect fundamental social principles – such as principles of distributive justice and dessert – the need for careful attention to this difference in cultural values is of fundamental importance. This, we note, and remind those considering such transplantation, is more than just a question for competition policy analysts and economists; it involves issues in the rubric of developmental and behavioural economics as well as cultural anthropology.

These considerations also demonstrate that criminalisation of cartel conduct is not the panacea which it is often felt to be. Criminalisation will be justified only to the extent that it underscores the values which a regime already possesses. Our earlier discussion of the introduction of cartel laws into China and Japan points to this.[100] While criminalisation can have an exhortative effect (to criminalise a certain behaviour draws people's attention to the undesirability of that behaviour in the hopes that they will avoid it), it is very easy to overstate this effect. As the lack of cartel prosecutions (at least until recently) in Japan attests, criminal laws, when they are 'out of synch' with other social values, will tend to be ignored or conveniently 'forgotten'.

However, should criminalisation of cartels be introduced, those contemplating developing a cartel control regime should also keep in mind that criminalisation is only one tool in the metaphorical fight against cartels. Private enforcement, through an effective regime, and leniency programmes as intelligence and evidence gathering tools are also important. The relationship among these three sorts of programmes needs to be kept in mind, and how they interact must be fully considered. At present, the EU is in a bit of almost needless uncertainty due to the outcome of the *Pfleiderer* case at the ECJ.[101] The result of that case is European-wide uncertainty over whether the contents of leniency applications are subject to disclosure in subsequent civil actions. By holding that this was a matter for national law to determine, it is appropriate to suggest that the ECJ added to confusion by failing to articulate a clear pan-European standard, thereby reducing the attractiveness of administrative leniency (out of fear of enhanced private damages). This result arises simply from a failure to explicitly recognise the interplay of these three elements, and grapple with the consequences of this relationship.

Effective leniency programmes as a means of obtaining information require the existence of strong criminal or administrative sanctions to act as a threat, or stick, so the carrot or reward of leniency will be sought. Again, policy-makers need to consider whether the values which drive such programmes (generally self-interested individualism) are reflected in the society into which the cartel control regime is imported.

[100] See text accompanying note 93.

[101] Case C-360/09 *Pfleiderer AG* v. *Bundeskartellamt* (14 June 2011) NYR.

Criminalisation is often touted for its deterrent effect. Hammond's claim about the use of criminal penalties and its effect on recidivism since July 1999 is a case in point.[102] However, deterrence does not depend exclusively on the existence of *criminal* sanctions (i.e. criminal sanctions are not a necessary condition for an effective deterrent regime), nor are criminal sanctions a sufficient condition. Deterrence requires the existence of consequences viewed as adverse by those who are intended to be deterred. As people are products of their culture, what is adverse is to a great extent culturally determined: social ostracism is more unpalatable in cultures which place an emphasis on social relationships over individual conduct. Likewise, cultural toleration of uncertainty will have a bearing on the efficacy of a measure's deterrent effect.

Administrative sanctions, although typically directed at the firms which engage in collusive activities, can have at least a limited deterrent effect. The fines meted out by the EU Commission have some deterrent effect, though this is muted as these fines are – in themselves – insufficient to provide an effective financial deterrent.[103] By imposing such fines on firms, the legal regime administered by (in the EU's case) the Commission imposes a duty on firms to monitor and accept responsibility for their agents' conduct.

Likewise, private remedies can also add to the arsenal of deterrence. While private enforcement of competition law has been a peripheral aspect of this present work, the significance of such remedies must not be underestimated. We noted in our discussion of the US regime that such remedies were developed and later enhanced to supplement public enforcement. However, in considering the viability of a private enforcement regime (or private enforcement element to the regime), a number of factors must be kept in mind.

First, private enforcement typically is a late addition to cartel control. The US experience shows this; its development in Europe only crystallised post-2001 with the ECJ's decisions in *Courage* v. *Crehan*[104] and *Manfredi*.[105] This was some thirty-two years after *Consten and Grundig*.[106] Given the fragmented nature of actions for damages

[102] See p. 106, above. [103] See the argument on pp. 97–101.

[104] Case C-453/99 *Courage Ltd* v. *Bernard Crehan* [2001] ECR I-6297, 5 CMLR 28.

[105] Case C-295–289/04 *Vincenzo Manfredi* v. *Lloyd Adriatico Assicurazioni* [2006] ECR I-6619, 5 CMLR 17.

[106] Cases 56 & 58/64 *Consten SaRL and Grundig-Verkaufs-GmbH* v. *Commission* [1966] ECR 299, CMLR 418.

resulting from the multiplicity of Member State private law regimes, it would be a fair comment to note that the European system is still (at least in comparison to the US system) in an infant stage. Additionally, in many relevant respects, the UK's private regime is also underdeveloped.[107] Accordingly, those contemplating private enforcement as a component of cartel control need to recognise that the development of such a regime into an appropriate means is unlikely to be instantaneous.

Second, those considering developing a private element to a cartel control regime must consider the existing legal institutions, particularly those which concern the redress of harms. It is certainly an easier task to add a new cause of action to an existing regime, than create such a regime from scratch. In a similar fashion, in formulating a private regime, there may be room to consider a cultural dimension to redress, particularly when an individually small amount of harm is done to a group of people. This is a characteristic of many competition harms to consumers. In societies which accept collective responsibility and harm, conceptions of collective redress and the ability of the legal system to take into account such 'group' harms need to be considered as part of the transplantation process. The recognition that such cultural values have this sort of implication for a system of private enforcement of competition law has apparently not been realised by those studying the globalisation of private enforcement of competition law.[108] This is hardly a criticism of those working in that area, as Hofstede's insights have only recently been applied to competition law, and this application to date has been limited to the analysis of a nation's response via its public law to the problem of cartels.

Third, and foremost, private enforcement is brought in to supplement and further strengthen a public regime. Senator Sherman's view of 'Private Attorneys-General' who have their own incentives and can use their own resources to enhance the efforts of a possibly overworked public agency is an appropriate insight here. Underlying this is the condition that the public authorities are effective.

[107] See, for instance, the Department for Business, Innovation and Skills' Consultation, *Private Actions in Competition Law: A Consultation* and OFT, *Private Actions in Competition Law: Effective Redress for Consumers and Business.*

[108] For instance, none of the contributions to Foer and Cuneo (eds.), *The International Handbook of Private Enforcement of Competition Law* discuss this issue to any extent.

An ineffective regime is little deterrent. Lack of efficacy can result from a number of factors: a poorly drafted competition ordinance, an ill-skilled or under-resourced investigatory or prosecutorial body, a judiciary which has yet to develop the expertise necessary to understand the potentially complex nature of evidence and arguments presented in competition matters – just to name a few such factors. The UK experience to date has provided some evidence of this. The drafting of the original cartel offence found in section 188 of the Enterprise Act 2002 shows the consequences of poorly drafted legislation. The collapsed BA trial of May 2010 is evidence of the need for appropriate training and developed skill sets, in spite of the investigatory and prosecutorial bodies being well funded.

But it is funding which will be an issue for those regimes which are in the process of developing their regimes. Funding is needed for training (of the investigators, the members of the authority and the judiciary), for investigation and prosecution of offences. It is not feasible that such expertise can be obtained quickly or inexpensively. It is also not likely that, once obtained, such expertise will produce immediate and visible returns. This presents something of a dilemma for those responsible for allocating resources in those countries contemplating the introduction of a competition regime. Although a competitive market may facilitate that nation's developmental goals, the investment in agencies which may enhance such a market may not become apparent for years. However, the return on investment in other areas (infrastructure, health, and education – to name just three) may well be more apparent and immediate. There is no clear, unique solution to this problem. However, the problem needs to be directly confronted, as with all decisions which involve the allocation of finite resources, to force a forthright discussion of the benefits of the alternatives and their consequences.

The final, and possibly most significant, point of best practice is the insight that cartel control is a corporate governance problem as much as it is a problem of individual criminal behaviour. To this extent, anti-cartel regimes must work alongside corporate governance regimes in an effort to control the misbehaviour which manifests itself as economic collusion. Few cartels result from price-fixing agreements with competitors negotiated and executed at the Board level. This agreement and implementation occurs down the corporate ladder. Two points of practice thus need to be drawn from this observation.

First, to the extent that this sort of collusion is not uniquely a 'competition law' problem, a narrow and competition-only focus is unlikely to be the best means of tackling the problem of economic collusion.[109] Second, corporate governance issues are to a great extent issues which can be, and traditionally are, dealt with through the establishment of a set of rewards and punishments. But, as this last chapter has suggested, cultural values play a significant role in determining the incentive structure to which people will respond. As Hofstede's work identifies a number of axes on which such values will centre, it is a fairly inescapable suggestion that a 'one size fits all' remedy will be a recipe for failure, whether the remedy is suggested for a corporate governance regime or an anti-cartel regime.

A central theme of this work, which has been particularly developed in this chapter, is to recognise that the market is not merely an institution (whether metaphorically or literally) in which goods and services are exchanged. Rather the market serves a social function, as a means of distributive justice chosen by a society. As such it can serve a number of goals, such as exchange and distribution, and quite possibly redistribution and social insurance.

In a paradigmatic liberal system of justice, free exchange is the dominant ideal or value of the market. The principles surrounding free exchange imply that the rules by which the exchange is made are open and known to all. By colluding, the cartelists violate this fundamental axiom of free exchange. This is what we initially identified as the wrong done by cartel activity. However, there is no unique flavour of liberalism. To the extent that other values are added to the conception of the market's purpose, particularly for distributive means (i.e. other than mere exchange), the 'flavour' of liberalism changes.

It has been clear from this chapter's discussion that responses to the problem of cartelisation cannot be effected without an understanding of the differing social dimensions to the marketplace. As a result, it is therefore wise to suggest that any sort of global convergence of anti-cartel laws which extends beyond a watered down, lowest common

[109] Accordingly, though there may be merit in the ICN's vision of itself as 'It is all competition, all the time', it is suggested that it may be appropriate to go beyond 'all competition', at least some of the time. While 'all competition' may be effective in focusing on what is at issue, 'all the time' may add blinkers to those looking for solutions. For this vision of itself, see the ICN's Factsheet.

denominator exhortation is likely to be unrealistic. However, this does not mean the end of transnational attempts to deal with the problem. Convergence at the regional level is a more appropriate solution, as it is in regions that nations are likely to find a common alignment along Hofstedian axes.

Conclusion

Our previous discussion has identified a number of themes which must be considered in any discussion of the origins and justification of antitrust law. We have been concerned not merely with the law as it stands today in the US, EU and the UK, but more importantly with how it arrived at its present state, and, given this development, how criminal sanctions can be justified in an anti-cartel regime. In particular, we have looked at the possibilities of global convergence of such regimes. Our conclusions regarding the appropriateness of criminalisation as an appropriate universal response to combat the phenomenon of cartelisation are somewhat sceptical.

Criminalisation has worked well in the US. Indeed anecdotal evidence suggests that fear of the imposition of American criminal sanctions has had a remarkable deterrent effect, eliminating recidivist behaviour, and likely discouraging potential cartelists from engaging in activity that would otherwise affect the American market. However, the American system arose from peculiar, nineteenth-century historical, social and economic origins, which were peculiar to that part of the world. Likewise, the development of the American system proceeded along its own unique trajectory due to economic and political influences which it faced. However, it is certainly clear that other jurisdictions do not have similar historical origins for their competition regimes, nor have they faced comparable political, economic and social circumstances to the US.

8.1 The normative background to cartel criminalisation

Our analysis began by considering the justification for criminalising cartel behaviour. We examined the view, commonly expressed by those in charge of antitrust authorities, that such behaviour could be immediately viewed as theft, and equivalently treated – with the resulting moral and criminal opprobrium that theft deserves. We found this position wanting. To put it in logician's terms: for this inference to be valid, additional intermediate premises need to be added. Indeed, this was the case with all the usual arguments that are often mustered to 'demonstrate' the 'harms' inflicted by cartel activity.

The first chapter of this work examined these arguments in an effort to establish a normative (or moral) ground on which to justify the criminalisation of hard-core cartel activity. The five commonly cited arguments are all, at least in the form in which they are commonly presented, wanting. Our argument started with a consideration of the *sui generis* nature of the criminal law.

Criminal law is society's most coercive institution. Breaches of criminal law result in significant sanctions: an individual can be deprived of their liberty and property for no other reason than the fact that they have violated this law. There is no compensatory or redistributive motivation for this 'taking' of property or liberty. In a society which values individual liberty and freedom from unnecessary interference from others – including the state – there must be at minimum some prima facie justification for such use of this coercive apparatus.

A liberal society is characterised by this recognition of the need to respect individual liberty. While liberalism differs from libertarianism, and as such the promotion and protection of individual liberty may not be the holy grail of liberal society, liberalism nevertheless shows a healthy respect for individual liberty. Accordingly, when a liberal institution seeks to curtail individual liberty, it is, prima facie, not unreasonable to seek a justification for such a limitation. Our analysis indicated that a traditional 'harm to others' basis, having its origins in the thought of John Stuart Mill, is appropriate.

But not all harms can serve as a justification for invoking the criminal law to prevent them. Most harms are far too trifling to be protected by the criminal law. Rather, as we argued, the sorts of harms which the criminal law ought to protect are those harms which result from a setback to an individual's welfare interests, which are the most fundamental of our interests. Welfare interests are the foundation upon which our survival depends: these are matters such as health, security and economic interests.

As we have seen, none of the five harms typically ascribed to cartel activity are those sorts of harms which result from a setback to welfare interests. The main criticism directed at cartel behaviour is that they, in effect, raise prices to consumers, making them pay more for the product or service purchased. It is in virtue of this appropriation of consumer surplus that rhetorical allegations of 'theft' are levelled at those engaged in cartel behaviour. But there is a significant difference between a transaction engaged in at a cartelised price and losing property through theft. The former is voluntary, and the latter is – by definition – involuntary.

A consumer who buys (say) beer, replica sports kits or bathroom fittings does so voluntarily. The purchase is made precisely because the price which the consumer paid was below the consumer's reservation price. There is no involuntary deprivation of the consumer's property. While it may be true that the consumer paid more than he or she would have, had the price not been 'fixed', merely overpaying for a good or a service does not mean one has been a victim of theft. While we may feel that we have been 'ripped-off' when we discover that we have been a victim of price-fixing, we only use this term in a rhetorical manner. Furthermore, and significant for this analysis of the justification for the criminalisation of hard-core cartel activities, while a consumer who may be the victim of price-fixing may be harmed, in the sense that he or she has less money than he or she may otherwise have had, it is far from clear that this sort of harm goes to those interests which the criminal law ought to protect.

Likewise, the remaining so-called 'harms' commonly ascribed to cartel activity, when carefully examined in the light of the justifications for the use of criminal sanctions, can also be viewed as inappropriate candidates for this sort of protection. Deadweight losses are created by the increased (or 'fixed') price exceeding a consumer's reservation price, making the desired good unaffordable for the consumer. The harm here is one of a frustrated (non-)consumer, and is certainly not a harm associated with a setback to welfare interests, of the sort that the criminal law ought to protect. Indeed, Sir Michael Jagger's well-known rejoinder of 'you can't always get what you want', may be appropriate to dismiss this claim.

In a similar vein, stunting the production of new products (and improved processes) is also not amenable to control via the criminal law. 'Improved' processes are more efficient processes (i.e. able to produce the same good less expensively), thereby reducing a producer's costs, which can in turn be passed on to the consumer. Thus the result of hindering 'improvement' to production processes is merely to prevent the reduction of prices to consumers. As harm, it is equivalent to the increase in price caused by price-fixing, earlier discussed and dismissed. The claims regarding purported harms occasioned by cartel behaviour preventing the development of novel products are nonsensical. Such claims suggest that one can be harmed by being deprived of non-existent products, and that such harm should be prevented through the use of criminal sanctions. The absurdity of this claim can be seen in that it would support the argument that, say, Shakespeare was somehow harmed by his being deprived of electronic word processing during the writing of his corpus.

Creating social waste, i.e. the argument that monopolists and cartelists expend resources to maintain and preserve their positions, are more properly viewed as a wealth transfer to other industries (e.g. regulation, the political elite, and – perhaps in the case of cartels – owners of airport and resort hotels). Given its nature, criminal law is not the appropriate means of controlling such wealth transfer. Furthermore, managerial slack (i.e. Leibenstein's 'X-inefficiency') is a result of the agency relationships inherent in any organisational relationship when the interests of the agent and the organisation diverge. While this behaviour may be harmful in the sense that such behaviour may not maximise value for owners or other corporate stakeholders, control of such behaviour is presumably best done through a realignment of incentives within an (and tailored for each) organisation, rather than a jurisdiction-wide criminal regime.

It is not suggested that price-fixing activity is not harmful. After all, a consumer who has to pay more as a result of a higher, non-competitive price has less money after the transaction than she otherwise would have and is thereby harmed. Someone who cannot afford a product due to the inflated non-competitive price is harmed by having a desire frustrated. But we suggest that harms of this sort are not the types of harms for which it is appropriate to use the criminal law to eliminate.

Rather our view is that the primary harm done by price-fixing activity is its effect which it has on society's chosen means of distributive justice: the market. A liberal society uses a market for the allocation (i.e. distribution) of goods, not exclusively because it is the most efficient means of distribution, but also because it is the means of distribution that maximises individual freedom of choice given the alternatives open to society. The market, in a liberal society, is thus a fundamental social institution, and as such – as we argued – deserves the protection of the criminal law.

Market manipulation can therefore be properly viewed as a harm inflicted on a significant social institution. In many respects this harm is comparable to the harm done by tax evasion. Taxation is a means by which governments raise funds to provide for institutions to benefit society generally. At minimum these include public goods (and public good-like) institutions such as external and internal security (national defence, police and other related institutions), public health, and means of democratic participation. Failing to contribute one's share of taxes is a form of free-riding, creating a self-exception. The free-rider takes the advantages of the institution, yet is unwilling to contribute to the burdens of the institution.

In a situation of market abuse, the abuser expects others to play by the rules (and encourages the belief that the abuser is playing by the rules), yet the abuser does not play by the rules when it is in their benefit not to so do. For instance, in a situation of insider trading, the person trading on undisclosed information relies on other players in the market to act under the belief that the market was fair, at least in the sense that all relevant information was disclosed. The 'insider', however, creates a self-exception to this, and takes personal advantage of the situation. Among the reasons for prohibiting insider trading is that if this practice becomes common (or in Kantian terms, 'generalised') the integrity of capital markets is cast into doubt, thereby undermining their institutional stature.

Price-fixing is similar. In a liberal market economy, a purchaser expects to take advantage of a competitive market, and thereby obtain a desired good at a competitive price. A price-fixer knows this, but clandestinely causes the price to be set at a super-competitive level, thereby appropriating some of the consumer surplus to itself. Were the price-fixer's hidden agenda to become generalised, the institution of the market, which serves as the principle of distribution in liberal economies, is undermined. The appropriate analogy is to a fixed sporting event. It is often said that match-fixing undermines the game. But this is nothing more than a shorthand manner of stating that match-fixing undermines the spectator's confidence in believing that what they are seeing is a real match of skill, as opposed to pre-arraigned theatre.

Likewise price-fixing undermines a market participant's confidence in the integrity of the market, and here it is the market generally – and not a particular (e.g. capital) market. That price-fixing affects the market in a generalised manner is of significance. In the sort of society in which we live, and to which a competition regime is applicable, citizens are compelled to engage in market transactions on an ongoing basis. This is the significance of a market-based system of distribution within a society. Any sort of market manipulation which undermines participants' confidence in market integrity strikes at the core of a fundamental social institution. This, we have argued, justifies the use of the coercive power of the state – in the form of the criminal law – to prevent. We note that this justification of criminalisation is entirely independent of considerations of harm *directly* done to consumers.

Direct harm to consumers could potentially serve as an additional reason for justifying the use of criminal sanctions to prevent so-called hard-core cartel activity. However, to justify this conclusion an intermediate premise is needed, and such a premise is necessarily dependent on the individual nature of a particular legal system, and not a market economy generally. If consumers are granted an explicit property right in consumer surplus, then – and only then – will price-fixing activity constitute theft. As we have noted, the American regime does this – we shall return to this point briefly.

8.2 A pragmatic justification for cartel criminalisation

In addition to the moral, or normative, reasons why criminalisation of cartel activity is justified, we have also seen two strong pragmatic grounds for the criminalisation of price-fixing behaviour, at both the firm and the individual level. Sanctions at the firm level are related to the nature of the modern business organisation, and the agency model used in its operation. Sanctions at the individual level are justified to supplement control of opportunistic behaviour by agents.

Unwanted conduct (from the perspective of the business' owners) arises, to a great extent, from the need to delegate responsibility within the organisation, and the resulting inability to constantly monitor the activities of those tasked with performing them. The interests of the agent often diverge from the interests of other stakeholders in the company (e.g. owners/shareholders, other employees, creditors). In pursing their own interests, the agents' actions can have detrimental consequences for other stakeholders. The imposition of criminal sanctions on firms whose agents misbehave provides an incentive to monitor and control their activity.

The evidence of the genesis of cartel behaviour shows that price-fixing agreements almost inevitably originate down the 'corporate ladder' from the boardroom. Although the Fine Art Cartel (and possibly a few others) may be viewed as exceptions to this, these may be the rhetorical 'exceptions which prove the rule'. Price-fixing typically occurs at the level of sales and marketing executives, rather than in the boardroom. Consequently, attacking this phenomenon, and effectively imposing criminal liability on the firm, requires a rule of corporate liability other than the so-called *Tesco* rule.

Vicarious liability, as it effectively imposes a duty on the firm to monitor its agents, is the appropriate rule. And, as also argued, such a rule should not permit an exception for due diligence in supervision or for the existence of 'adequate safeguards'. It has been argued that these latter exceptions (defences) to a rule of vicarious liability are justified only on the condition that the activity sought to be controlled has social worth. However, given the pernicious effect which price-fixing has on the market, this condition is not satisfied. There is no such thing as an efficient level of price-fixing.

Further, the imposition of individual criminal liability serves as an additional deterrent to liability imposed at the firm level. First, by imposing sanctions on the agent, it ensures that the agent's pursuit of his own self-interest at the potential expense of his employer is not costless. If the only sanction imposed were imposed on the firm, the agent may escape any personal cost for the activity. (Indeed, were the sanction imposed several years after the activity, the agent could have possibly retired or moved on to other employment, avoiding even those sanctions an employer could impose.) Individual criminal liability aids in addressing the agency issue.

Second, imposition of individual criminal liability for price-fixing adds a much-needed supplement to the deterrent effect which sanctions on firms have. Becker's calculus shows us that if a risk-neutral individual is to be deterred from engaging in a practice (criminal or other), the expected costs of engaging in that practice must exceed its expected benefits. However, the data regarding the benefits which price-fixers yield from their activities indicate that this behaviour is not only extremely profitable, but likely exceeds the costs imposed by fines (at least in Europe). Merely increasing fines, however, is not an adequate response.

The economic data surrounding cartel overcharges and durations indicate that in many cases a fine with appropriate deterrent effect would have a bankrupting effect on the firm in question. As such a firm's exit would further concentrate an already uncompetitive market, this consequence is undesirable. However, should the sanctions be insufficient, they will be an annoyance, a tax or licence fee on cartel activity. There is thus a gap between a sufficient level of sanctions to have appropriate deterrent effect, and the level at which they can be applied without having an anti-competitive effect in a given market. We have argued that a practical effect of individual criminal liability for competition offences is to fill this 'deterrence gap'. These practical reasons provide powerful, though pragmatic, arguments for the use of criminal sanctions in enforcing competition law. The pragmatic arguments become stronger if they are – as we argue they should – taken as being supported by our initial moral (or normative) arguments.

8.3 Scepticism about the expansion of criminalisation: the US , EU and UK regimes examined

These normative and pragmatic considerations act as benchmarks for us to examine the competition regimes of the US and EU. The US regime is often viewed as a paradigm to be emulated by other regimes. Indeed, from the perspective of deterrence, it is effective, as the lack of recidivism since 23 July 1999 attests. The EU system can be fairly viewed as growing teeth: becoming more effective in the fight against cartels, yet with its own weaknesses. As we have witnessed, in order to strengthen the system, academic commentators have suggested enhancing it by incorporating criminal sanctions into it.

Our historical considerations of American competition law showed an almost consistent focus on the desire to protect consumer welfare and to – in effect – assign a property right in consumer welfare to consumers. Although, considering the Sherman Act in the closing decades of the nineteenth century, they would not have been aware of the term 'consumer surplus', it is clear that by protecting a buyer's ability to pay lower prices in the face of cartel activity, these legislators and judges were protecting consumer surplus. While American merger control law is often, and fairly, criticised as possessing differing and confusing goals, such a criticism cannot be directed at American cartel control law. Collusion (i.e. price-fixing) and related behaviour, with their attendant appropriation of consumer surplus, have been consistently regarded as (to use Justice Scalia's words) 'the supreme evil of antitrust'.[1]

Initial disagreement about the extent of the Sherman Act's scope – whether it extended to all agreements or merely 'unreasonable' ones – and the Depression era proved to inject a bit of initial uncertainty in the judicial interpretation of that Act. However, this uncertainty was soon resolved by the Supreme Court. The 1927 case of *Trenton Potteries* indicated the Court's view of the dangers of holding a price-fixing agreement to be 'reasonable', irrespective of any social gains. This view was

[1] *Verizon Communications Inc.* v. *Law Offices of Curtis V Trinko LLP* 540 US 398, 408, 124 S Ct 872, 879 (2004).

to remain a constant theme in subsequent jurisprudence, thereby providing a fulcrum point by which the Depression-era case of *Appalachian Coals* could eventually be distinguished into obscurity.

In the last thirty-five (or so) years American courts have developed a greater economic sensitivity. It is certainly no coincidence that this sensitivity mirrored the publication of Bork's *The Antitrust Paradox* and the ascendency of the Chicago school's approach to antitrust law. However, it is fair to say that, though this sensitivity may be influential on matters such as merger control and vertical agreements, it has done little to erode the longstanding suspicion which the courts have had toward collusive horizontal agreements.

As *NCAA* indicates, economic sensitivity towards horizontal arrangements merely requires a 'quick look' at the industry structure to determine whether the product delivered requires some form of cooperation. As the case law shows, sports leagues require this element. Professional associations and Universities in their delivery of financial aid packages to prospective students do not. If the restraint is a naked restraint, and the industry does not require cooperation for the delivery of the good, no further analysis is necessary.

So in spite of the increasing reliance on microeconomic analysis in American antitrust law generally, there has been little weakening of the universal condemnation of the effects of collusion. Whether this is expressed as (in Sherman's original Bill) any practices 'which tend to advance the cost to the consumer of any article', as (in *NCAA*) diminishing consumer preference, or even (as Justice Scalia rhetorically expressed it) 'the supreme evil of antitrust' is irrelevant: the overwhelming goal of American anti-cartel laws has been to protect consumer welfare. In effect the Sherman Act is an assignment of a property right in consumer surplus, and it does so to the greatest extent constitutionally permitted.

Notwithstanding this assignment of property rights, American antitrust will also examine the effects of a practice on the market, and the importance of – in effect – the rules of the market. *Topco* is illustrative of this point. Justice Marshall's comments[2] well illustrate the view that the Sherman Act serves as an economic 'Bill of Rights', ensuring that competitors can interact in the market free of any hindrance of foreclosure from private groups. These remarks echo the majority's view in *Northern Pacific Railway*[3] that the economic charter advanced by the Sherman Act yields (among other things) the best allocation of resources, the highest

[2] Quoted above, p. 146. [3] Quoted above, p. 144.

quality of goods and the lowest prices. A competitive market, characterised by an absence of private forces imposing hidden rules, promotes consumer welfare.

By promoting consumer welfare and when viewed by an American public in this way, the anti-cartel programme of the Sherman Act can be seen very positively. Rightly or wrongly, cartel control is viewed as saving consumers significant sums. This popularity has been enhanced by judicious case selection on the part of the DOJ which went hand-in-hand with an increase in penalties imposed on both firms and individuals convicted of hard-core cartel offences. Its popularity has enhanced its effectiveness: in those cases which go to trial, juries are willing to convict, and recidivism is low to non-existent. In turn, its effectiveness has made it one of the most feared systems internationally. Anecdotal evidence suggests that international cartels will avoid affecting the American market out of fear of the consequences. And it is precisely because of its effectiveness that other jurisdictions look toward it as a source of inspiration.

In contrast, the EU's competition system does not have an underlying economic 'Bill of Rights'. Rather, this system is built upon two European treaties having their origins in earlier treaties and associated political compromises. Our examination of the historical and intellectual antecedents to the post-Lisbon regime shows that European law expresses neither a clear, unique goal of the role of competition policy within an integrated Europe nor a conception of the market which is amenable to the notion that consumer welfare is the primary goal to be protected by competition policy.

Our brief review of the European intellectual climate which surrounded the years preceding the signing of the early treaties was heavily influenced by ordoliberalism. This economic philosophy viewed the market differently from Anglo-American liberalism. In the ordoliberal conception of market regulation, the goal of the competition is to prevent abuse of market players from concentration of power by other players (whether private or governmental in nature). If protection of consumer surplus was ever a consideration for the ordoliberals, it was only secondary to other considerations.

The notion of freedom from economic concentration and its resulting market abuse was also appealing to those who put themselves in charge of reconstructing the Continental economy after the Second World War. Cartels and other means of economic cooperation were rightly viewed as being an integral feature of the German war-machine, and thus an economic feature which had to be eliminated to prevent re-militarisation on the Continent. An anti-cartel law of the Sherman Act sort would facilitate this industrial deconcentration.

Analysis of these intellectual roots has shown that although there is an element of truth in both of the above accounts, neither alone explains the background to the early treaties. Additionally, those negotiating (and influencing the negotiations of) a Common Market also gave consideration to market integration stimulated by desires to rebuild the Continent through expanding its industrial production by providing an expanded market. Additionally, when interlinking the economies of its states, there was the anticipation that such linkage would promote a lasting peace.

In a very real sense, then, market integration can be seen as the original conception of a 'European market'. This would be a market where goods, services, capital and payments could be readily transferred across formerly hostile frontiers, without barriers – imposed either publically or privately – to hinder such a flow. Competition law, in the early days of the Common Market, served as the handmaiden of market integration. While the Commission's enforcement priorities may have changed in the past two decades, market integration nevertheless remains an important objective of EU competition policy.

Significantly, although the European treaties view a competitive market as a goal of the Union, competition is only one goal among many. Our analysis suggests that a competitive market has never been *the*, in the sense of exclusive, goal of the EU or its predecessors. At best, it was *one of* the goals: important, yes, but not unique. Further, in the context of a post-Lisbon Europe, it is far from clear that if there were a hierarchy of Treaty goals, completion would be near the top.

The significance of this is evident. Preservation of consumer welfare cannot be viewed as the overwhelming goal of European competition law. To do so likely reads the treaties' articles in isolation, and ignores the provisos of TEU Article 3(3), which indicates that the Union should work for a 'social market economy'. This is a dramatically different concept of a market than that protected by the Sherman Act.

This multiplicity of market goals casts doubt on what the rules of 'the European market' are. A social market economy not only uses the market as a means of economic distribution, but it also uses it to achieve other social goals, as its name suggests. It can thereby advance employment objectives, regional considerations, and environmental concerns, among others. It is the consistency with social concerns that obscures the objectives of the market within the EU. Although market segregation may be an unequivocal *malum*, there are few – if any – others.

Given this equivocal nature of market goals which encompass both economic and social agendas, arguments for criminalising market collusion at the European level are somewhat difficult to make. It is clear that a set of producers who collude to raise the price of a good so that they may appropriate consumer surplus to themselves, clearly play 'fast and loose' with the rules of any market. However, it is also clear that the mere appropriation of consumer surplus, in the absence of a contrary assignment of a property right in it, is not an appropriate target for criminal sanctions. We note that it would be a significant mistake to read the European treaties as providing such an assignment of a property right. Further, as social considerations – as an example, for environmental or developmental considerations – may motivate such an appropriation of consumer surplus, the argument for such collusive behaviour to be criminalised becomes even murkier.

Given that criminal laws, to be viewed as legitimate to the members of a society that these laws purport to govern, must be accepted by its members, social attitudes towards a given activity are significant considerations in assessing the legitimacy of criminalising certain forms of behaviour. In our earlier discussion, we noted an almost ambivalent attitude towards price-fixing in many parts of Europe. Further, and more significant for our present purposes, we can rightfully ask whether there is a consistent, European-wide conception of what the market is, and thus what competition in it should entail. The remarks of former President Sarkozy regarding the altered nature of the competition provisions in the Lisbon Treaty suggest a divergence of attitudes within the Union.[4] Further, the divergence may not be merely a Franco–Anglo divide: the experience in transitioning from a command to market economy of those Member States that joined on and after 2004, may suggest yet another, and potentially different, view of the relationship between the market and society. We therefore must remain somewhat sceptical of the legitimacy of a harmonised, European-wide criminal, anti-cartel regime.

Our examination of the UK's regime further underscores this scepticism. The British treatment of cartel activity tells against the suggestion that there is a common 'English-speaking' legal response to this sort of collusion, which is articulated well in the American paradigm. Since the

[4] See p. 202.

late eighteenth and early nineteenth century, and the subsequent spread of laissez-faire liberalism, price-fixing per se has never been viewed as particularly pernicious. What drew a legally benign activity into the ambit of criminality was some other element beyond the agreement – fraud or some other similar activity. This is well discussed and documented in the speech delivered in the House of Lords in *Norris*.

With this as the background, it is fairly easy to see how 'dishonesty' became an element in section 188 of the Enterprise Act 2002. It merely reflected the underlying values of the legal regime. But by so reflecting these values, it in fact 'killed' the offence. The requirements of the *Ghosh* test for dishonesty, and the need to convince a jury that the conduct complained about was dishonest, made prosecutions impossible. The OFT's lamentable record in securing convictions is to a great deal a result of this element.

In reforming the offence, Parliament is considering replacing 'dishonesty' with a secrecy element. Again, it is not price-fixing *simpliciter* which is the wrong; rather it is price-fixing done in a clandestine manner which is the gravamen of the offence. From a pragmatic perspective, it is difficult to see how this alteration will improve the efficacy of the offence. Instead of considering the honesty of the cartel participants, jurors will now be called on to assess the transparency of their arrangements. In effect, the jury's former task of deliberating on the morality of commercial agreements will be transformed into a consideration of murky sales or bidding practices. If convictions are unlikely to result, the practical effect of deterrence is muted.

In addition, if part of the drive for an improvement of the offence was a desire to somehow harmonise the UK regime with, say, the American regime, to avoid another *Norris*-type embarrassment, the reformed offence is no improvement. The openness element of the offence results in the UK's criminal cartel offence being an outlier in the international community. This may have a significant impact on the UK's ability to interact with other national authorities. To the extent that double criminality is necessary for extradition, the unique nature of the UK offence will make this form of cooperation impossible. To the extent that double criminality may be a necessity for the sharing of evidence or intelligence among authorities, the unique nature of the proposed offence is also a concern.

Notwithstanding these pragmatic concerns telling against the efficacy of the UK offence (whether as originally formulated by section 188 of the Enterprise Act or as proposed to be revised by the 2012 Bill), it is suggested that the offence indeed captures what has been shown to be the core of the harm done by economic collusion. Economic collusion is wrong, it is argued, not because it involves the appropriation of consumer surplus, but because it does so in a clandestine manner.

The core harm done by the cartelist was this surreptitious self-exception to the general principle that the 'rules of the market' be known to all. Given the fundamental role played by the market within a liberal society, this clandestine behaviour in fact strikes at a fundamental institution of a liberal society: the market. A liberal society adopts the market as its means of distributive justice. It does so because the market is that means by which individuals can freely determine their choices. The need for transparency in the 'rules' of the market, in particular that they be known in advance to all participants, hits at the very reason why the market is chosen in the first place. And in light of the fundamental role played by the market in liberal society, it has been argued that such a society is justified in using the criminal law to protect this institution of distributive justice.

To the extent that the UK regime has been unsuccessful in putting cartelists behind bars, it is a failure. To the extent that this lack of 'success' reduces the deterrent effect of the offence, the offence is a failure. The UK offence accurately captures the crux of the harm found in economic collusion. And in so doing it shows that a separate set of values (no matter how much of an outlier in the international stage it is, or how unworkable it may be from a practical perspective of obtaining convictions and extraditing accused), indeed has a normative backing.

The set of values possessed by the UK regime is different from those values found in the US's regime. It is noteworthy that these two jurisdictions are cultures which are aligned on similar Hofstedian cultural axes. Yet the response to the same activity is profoundly different. The EU (to the extent we can extrapolate Hofstedian traits onto a transnational institution) shares similar values. Likewise, the EU response to economic collusion in the form of cartel activity is markedly different from that of either the US or UK. One can only conclude that the divergences in values inherent in these three regimes are somewhat greater than they are generally held to be.

8.4 Scepticism about internationalisation

Indeed, this close examination of these three regimes provides a foundation which we can use to begin to draw a sceptical conclusion about either the practical success of an effective global convergence project for cartel control, or the normative merits of suggesting such a topic. It can rightly be asked that if three regimes, otherwise so similar in values and cultural outlook, cannot agree on the fundamental reasons for the control of economic collusion, is it appropriate to suggest that other nations follow them?

This scepticism should extend beyond the borders of Europe and North America. While much has been said about the effectiveness of the American regime – and it is this effectiveness that makes it worthy of emulation – our analysis indicates that it may not be appropriate to uncritically transplant such a regime abroad. A similar argument can be made about the EU and UK regimes.

The EU regime developed initially as an adjunct to the completion of the internal market. The Treaties prohibited private enterprises from doing what governments were also prohibited from doing – fragmenting the market. This purpose of the European competition agenda was never a part of the agendas of the US or UK: there was no need perceived to use a competition regime to complete the American or British markets.

But completing the market was only one purpose of European competition law. European competition law, as Article 101(3) states, can also be used as a means to 'improv[e] the production or distribution of goods or to promot[e] technical or economic progress, while allowing consumers a fair share of the resulting benefit'. As such, the EU regime *also* protects consumer surplus, as *one of* its goals. The incorporation of multiple goals into the European project, as a result of the historical and political circumstances unique to Europe since the Second World War casts doubt on the extent to which its underlying substantive vision can readily be received abroad.

The UK's regime, too, may be a difficult sell abroad. A jurisdiction will adopt or import an antitrust regime from abroad for a number of reasons; primary among these will be the regime's efficacy (in terms of deterrent effect and/or the ability of the political authorities to 'sell' the proposed regime to the relevant interested constituencies) and the sort of regime contemplated by any international agreements to which the importing state may be a party. While the UK regime, for reasons we have explained, may have its normative advantages, the UK experience shows that it is not an effective piece of legislation (at least in the form found in section 188 of the Enterprise Act 2002[5]). Given this lack of deterrent effect, it is unlikely to be viewed as a viable pattern on which to

[5] It is obviously premature to speculate on the efficacy of the revised UK offence.

frame the cartel offence in a jurisdiction which is in the process of developing its own regime.

These considerations show our scepticism towards the use of the US, EU and UK regimes as patterns to be emulated by other jurisdictions. To use the transplant surgery metaphor, these considerations go to the suitability of these regimes as metaphorical organ donors. In continuing with this metaphor, the suitability of recipient regimes must also be considered.

The previous chapter's discussion of Geert Hofstede's work and its implications for legal norms raises our scepticism about the viability of wholesale convergence of anti-cartel regimes. Hofstede's analysis shows that there are multiple spectrums of cultural values which are of relevance to the design of legal and political institutions. These attitudes in turn shape not just the responses to legal regimes, but also (and more significantly for our purposes) social attitudes towards the legitimacy of the measures adopted by these regimes.

To the extent that the market represents a society's means of distributive justice, it incorporates significant social norms into its practices. The liberal paradigm of atomistic individuals, interacting freely with each other in an effort to maximise their interests, is very much the conception of society and the market built around the Anglo-American axes of Hofstedian values. Atomism and individual action, and the pursuit of individual interests, are fundamental features of this Anglo-American social construct.

As a result of these features, those possessing such values regard certain forms of conduct within the marketplace as not just unacceptable, but as sufficiently fundamentally wrong so as to deserve society's most extreme form of condemnation – the use of criminal sanctions to proscribe that activity. However, in a social context where different, collectivist and cooperative values are pervasive, the manifestation of these values in the marketplace is less likely to attract social condemnation. As a consequence of this lack of disapproval, jurisdictions possessing such values are unlikely to be receptive of the need (or merit) of criminalising economic collusion. Such regimes are either unlikely to criminalise such behaviour; or, if it is criminalised, are unlikely to treat the behaviour as a matter deserving of great censure. In this regard, China provides a good example of the former – cartelisation is not a criminal matter in China. Japan provides a good example of the latter. It – though having criminal cartel laws 'on the books' for a relatively lengthy amount of time – has only recently begun to prosecute individuals.

Further, a person's cultural background is influential on how he or she will respond to the various stimuli and incentives are presented to them. Cartel control and criminalisation are inherently about establishing programmes which provide appropriate incentives for firms and individuals to not only not engage in this behaviour, but – in the face of a leniency programme – to provide information to the authorities about the activities of oneself and one's co-conspirators. The conventional model of cartel control, inherent in both of these types of programmes and viewed as fit for 'export', involves providing appropriate incentives for individuals to act in a certain way.

These incentives provided by the cartel control regimes which are touted for export – as we have argued – are predicated on a cultural assumption of atomistic action by self-interested individuals. Sanctions on, and rewards to, individuals 'work' only if the individuals feel that their interests are all that is to be taken into account in the relevant decision-making process. If, on the other hand, other – perhaps 'collective' – interests are involved in an individual's assessment of how to respond, then the immediate transplant of Anglo-American style regulatory and leniency regimes is unlikely to be a success.

Hofstede's results thus present a significant challenge for those who wish to suggest the desirability of a globally converged system of cartel control. First, the 'standard' means of control (where 'standard' is used in the sense of the US/EU-type regime which is held to be the ideal pattern for international convergence) may provide for incentives which, due to cultural differences, may not be effective. Appeals to individual interest may fall on deaf ears when the pursuit of individual benefit at the expense of a collective good (or goal) may result in the social (and economic) ostracism of that individual. As a result, this standard regime is unlikely to be successfully imported into a jurisdiction in which values different from those found in the Anglo-American core are prominant. And even if such jurisdictions were to adopt such a standard model, given the cultural differences, such a regime would find its normative force weakened, with nullification by the inaction of the authorities (and/or their political masters) a strong possibility.

Further, collectivist cultures, by definition, will be disposed to collective action. Such action, when extended into commercial practice, can serve as the basis for the collusive behaviour viewed to be at the core of hard-core cartel activities. The implication of this is evident: societies which, due to their cultural disposition, most 'need' an anti-cartel regime, are less likely to either accept or enforce such a regime.

Although this consequence has been noted by some scholars,[6] they represent a minority.

This cultural dimension has implications not just for sanctions against individual activity which facilitates cartel practices and incentives to provide information about the operation of cartels, but also to other means which can be used to control the likelihood that such collusion occurs. To a great extent, this sort of collusive behaviour has its roots in how business organisations are governed. It is also a corporate governance problem.

Corporate governance regimes are also inherently incentive and sanction setting systems. Any concerns which we have noted about the interplay between cultural values and anti-cartel regimes are also equally, if not more, pressing for such governance regimes. This observation is a consequence of the role which these sorts of organisations play within the marketplace and our thesis of the relationship which market values have to the principles of distributive justice adopted by a society.

This study has therefore resulted in both positive and negative results, all of which must be considered by those considering specific cartel control regimes for their utility as part of a general global convergence project of competition regimes. The negative results are principally in regard to the viability of an effective global convergence project. The present writer is sceptical about whether such a regime could become successful.

For such a project to work, the US and EU, as the main 'players', will need to be involved. Yet the values of the US and EU (to the extent that these two regimes share common values), are predicated on cultural foundations which are not necessarily shared globally. Given the need for importing regimes to share such values so that they can effectively implement such a regime, there is scepticism about how effective such global transplantation could be.

This scepticism stems from the need to develop a wide agreement on the content of provisions of a converged regime, which would include not just definitions of 'offences' but also likely the development of leniency (and other intelligence-gathering) programmes and means for the transmittal of evidence and accused. Given the plurality of values worldwide, it is doubtful that any grand, wide-ranging project can establish this in any meaningful way. A more likely result will be a watered-down, lowest common denominator form of guidance.

6 See, e.g., Cheng, 'How Culture May Change', 213–18.

Regional convergence is a viable alternative to a global project. A regional focus is likely to be more amenable to capturing common cultural values. Likewise, insofar as trade patterns and trade agreements are becoming more regionally oriented, there is a greater incentive among those participating in such commerce and agreements to converge their regimes at the regional level than at the global level. This is one of the important positive results of the present work: to suggest that regionalism is the way to proceed in the future consideration of international cartel control regimes.

Another significant result of this work has been to show that cartel control, along with any other legal regime, has significant normative and cultural elements to it. Cartel control is inherently normative. A cartel control regime seeks to promote or protect certain values in the market. And the market, we saw, is one of the (if not the) fundamental means which a society uses as a principle of distributive justice. The market thus reflects the norms of a society. Accordingly, from this basis, there can be no 'one size fits all' solution to the problem of cartel control.

Given the variance in such norms, talk of effective cartel control is more than just an exercise in which lawyers, policy analysts and economists specialising in industrial organisation should engage. Cartel control, particularly when pursued via the criminal law, is inherently about setting incentives to modify *people's* behaviour. When done at the global level it modifies *peoples'* behaviour. Consequently, the disciplines of behavioural economics and cultural anthropology will contain insights which can be applied in addressing the problem. Our discussion of best practices in internationalisation has recognised this and as a result proposed suggestions to take this discipline's insights into account when international solutions are proposed or designed. This, it is hoped, will be the positive conclusion to be drawn from this work.

BIBLIOGRAPHY

'Capital punishment: an offence against victims' relatives', *The Guardian* (Manchester and London), 7 April 2011, available at www.guardian.co.uk/commentisfree/cifamerica/2011/apr/07/capital-punishment-texas

'ICC tribunal bans Pakistan Test captain Salman Butt for 10 years', *The Observer* (London), 6 February 2011, available at www.guardian.co.uk/sport/2011/feb/06/pakistan-cricket-bettting-scandal-test-match

'Japanese sumo wrestling tournament cancelled over bout-fixing allegations', *The Guardian* (Manchester and London), 6 February 2011, available at www.guardian.co.uk/world/2011/feb/06/sumo-match-fixing-corruption-japan

'No restorative justice for those bereaved by Potters Bar', *The Guardian* (Manchester and London), 21 March 2011, available at www.guardian.co.uk/commentisfree/2011/mar/21/potters-bar-train-crash-accountability

'Sisters granted parole in return for kidney donation', *The Guardian* (Manchester and London), 31 December 2010, available at www.guardian.co.uk/world/2010/dec/31/mississippi-sisters-parole-kidney?INTCMP=SRCH

'Trade troubles: Russia should embrace constraints of WTO membership', *Financial Times*, 10 December 2012, available at www.ft.com/cms/s/0/27d887aa-4095-11e2-aafa-00144feabdc0.html#axzz2HwEe02Jj

'WTO issues loom over EU–Russia summit', *Financial Times*, 21 December 2012, available at www.ft.com/cms/s/0/1b4a38da-4b4e-11e2-88b5-00144feab49a.html#axzz2HwEe02Jj

Alchian, Armen A. and Harold Demsetz, 'Production, Information Costs, and Economic Organization' (1972) 62 *American Economic Review* 777

Allender, S. R. Balakrishnan, P. Scarborough, P. Webster and M. Rayner, 'The Burden of Smoking-related Ill Health in the UK' (2009) 18 *Tobacco Control* 262

Allens Arthur Robinson (A Firm), *'Corporate Culture' as a Basis for the Criminal Liability of Corporations* (Prepared by Allens Arthur Robinson for the United Nations Special Representative of the Secretary-General on Human Rights and Business) (Sydney, February 2008)

Almunia, Joaquín, 'Competition Policy for Innovation and Growth: Keeping Markets Open and Efficient', European Competition and Consumer Day, Copenhagen, 8 March 2012, available at http://europa.eu/rapid/

pressReleasesAction.do?reference=SPEECH/12/172&format=HTML&aged=0&language=EN&guiLanguage=en

American Presidency Project: Republican Party Platforms, available at www.presidency.ucsb.edu/ws/index.php?pid=29627#ixzz1mw6Mx7pz

Anderson, David and Rachel Cuff, 'Cartels in the European Union: Procedural Fairness for Defendants and Claimants' (2011) 34 *Fordham International Law Journal* 385

Andreangeli, Arianna, *EU Competition Enforcement and Human Rights* (Edward Elgar, 2008)

'Competition Law and Human Rights' in Ioannis Lianos and D. Daniel Sokol (eds.), *The Global Limits of Competition Law*, 22–36

Archibald, Todd, Kenneth Jull and Kent Roach, 'The Changed Face of Corporate Criminal Liability' (2004) 48 *Criminal Law Quarterly* 367

Arlen, Jennifer, 'The Potentially Perverse Effects of Corporate Criminal Liability' (1994) 23 *Journal of Legal Studies* 833

Arlen, Jennifer and Renier Kraakman, 'Controlling Corporate Misconduct: An Analysis of Corporate Liability Regimes' (1997) 72 *New York University Law Review* 687

Ashenfelter, Orley and Kathryn Graddy, 'Anatomy of the Rise and Fall of a Pricefixing Conspiracy: Auctions at Sotheby's and Christie's' (2005) 1 *Journal of Competition Law and Economics* 3

Ashurst (A Firm), *Study on the Conditions of Claims for Damages in Case of Infringement of EC Competition Rules* (Part One: Comparative Report) (Publications Office of the European Union, 2004)

Study on the Conditions of Claims for Damages in Case of Infringement of EC Competition Rules (Part Two: Economic Report) (Publications Office of the European Union, 2004)

Austin, John, *The Province of Jurisprudence Determined* (1832) (London, Lowe and Brydon, 1955)

Bailin QC, Alex, 'Doing Away with Dishonesty' (2011) 10 *Competition Law Journal* 169

Bassow, Leonardo J. and Thomas W. Ross, 'Measuring the True Harm From Price-Fixing to Both Direct and Indirect Purchasers' (2010) 57 *Journal of Industrial Economics* 895

Baye, Michael R. and Joshua D. Wright, 'Is Antitrust Too Complicated for Generalist Judges? The Impact of Economic Complexity and Judicial Training on Appeals' (2011) 54 *Journal of Law and Economics* 1

Becker, Gary S., 'Crime and Punishment: An Economic Approach' (1968) 76 *Journal of Political Economy* 169

Beitz, Charles R., 'Rawls's Law of Peoples' (2000) 110 *Ethics* 669

Berghahn, V., *The Americanization of West German Industry* (Cambridge University Press, 1986)

Bishop, Simon and Mike Walker, *The Economics of EC Competition Law: Concepts, Application and Measurement* (3rd edn, London, Sweet & Maxwell, 2010)

Blackstone, William, *Commentaries on the Laws of England* (1753) (Philadelphia, Lippincott, 1893)

Bonefeld, Werner, 'Freedom and the Strong State: On German Ordoliberalism' (2012) 17 *New Political Economy* 633

Bork, Robert, *The Antitrust Paradox: A Policy at War with Itself* (revised edn, New York, Basic Books, 1993)

Bosch, Jean-Claude and E. Woodrow Eckhart Jr, 'The Profitability of Price Fixing: Evidence from Stock Market Reaction to Federal Indictments' (1991) 73 *Review of Economics and Statistics* 309

Boudewijn, Bouckaert and Gerrit De Geest (eds.), *Encyclopedia of Law and Economics* (Cheltenham, Edward Elgar, 1996–2000)

Bowen, Francis, *The Principles of Political Economy Applied to the Conditions, Resources and Institutions of the American People* (2nd edn, Boston, Little Brown, 1859)

Braithwaite, John, *Corporate Crime in the Pharmaceutical Industry* (Abingdon, Routledge, 1984)

Bright, Christopher, 'EU Competition Policy: Rules, Objectives and Deregulation' (1996) 16 *Oxford Journal of Legal Studies* 536

Brisimi, Vasiliki and Maria Ioannidou, 'Criminalizing Cartels in Greece: A Tale of Hasty Developments and Shaky Grounds' (2011) 34 *World Competition* 157

Bryant, Peter G. and E. Woodrow Eckard, 'Price Fixing: The Probability of Getting Caught' (1991) 73 *Review of Economics and Statistics* 531

Buch-Hansen, Hubert and Angela Wigger, *The Politics of European Competition Regulation: A Critical Political Economy Perspective* (Abingdon, Routledge, 2011)

Bucy, Pamela H., 'Corporate Ethos: A Standard for Imposing Corporate Criminal Liability' (1991) 75 *Minnesota Law Review* 1095

'Indemnification of Corporate Executives Who Have Been Convicted of Crimes: An Assessment and Proposal' (1991) 24 *Indiana Law Review* 271

Burrows, Paul, 'Product Liability and the Control of Product Risk in the EC' (1994) 10 *Oxford Review of Economic Policy* 68

Calabresi, Guido and A. Douglas Melamed, 'Property Rules, Liability Rules, and Inalienability: One View of the Cathedral' (1972) 85 *Harvard Law Review* 1089

Camatsos, Stratis G. and Albert A. Foer, 'Cartel Investigations in the USA: A Primer' (American Antitrust Institute, Working Paper No. 07–05, 13 March 2007)

Canada Competition Bureau, *Immunity Program under the Competition Act* (7 June 2010), available at: www.competitionbureau.gc.ca/eic/site/cb-bc.nsf/eng/03248.html

Leniency Program (29 September 2010), available at www.competitionbureau.gc.ca/eic/site/cb-bc.nsf/eng/03288.html

Carden, Art, 'Beliefs, Bias, and Regime Uncertainty after Hurricane Katrina' (2008) 35 *International Journal of Social Economics* 531

Cengiz, Firat, 'Passing-On Defense and Indirect Purchaser Standing in Actions for Damages against Violations of Competition Law: What can the EC Learn from the US?' (University of East Anglia Centre for Competition Policy, Working Paper 07–21)

Ceres, Katalin J., Maarten Pieter Schinkel and Floris O. W. Vogelaar (eds.), *Criminalization of Competition Law Enforcement: Economic and Legal Implications for the EU Member States* (Cheltenham, Edward Elgar, 2006)

Cheffins, Brian R., *Company Law: Theory, Structure and Operation* (Oxford University Press, 1997)

Cheng, Thomas K., 'How Culture May Change Assumptions in Antitrust Policy' in Lianos and Sokol (eds.), *The Global Limits of Competition Law*, 205–20

'Convergence and Its Discontents: A Reconsideration of the Merits of Convergence of Global Competition Law' (2012) 12 *Chicago Journal of International Law* 433

Clarkson, C. V. M., 'Kicking Corporate Bodies and Damning Their Souls' (1996) 59 *Modern Law Review* 557

Coase, Ronald H., 'The Lighthouse in Economics' (1974) 17 *Journal of Law and Economics* 357

Coffee, John C., '"No Soul to Damn: No Body to Kick": An Unscandalized Inquiry into the Problem of Corporate Punishment' (1980) 79 *Michigan Law Review* 386

Collins, Kathleen Murtaugh, 'Harmonizing the Antitrust Laws of NAFTA Signatories' (1994) 17 *Loyola of Los Angeles International and Comparative Law Journal* 157

Combe, Emmanuel, Constance Monnier and Renaud Legal, 'Cartels: The Probability of Getting Caught in the European Union' (Cahiers de Recherche PRISM-Sorbonne / CR-07–01–03 (March 2008))

Congressional Record S 1, 51st Cong., 1st Sess, (March 1890), reprinted in Joseph L. Greenslade, 'Labor Unions and the Sherman Act: Rethinking Labor's Nonstatutory Exemption'

Connor, John M., 'Effectiveness of Antitrust Sanctions on Modern International Cartels' (2006) 6 *Journal of Industry, Competition and Trade* 195

Global Price Fixing (Heidelberg/Berlin, Springer, 2007)

'The Great Global Vitamins Conspiracies, 1985–1999', (4 September 2008), available at http://ssrn.com/abstract=886968

'Cartel Amnesties Granted: Worldwide Whistleblowers' (Working Paper, 20 May 2009), available at http://ssrn.com/abstract=1285469

'Recidivism Revealed: Private International Cartels 1990 – 2009' (2010) 6 *Competition Policy International* 101

'Has the European Commission Become More Severe in Punishing Cartels? Effects of the 2006 Guidelines' [2011] *European Competition Law Review* 27

'Global Cartels Redux: The Lysine Antitrust Litigation (1996)' in John E. Kwota, Jr and Lawrence J. White (eds.), *The Antitrust Revolution: Economics, Competition, and Policy*

Connor, John M. and C. G. Helmers, 'Statistics on Private International Cartels' (American Antitrust Institute (AAI), Working Paper No. 07–01 (10 January 2007), available at http://ssrn.com/abstract=1103610

'Statistics on Modern Private International Cartels, 1990–2005' AAI Working Paper No. 07–01 (American Antitrust Institute, 10 January 2007)

Connor, John M. and R. H. Lande, 'How High Do Cartels Raise Prices? Implications for Optimal Cartel Fines' (2005) 80 *Tulane Law Review* 513

Cook, Philip J. and Jens Ludwig, 'The Social Costs of Gun Ownership' (2006) 90 *Journal of Public Economics* 379

Corpus Juris Secundum

Crawford, James, *The International Law Commission's Articles on State Responsibility: Introduction, Text and Commentary* (Cambridge University Press, 2002)

Culpepper, Dreda and Walter Block, 'Price Gouging in the Katrina Aftermath: Free Markets at Work' (2008) 35 *International Journal of Social Economics* 512

Dabbah, Maher M., *International and Comparative Competition Law* (Cambridge University Press, 2010)

Dam, K. W., 'Class Actions: Efficiency, Compensation Deterrence, and Conflict of Interest' (1975) 4 *Journal of Legal Studies* 47

De, Oindrila, 'Analysis of Cartel Duration: Evidence from EC Prosecuted Cartels' (2010) 17 *International Journal of the Economics of Business* 33

Dennison, S. R., 'The British Restrictive Trade Practices Act of 1956' (1959) 2 *Journal of Law and Economics* 64

Department for Business, Innovation and Skills, *A Competition Regime for Growth: A Consultation on Options for Reform* (BIS, March 2011)

Growth, Competition and the Competition Regime: Government Response to a Consultation (BIS, March 2012)

Private Actions in Competition Law: A Consultation on Options for Reform (BIS, April 2012)

Department of Trade and Industry, *A World Class Competition Regime* (Cm. 5233) (HMSO, 30 July 2001)

Department of Transport, *M V Herald of Free Enterprise: Report of Court No. 8074, Formal Investigation* (HMSO, 1987)

De Smet, Dieter, 'The Diametrically Opposed Principles of US and EU Antitrust Policy' [2008] *European Competition Law Review* 356

Devlin, Patrick, *The Enforcement of Morals* (Oxford University Press, 1965)

Diskant, Edward B. 'Comparative Corporate Criminal Liability: Exploring the Uniquely American Doctrine through Comparative Criminal Procedure' (2008) 118 *Yale Law Journal* 126

Djelic, Marie-Laurie, 'Does Europe Mean Americanization? The Case of Competition' (2002) 6 *Competition and Change* 233

'From Local Legislation to Global Structuring Frame: The Story of Antitrust' (2005) 5 *Global Social Policy* 55

Dresher, Melvin, *Games of Strategy: Theory and Applications* (Englewood Cliffs NJ, Prentice-Hall, 1961)

Duquette, Jerold J., *Regulating the National Pastime: Baseball and Antitrust* (Westport CT, Greenwood, 1999)

Easterbrook, Frank and Daniel R. Fischel, 'The Proper Role of a Target's Management in Responding to a Tender Offer' (1981) 94 *Harvard Law Review* 1161

Edwards, Corwin D., *Control of Cartels and Monopolies: An International Comparison* (New York, Oceana, 1967)

Ehlermann, Claus-Dieter and Isabela Atanasiu (eds.), *European Competition Annual 2006: Enforcement of Prohibition of Cartels* (Oxford, Hart, 2007)

Ehlermann, Claus-Dieter and Mel Marquis (eds.), *European Competition Law Annual 2008: Anititrust Settlements under EC Competition Law* (Oxford, Hart, 2010)

Eichanwald, Kurt, *The Informant* (New York, Random House, 2000)

Ekelund, Jr, Robert B. and Robert F. Hébert, *A History of Economic Theory and Method* (4th edn, Long Grove, Illinois, 1997)

Elzinga, Kenneth G. and William Brett, *The Antitrust Penalties: A Study in Law and Economics* (Yale University Press, 1976)

Euken, Walter, *Grundsätze der Wirtschaftspolitik* (1952)

European Commission, Cartel Fines, available at http://ec.europa.eu/competition/cartels/cases/cases.html

Communication de la Commission, du 27 mai 1970, concernant les accords d'importance mineure qui ne sont pas visés par les dispositions de l'article 85 paragraphe 1 du traité instituant la Communauté économique européenne [1970] OJ C64/1

First Report on Competition Policy (Publications Office of the European Union, 1972)

Twelfth Report on Competition Policy (Publications Office of the European Union, 1982)

Green Paper on Vertical Restraints COM (1996) 721 final (22 January 1997)

White Paper on Modernisation of the Rules Implementing Articles 85 and 86 of the EC Treaty Commission Programme No. 99/027 (Brussels, 28 April 1999)

Green Paper on the Review of Council Regulation (EEC) No. 4064/89 COM (2001) 745 final (Brussels, 11 December 2001)

Twenty-Seventh Report on Competition Policy SEC(98) 636 available at http://ec.europa.eu/competition/cartels/statistics/statistics.pdf

Thirty-First Report on Competition Policy (2001) (Publications Office of the European Union, 2002)

'Antitrust: Commission fines 17 bathroom equipment manufacturers € 622 million in price fixing cartel', IP/10/790 (Brussels, 23 June 2010), available at http://europa.eu/rapid/pressReleasesAction.do?reference=IP/10/790&format=HTML&aged=1&language=EN&guiLanguage=en

'Antitrust: Commission opens proceedings against Johnson & Johnson and Novartis', IP/11/1228 (21 October 2011), available at http://europa.eu/rapid/pressReleasesAction.do?reference=IP/11/1228&format=HTML&aged=0&language=EN&guiLanguage=en

Communication from the Commission to the European Parliament, the Council, the European Economic and Social Committee and the Committee of the Regions, *Report on Competition Policy 2011* (SWD (2012) 141 final)

'Antitrust: Commission enforcement action in pharmaceutical sector following sector inquiry' (30 July 2012), available at http://europa.eu/rapid/pressReleasesAction.do?reference=MEMO/12/593&format=HTML&aged=0&language

Ezrachi, Ariel and Hassan Qaqaya, 'UNCTAD's Collaborative Information Platform' [2012] 4 *Concurrences* 204–7

Faull, Jonathan and Ali Nikpay, *The EC Law of Competition* (Oxford University Press, 2007)

Federal Trade Commission (FTC) Press Release, 'Google Agrees to Change Its Business Practices to Resolve FTC Competition Concerns In the Markets for Devices Like Smart Phones, Games and Tablets, and in Online Search' (3 January 2013), available at www.ftc.gov/opa/2013/01/google.shtm

Feinberg, Joel, *Harm to Others* (Oxford University Press, 1984)

Offense to Others (Oxford University Press, 1985)

Harm to Self (Oxford University Press, 1986)

Harmless Wrongdoing (Oxford University Press, 1988)

Fisher, Franklin M., 'The Social Costs of Monopoly and Regulation: Posner Reconsidered' (1985) 93 *The Journal of Political Economy* 410

Fisse, Brent, 'Corporate Criminal Responsibility' (1991) 15 *Criminal Law Journal* 166

'Criminal Law: The Attribution of Criminal Liability to Corporations: A Statutory Model' (1991) 13 *Sydney Law Review* 277

Foer, Albert A. and Jonathan W. Cuneo (eds.), *The International Handbook of Private Enforcement of Competition Law* (Cheltenham, Edward Elgar, 2010)

Fuller, Lon, *The Morality of Law* (Yale University Press, 1964)

Anatomy of Law (New York, New American Library, 1969)

Gal, Michal S., 'Review Essay: New Perspectives on International Antitrust' (2012) 106 *American Journal of International Law* 401

Geradin, Damien and David Henry, 'The EC Fining Policy for Violations of Competition Law: An Empirical Review of the Commission Decisional

Practice and the Community Courts' Judgements' (2005) 1 *European Competition Law Journal* 401

Gerber, David J., 'Constitutionalizing the Economy: German Neo-liberalism, Competition Law and the "New" Europe' (1994) 42 *American Journal of Comparative Law* 25

Law and Competition in Twentieth Century Europe: Protecting Prometheus (Oxford University Press, 1998)

Global Competition: Law, Markets, and Globalisation (Oxford University Press, 2010)

Giocoli, Nicola, 'Competition versus Property Rights: American Antitrust Law, the Freiburg School, and the Early Years of European Competition Policy' (2009) 5 *Journal of Competition Law and Economics* 747

Givelber, Daniel, 'Cigarette Law' (1998) 73 *Indiana Law Journal* 867

Gobert, James, 'Corporate Criminality: Four Models of Fault' (1994) 14 *Legal Studies* 395

Gobert, James and Maurice Punch, *Rethinking Corporate Crime* (London, Butterworths/LexisNexis, 2003)

Goyder, Joanna and Albertina Albors-Llorens, *Goyder's EC Competition Law* (5th edn, Oxford University Press, 2009)

Greenslade, Joseph L., 'Labor Unions and the Sherman Act: Rethinking Labor's Nonstatutory Exemption' (1988) 22 *Loyola University of Los Angeles Law Review* 151

Guzman, Andrew T. (ed.), *Cooperation, Comity, and Competition Policy* (Oxford University Press, 2010)

Hammond, Scott D., 'The Evolution of Criminal Antitrust Enforcement Over the Last Two Decades', The 24th Annual National Institute On White Collar Crime Presented by the ABA Criminal Justice Section and the ABA Center for Continuing Legal Education, Miami, 25 February 2010, available at www.justice.gov/atr/public/speeches/255515.htm

Hammond, Scott D. and Belinda A. Barnett, 'Frequently Asked Questions Regarding the Antitrust Division's Leniency Program and Model Leniency Letters' (19 November 2008)', available at www.justice.gov/atr/public/criminal/239583.htm

Hansard, House of Commons Debates (June 1844)

House of Commons, Standing Committee B, 23 April 2002

House of Commons, Public Bills Committee, 10 July 2012

Harding, Christopher and Julian Joshua, *Regulating Cartels in Europe* (2nd edn, Oxford University Press, 2010)

Hart, H. L. A., *Essays in Jurisprudence and Philosophy* (Oxford University Press, 1983)

'Positivism and the Separation of Law and Morals' in *Essays in Jurisprudence and Philosophy*

Punishment and Responsibility: Essays in the Philosophy of Law (2nd edn, Oxford University Press, 2008)

Hayek, Friedrich, *The Constitution of Liberty* (University of Chicago Press, 1960)

Law, Legislation and Liberty Volume 1: Rules and Order (University of Chicago Press, 1973)

Law, Legislation and Liberty Volume 2: The Mirage of Social Justice (University of Chicago Press, 1976)

Law, Legislation and Liberty Volume 3: The Political Order of a Free People (University of Chicago Press, 1979)

Hittinger, Carl W. and Jarod M. Bona, 'The Diminishing Role of the Private Attorney General in Antitrust and Securities Class Action Cased Aided by the Supreme Court' (2009) 4 *Journal of Business and Technology Law* 167

Hobbes, Thomas, *Leviathan* (1651)

Hodge, Tom C., 'Compatible or Conflicting: The Promotion of a High Level of Employment and the Consumer Welfare Standard under Article 101' (2012) 3 *William and Mary Business Law Review* 59

Hofstadter Richard, 'What Happened to the Antitrust Movement' in *The Paranoid Style in American Politics and Other Essays* (New York, Vintage, 1967)

Hofstede, Geert, *Culture's Consequences: Comparing Values, Behaviors, Institutions, And Organizations Across Nations* (2nd edn, London, Sage Publications, 2001)

Hovenkamp, Herbert, 'Regulatory Conflict in the Gilded Age: Federalism and the Railroad Problem' (1988) 97 *Yale Law Journal* 1017

Federal Antitrust Policy: The Law of Competition and Its Practice (4th edn, St Paul MN: West, 2011)

Howell, Beryl A., 'Sentencing of Antitrust Offenders: What Does the Data Show?' (US Sentencing Commission, 2010), available at www.ussc.gov/About_the_Commission/About_the_Commissioners/Commissioner_Bios.cfm

Hyytinen, Ari, Frode Steen and Otto Toivanen, 'Cartels Uncovered', Working Paper (OR 1105), Katholieke Universiteit Leuven, Department of Managerial Economics, Strategy and Innovation, Faculty of Business and Economics (11 March 2011), available at SSRN http://ssrn.com/abstract=1793665

Informant, The (Warner Brothers; Gregory Jacobs, Producer, 2009)

International Competition Network, *Defining Hard Core Cartel Conduct: Effective Institutions, Effective Penalties* (Office for Official Publications of the European Communities, 2005), available at www.internationalcompetitionnetwork.org/uploads/library/doc346.pdf

International Competition Network, 'Factsheet', available at www.internationalcompetitionnetwork.org/uploads/library/doc608.pdf

International Cricket Council, Press Release, 'ICC reaction to decision of independent Anti-Corruption Tribunal', available at http://icc-cricket.yahoo.net/newsdetails.php?newsId=13066_1296983640

Ioannidou, Maria, 'Reforming UK Competition Law Regime: The Consumer Perspective' (2012) 11 *Competition Law Journal* 28

Italianer, Alexander (Director General for Competition, European Commission), Roundtable Conference with Enforcement Officials, American Bar Association Section of Antitrust Law, Spring Meeting, Washington DC (23 April 2010), quoted in John M. Connor, 'Has the European Commission Become More Severe in Punishing Cartels? Effects of the 2006 Guidelines'

'Trends in Cartel Enforcement and Policy', ICN Annual Conference 2010, Istanbul Cartel Working Group, Session 29 (April 2010), available at http://ec.europa.eu/competition/speeches/text/sp2010_02_en.pdf

Jensen, Michael C., *Foundations of Organizational Strategy* (Harvard University Press, 1998)

A Theory of the Firm: Governance, Residual Claims and Organizational Forms (Harvard University Press, 2000)

Jensen, Michael C. and William H. Meckling, 'Theory of the Firm: Managerial Behavior, Agency Costs and Ownership Structure' (1976) 3 *Journal of Financial Economics* 305, reprinted in Michael C. Jensen, *Foundations of Organizational Strategy*

Jevons, William Stanley, *The Coal Question: An Inquiry Concerning the Progress of the Nation, and the Probable Exhaustion of our Coal-mines* (1865)

Jewkes, John, 'British Monopoly Policy 1944–56' (1958) 1 *Journal of Law and Economics* 1

Jones, Alison and Brenda Sufrin, *EU Competition Law: Text, Cases and Materials* (4th edn, Oxford University Press, 2011)

Kahn-Freund, Otto, 'On Uses and Misuses of Comparative Law' (1974) 37 *Modern Law Review* 1

Kant, Immanuel, *Fundamental Principles of the Metaphysic of Morals* (1785)

The Metaphysics of Morals (Mary Gregor, trans. and ed.) (Cambridge University Press, 1996)

Karier, T., 'Unions and Monopoly Profits' (1985) 67 *Review of Economics and Statistics* 34

Karpel, Amy Ann, 'The European Commission's Decision on the Boeing-McDonnell Douglas Merger and the Need for Greater U.S.-EU Cooperation In The Merger Field' (1998) 47 *American University Law Review* 1029

Karpoff, Jonathan A. and John R. Lott Jr, 'The Reputational Penalty Firms Bear from Committing Criminal Fraud' (1993) 36 *Journal of Law and Economics* 757

Kennedy, Duncan, 'The Role of Law in Economic Thought: Essays on the Fetishism of Commodities' (1985) 34 *American University Law Review* 939

Khan, B. Zorina, 'Antitrust and Innovation before the Sherman Act' (2011) 77 *Antitrust Law Journal* 757

Khanna, V. S., 'Corporate Criminal Liability: What Purpose Does It Serve?' (1996) 109 *Harvard Law Review* 1477

Kirby, M. W., 'Government Intervention on Industrial Organization: Coal Mining in the Nineteen Thirties' (1973) 15 *Business History* 161

Klawiter, Donald C., 'US Corporate Leniency after the Blockbuster Cartels: Are We Entering a New Era?' in Claus Dieter Ehlerman and Isabela Atanasiu (eds.), *European Competition Law Annual 2006*, 489–509

Kraakman, Reiner et al. (eds.), *The Anatomy of Corporate Law: A Comparative and Functional Approach* (2nd edn, Oxford University Press, 2009)

Kroes, Neelie, 'European Competition Policy - Delivering Better Markets and Better Choices', European Consumer and Competition Day, London, 15 September 2005, available at: http://europa.eu/rapid/pressReleasesAction.do?reference=SPEECH/05/512&format=HTML&aged=0&language=EN&guiLanguage=en

'Tackling Cartels - A Never-ending Task', Anti-Cartel Enforcement: Criminal and Administrative Policy - Panel session, Brasilia, 8 October 2009, available at http://europa.eu/rapid/pressReleasesAction.do?reference=SPEECH/09/454&format=HTML&aged=0&language=EN&guiLanguage=en

Kwota, Jr, John E. and Lawrence J. White (eds.), *The Antitrust Revolution: Economics, Competition, and Policy* (5th edn, Oxford University Press, 2009)

Lande, Robert H., 'Are Antitrust "Treble" Damages Really Single Damages?' (1993) 54 *Ohio State Law Journal* 115

'Five Myths About Antitrust Damages' (2006) 40 *University of San Francisco Law Review* 651

Lande, Robert H., and Joshua P. Davis, 'Benefits from Private Enforcement: An Analysis of Forty Cases' (2008) 42 *University of San Francisco Law Review* 879

Lanzillotti, Robert F., 'The Great School Milk Conspiracies of the 1980's' (1996) 11 *Journal of Industrial Organization* 413

Law Commission, *Criminal Law Involuntary Manslaughter - An Overview* (Consultation Paper No. 135) (HMSO, 1994)

Legislating the Criminal Code Involuntary Manslaughter (Item 11 of the Sixth Programme of Law Reform: Criminal Law, Law Com. No. 237) (HMSO, 1996)

Criminal Liability in Regulatory Contexts: A Consultation Paper (Consultation Paper No. 195) (HMSO, 2010)

Law Commission and the Scottish Law Commission, *Company Directors: Regulating Conflicts of Interests and Formulating a Statement of Duties* (September 1999) (Law Com. No. 261, Scot Law Com. No. 173) (HMSO 1999).

Lee, Ki Jong, 'Culture and Competition: National and Regional Levels' (2008) 21 *Loyola Consumer Law Review* 33

Leibenstein, Harvey, 'Allocative Efficiency vs. X-Inefficiency' (1966) 56 *American Economic Review* 392

Leiber, Francis, *Encyclopedia Americana* (1831), vol. IX, 150 available at http://quod.lib.umich.edu/m/moa/AJD6870.0009.001/152?rgn=full+text;view=imageca

Leppard, Marie, 'The Reform of the UK Competition Regime: What can be Learnt from France?' (2012) 11 *Competition Law Journal* 219

Letwin, William L., 'The English Law Concerning Monopolies' (1953) 21 *University of Chicago Law Review* 355

'Congress and The Sherman Antitrust Law: 1887–1890' (1956) 23 *University of Chicago Law Review* 221

Lever, Jeremy and John Pike, 'Cartel Agreements, Criminal Conspiracy and the Statutory "Cartel Offence": Part 2' [2005] *European Competition Law Review* 164

Lianos, Ioannis and D. Daniel Sokol (eds.), *The Global Limits of Competition Law* (Stanford University Press, 2012)

Locke, John, *Second Treatise on Government* (1689)

Lott, Jr, John R., 'The Level of Optimal Fines to Prevent Fraud When Reputations Exist and Penalty Clauses are Unenforceable' (1996) 17 *Managerial and Decision Economics* 363

Lovett, A. W., 'The United States and the Schuman Plan: A Study in French Diplomacy 1950–1952' (1996) 39 *Historical Journal* 425

Lucas, Arthur F., 'A British Experiment in the Control of Competition: The Coal Mines Act of 1930' (1934) 48 *Quarterly Journal of Economics* 418

Marshall, Alfred, *Principles of Economics* (1890) (8th edn, London, Macmillan, 1920)

May, James, 'Antitrust Practice and Procedure in the Formative Era: The Constitutional and Conceptual Reach of State Antitrust Law, 1880–1918' (1987) 135 *University of Pennsylvania Law Review* 495

'Antitrust in the Formative Era: Political and Economic Theory in Constitutional and Antitrust Analysis, 1880–1918' (1989) 50 *Ohio State Law Journal* 257

Meese, Alan J., 'Debunking The Purchaser Welfare Account of Section 2 of The Sherman Act: How Harvard Brought us a Total Welfare Standard and Why We Should Keep It' (2010) 85 *New York University Law Review* 659

Melícias, Maria João, '"*Did They Do It?*" The Interplay Between the Standard of Proof and the Presumption of Innocence in EU Cartel Investigations' (2012) 35 *World Competition* 471

Mercer, Helen, *Constructing a Competitive Order: The Hidden History of British Antitrust Policies* (Cambridge University Press, 1995)

Mill, J. S., *Principles of Political Economy* (1848)

On Liberty (1859), reprinted in J. M. Robson (ed.), *The Collected Works of John Stuart Mill Vol. XVIII: Essays on Politics and Society* (University of Toronto Press, 1977)

Mitchell, B. R., *British Historical Statistics* (Cambridge University Press, 1988)

Monopolies and Restrictive Practices Commission, *Report on the Supply of Dental Goods* (1 December 1950), available at http://webarchive.nationalarchives.gov.uk/20111202195250/ http://competition-commission.org.uk/rep_pub/reports/1950_1959/001dental.htm

Collective Discrimination: A Report on Exclusive Dealing, Collective Boycotts, Aggregated Rebates and other Discriminatory Trade Practices (Cmd 9504) (HMSO, 1955)

Montesquieu (Charles-Louis de Secondat, baron de La Brède et de Montesquieu), *De L'Esprit des Lois* (1748)

Montgomery, W. David, Robert A. Baron and Mary K. Weisskopf, 'Potential Effects of Proposed Price Gouging Legislation on the Cost and Severity of Gasoline Supply Interruptions' (2007) 3 *Journal of Competition Law and Economics* 357

Monti, Giorgio, 'Article 81 EC and Public Policy' (2002) 39 *Common Market Law Review* 1057

EC Competition Law (Cambridge University Press, 2007)

Monti, Mario, 'Competition enforcement and consumers – a stable link in times of change', Speech delivered at European Competition Day, Athens, 14 February 2003, available at http://ec.europa.eu/competition/speeches/index_speeches_by_the_commissioner.html

Motta, Massimo, *Competition Policy: Theory and Practice* (Cambridge University Press, 2004)

'On Cartel Deterrence and Fines in the European Union' [2008] *European Competition Law Review* 209

National Health Service Information Centre, *Lifestyles Statistics, Statistics on Alcohol: England*, 2010, available at http://www.ic.nhs.uk/webfiles/publications/alcohol10/Statistics_on_Alcohol_England_2010.pdf

Negrinotti, Matteo P., 'Review' (2009) 5 *Competition Law Review* 215, available at www.clasf.org/CompLRev/Issues/Vol5Iss2ReviewNegrinotti.pdf

Newbould, Gerald D., *Management and Merger Activity* (Liverpool, Guthsted, 1971)

Note, 'Legislation' (1932) 32 *Columbia Law Review* 347

Nozick, Robert, *State, Anarchy and Utopia* (New York, Basic Books, 1974)

Odudu, Okeoghene, *The Boundaries of EC Competition Law: The Scope of Article 81* (Oxford University Press, 2009)

Office of Fair Trading, *Proposed Criminalisation of Cartels in the UK* (Report by Sir Anthony Hammond and Roy Penrose) (OFT 365) (OFT, November 2001)

Guidance as to the Appropriate Amount of a Penalty (OFT 423) (OFT, December 2004)

'Predicting Cartels', Economic Discussion Paper No. 773 (OFT, March 2005)

'Private Actions in Competition Law: Effective Redress for Consumers and Business' (Discussion paper) (OFT916) (OFT, April 2007)

Press Release, 'Lactalis McLelland agrees early resolution in dairy retail price initiatives investigation', 22/08, 15 February 2008, available at www.oft.gov.uk/news-and-updates/press/2008/22-08

Project Condor Board Review (OFT, December 2010)

Applications for Leniency and No-action in Cartel Cases OFT's Detailed Guidance on the Principles and Process: A Consultation on OFT Guidance (OFT 803con) (OFT, October 2011)

Guidance as to the Appropriate Amount of a Penalty (OFT 423rev) (OFT, September 2012)

Omerod, David, *Smith and Hogan's Criminal Law* (12th edn, Oxford University Press, 2008)

Organisation for Economic Co-operation and Development, Directorate for Financial, Fiscal and Enterprise Affairs Competition Committee, Report On The Nature And Impact of Hard Core Cartels And Sanctions Against Cartels Under National Competition Laws DAFFE/COMP(2002)7 (OECD, 2002), available at www.oecd.org/dataoecd/16/20/2081831.pdf

Hard Core Cartels: 2000 (OECD, 2000)

Hard Core Cartels: Recent Progress and Challenges Ahead (OECD, 2003)

Principles of Corporate Governance (OECD, 2004)

Directorate for Financial and Enterprise Affairs Competition Committee, Latin American Competition Forum – Session I: Competition Provisions in Regional Trade Agreements – Note by the United States 10–11 September 2008, Panama City, DAF/COMP/LACF/WD(2008)1, 19 August 2008

Competition Law and Policy In Mexico: An OECD Peer Review (OECD, 2004)

Guidelines for Multinational Enterprises (OECD, 2011)

'What We Do', Website www.oecd.org/about/whatwedoandhow/

Oxera (A Firm), *Quantifying Antitrust Damages: Towards Non-Binding Guidance for Courts* (Publications Office of the European Union, 2009)

Page, William H., 'Background Note Policy Choices In Defining The Measure Of Antitrust Damages' (2009) *OECD Journal: Competition Law and Policy* 48

Paley, William, *The Principles of Moral and Political Philosophy* (1785) (Indianapolis, Liberty Fund, 2002)

Patel, Ruchit, 'The Removal of Dishonesty from the Cartel Offense and the Publication Defense: A Panacea?' *CPI Antitrust Chronicle*, May 2012 (1)

Pearsall, Judy, *Concise Oxford English Dictionary* (10th edn, revised 2002)

Peritz, Rudolph J. R., *Competition Policy in America: History, Rhetoric, Law* (revised edn, Oxford University Press, 2000)

Peyer, Sebastian, 'Private Antitrust Litigation in Germany from 2005 to 2007: Empirical Evidence' (2012) 8 *Journal of Competition Law and Economics* 331

Pietri, N., *Evolution Economique de l'Allemagne du Milieu du 19è Siècle à 1914* (SEDES, 2002)

Pinto QC, Amanda and Martin Evans, *Corporate Criminal Liability* (London, Sweet & Maxwell, 2008)

Polinsky, A. Mitchell and Steven Shavell, 'Should Employees Be Subject to Fines and Imprisonment Given the Existence of Corporate Liability?' (1993) 13 *International Review of Law and Economics* 239

'The Optimal Tradeoff between the Probability and Magnitude of Fines' (1979) 69 *American Economic Review* 880

'Public Enforcement of Law' in Boudewijn Bouckaert and Gerrit De Geest (eds.), *Encyclopedia of Law and Economics*

Porter, Robert H, 'Detecting Collusion' (2005) 26 *Review of Industrial Organization* 147

Posner, Richard, 'The Social Cost of Monopolies and Regulation' (1975) 83 *Journal of Political Economy* 415

'An Economic Theory of the Criminal Law' (1985) 85 *Columbia Law Review* 1193

Proos, Aini, 'Competition Policy in Estonia' in Katalin J. Cseres, Maarten Pieter Schinkel and Floris O.W. Vogelaar (eds.), *Criminalization of Competition Law Enforcement* 307–11

Raphael, M., *Blackstone's Guide to the Bribery Act 2010* (Oxford University Press, 2010)

Rawls, John, *A Theory of Justice* (1971) (revised edn, Harvard University Press, 1999)

The Law of Peoples (Harvard University Press, 1993)

Robertson, Aidan, 'The Reform of UK Competition Law – Again?' [1996] *European Competition Law Review* 210

Rockefeller, E. S., *The Antitrust Religion* (Washington DC, Cato Institute, 2007)

Rodger, Barry J. and Angus MacCulloch, *Competition Law and Policy in the EC and UK* (3rd edn, Abingdon, Routledge-Cavendish, 2004)

Rubenstein, William B., 'On What A "Private Attorney General" Is – And Why it Matters' (2004) 57 *Vanderbilt Law Review* 2129

Ruger, J. P., 'Democracy and Health' (2005) 98 *QJM: An International Journal of Medicine* 299

Salinger, Michael A., 'Tobin's *q*, Unionization and the Concentration-Profits Relationship' (1984) 15 *Rand Journal of Economics* 15

Samuelson, Paul A., 'The Pure Theory of Public Expenditure' (1954) 36 *Review of Economics and Statistics* 387

Schinkel, Maarten Pieter, 'Effective Cartel Enforcement in Europe', Amsterdam Center for Law & Economics, Working Paper No. 2006–14 (August 2007), available at http://ssrn.com/paper=948641

Sealey, Raphael, 'Aristotle, *Athenaion Politeia* 57.4: Trial of Animals and Inanimate Objects for Homicide' (2006) 56 *Classical Quarterly* (N.S.) 475

Segerson, Kathleen and Tom Tietenberg, 'The Structure of Penalties in Environmental Enforcement: An Economic Analysis' (1992) 23 *Journal of Environmental Economics and Management* 179

Sen, Amartya K., 'Isolation, Assurance and the Social Rate of Discount' (1967) 81 *Quarterly Journal of Economics* 112

Development as Freedom (Oxford University Press, 1999)

Serious Fraud Office, Press Release, 'Sports Direct plc and JJB Sports plc', 19 October 2010, available at www.sfo.gov.uk/press-room/latest-press-releases/press-releases-2010/sports-direct-plc-and-jjb-sports-plc.aspx

Shavell, Steven, 'Strict Liability versus Negligence' (1980) 9 *Journal of Legal Studies* 1

Sigfried, John J. and Molly Gardner Burba, 'The College Football Association Television Cartel', Department of Economics, Vanderbilt University, Working Paper 03-W20 (September 2003)

Simonsson, Ingeborg, *Legitimacy in EU Cartel Control* (Hart, 2010)

Smith, Andrew O., 'The Manufacture and Distribution of Handguns as an Abnormally Dangerous Activity' (1987) 54 *University of Chicago Law Review* 269

Smith, Lewis, 'Sale of human organs should be legalised, say surgeons', *The Independent* (London), 5 January 2011, available at www.independent.co.uk/life-style/health-and-families/health-news/sale-of-human-organs-should-be-legalised-say-surgeons-2176110.html

Stephan, Andreas, 'The Bankruptcy Wildcard in Cartel Cases' [2006] *Journal of Business Law* 511

'Survey of Public Attitudes Towards Price-Fixing and Cartel Enforcement in Britain' (2008) 5 *Competition Law Review* 123

'See No Evil: Cartels and the Limits of Antitrust Compliance Programs' (2010) 31 *Company Lawyer* 231

'Cartel Laws Undermined: Corruption, Social Norms and Collectivist Business Practices' (2010) 37 *Journal of Law and Society* 345

'How Dishonesty Killed the Cartel Offence' [2011] *Criminal Law Review* 446

Stephen, James Fitzjames, *Liberty, Equality, Fraternity* (1874) (reprinted, Indianopolis, The Liberty Fund, 1993)

Story, Joseph, 'Natural Law' in Francis Leiber, *Encyclopedia Americana* (1831)

Sullivan, G. R., 'The Attribution of Culpability to Limited Companies' (1996) 55 *Cambridge Law Journal* 515

Sullivan, Lawrence A. and Warren S. Grimes, *Law of Antitrust: An Integrated Handbook* (2nd edn, St Paul MN, West, 2006)

Summers, Scott, 'What Should the Dishonesty Element of the UK Cartel Offence be Replaced With?' (2012) 11 *Competition Law Journal* 53

Sykes, Alan O., 'The Boundaries of Vicarious Liability: An Economic Analysis of the Scope of Employment Rule and Related Legal Doctrines' (1988) 101 *Harvard Law Review* 563

'Comparative Advantage and the Normative Economics of International Trade Policy' (1988) 1 *Journal of International Economic Law* 49

Taylor, Martyn, *International Competition Law: A New Dimension for the WTO?* (Cambridge University Press, 2006)

Tesco, *Annual Report 2010*

Thorelli, Hans, 'Antitrust Policy in Europe: National Policies after 1945' (1958) 26 *University of Chicago Law Review* 222

Townley, Christopher, *Article 81 and Public Policy* (Oxford, Hart, 2009)

H M Treasury and Department of Trade and Industry, *The UK's Competition Regime* (Department of Trade and Industry, July 2001)

Trebilcock, Michael, Robert Howse and Antionia Eliason, *The Regulation of International Trade* (4th edn, Abingdon, Routledge, 2012)

Tullock, Gordon, 'The Welfare Costs of Tariffs, Monopolies, and Theft' (1967) 5 *Western Economic Journal* 224

United Kingdom, House of Lords Select Committee on the European Union, *Fourth Report* (HL 33, Ordered printed 29 February 2000)

United Nations, Conference on Trade and Development (UNCTAD), Model Law on Competition

Competition Provisions in Regional Trade Agreements: How to Assure Development Gains (New York: United Nations, 2005)

United Nations, Set of Principles and Rules on Competition, TD/RBP/CONF/10/Rev. 2

Resolution 35/63 (General Assembly, Thirty-Fifth Session, 83rd Plenary Session, 5 December 1980)

United States, Antitrust Modernization Commission, *Report and Recommendations* (Washington, April 2007)

United States Court Service, 'U.S. District Courts – Civil Cases Commenced, by Basis of Jurisdiction and Nature of Suit, During the 12-Month Periods Ending June 30, 2009 and 2010' available at www.uscourts.gov/uscourts/Statistics/StatisticalTablesForTheFederalJudiciary/2010/C02Jun10.pdf

'U.S. District Courts – Civil Cases Commenced, by Basis of Jurisdiction and Nature of Suit, During the 12-Month Periods Ending June 30, 2010 and 2011', available at www.uscourts.gov/uscourts/Statistics/StatisticalTablesForTheFederalJudiciary/2011/C02Jun11.pdf

United States Department of Justice, Antitrust Division, *An Antitrust Primer for Federal Law Enforcement Personnel*, 2005, available at www.justice.gov/atr/public/guidelines/209114.htm

'Division Update Spring 2012', available at www.justice.gov/atr/public/division-update/2012/criminal-program.html

United States Department of State, *Decade of American Foreign Policy*, 1941–49 (Washington, 1950) (Item 17: Berlin (Potsdam) Conference)

United States Federal Trade Commission Press Release, 'Google Agrees to Change Its Business Practices to Resolve FTC Competition Concerns In the Markets

for Devices Like Smart Phones, Games and Tablets, and in Online Search' (3 January 2013), available at: www.ftc.gov/opa/2013/01/google.shtm
United States Sentencing Commission, *Guidelines Manual* (November 2010)
United States Sentencing Commission, Office of General Counsel, *Chapter Eight Fine Primer: Determining the Appropriate Fine Under the Organizational Guidelines* (USSC March 2012), available at www.ussc.gov/Legal/Primers/Primer_Organizational_Fines.pdf
Utton, Michael A., 'Fifty Years of U.K. Competition Policy' (2000) 16 *Review of Industrial Organization* 267
Cartels and Economic Collusion: The Persistence of Corporate Conspiracies (Cheltenham, Edward Elgar, 2011)
Van Rompuy, Ben, 'The Impact of the Lisbon Treaty on EU Competition Law: A Review of Recent Case Law of the EU Courts', *CPI Antitrust Chronicle* December 2011 (1) available at http://ssrn.com/abstract=1970081
Vanberg, Viktor J, 'The Freiburg School: Walter Euken and Ordoliberalism', Freiburger Diskussionpapiere zur Ordnungsökonomik/Freiburg Discussion Papers on Constitutional Economics No. 04/11 (2011)
Villarejo, Cecilio Madero (Acting Deputy Director General, Directorate General for Competition, European Commission) at the Annual Conference on European Antitrust Law, Academy of European Law (ERA), Brussels, 3 March 2011, available at http://ec.europa.eu/competition/speeches/ text/sp2011_02_en.pdf
Viscusi, W. Kip, Joseph E. Harrington and John M. Vernon, *The Economics of Regulation and Antitrust* (3rd edn, Cambridge MA, MIT Press, 2005)
Vogelaar, Floris O. W., *The European Competition Rules: Landmark Cases of the European Courts and the Commission* (2nd edn, Europa, 2007)
Vollmer, Christof, 'Experience with Criminal Law Sanctions for Competition Law Infringements in Germany' in Cseres, Schinkel and Vogelaar (eds.), 257–69
Walker, Amasa, *The Science of Wealth: A Manual of Political Economy – The Laws of Trade, Currency, and Finance* (Boston, Little Brown, 1866)
Wardhaugh, Bruce, 'From Natural Law to Legal Realism: Legal Philosophy, Legal Theory and the Development of American Conflict of Laws Since 1830' (1989) 41 *Maine Law Review* 307
'Closing the Deterrence Gap: Individual Liability, the Cartel Offence and the BIS Consultation' (2011) 10 *Competition Law Journal* 175
'A Normative Approach to the Criminalisation of Cartel Activity' (2012) 32 *Legal Studies* 369
'The Cartel Offence Within A "World Class" Competition Regime: An Assessment of the BIS Consultation Exercise and its Results' (2012) 8 *European Competition Journal* 573
Wayland, Francis, *The Elements of Political Economy* (Leavitt Lord, 1837)
Weiss, Wolfgang, 'Human Rights and EU Antitrust Enforcement' (2011) 32 *European Competition Law Review* 186

Werden, Gregory J, Scott D. Hammond and Belinda A. Barnett, 'Recidivism Eliminated: Cartel Enforcement in the United States Since 1999', Georgetown Global Antitrust Enforcement Symposium, Washington DC, 22 September 2011, available at www.justice.gov/atr/public/speeches/speech-hammond.html

Werden, Gregory J and Marilyn J. Simon, 'Why Price Fixers Should Go to Prison' [1987] *The Antitrust Bulletin* 917

Whelan, Peter, 'A Principled Argument for Personal Criminal Sanctions as Punishment under EC Cartel Law' (2007) 4 *Competition Law Review* 7

Whish, Richard P. 'Recent Developments in Community Competition Law 1998/99' [2000] *European Law Review* 219

Competition Law (6th edn, Oxford University Press, 2009)

Whish, Richard P. and David Bailey, *Competition Law* (7th edn, Oxford University Press, 2012)

Wilgus, H. L., 'The Standard Oil Fine' (1907) 6 *Michigan Law Review* 118

Wilks, Stephen, *In the Public Interest: Competition Policy and the Monopolies and Mergers Commission* (Manchester University Press, 1999)

Williamson, Oliver, 'Economies as an Antitrust Defense: The Welfare Trade-offs' (1968) 58 *American Economic Review* 18

The Economics of Discretionary Behavior: Managerial Objectives in a Theory of the Firm (Englewood Cliffs NJ, Prentice-Hall, 1974)

Wils, Wouter P. J., *Principles of European Antitrust Enforcement* (Oxford, Hart, 2005)

Efficiency and Justice in European Antitrust Enforcement (Oxford, Hart, 2008)

'Is Criminalization of EU Competition Law the Answer?' in Ceres, Schinkel and Vogelaar (eds.), 60–109

World Trade Organization, Working Group on the Interaction between Trade and Competition Policy, Provisions On Hardcore Cartels: Background Note by the Secretariat, 20 June 2002, WT/WGTCP/W/191

Wright, Joshua D. and Angela M. Diveley, 'Do Expert Agencies Outperform Generalist Judges? Some Preliminary Evidence from the Federal Trade Commission' (2013) 1 *Journal of Antitrust Enforcement* 82

INDEX